AF260529

"We humans have an unending propensity to find our security and value everywhere but Christ. As such, it has always been necessary for the church to become aware of how the idols of its age are drawing it away from its mission. In this compelling book, Sherwin raises a prophetic voice inviting us to see how we have become enamoured by idols in our own time. We've substituted an embodied faith that makes a difference in this present world for spiritual escapism. We've traded the power of Christ's love and humility for power rooted in influence, celebrity, and politics. We've giddily taken over the Spirit's task of judgement, evaluating everyone around us, narrowing the definition of the Gospel until we are clear about who is in and who is out, with our own hand comfortably guarding the gate. The resulting brand of Christianity feels obvious and familiar to us, but it has so little in common with the vibrant faith and practice of Jesus' first followers. With honesty, vulnerability, and thoughtful theological reflection, Sherwin invites us to hear again the voice that animated those first Christians—we can be a part of the community that incarnates Jesus, participating in God's masterwork of restoration that is truly good news for all humanity and, indeed, for the whole cosmos. This is a message the church in our age desperately needs."

**—Marc Alan Schelske, Teaching Elder of Bridge City Community Church in Milwaukie, Oregon; author of *The Wisdom of Your Heart: Discovering the God-given Purpose and Power of Your Emotions*.**

Black Coney Press, 2019

ISBN 978-1-9162672-0-6 (Paperback)

A CIP catalogue record for this book is available from the British Library

Cover and interior design by Tristan Sherwin

Cover and interior photography by Amelia Stura

Scripture quotations marked (CJB) are taken from the Complete Jewish Bible Copyright © 1998 by David H. Stern. Published by Jewish New Testament Publications, Inc. www.messianicjewish.net. Distributed by Messianic Jewish Resources Int'l. All rights reserved. Used by permission.

Scripture quotations marked (NLT) are taken from the Holy Bible, New Living Translation, copyright © 1996. Used by permission of Tyndale House Publishers, Inc., Wheaton, Illinois 60189. All rights reserved.

Scripture quotations marked (NKJV) are taken from the New King James Version. Copyright © 1982 by Thomas Nelson Inc. Used by permission. All rights reserved.

Scripture quotations marked (RSV) are taken from the Revised Standard Version of the Bible, copyright © 1946, 1952, and 1971 National Council of Churches of Christ in the United States of America. Used by permission. All rights reserved.

Scripture quotations marked (NRSV) are taken from the New Revised Standard Version Bible, copyright © 1989, National Council of Churches of Christ in the U.S.A., and are used by permission. All rights reserved.

Scripture quotations marked (The Message) are taken from THE MESSAGE. Copyright © 1993, 1994, 1995, 1996, 2000, 2001, 2002. Used by permission of NavPress Publishing Group.

Scripture quotations marked (NIV) are taken from the Holy Bible, New International Version Anglicised Copyright © 1979, 1984, 2011 Biblica. Used by permission of Hodder & Stoughton Ltd, an Hachette UK company. All rights reserved. 'NIV' is a registered trademark of Biblica UK trademark number 1448790.

To the memory of Tom Wedall,

With belated thanks for that one, brief conversation and for the gift

of a sentence that has prophetically haunted me throughout the years

of my pilgrimage with Christ: 'Never neglect the Resurrection!'

Tristan Sherwin

# LIVING THE DREAM?

The Problem with Escapist,
Exhibitionist, Empire-Building
Christianity

# CONTENTS

# FOREWORD

The way believers work out their faith is always within a context. For, as persons, we are inevitably situated. We live positioned in time, in geography, in culture, influenced by prevailing moral and philosophical ideas. This does not mean, of course, that we are consciously aware of any of these. Far more often, the contours which shape our experience of life are seen to be 'normal.' Their values structure our society. They frame its laws, politics, and economics; they direct the curricula in our educational institutions. And they make it easy for each succeeding generation to see itself as more enlightened than the generations of its parents and grandparents.

Those of us who study history or philosophy, however, are conscious that such 'normalization' carries with it a false assumption of neutrality. It is dangerous to maintain that 'we see things like this, because this is how they are.' For are they? Familiarity often lulls us into accepting the very things we should be questioning. It prevents us from recognizing that undergirding the way societies think and act lie deep-seated world views which contain their own assumptions about human life, meaning, morality, truth and God.

This can even affect how we understand and relate to the Christian faith. Christianity itself offers us an authentic world view—a framework of meaning, from which we can begin to see the reality that surrounds us, in its wonderful depth and coherence. It is one we learn from the unfolding narrative of the Bible in the many varied forms of literature we find there. It is also one which finds its ultimate meaning in the New Testament revelation of Jesus the Christ, as the Incarnate Word of God. But all too often, competing, prevailing world views lodged solidly in our cultural mindset can intrude into the reading of the Bible and distort our understanding. We listen as opponents of Christianity fail to grasp its most fundamental concepts and parody the text, missing the point. We listen also as Christians attempt to justify very strange concepts or incongruences, because they believe God is asking them to believe these. And the clarity and relevance of Christian truth for our own generation becomes blurred by confusion and misrepresentation.

So this book rightly recognizes and identifies many of the 'isms' that intrude into our interpretation of the truth God offers us. For, whether they be escapism, nationalism, materialism, exhibitionism, consumerism, individualism, militarism or a dozen others, their impact will leave us with a shrunken or unrecognizable Gospel, and affect our own faith lives. Corruptions of the Christian faith leave everyone impoverished. Yet in *Living the Dream?* Tristan Sherwin does more than offer us warnings. He invites us back into the living text of the Bible, so we can read it better. He tackles tricky passages, and articulates the many questions that people ask, engaging with them in an open, thoughtful way. He acknowledges an unfolding, progressive revelation and points to the Hebrew Scriptures as 'a self-critical window on itself, (which) constantly refines and challenges its own views.' He challenges misleading representations of God, especially those which describe a violent, vengeful autocratic deity. Instead, he points to the radical self-emptying love of Christ's Cross as 'the pattern through which the world is saved and reconciled.'

With theology woven through a mosaic of film, stories, family outings, and international news, we are reassured in our recognition that Christianity speaks into every area of our life and culture today. And this takes us inevitably from thinking about the Christian vision, into the question of how we should live it out in our own lives and relationships. No author can answer this question for us, however. The routes we take and the visions we embrace are our own responsibility before God. For some of us the path might be hard. Yet, whoever you are, and whatever turmoil you might have encountered, I believe that by the time you reach the final pages, you will be more conscious that a Christian way forward is a joyful challenge for any human being. And Christ's love is available to every one of us to help us meet that challenge. For God's kingdom will surely come closer in our own culture, when God's Spirit lifts our human spirits and fills us with a deeper vision of God's intent for the world.

— Elaine Storkey, author of *Scars Across Humanity*

# oo | INTRODUCTION

I shoplifted a wristwatch eighteen months ago

In my defence, it *was* an accident. Honest! It had been a long day for us as a family, and the end of it found Steph and me floundering around a supermarket for what seemed like hours (it was probably twenty minutes, in retrospect). I was fatigued, and the kids were bouncing around and pestering for things in their end-of-the-day hyperactivity. Plus, my depression was causing me to have what I would call a 'grey day'. So I wasn't fully with it, so to speak.

I'm not making excuses. In hindsight, I can easily see where I went wrong. *I* had the handheld scanner, and I know that it was *my* task to scan every item we placed into the trolley. But for some unknown reason, after relenting to our youngest's demands to spend his unearned Christmas money on a cheap wristwatch, I failed to do my duty. I just pushed the trolley towards him, he placed the watch inside, and then we all mooched over to the food section of the store, where we spent another twenty or so minutes. We then walked to the self-checkout tills, I transferred the data from the handheld scanner to the till, I paid, packed, and then drove home. Through all of this, *we* (not *I*, officer) were unaware of the felony that had taken place. I did—hand on heart—believe we had paid for every item in our possession.

It's easily done. Although I'm not sure you're totally convinced.

When we arrived home, though, it wasn't long before the ugly, hideous truth of our misdemeanour revealed itself, as our son attempted to try on his new contraband.

Upon opening the packaging, we discovered that a plastic clasp on one of the watch straps had snapped beyond repair. So inevitably, like any good consumer who knows their rights, I went to the carrier bag to fish out the receipt. We reuse our shopping bags, and I have a nasty habit of leaving all of the shopping receipts in the bottom of them. So I picked up what I thought was the latest receipt and combed through the itemised list, looking for the watch to make sure it was the correct one. Lo and behold, the watch wasn't on there, so I picked up another… and another… and another… until I had scrutinized all fifty of them. I then searched my coat pockets. And my trouser pockets. And then my wallet. No luck there, either.

As I paused to ponder this mystery, a gnawing doubt crept towards the forefront of my mind. I returned to the shopping bag and started going through the receipts again, this time looking at the dates, and that's when my suspicions were confirmed.

Instantly, the whole scene in the shop replayed in my head. I knew what I had done. I knew I hadn't scanned that cheap £7 watch. I could only confess: 'Steph, *we've* stolen a watch.'

I'll be honest with you. The thought of returning this broken watch to the store seemed like a huge waste of effort. They'd only throw it away, anyway, I reasoned. And it was cheaply made, I thought, so do we really want to get a replacement? Additionally, no one knew we had it. So why should I waste my time taking back something that no one knows I have, and that they'll only throw away upon return? I might as well throw it in my own bin and save all of us the hassle. But, in my attempts to be an honest person, I had to return the watch. And plus, my son still wanted a watch; he was distraught to discover that it was broken, and was "desperate" to replace it. So I had to return to the scene of our crime.

I decided I would take the watch back the next day. I would explain how I forgot to scan it, I'd then pay for the watch, and I'd get a replacement. No worries. I was sure they'd understand. I was sure they'd find the whole thing comical. I even imagined myself standing at the customer service desk, laughing with the store's clerk like we were old friends. What could go wrong?

Answer: Steph.

Or, to be more precise: Steph had just gotten a brainwave.

Steph's a bargain hunter, by the way, and like many, she hates the idea of wasting money on cheap 'tat'. She hadn't wanted to buy the watch in the first place, and now saw the broken watch as an opportunity to get something of better quality. So, while I was hunting through receipts, Steph—acting on the belief that we had paid for the watch and whilst seeking to comfort our heartbroken son—was busy searching online for a better deal than the broken, cheap, plastic tat we'd "purchased". Apparently, I soon discovered after my confession, while I was knee-deep in shopping receipts and frantically rummaging for redemption, Steph had made an online purchase.

Which was a good move by Steph. But this totally messed up my fantasised ending of us all stood at the customer service counter, laughing together like it was the end of some US sitcom. And no amount of me pleading with Steph that this had now ruined my well-crafted story arc, would persuade her to cancel the order and let me get a replacement from the store. 'They'll understand', was the only consolation offered to me, along with, 'stop being a wimp.'

So I went to return the broken watch; a watch that *we* had (unintentionally) stolen, but that *we* hadn't broken, and that *Steph* didn't want a replacement for.

Of course, you're reading this, and I suppose it makes sense to you. But that's only because I've finally arrived at a place where I can relate this tale in a fairly ordered fashion. However, the next day, as I stood in line at the return's desk, I had no idea of where to begin.

When my turn came round, I did my best to explain. I started with, 'I've come to return this watch…', and it went downhill from there very quickly. The customer service clerk must have asked me to explain the situation three times. And not knowing what transaction needed to be typed into his computer—or whether there was anything that needed to be typed into his computer—he then called over his manager for advice. I explained it to her at least three times as well. And through every reiteration of the story, questions would arise.

'So you want a refund?'

'No, I didn't pay for it.'

'Do you want a replacement?'

'No. I don't want it. I don't want another one, either. I just want to return it… we're getting another one from somewhere else.'

'But you're returning it because it's broken?'

'Yes. But I didn't break it, I stole it; accidentally. So I was going to return it anyway, but I thought you would want to know that it's broken…'

And on, and on it went. The story didn't make sense, and the baffled looks on their faces proved it. As did the curious and puzzled looks on the faces of the other customers waiting in the queue behind me.

After twenty minutes of awkward conversation, they took the watch out of my hands and placed it on the counter behind them. They still didn't get it. They had only conceded to the weirdness of the situation. But to lighten the mood, and to hopefully achieve my sitcom vision of a scene of laughter, I asked for a receipt of return.

I shouldn't have…

I can't blame the clerks at the supermarket for giving me those funny looks. It was a difficult story to understand. And I have no idea of what conclusions they formed after I left. Although, now that I think about it, I guess the fact that I've always been "randomly" selected for a security check at the self-checkout ever since tells me everything I need to know.

## DAZED AND CONFUSED

The reality, though, is that some stories are hard to follow. But deep down within all of us, there's this ingrained idea that stories must make some sort of sense if they're to be called stories, and not riddles.

It reminds of when the final episode of the show, *Lost*, aired on Television. The day after that episode premiered, I went to work believing I had understood it all; that I had grasped the imperative conclusion of its sixth season and had therefore understood what the show had been about since season one. But when I got the chance to share my view at the coffee machine, my opinion clashed sharply with the interpretations of two of my workmates.

Like a good number of people around the world, one of my friends was adamant that the finale had confirmed that the entire cast of characters had been dead since the first episode and that the mysterious island, which Oceanic Flight 815 had crashed on, was purgatory. I'm still not convinced that's right, regardless of how popular an idea it is. To me, that ending doesn't make any sense of the show.

For my other friend, that final episode ruined everything. He'd been *Lost's* biggest fan since it had started airing back in 2004. This was the show that he proudly hailed as the best piece of TV ever produced. But within the space of sixty minutes, his whole outlook turned a full one-eighty. In his opinion, that one episode had made a mockery of the previous 120 episodes. It had totally diverted from the main story and had answered no questions whatsoever. And to this day, my friend Matt treats the name of the show as a swear word. I risk my life uttering its name in his presence.

I can see where he's coming from. It made no sense. And, I feel, stories have got to make sense.

I'm not saying that stories can't have any depth, or multiple layers, or several micronarratives moving along and developing at the same time. I'm not saying that there cannot be a good number of principles, morals, or multiple life-lessons to glean along the way, or even a lingering sense of mystery. The best stories ever written possess all these things.

But the bigger story—the wider metanarrative of it all—has got to make some sense if we're to understand how the smaller scenes play out within it. The bigger story is what's imperative to the detail; it's what we want to know when we ask what a film, or a book, or a song, or the meaning of life, is all about. And even if you hold to there being no meaning to life, then that's still a metanarrative; you've made the idea of there being no ultimate meaning the backdrop to everything that happens in the foreground.

Whatever direction you take, the BIG story is always there. The big story is what we want to know, and what we try to communicate when asked. The big story is what the clerks at the supermarket couldn't grasp. The big story—as espoused by its final episode—is what changed my friend's opinion of *Lost*.

So I've written this book to explore that bigger story.

No, I'm not exploring the fan-theories about *Lost*. And no, I'm not going to discuss the character Kate, and her wrong decision of choosing Sawyer instead of Jack, either (even after all these years, I'm still too upset to talk about that at any depth).

But I do want to walk through the narrative of the Bible. Which is a tough task because it's a huge story which features a wide cast—an ancient story that continues to inspire writers, artists, poets, and film-makers to this day. To some extent, the Bible is not even *a* story. It's a compilation of many stories, experiences, episodes and eras. It's got layers and micro-narratives galore. So there's no way that I am going to look into every single part that contributes to forming the whole corpus of the Jewish and Christian Scriptures.

All I want to do here is to get us to think through the wider, larger, all-encompassing metanarrative through which the Scriptures move us.

Why?

Well, mainly because I'm tired of the confusion that exists around this story. I love this story, but my passion for it has subsequently developed into an irritation towards alternative ideas about this story's meaning. In particular, there are three pseudo-versions of this beautiful and complex story's thrust that I take issue with. Three versions that have also sadly glued themselves into the cultural perception of what Christianity is all about.

One of those is the idea of dominance. History testifies of Christianity being used as a means to take over and control as much of the world as possible. God, in this version, is seen as the one who sponsors political power plays—whether that be the post-Constantine Roman Empire,

Europe under Christendom, or even, in modern history, America. The metanarrative of this style of Christianity is that a select "we" are the divinely-elected elite, called to bring the world into peaceful order with as much force as necessary. It's militant, power-hungry, often nationalistic, and always oppressive. This is what I would call Empire-Building Christianity.

A second, prevalent idea surrounding Christianity, is that it's anti-material and hyper-spiritual. In this idea, Jesus is the golden ticket, guaranteeing us a seat on God's bus so that we can escape the material realm and pass into a blissful, disembodied state after death. In this stance, God isn't a fan of what Hal Lindsey's malign ideas dubbed the 'late great planet Earth'; it's become filthy, wretched and beyond repair. This being the case, God is out to destroy the world, but don't cry over this, because it's our souls that God wants to save anyway. There's a lot of Greek (not Jewish) thought which has led to this understanding of the biblical story, and it's held sway in the Western Church for a long time. This is what I would call Escapist Christianity; it's a scenario in which we're seeking to avoid the constraints of the material life, or the fate of the Earth, or in which we're seeking to escape a post-mortem, fire and brimstone eternity. One way or another, the story of Scripture is studied in the manner of a survivor's guide, as we try to discover the secrets of getting our disembodied humanity (our souls) out of here.

The third trend is found in the prosperity versions of the story, where there's a preoccupation with getting what we want, when we want, if we click our heels together in the right way. It's a hedonistic and overtly individualistic approach, with its focus being on self-promotion, self-satisfaction and self-actualisation. Some versions of these ideas are easy to spot and are rightly avoided by many Christians. But the subtler stuff, and the ideology behind it, is still small enough to slip through the cracks in our creeds and turn the story of Scripture into an allegory of self-discovery. Especially within the streams that I belong to: the Charismatic and Pentecostal movements. Our conferences, our books, our Bible studies, etc., seem to pulsate with self-help therapy, placebo-clichés, individualism, consumerism and an over-focus on entertainment.[1] I call this version, Exhibitionist Christianity. It may not long for financial reward (and often doesn't), but its focus on the prosperity of the self takes theology and inverts it to Me-ology. It views God as a genie. It treats Jesus as a mascot. And it makes the Spirit into a euphoria-inducing, performance-enhancing drug.

These three versions will pop up again and again as we journey through the following pages together, and hopefully, as we hold them up against the actual story, we'll be able to see how perverse, self-indulgent, and malign these alternatives are. To a great extent, all three versions could fall under the category of the "prosperity gospel" because of their infatuation with the idea of human transcendence. Even within the streams that do not teach a "name-it, claim-it" exhibitionist attitude towards power, possessions and personal success, the ideas of political/global dominance (Empire-Building), or abandoning the economic and ecological world to some doomsday event (Escapist), can still leave an infectious taint on a beautiful story that is really about the Kingdom of God.

The problem I have—and I am not alone in this—is that in every one of the alternative versions of the story, there is a focus on *I* (or even a select *we*) living some version of the human dream. These versions also make the Earth look like a disposable prop, and they make serious character statements about God. And when our image of God is perverted, our expression of God, or "God's will", is also perverted.

However, the Judaeo-Christian dream, as told in the Bible's grand narrative, has never been the transcendence or transmigration of humanity into some heavenly sphere, or into global dominance, or into our ideas of the perfect me. The central focus of this story, its main melody, has always been the descent and dwelling of God on Earth.

We're going to explore this story, in a roundabout way, through this book. Because if we can get the metanarrative of the story correct, if we can hear the pulse behind this age-old song, I believe we'll be in a better position to understand what it means to declare ourselves as followers of Jesus.

## BLOWING MY TRUMPET

As a matter of importance, I need to add here that this book isn't a denominational thing. This isn't me holding up my own tribe as the answer to it all. Far from it. My tribe isn't flawless. Moreover, over the past few years, I've found myself increasingly tribe-less. I've found myself listening to and agreeing with more voices that are outside of the Pentecostal communion than within it. That's not to say that I no longer regard myself as Pentecostal; I can "boom-shaka-lakka" as well as the next person, but being Pentecostal isn't my aim. Maybe it's because I'm from a non-Christian background originally, and I'm what some people would term a 'first-generation Pentecostal', but my goal is to be a disciple of Jesus, and I feel that there is much that we Pentecostals have to learn from the more liturgical, sacramental and contemplative branches of the church that can help with this.

In all quarters of the Western Church, though, these three alternative ideas on Christianity can be present or absent. No quarter is immune to their influences. But that's not to say that every church or Christian is under their influence, either. There are voices in each quarter of Christianity that speak either for or against these things. But because I'm from the Pentecostal/Charismatic section, I'll obviously be taking prophetic aim at those in my own camp. That may make us sound worse than we are, so I'll apologise for this in advance. We're not all that bad, and there's beauty and truth I have gleaned from within Pentecostalism that I will cherish always—regardless of wherever I end up in the future. That said, I'm well aware that some of what I've written here will clash sharply with my single-generation roots. I could, and will, I suspect, lose friends over this.

Unlike my first book, *Love: Expressed*, there's a bit more of a theological slant here. But I've done my best to convey what I have to say in a way that isn't overwhelming. Hopefully, the words that follow will maintain a degree of depth and still move at a good pace. To help with that flow, I've avoided heavy theological words or other jargon as much as possible. And where I couldn't avoid this, I've made sure to include some explanation in the endnotes.

I'm aware that some of my non-Christian friends will be reading this too; you'll be able to follow this, and it might surprise you. To my Christian friends, it should surprise you as well. Whoever you are, we'll take this journey slowly—a step at a time. There'll be a bit of going back and forth, there'll inevitably be some overlap, and some things might make better sense on the second time through. But we will get there in the end as long as we keep putting one foot in front of the other.

I should warn you: you're entering my wrestling match here; it's a tug-of-war that I've been engaged in for the past decade, and that certainly isn't going to come to an end tomorrow. This book will not give you all the answers, but I am hoping that it sparks enough of the right questions.

In short, this book won't settle you. If it does, then I've failed. My hope is that it will shake our Empire-Building, Escapist, Exhibitionist Christian tendencies to their foundations, and that it will take its place alongside the other voices that also march and blow their trumpets around these forbidding, foreign walls, hoping for their collapse. Who knows, maybe, by the end of this, we'll all be in a better position to know what it is to live the dream of God.

— Tristan Sherwin.

# LIVING THE DREAM?

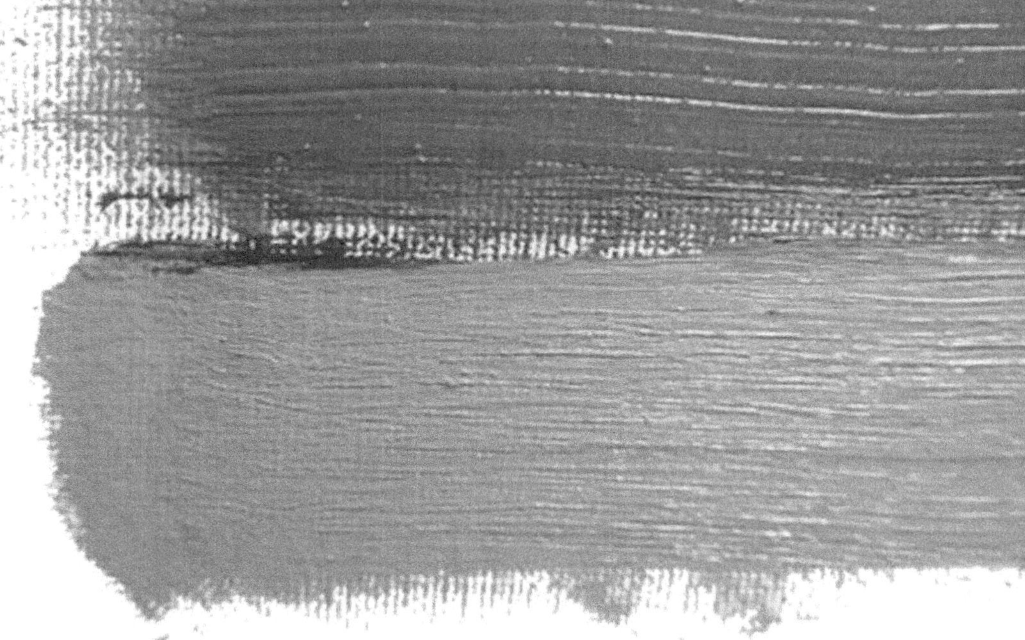

# PROLOGUE

In the beginning God created the heavens and the earth. The earth was unformed and void, darkness was on the face of the deep, and the Spirit of God hovered over the surface of the water.

Then God said, "Let there be light"; and there was light. God saw that the light was good, and God divided the light from the darkness. God called the light Day, and the darkness he called Night. So there was evening, and there was morning, one day.

God said, "Let there be a dome in the middle of the water; let it divide the water from the water." God made the dome and divided the water under the dome from the water above the dome; that is how it was, and God called the dome Sky. So there was evening, and there was morning, a second day.

God said, "Let the water under the sky be gathered together into one place, and let dry land appear," and that is how it was. God called the dry land Earth, the gathering together of the water he called Seas, and God saw that it was good.

God said, "Let the earth put forth grass, seed-producing plants, and fruit trees, each yielding its own kind of seed-bearing fruit, on the earth"; and that is how it was. The earth brought forth grass, plants each yielding its own kind of seed, and trees each producing its own kind of seed-bearing fruit; and God saw that it was good. So there was evening, and there was morning, a third day.

God said, "Let there be lights in the dome of the sky to divide the day from the night; let them be for signs, seasons, days and years; and let them be for lights in the dome of the sky to give light to the earth"; and that is how it was. God made the two great lights — the larger light to rule the day and the smaller light to rule the night — and the stars. God put them in the dome of the sky to give light to the earth, to rule over the day and over the night, and to divide the light from the darkness; and God saw that it was good. So there was evening, and there was morning, a fourth day

God said, "Let the water swarm with swarms of living creatures, and let birds fly above the earth in the open dome of the sky." God created the great sea creatures and every living thing that creeps, so that the water swarmed with all kinds of them, and there was every kind of winged bird; and God saw that it was good. Then God blessed them, saying, "Be fruitful, multiply and fill the water of the seas, and let birds multiply on the earth." So there was evening, and there was morning, a fifth day.

God said, "Let the earth bring forth each kind of living creature — each kind of livestock, crawling animal and wild beast"; and that is how it was. God made each kind of wild beast, each kind of livestock and every kind of animal that crawls along the ground; and God saw that it was good.

Then God said, "Let us make humankind in our image, in the likeness of ourselves; and let them rule over the fish in the sea, the birds in the air, the animals, and over all the earth, and over every crawling creature that crawls on the earth." So God created humankind in his own image; in the image of God he created him: male and female he created them. God blessed them: God said to them, "Be fruitful, multiply, fill the earth and subdue it. Rule over the fish in the sea, the birds in the air and every living creature that crawls on the earth." Then God said, "Here! Throughout the whole earth I am giving you as food every seed-bearing plant and every tree with seed-bearing fruit. And to every wild animal, bird in the air and creature crawling on the earth, in which there is a living soul, I am giving as food every kind of green plant." And that is how it was. God saw everything that he had made, and indeed it was very good. So there was evening, and there was morning, a sixth day.

Thus the heavens and the earth were finished, along with everything in them.

On the seventh day God was finished with his work which he had made, so he rested on the seventh day from all his work which he had made. God blessed the seventh day and separated it as holy; because on that day God rested from all his work which he had created, so that it itself could produce.

— B'resheet (Genesis) 1:1 - 2:3,

Complete Jewish Bible (CJB)

# PART 01 | DIVINE ORIGINS & HUMAN TRAJECTORIES

In the beginning God created the heavens and
the earth.
– Genesis[2]


Thou hast made us for thyself, O Lord, and our
heart is restless until it finds its rest in thee.
– St Augustine of Hippo[3]


Man is best defined not as a 'logical' but as a
'Eucharistic' animal. He does not merely live in
the world, think about it and use it, but he is
capable of seeing the world as God's gift, as a
sacrament of God's presence and a means of
communion with him.
– Bishop Kallistos Ware[4]


I sometimes think that God in creating man
somewhat overestimated his ability.
– Oscar Wilde[5]

# 1.1 | MINE!

Our youngest child is addicted to a computer game called Minecraft™.

If life could be as he wanted it—if his dream could become reality—each day would consist of spending his waking hours immersed within this environment of pixels. For those of you who have miraculously escaped the news of this particular computer game, the premise is extremely simple: You mine, and yes—you guessed it—you craft, in a virtual world where everything is formed by blocks. And I mean everything. With the exception of the round eggs that the square chickens lay and the odd corner of rail track, Minecraft takes a purist approach to right angles. The vivid landscapes of mountains and forests, and the pigs, Mooshrooms, people and monsters which inhabit them, are all fashioned from blocks.

Cubes.

Cuboids.

No arcs, bends or radii allowed.

When you first enter this rectilinear paradise/purgatory (depending on how you want to look at it), you'll find yourself being launched into a land stocked full of resources; a dystopian, unblemished canvas, where, after excavating the raw materials and mixing them with huge dollops of imagination, you can 'build whatever you like'—to use my son's terminology. The terrain's loaded up, and ready and waiting for you to breathe your personality all over it. Every nanobyte of this pixelated world and all it contains belongs to *you*, and *you* are free to do whatever *you* desire to do with it—within programming limits, of course. And so long as it doesn't require curves.

As far as computer games go, Minecraft has split opinion in our home. As parents, Steph and I love the creative aspect of the game; our son has to imagine and execute his ideas. This is far better, we feel, than following predetermined stories which only help to refine the motor skill of 'button-bashing'.

That aside, Steph's still nicknamed the game 'Bore-Craft'; it's hardly entertaining to watch and the soundtrack either lulls you to sleep or drives you insane.

I, on the other hand, differ. I was intrigued by this world of perpendicular possibilities and took a more direct approach; which involved grabbing a control-pad and tagging along with Eaden in his virtual experiences. It was time for a Dad-and-Lad team-up as we began to cast our artistic vision into the world.

But that's when the problems started.

It goes without saying that *you* can't build the world as *you* would want it when there's two of *you* on the scene. Instead, it's dappled with "make do's" and conflict.

Why? Well, I could blame it all on the fact that my eight-year-old takes a different approach to mine when it comes to construction; after all, he's not here to defend himself. But I'll hold my hands up and confess that I'm equally responsible for the chaos that ensued.

All right, I'll admit it; it's all my fault.

Call me a traditionalist, but when *I* build a wall, and the game offers me the raw materials of brick, stone, or purple wool, I'm going to avoid the latter. Even pixelated wool probably lacks the strength and integrity that I believe is required of a wall. Not to mention the devastation that a torrent of rain would cause! But not my son, Eaden. Oh no. It's wool all the way; as above, so below. Wool walls, combined with wool roofs, and wool fireplaces.

And when there is no wool left? Slime.

Not only did we clash on materials, but colour schemes presented further tensions. I wanted sandstone walls, terracotta roof tiles, and nice oak flooring—all in their natural, realistic hues, please. Is that too much to ask? But not my son—my beautiful, wonderful son, whom I happen to love very much, I should add. His world was a collage of vibrant contrasts; an explosion of colour. Like it had been caught between a giant game of paintball and a Holi Festival.

All of this drove me round the bend—or at least a faceted version of a bend.

We both had different ideas; our dreams clashed, our wills collided, and the world we were crafting became collateral damage caught up in the procession of our egos. Instead of paradise, a dystopia of division and disharmony emerged.

Nothing demonstrates this more than my granite-grey Norman castle standing in the looming shadow of a giant statue of *Sponge Bob Square Pants* (made of wool, of course).

It turned out that the virtual world of Minecraft wasn't big enough to house both of us; we both couldn't play God.

## PYRAMIDS

But imagine for a moment a world that *was* big enough. And then populate it with over seven billion people.

Seven billion ways.

Seven billion wills.

Seven billion dreams.

Within that world, there would be an existence of harmony amongst certain groups of people—places where dreams would merge and a kind of "truce" would occur on a macro-sociological scale. But between the other groups, and in the cracks of those that appeared to be cohesive at large, dreams would clash, tensions would intensify, and oppression, struggle and disharmony would exist.

Give those seven billion inhabitants the same, shared volume of resource, the same building blocks—the raw material of our planet—and there will be those who gather and hoard mass quantities of it from others; along with those who would steal, kill and conquer in order to control that resource; and many who would be left with nothing at all. Unlike players of Minecraft, we're not so geometrically restricted when we build. And yet, despite the abundance of geometric options available to us, there's always one shape that consistently emerges. Whether we consider things physically, socially, politically, technologically, religiously, or economically, pyramids always seem to arise. And at the top of those pyramids, within the fraction that controls and owns much, a further subdivision of people will exist; those who, motivated through individualistic or tribal tendencies and driven by materialistic and consumeristic greed, will unbelievably hold to the notion that they have hardly anything at all.

Then tell that fraction—the well-resourced and "blessed" part—to go and live their dreams; go and fill the world with their personality and make it theirs! Then stand back and observe as things go crazy. Especially as that privileged fraction doesn't recognise that from much of the world's perspective, they're *already* living the dream. That fact rarely enters into the brains of the few. They don't see what their global neighbours have or haven't got, so appreciation only ever peaks in the stunted form of gratitude, and never matures into generosity. Instead, what captures their attention and grabs at their hearts, is what those next door possess or what the industrial, money-grabbing conveyors of dreams tell us we should have. And so the grasping for more—more power, more resource, more *mining* of what we feel is rightfully *mine*—continues to play on a perpetual loop.

It's difficult to resist the human compulsion to *mine*; to covet, take, control, horde and label as *mine* as much as possible. To act in opposition to this drive, to label things as *yours* or *ours*, seems unnatural at times within the Western hemisphere. Unless, of course, it's with regards to those things which are undesirable, like war, poverty, disease and disaster.

As a result of all this mining, a world of contrasts emerges, and the contrasts should hit us hard. For many in our world, the biggest causes of death are malnutrition, disease, and war. For others, its greed, health problems related to obesity, and lack of exercise.

It's rather out-of-balance, isn't it? The world, as it currently finds itself, is full of more stark and disturbing disparities than that of a Norman castle with *Sponge-Bob* as its neighbour.

And yet, are any of us living the dream? It seems the more we try to make the world in our image, the more problems arise. It's suffocating, to some extent. Life, *real* life—whatever we believe that consists of—gets stifled as we, alongside everyone else, fight to breathe our expression of self into the world. Like continually breathing into a paper bag, it feels good at the start, cathartic almost, to fill the world with *I*. But if we do it for long enough, we end up choking; choking on our own expression. We keep breathing heavily into this paper bag called self, trying to expand it further, because we've been sold the lie that there is enough for all of us to have as much as we want, whenever we want, however we want it. Sadly—but also thankfully—this isn't true.

Russian novelist Fyodor Dostoyevsky poignantly wrote:

> The world says: "You have needs—satisfy them. You have as much right as the rich and the mighty. Don't hesitate to satisfy your needs; indeed expand your needs and demand more." This is the worldly doctrine of today. And they believe that this is freedom. The result for the rich is isolation and suicide, for the poor, envy and murder.[6]

It goes without saying that *you* can't build the world as *you* would want it when there is more than *you* on the scene.

But I'm not talking solely about the world here.

Within some branches of Christianity, the Minecraft way of thinking is not too far beneath the surface: The world and all it contains belongs to you, and you can do whatever you want to do with it—within faceted moral limits—because God wants what you want. God is for *you*, after all, and against those who would disagree with your colour scheme or choice of building materials. Repeating the "worldly doctrine" that Dostoyevsky expressed, some streams even tell us to expand our needs; believe and pray for bigger and for more and never doubt your "God-given potential" (which can be a veiled way of talking about demanding what you want). Accumulating wealth and resource within this theological framework is then understood as a blessing, ordained by God as proof of your devotion and "special-ness" in comparison to everyone else. Proof that God wants more of *me* and less of *them*. Or more like *me*, and less like *them*.

Mining is the goal, and losing, or so this way of thinking believes, is not what following Jesus looks like. *'Laying your life down for the Gospel'*, is interpreted as *'Be prepared to go through hell to get what you want'*, and *'Picking up your cross'* is taken as the price-tag on our own dreams coming to fruition; the cost of self-realisation and self-actualisation. In the Prosperity, Self-help, Seven-steps-to-success "gospels", *you* is the image that is called to be expressed on the world's stage. And the world has become sadly distorted as a stage for human ego; a temporary proving ground full of resource for the transcendence of *our* humanity.

Winning, achieving your personal goals and life-hacks are the commission, benediction and liturgy of the modern age. Consumerism, Materialism, and Individualism have crept into the body of Christ like a cancerous parasite. So instead of resembling an organism of blessing to the world, we often resemble a self-serving hive of ego.

Maybe it's only a coincidence that the bestsellers at my local Christian bookshop don't look all that different from the contents of a gamer's "hints and tips" guide to Minecraft?

Admittedly, some of this isn't too easy to detect; it's not glaringly obvious all the time. It's often subtly wrapped up in the guise of religion, accompanied by faux incense and smoke (glitz and glamour), and acted out to a soundtrack of praise. And in the euphoria-steeped moments of this charade, it's easy to find yourself being dragged along with the current. As I said, the human compulsion to *mine* is a difficult tendency to resist. Especially when it's being endorsed. But if we would only pause to consider for a moment on a Sunday morning, and like Dorothy from the *Wizard of Oz*, if we only had the courage to draw back the curtain on our theology, maybe we too would discover that there is no divine life pulsating through this form of religion, other than the man-made, man-operated, smoke-and-mirrors light show.

Then again, would we want this not to be about *us*? Perhaps we'd prefer to keep the curtain? Maybe we're worried that if we did pull back the drapes on our religion, we'd catch a glimpse of *me* behind the veil, pushing all the pedals and pulling all the levers?

But what if—and I know I might have to stretch some thinking here—this life isn't about *me*, or *I*, or solely even *us*? What if the world isn't a stage or a testing ground? What if all of this is not about *you* at all, but about *everything*? And by everything, I mean everything. Including all the things we would prefer to write off as the construction materials for the citadels of our egos.

What if the centre of all this, the purpose of all this, wasn't to *mine*?

It's time to reboot the programming. So with that in mind, let's go back to the beginning.

But what do I mean by *beginning* exactly?

# 1.2 | SUBSTANCE ADDICTION

What follows may seem like a strange and unnecessary abstraction, especially at the start of the book, but I want you to know that it's essential. I need to talk about the book of Genesis (which will feature heavily in the book ahead of us), and in particular about the creation stories and how I understand them.

Of all the stories contained in the Bible, the creation accounts of Genesis probably rank high up in the list of the most controversial. The opening eleven chapters alone are a hotbed for discussion and the litmus test for many on how *true* you are in being a *true* Christian.

Trust me when I say that nothing heats up the room like a discussion on the historical reliability of the Bible's account of cosmological and human origins.

Which is shocking, because when it comes to the stories of Genesis, why don't we get nearly so impassioned when we debate the injustice of Dinah's rape? Or the ongoing, revolting development of patriarchy? Or the idea of a God who could be haggled with over the destruction of the people living in Sodom and Gomorrah?

But I digress.

Sadly, the creation stories have been terribly misused over recent centuries and decades. At one extreme, they've become rhetorical devices against any other narratives or scientific theories that propose alternative understandings of the world's formation. Sadly, this use as a trump-card has a) weaponised the story, and b) become a huge faith barrier to anyone who struggles with reading this account literally. At the other extreme, the creation accounts have been reduced to fairy-tales, not unlike the stories of the Brothers Grimm; this has resulted in the stories being viewed as if they are saying nothing of importance to intellectual people, with the exception of trite, clichéd morals.

But Genesis is important, for understanding the trajectory of the grand narrative of the Bible's story, and especially in the light of what I'm trying to say in this book. For me, and many others who don't read the Genesis creation stories literally, these stories are of priceless value; they encapsulate the blueprint of God's dream for the Earth and humanity, and they are a pattern of the Gospel.

But let's step back, and take this slowly over this section and the next.

A couple of years ago I picked up a book in a shop, turned to the Introduction and read the first line, which went something like this: 'The Bible was the first scientific textbook…' I cringed, rolled my eyes to the back of my head, and placed the book back with its counterparts.

It may have been an excellent book, and maybe I should have given it more time to explain itself. But I struggle with the analogy of Scripture as a modern textbook of any sort, especially a science one. Not only are there many better examples of ancient cosmology, astronomy and medical texts, which are more suited as competitors for being the first "science textbooks" (and which, by the way, bear no literary resemblance to the opening of Genesis or to any other ancient creation stories), but to classify "In the beginning God created the heavens and the earth" as *science* seems to be pushing the definition's boundaries.

Of course, if we mean *science* in the broadest of terms, and trace it all the way back to its Latin root verb, *scire*, meaning *to know*, then yes, Genesis is revealing something important for us *to know*. However, I'm deeply suspicious that it's not the physical processes that our universe or mankind emerged from. For many of my friends, atheist and theist alike, that may come as a shock. But I take my science from science books, not Scripture.[7] Because of this, I find it difficult to harmonize the science with Genesis if I have to understand the latter as a scientific account of *how* and *when* everything within the material realm appeared in history.

I've not always held this view; my mind has changed over the years—but that's another story. But I know I'm not alone in this opinion or this kind of 'conversion'. The whole debate on the scientific validity of Genesis has developed all manner of theological clusters, including Young Earth Creationists, Old Earth Creationists, Theistic Evolutionists, and advocates of Intelligent Design. It's also worth stating that this debate isn't something new because of the challenges of recent theories like Evolution. This conversation—to put a diplomatic label on what has not always been so amicable—has been going on for two millennia, at least. And I'm not convinced it will stop in my time.

I know that there's a temptation to read Genesis as a scientific text, especially where there appears to be an overlap with scientific discovery. I've done this myself. Yes, it's interesting that Genesis mentions the creation of biological systems and not of a God who has to wave a magic wand each time for something to happen (e.g. trees and animals which produce after their own kind, and the regular motion of the Sun and Moon). The biblical story displays an ecological model of the world which is self-functioning and which doesn't need to be divinely micromanaged. An idea way ahead of its time, some may argue, and that agrees with what we have and can observe. Such overlaps sound promising.

However, there are many instances where Genesis mentions things that are glaringly out of sync from the material-origin viewpoint of the 21$^{st}$ century.

To highlight a few:

Light existing before the Sun was made? We've all spotted that one, so let's not pretend it isn't there. So if this "Light" is to be taken as the material creation of what we know emanates from the Sun—quantum packets of energy that we label as photons—then we've got a problem. And we're only at verse three. When you jump forward to Day Four, the day in which the Sun and Moon are established, something else stands out. The Moon is called a great light, a lamp, like the Sun; indistinguishable from each other, with the exception of one being prominent at night. But the Moon isn't a light at all. It doesn't produce light; it's not self-luminescent. A better description of the Moon would be a mirror; as we now know that the light it appears to produce is a reflection/refraction of the light from the Sun.

Or what about Day Two of this Creation Saga (verses 6-8), where the *primordial waters* are divided into the *waters above* and the *waters below*? It's easy to miss this, or dismiss it and not give it much thought. But this verse is clearly referencing an ancient understanding of the structure of the cosmos; a model which envisaged all that exists being sandwiched between two firmaments of water. The bottom firmament of water was separated again on Day Three, being gathered into one place to reveal the dry ground which would bring forth plants (also mentioned in Day Three) and all manner of wildlife (Day Six). The upper firmament, the waters above, was seen as a liquid ceiling which was suspended (held back) a fixed distance away from the Earth, and upon which the stars, Sun and Moon sailed back and forth.

In other words, Outer Space, as we now know it, appears to be non-existent in this model of the universe. When you think about it, no mention whatsoever is made of a wider universe within Genesis, let alone our local solar system that contains other planets. Stars aren't seen as potential solar systems, as we now know them to be; the writer of Genesis simply posits that the stars are lights to illuminate the Earth. It's just us (Earth), surrounded by the water that has been separated by God; just us, existing in the space between a liquid floor and a liquid ceiling. (I'll be coming back to this *Earth sandwich*, so please keep it in mind).

And what about where the story starts? According to verse two, before anything else is made, Earth already exists in a *void* and *formless* state. Before light, and before our Sun. How it got there is anyone's guess, and what exactly does the text mean by *formless*? Could this phrase be key to how we should read this story? But we'll put these questions to one side for a moment, because for those of us who want to claim that Genesis One is the historical—though short—version of how everything came out of nothing, then we have an obvious problem; our planet already exists at the beginning. This particular portion of the tale doesn't start with nothing, but with something. This should cause us to think about what this *beginning* in Genesis represents. Is this the *very* beginning, what some Christians would want to call the moment prior to the Big Bang, or is this the beginning of something else? With Earth already on the scene, I suggest something else. Maybe, to tease you with what is ahead, this isn't about the making of the world at all, but the ordering of the world?

Before moving on, could I also mention the glaring omission of Mr and Mrs Tyrannosaurus Rex and their fellow associates? Hey, I'm a Dad, so that question pops up. And stories of there not being enough room on Noah's Ark, or that the family Rex wasn't allowed admission by Noah because of their ferocious appetites, don't explain this problem away.

You see, when we try and read the origin stories of Genesis through our 21st-century empirical lens of material origins, all manner of holes begin to appear.

## MYOPIC STORIES

So, is that it? Is Genesis wrong? No. But maybe our expectations of what we think it is saying are.

For a start, we need to acknowledge that *our* current understanding of Creation's form would not have been in the minds of the original author(s) or their audience.[8] They would have understood and spoken about the structure of the vast cosmos through their own ancient culture's lens. Like us, there would be limits to what they would have known and been able to explore. Their knowledge of the world would have had gaps, and they would have had endless stories trying to explain and fill in those gaps.

We must also accept that within the gulf of time that has passed between the ancient and the modern worlds, the structure of the universe has been transformed dramatically. Not physically, of course, but conceptually. We've filled in some of those knowledge gaps with better information; actual data has replaced speculation. Believing, in some places, has been superseded with seeing. Additionally, through our exploration of the world, we've also stumbled upon new gaps; there are new questions, new limits, new mysteries. And these new gaps continue to challenge what we once thought we knew with certainty. Our ever-expanding view of our universe hasn't stopped growing. We're still uncovering, theorising and testing the limits of what we know about this place we call home.

It's not that any of us are wrong, as such, but no matter where we stand in history, all of our greatest theories are approximations. Over time, we get closer to clarifying the truth, but the "blurred" edges to our knowledge still remain. As the Roman philosopher Seneca put it, way back in the first century:

> [K]nowledge will be unfolded only through long successive ages. There will come a time when our descendants will be amazed that we did not know things that are so plain to them [...].[9]

Seneca's words in the context of his own time (which was also an enlightened age, full of intellectual pursuit) are equally applicable to ours. One day, we will be seen as prehistoric. Which makes you wonder how much of today's current scientific thinking will still be *current* in another three millennia? How many of our greatest theories—the stories we currently tell—will be thought of as primitive and akin to the Earth sandwich?

Of course, we don't need to wait millennia to see these sorts of changes in ideas. The past five centuries alone have seen enormous paradigm shifts in how we understand the universe and our place in it, shifts that have been both revolutionary and challenging, not only to the religious world but to the world as a whole.

Take something as straightforward as a Heliocentric Solar System.[10] The idea of the Earth orbiting the Sun has gained ground only in recent history. Such a theory would have been totally foreign to the original audience of the Genesis origins story. As I've said, the modern, proven and observable model of our Solar system—one that exists within a galaxy of other solar systems, which is but one galaxy contained within a universe full of galaxies—doesn't match with Genesis' model of the Earth (on its own) being sandwiched between the water above and the water below. We've moved forward in our understanding; from the idea of an Earth sandwich, through the phase of thinking that our Earth was the centre of the universe (a Geocentric view), and eventually to the modern acknowledgment of a Sun-centric (Heliocentric) solar system which is far from the heart of the Cosmos (and by the way, there have been many other alternatives along the way). And it goes without saying that this transition wasn't easy or free of controversy.

It was roughly five hundred years ago when the heliocentric model of our solar system began its upward struggle for dominance, as it contended against the scientific views of its day and the biblical interpretations of the religious authorities—both of which held to the idea of the Sun revolving around a stationary Earth.[11] Even though the "new" theory's main protagonists shared the Christian faith, they were still labelled heretics and persecuted by those who adamantly refused, on biblical grounds, to accept what we know as true.[12]

We may feel embarrassed about the resistance of these people. We might even want to call them stupid or fundamentalist from our privileged vantage point of hindsight. But are we any better? They believed that to embrace the idea of an orbiting Earth was to move away from the literal words of the Bible which speak of the Earth's foundations being immovable. Many Christians today do the same when it comes to Inflationary Cosmology and Evolution.

And yet, unlike a number of Bible readers today, those who embraced this new scientific understanding of the solar system didn't abandon Scripture, they learnt to reread it. They didn't see the choice being between scientific discovery and the Bible. They saw that the choice lay with their method of interpretation. I know this because the way in which some of us today understand and use Scripture to defend it against further scientific progress (ironically) is a product of how they came to interpret it.

Some of these methods don't always work though. They create more problems than they solve by hiding (or selectively overlooking) what the text clearly alludes to. They're interpretation methods which are quick to point out texts which speak of the circumference of the Earth (because they appear to agree with our epoch's awareness of the world as a globe), and which are more than happy to downplay the texts which speak of the world having four corners. Such methods fail—and create further contradictions—because they still prioritise the reader's world view and language over the writer's world view and language. Tensions arise because we try superimposing our world view over an ancient one, silencing what the ancient writers are trying to communicate. So when it comes to reading the creation stories, we have people who reject (or who are innocently ignorant of) the Earth sandwich with which Genesis begins, and who automatically interpret the opening of the creation account as if it's describing the Big Bang—which it certainly isn't.

What a strange contradiction this then creates for those who claim that the Genesis creation account should be understood literally. The same modern, plain-text-reading Christians who happily embrace the idea of our Earth revolving around the Sun (and hold to this as being biblical), also say that the creation account of Genesis should be read as historical fact—literal, unchanging truth, to be understood as what we would have seen unfolding if we had been there to witness it firsthand.

I'll be blunt; if you want to take Genesis *literally*—as the factual, historical and chronological, scientific account of the material formation of the structure of the universe—then you're going to have drop our model of the solar system, surely?

## ETHNOCENTRISM

To be perfectly clear, I don't feel that this is the choice we need to make. Instead of pitting Scripture against science, what we need to do is start reading the creation accounts *literarily*. What I mean by that is this: we need to respect the Bible as an *Ancient Text*, which requires a thoughtful reading, and stop treating it like a modern textbook, which can be read at a simple, surface level. We can't abandon the world view out of which Scripture was written and replace it with our own. Additionally, we can't assume that everything that the ancient world said was to be understood in a rigid, dumbed-down, literal sense, free of connotation and poetic flourish.

As ancient texts, the manuscripts which have been compiled together to form the Bible utilise a number of different genres in order to communicate what they have to say. Historical dramas, parables, poetry and hymns find themselves braided in with genealogies, laws and proverbs. And all of this is saturated with figurative language; much like language today. The Bible is full of euphemism, idiom, hyperbole, wordplay, allegory and anthropomorphisms. Scholars who study the original language of the Bible point this out all the time, and pull wonderful insights out of the Bible because of it; insights which contain a measure of depth, beauty and truth that literal description would fail to capture. When it came to communicating something important, the ancient writers of Scripture, like modern storytellers, didn't see symbolic/emotive language as secondary to the technical language that we're used to in textbooks, it was preferred.

We still prefer symbolic speech today. We say things all the time which are not meant to be taken literally, but which are still used to adequately convey truth in some sense. To illustrate this point with a topical example, how many of us still say, 'The Sun rises in the east, and it sets in the west'?

Now there's nothing wrong with that, is there?

Apart from it being a lie. Or, at least it would be if we all took it as a literal description of the Sun's movements.

We know the Sun doesn't move in relation to us. We know it's incapable of rising or setting; it goes neither up, down, left nor right. The Sun is one of the most stationary objects in our solar system (thankfully, otherwise our planet would be in a right mess).[13] But when people say things like this, we know what they're getting at. We know what they are describing and what they are not—we understand the limits and the adequacy of the pictures they are using.

We may not take figurative speech literally, but that doesn't mean that figurative speech isn't describing how things *really* are. All we're doing is employing a more germane way of getting that reality across. Which can be confusing, if we are not discerning.

Sometimes we jump out of our skin, or die laughing, or find ourselves barking up the wrong tree and beating around the bush. Life isn't always a bed of roses, is it? Once in a blue moon, we find ourselves feeling a bit under the weather, or green with envy because someone has stolen our thunder, or we see red because someone has let the cat out of the bag about something that we were keeping behind closed doors. My son frequently protests that it'll take him a million years to tidy his room, and I regularly tell him that it will only take a second if he pulled his finger out and shifted his backside into gear. Which is true—I'm not pulling his leg.

Sometimes, we need to take how things are communicated with a pinch of salt. But of course, feel free to sit on the fence about this. After all, my argument could be full of holes.

You see, some of our rereading of the Bible, in order to keep it as literal as possible, is bogus. Flat understandings don't even work in modern conversations. And it doesn't work with the Bible because doing so disrespects its literary forms, its cultural characteristics, its authors' voices and their audience's ears. It rejects both the way in which the ancient world thought and the way in which the ancient world communicated. Flat, literal readings lead us to slice and splice, and cut and paste the modern, Western way of thinking into the ancient, Eastern way, resulting in all sorts of confusing interpretations. Personally—and this isn't solely my view, or even a modern view—the better way of reading and understanding Scripture isn't to pull it into the twenty-first century, but to keep it where it was written.

Reading Scripture is akin to eavesdropping on the conversation of someone who comes from another time and another place. So if we aren't prepared to wrestle with the cultural and historical context of when and where the conversation is taking place—or prepared to enter into the thinking of those involved in that conversation—then we're likely to walk away with the wrong impression, spreading Chinese whispers of what was never intended. As modern readers of an ancient book, we must tread carefully and reverently.

This doesn't mean abandoning what the Bible has to say to us today. But it does require us to stop pitting it against a world view that it wasn't responding to, or in conversation with. We must hear Scripture's conversation with its own world first, before translating it into ours—including the book of Genesis.

Yes, doing this will highlight the differences in world views; there will be obvious clashes between what was once thought and what we have now observed. And yes, this might lead us to ask why the Bible would tell *us* a story which isn't true; why would the Bible tell *us* about an Earth sandwich and not a solar system? More so, why would God lie to *us*, if God is indeed the voice whispering in the authors' ears, telling them what to say?

Firstly, this story wasn't told to *us*, it was told to, and by, those in the ancient world. And secondly, assuming that God is the unfiltered voice inspiring these storytellers, it's entirely possible that God—if God knows anything about communicating with people—accommodated to what people currently understood or thought in order to move them forward to a new level of understanding. Like any good teacher, surely God knows how to teach in a way that people can grasp. In other words, there's nothing odd about the Bible using the ancient model of the Cosmos to talk to ancient people about God's role in the forming of the Cosmos and about God's continued work within the Cosmos.[14]

Whatever Genesis had to say to its ancient audience, it said it using the framework of its ancient audience's culture and time—with a few important tweaks, which we'll come to shortly. Therefore, the ancient stories of the arrangement of the cosmos and how it came to exist are underlying and infused and reflected within the Genesis story. There's accommodation to, conversation with and challenge of the views already in existence; there is a level of continuity and also discontinuity between the picture Genesis presents and the framework that the ancient world held. This should help us to see that the writers of Genesis weren't attempting to change the ancient world's scientific stance on the universe, but their understandings of God and God's purposes. As such, those ancient views of cosmology do not have to be agreed with in order for us to grasp and affirm the heart of Genesis' message.

How do we get to the heart of that message?

Maybe by distinguishing where the story of Genesis is discontinuous within its own historical context and not our own? But because we only ever notice how it differs from today's ideas and priorities about the history of the universe, we think that the subject matter of Genesis is the material origins of the universe. We notice differences that the ancient world wouldn't have given a second thought to.

Our struggle is that as products of the twentieth and twenty-first centuries, we're more inclined to read Genesis against the background of the twentieth and twenty-first centuries. Or, to put that another way, we decide and alternate the agenda of Genesis' message by asking it the questions we are currently faced with. We suffer historical amnesia and forget that Genesis was written for and by an entirely different historical population facing an entirely different set of questions.

Come to think of it, it's rather arrogant to presume that Genesis was written solely *to* us; addressing the questions of our time, in our materialist, post-Enlightenment, Western culture. This is what is called an *ethnocentric* interpretation of Scripture, a way of reading which prioritises *our* time, *our* culture, *our* values and *our* ways of thinking as the only lens through which Scripture can be properly understood.

## MACHINE MEN, WITH MACHINE MINDS[15]

Saying that Genesis wasn't written *to* us, doesn't mean that Genesis hasn't got anything important to communicate to us. On the contrary, Genesis has lots to say to us, as I hope this chapter (and this book) makes clear. But the questions the creation story addresses are not our twenty-first century, material- and mechanics-driven questions about Cosmogony and Cosmology. We ask many *How?* questions with regards to processes. The ancients would have also been inclined to ask *How?* But their approach and ours are not the same.

Scholar John H. Walton, in his excellent book *The Lost World of Genesis One*, suggests that we, in the modern world, have a knack of thinking about the cosmos as a machine, and consequently we want to know how and when it was manufactured. There's a dominantly materialistic agenda to our thinking, and interpretation, therefore, of Genesis. The ancients, however, didn't liken the cosmos to a machine but thought of it more like a kingdom. Because of this, the questions Genesis addresses aren't regarding the material origins of the world at all, but about its function, its purpose and how it is ruled. We want to know how it was all made; they wanted to know how it was all run. In other words, we in the twenty-first century have a substance addiction; we think substance—what things are made from—is everything. But, as Walton points out, the Bible's culture thought otherwise:

> Although we are aware of the physical world around us, we live in a world of functions. Materialism sees the functions of our world as the consequence of structures, that is, that objects or phenomena in our world function the way that they do because of their physical structures. In the biblical way of thinking, the objects and phenomena in the world function the way they do because of God's creative purposes [...]. The biblical way of thinking counters materialism when it insists that the most important part of the equation is God's purposes.
>
> Our world tends to subordinate the functional to the material. That is why ever since the Enlightenment (at least) we have generally believed that it is most important for us to think of creation in terms of the material. Our world has taught us to give priority to the material [...]. The Bible considers it much more important to say that God has made everything *work* rather than being content to say that God made the physical stuff.[16]

That's not to say that the Bible doesn't affirm God as the creator of all the substances that exist. It does, repeatedly.[17] Life, animate or not, isn't some random cosmic accident, or a strange, self-existing emergent property of clashing, erratic atoms; it exists because of divine intent. Because the Bible affirms this, and because it's speaking to a culture—unlike that of today—where everyone believed that a god or gods created all that exists, the Genesis account doesn't need to fixate on this as the purpose of its message. The emphasis here is not on substance but on divine *identity* and *intent*.

Even if Genesis was about answering how the material world came to exist—and I don't believe it is—it's striking how short and undetailed this account is. It's missing a wealth of information we would want; and what it does say, it says using poetic rhythm more than scientific terminology.

Imagine, for a moment, that God had told the author of Genesis everything about the mechanisms and processes that had brought about this vast universe, and that the author had then proceeded to write it down like some ancient version of Hawking's *A Brief History of Time* or Greene's *An Elegant Universe*. I've read those books; they're extraordinary books, and Brian Greene's is one of my all-time favourites. But even the one which describes itself as *Brief* is far from being brief (though it is a passing-glance description compared to what it could potentially have been).

Let's be honest, some of us struggle with reading the genealogies and the codified law sections of Scripture; how would we ever cope with passages about Relativity, Quantum Electrodynamics and the Periodic Table of Elements?

Personally, I'd love this. But Steph, despite being smarter than me, would still label this as a 'Yawn-athon'. And I imagine she wouldn't be alone.

Luckily for Steph, none of this is the priority for the authors of Genesis; *purpose* is in focus and *processes* hardly get a look in at all. The motivation behind their composition isn't to contemplate physics, examine biology or explain chemistry. The writers are not interested in addressing those things in this account; they're content to just write that God said, "Let the *earth* bring forth…". The age of the universe has no mention in this tale; it's not even an afterthought or a hanging question. The vast scope of the diversity of life on planet Earth only gets a slight nod; the menagerie of animals and the zoological beauty of plants, which make us gasp in awe for hours on end when watching shows like David Attenborough's *Planet Earth*, all seem rather understated in Genesis. Even humanity—whom we would classify as the pinnacle of biological life—doesn't grab much headline space in this account of creation. Earth gets more mentions than us, and we aren't even the climax of the story—God's *rest* is.

This finale tells us that the writers of Genesis had other things they wished to contemplate, namely God. Maybe then, taking all of this into account, it's best to read Genesis as a literary account of *purpose*;

> *God's* purpose;

> *God's Kingdom* purpose on Earth;

> *not* material origins?

Of course, to suggest such things sounds like I am challenging the authority of Scripture. So out of paranoia, I feel the need to state that I love the words of Scripture; I regard them highly. I treat the Bible with respect and awe, valuing its complexity, history, culture and voice(s). And I can never imagine a time when I will stop wanting to delve deeper into it.

I'm not challenging the Bible's authority, but merely, in this case, trying to define what that *authority* is and is not. It would take another book for me to grapple with what I think about describing the Bible as *Authoritative*, *Infallible*, and *Inspired*—all words that have had some huge baggage attached to them over the years. But for now, to touch briefly on this one area, I would suggest that to read Genesis as a scientific account of how our universe came to materially exist is to misunderstand what it *is* saying with authority. Actually, to misunderstand the message of any story—whether fact or fiction, written or spoken—is to demean what it's authoritatively conveying.

Personally, as someone who enjoys reading science books as well as theological treatises, I have no issues with holding scientific understanding and Genesis together. That doesn't mean I have no scientific questions. Of course I do; lots of them. I also have plenty of theological and hermeneutical questions about the Bible. But it's a false dichotomy to pit science against Genesis.[18]

The real question Genesis would have left on its original hearer's lips, and the question it should leave on ours also, is not, 'Did it happen like that?', but 'Who is this God?

# 1.3 | THE GOSPEL OF GENESIS: A DIVINE RÉSUMÉ

I want you to think of Genesis as a song, as an anthem about God's redemptive power and God's eventual dwelling within creation. Within this song, God saves the world from its oppression to a formless, dysfunctional and chaotic state and then, on the seventh day—the day made Holy—God descends, rests, and reigns within the temple of creation.

In many ways, the opening poem of Genesis was the Good News, the Gospel, of its day. In the same way that the story of the Exodus from Egypt would have been heard by the Jewish exiles in Babylonia, news of this kind of God, and of this kind of world-ordering power, would have been a seedbed of hope for those who desired liberation from slavery and oppression. Such a song would have brought strength to the dispossessed, to those who felt formless and void within their bondage and exile. Telling this story, singing this song, living in its light, would have enabled those in slavery to challenge the metanarrative that the current world order insisted upon. Especially when the controlling narrative's demeaning, dehumanising, and degrading views of you and your place in the world had been supposedly imposed by the "gods" who articulated those views of you and the world.

Genesis sings of a counter world order, and of a God who arranges the world in a way that is contrary to the coercive forces that were currently running the show. This is an anthem of revolution, a chant which challenged the foundations of the world's powerhouses. When reading the creation account of Genesis One within its own historical context of the Ancient Near East (ANE), it's not difficult to understand the theological and political punch that this song would have had.

Think of those who would have worshipped the Sun and Moon as gods, as divine beings who had control over the things of the Earth. Genesis challenges this thinking—like a cultural slap across the face—by stating that the Sun and Moon aren't powerful beings at all, but merely created objects, brought about in the same way as the plants and animals, and who therefore have no control over their own course, let alone the fate of Earth's population. For those who would deify the sea, or who would idiomatically use it to symbolise Chaos, the Genesis God is the one who comes and constrains this Chaos, parting the ancient waters, and bringing order out of them. God is the one who tames the primordial monster.[19]

Within the Genesis song, all that the world of the ANE worshipped, prayed to, appealed to, and tried to control and appease through sacrificial ritual and religious rites, are cast down from their transcendental status to the dust of the created order. These other cosmological and heavenly powers turn out to be frauds and fabrications. False hopes. Non-contenders.

Maybe one way to consider the Genesis One account then is to think of it as a Divine Résumé. Only the creator God is King; the other "gods" aren't even a reality.

In an ironic twist, then, what many of us today think of as a statement of *Theistic* faith, would have been originally heard as the *Atheistic* treaty of its day. Imagine the uproar that Friedrich Nietzsche's *God is Dead*, or Christopher Hitchens' *God is Not Great* have spawned in modern times, and you're close to the paradigm-smashing impact of Genesis in its own culture.

But not only is the known heavenly pantheon stripped of all its faux, man-made glory, *how* the true creator God goes about his work is also in stark contrast to the other claims in circulation.

Other ANE creation stories embellish tales of the world being formed by war or being accidentally brought into existence through the cataclysmic consequences of heavenly power-struggles, but Genesis proposes an alternative. Every component of creation is arranged, ordered and brought about in love. Nothing is surplus to requirement, or classified as the collateral damage of conflict, or treated like the unintended debris that a worker leaves behind. Differing from the other ANE accounts, creation—the vast scope of the universe—comes about not through the destructive means of tearing, ripping and corrupting the material world, but through the life-giving, organising utterances of God.

This is crucial to note; *God, according to Genesis, is not at war with all that is made. Neither does God use war to bring order to all that is made.* Order comes through God's *liberating* and *loving* proclamation.

It's *all* good. Every piece, pattern and purpose.

The phrase, '*it was good*', is echoed within the finale of every stanza of the creation poem. Each day's work is affirmed and admired by its artisan. And the final tasks to be completed within the sixth day culminate in the crescendo of '*very good*' being spoken over all that has transpired. God delights over erosion and tides, sunrise and nightfall, the multiplication of fauna and flora, spiders and humans. The water cycle, plate tectonics, the laws of thermodynamics and the space-bending power of gravity, are all met with applause. The substance and function of the cosmos are imbued with divine pleasure.

In summary, then, the *material* world is God's *good* creation, and this material existence, according to this ancient song, isn't a stage for humanity or a cage of bondage to our true, soulish nature; it's a display of divine craftsmanship. This is God's masterpiece. Creation is God's Temple (a concept we'll explore in the next section); a place made for God's glory to dwell in.

Before moving on, it's important that we take this in. If we are going to understand the Gospel, if we are going to grasp the dream of God, then we need to let this 'Genesis Gospel' saturate us.

The focal point of the Genesis Gospel is the resting and reigning place of God: God's Kingdom. In some modern versions of the Gospel, however, 'me' usurps the central position. And by 'me', some mean that reductionally elusive, non-material, "real" bit of me; the soul. As these versions go (versions that have replaced the Jewish thrust of the story with the Greek philosophy of Plato) God acts to rescue 'me' from this corrupted, evil material existence and take 'me' to a place that is existent, but in a non-material kind of way.

Not only does this not make any sense, but it misses the point of Genesis—by a long, long way. In Genesis, God liberates the world from the oppressive grip of Chaos and Darkness and then rests (reigns) within it. This is the thrust of the Gospel, not only in Genesis, but also throughout the corpus of the Old Testament and into the New.

We could say that in both the Incarnation and the Bodily Resurrection, God says a firm, 'yes', to the material world. Through becoming flesh, God rejects the view that the material of creation is evil; by becoming dust, God embraces and reaffirms its intrinsic 'very-goodness'. If God really is the Saviour and King of creation, then this isn't about souls, but about every *body* that exists within the epic spectrum of a neutrino to a nebula, and whatever is left to discover outside of those boundaries.

With humility, then, we must be willing to accept that the Gospel is not about *us*. It involves *us*. But it is much, much bigger than *you* and *I*.

I appreciate that not all Christians are eager to embrace the idea of science and Genesis being held together. The thing is, we could argue until we're blue in the face about the relationship between science and Scripture. And personally, which interpretation of Genesis you hold to doesn't concern me too much; I don't feel it's an essential to the faith. But regardless of the '*How it all came about*' questions, the bigger emphasis of this story cannot be overlooked; God's habitation in the Earth. And when we miss this emphasis and keep the rhetoric of Genesis to questions of 'Did it happen like that or not?', it's then that we are in danger of misunderstanding the purposes of God.

But let's not rush ahead. Let's dwell in this creation account a while longer, because as I've said, *dwelling* is what this story is about.

# 1.4 | THE IMMANENT GOD AND THE *IMAGO DEI*

The story of Genesis One would have resonated deeply with anyone in the ANE who had ever built a place of worship. Biblically speaking, the literary structure of Genesis is similar to the accounts of Moses building the Tabernacle, and Solomon constructing the Temple. The Genesis pattern is even echoed by the gospel writer John, as he arranges his account of the Jesus story to tell us of how God *tabernacled/dwelt* with his people.

So let's put the story this way.

In the beginning, God sets out to form a Temple, an environment that would house his glory. *Glory*, in this sense, isn't describing goosebumps, tingly-sensations, or nice shiny things. *Glory* is a way of saying *heavy presence*; a way of describing the fullness of a person's identity inhabiting a place.

When we first meet this place of habitation within this song though, it's found to be in a *formless* state. This term isn't describing a lack of shape (everything that exists has a form) but a measure of order; *formless* is the lack of *Shalom* (we'll come back to the idea behind this word later). In the beginning, God's chosen place of rest is in a state of chaos; enslaved and cloaked within darkness and disarray. But after brooding and lamenting over the surface of the world, the incandescence of God enters into the darkness and overcomes it with light as God's Spirit breathes blessings upon it; 'Let there be…'

According to Genesis, God liberates creation from its disordered state through the creative power of his word. And these divine words don't return void—colluding with and perpetuating the chaotic formlessness—they bring forth function and flourishing, life and order. As a song of rescue, Genesis follows the same rhythms of divine intervention that we observe in all the scriptural stories of exile-to-redemption: God leads from oppression to liberation, from darkness to light, from enslavement to vocation, from chaos to Shalom.[20]

With each liberating 'Let there be...', God removes the disorder and arranges the temple; defining the different "utensils" within it and separating them from each other through the act of *naming*. When something is named in Scripture, it's not about giving it a label, but setting it apart and calling it to a function. We see a similar thing when God calls people in the Bible to particular vocations, such as Abram (Abraham), Sarai (Sarah) and Jacob (Israel); God's renaming of them is a consecration.

So God names the Temple's utensils, separating the Sun from the Moon, the Day from the Night, and the Land from the Sea, etc. This is God's pattern every day throughout his sanctuary; naming and blessing as 'good'. Not a moral good, but a functional, 'that's as it should be' good. All are singing in harmony within the symphony of creation.

If you wanted a loose analogy, you could liken this process to buying and renovating a dilapidated house. Imagine walking through the front doors and into its musty interior, only to witness the thick layers of dust and mould, the rotten floorboards, the tattered furniture that's been strewn about, and the overall lack of purpose to any of its rooms. You pull the boards off the windows, allowing the light to filter into the empty spaces, and you slowly begin to walk through house stating, 'This will be the lounge, this will be the bedroom... we'll have a light there, a desk here, etc.' Over the following days, the work follows your vision and eventually what was once a formless house has become a home. God's work in creation is a similar affair, and if there's an encouraging aside to take from this story so far (a lesson that recurs throughout the Bible), it's that God is drawn to the broken and neglected things, and does the miraculous with them.

As I've said above, Moses' Tabernacle and Solomon's Temple both follow a similar procedure; their places of worship are organised by separating and consecrating the various utensils for their purposes within the dwelling place of the Lord.[21] Of course, after the work is done by both Moses and Solomon, after the place of worship is built and organised, there's still something left to happen: the *presence* of God (represented in the

Moses and Solomon stories as a cloud) has yet to arrive and dwell. But before this "arriving", something else needs to be set in place.

In the ANE, once a temple was completed, the final thing to be brought into the place of worship would be the *image* or the *ikon* of the deity to whom the house belonged. This *image* wouldn't be anything special in or of itself. Like idols of old, it could be made of stone, wood, or precious metals such as gold—the same materials that have also been used in forming the temple structure itself. It wasn't the material from which the *image* was made which set it apart from the rest of the temple; what made it different— *other*—was what would happen to it. What separated it from the rest of the Temple was the function given to it.

Once placed in the sanctuary, the *image* would be anointed; usually with oil, water, or maybe blood. Like the *image* itself, this anointing was metaphorical; it symbolised that the *image* had received something of the *life*, the *essence*, the *spirit*, the *breath* of its deity.

Sound familiar?

I should add here that this anointing didn't make the *image* divine. It was a consecration; a commissioning of its function to speak/mediate on behalf of god. Without the s*pirit*, the object would still remain *dead*, raw material (that *dead* is important to note). But with the *breath* of its god, it became an earthy object acting as a representative of divine life; a *living* stone. The *image* testified to the immanence of its deity; god was with us.[22]

Again, in the accounts of Moses' Tabernacle and Solomon's Temple, it's when this image's anointing is completed that the presence, the glory of God—usually represented by a dense cloud—comes and resides in the place of worship, subsequently making it holy. In the Genesis account, it's on the evening that follows the placing of this image when God 'rests' and blesses the seventh day as holy.[23]

For those of us who are familiar with the stories contained in the Bible, this will be firing all sorts of connections in our minds about *Oil* and *Breath* and the pouring out of God's Spirit within both the Old and New Testaments.

For now, though, a question, with a rather obvious answer, should be poised on our lips;

Who was this Imago Dei?

In the story of Genesis, within God's creation Temple, Humanity (in its plurality and diversity) was formed and commissioned to be the *image* of God. As Genesis One and Two poetically express it:

> Then God said, 'Let us make people in our image, to be like ourselves
> [...].'
> So God created people in his own image;
> God patterned them after himself;
> male and female he created them.[24]

> God formed a man's body from the *dust* of the ground and breathed into
> it the *breath* of *life*. And the man became a living person.[25]

I'm not going to look too closely into the other creation story of Genesis Two, here—I'll leave that for you to delve into when you reach the *Further Reading* section of this book and read from those who are better equipped than myself.

What I would say though, in agreement with the scholars Christopher Wright and John Walton, is that the *image* of God is not some biological property that we possess, but a calling upon humanity to represent and serve God. It's a *priestly* consecration.

In other words, we're not the *image of God* because we are human, as opposed to being a cat or a snail. We didn't come to inherit this property because it was latent within the matter from which we're formed; we are not constructed out of some alien substance, but are fashioned from the same chemical material as the rest of God's temple. We are but dust.

Bearing the image of God is not anatomical or physiological at all, but pneumatological. What I mean by that is this: it has nothing to do with our gender, hormones, genome, or the colour of our skin. Nor is it a measure of our physical ability or inability. It's nothing to do with any of our human attributes; it's got everything to do with God's Spirit living within us.

All that other stuff is the "dead", raw material. But the *Breath* (pneuma) is a gift that transforms our humanity into image bearers. It's God bestowing his presence, his essence, his likeness upon us, enabling us to reflect and witness to the immanent presence of God within our world.[26]

Humanity was anointed to look like God; called to reflect what God is like within the cosmic temple; to mediate divine life into creation. And to be clear, when I say what God looks like, I'm not talking about God having arms, legs and a pointy nose. Looking like God means being a living description of the Divine's nature and character. Humanity was to be God's parable, God's expression of self.

It's for this reason that the Ten Commandments forbid the making of images for worship. It wasn't only a warning against worshipping other gods. Underneath the second commandment is the fundamental understanding that God had already prepared himself an image: *Us*. And I mean *us*. Not *I*, or *me*, or *you*, or *them*, or *us* in the tribal sense. I'm talking about humanity as a whole.

Through how we lived with each other and through how we stewarded the Earth, God was to be made visible. Life, therefore, in all its social and cultural permeations, was worship; this includes science, technology, art, music, farming, trading, parenting, marriage, singleness and so on. Through all of it, we were to participate in the flourishing of God's vision for this planet. We were to join with God in ordering the temple; keeping it chaos-free by mediating God's life and expression into it. We would flourish, Life would flourish.

Except it doesn't look like that now, does it? Even the composer of the Genesis poem is writing from a point in time when things weren't as they ought to be; trying to answer the age-old question of 'Why is the world like this?' For them back then, as well as us today, it looked as if chaos still ruled.

Knowing that God gave such an important task to humanity, I can't help but echo the double-layered sentiment of Oscar Wilde: Did God overestimate our capability, or his own ability when forming humanity?

What went wrong?

In a nutshell, the human compulsion to *mine*.

# 1.5 | ALTERED IMAGES

The problem, as the story unfolds in the third chapter of Genesis, is that Humanity rebels. Unhappy with merely being an *image*, not wanting to be a signpost to something else, we shook off the divine image and decided to go it alone.

Of course, that's a narrow, simplistic view of the matter, and we will explore the deeper and more critical motivations behind this act later. For now, though, we'll stick to the simplified view and say that the temptation to be God—to hold all the cards and have all the power—was too difficult to resist (we will come back and have a closer look at this particular story in Parts 2 and 6).

Within the developing story, humanity's failure to image God is where *death* enters the scene.

Imagine a change in the movie soundtrack, if you like.

What kind of death is something that gets you thinking? Some theologians accept that Adam and Eve, representatives of the first people, would have been inherently mortal, not naturally immortal. Being made from dust was a typical ancient, symbolic way of describing mortality. Immortality was only available to them through having access to what is symbolised by the *Tree of Life*.

But putting that aside for a moment, surely death existed prior to what is commonly referred to as 'The Fall'? After all, trees and plants are said to reproduce after their own kind in Genesis 1:11-12, and we know how that works, right?

Trees produce fruit that contains seeds, which, if unpicked, falls to the ground where the flesh of the fruit begins to *rot*. As the fruit *decays*, the seed, which was concealed within the fruit, is released. Over the coming days, this seed will be buried by some animal or covered by dirt through some other means, and after a period of time, the seed will *deteriorate*, allowing what it is currently made of to cease being one thing and commence becoming something else.

Alternatively, something eats the fruit; maybe a bird, or a squirrel, or us. We also know how this process works. Digestion is a process in which a *breakdown* occurs between the chemical bonds of the food we've ingested. Our bodies *destroy* the fruit, *ripping* it apart and thereby reducing it to its fundamental components. Digestion is also a type of *death*; what goes in doesn't come out. Well, something comes out, we'll all admit, but it isn't what went in.

We feed on death. From the food we consume, we take the construction materials and energy that our bodies need in order to develop and live, whilst the stuff we can't use gets "thrown" out of our bodies as waste. And when a seed comes out in that, then it finds itself in an excellent batch of fertiliser. The seed, in turn, decays, emerging in new life via a process similar to digestion; it also takes from the fertilizer the construction material it needs.

Through this cycle of death and decay, a shoot of life emerges from the seed… which grows into another tree… which then goes on to produce more seed-bearing fruit, etc. This is the reason some people call it the circle of life.

I'm not meaning to go all Mufasa on you.[27] But at some level, an entropic, decaying mechanism which uses death to recycle life must have been at work.

So let's think of this *death* in a different way.

Have you ever had a numb arm?

We've all experienced this numb feeling at some point in time, I'm sure. Sometimes it's accompanied by that tingling sensation we've dubbed 'pins and needles'. If you can't remember this sensation right now, sit on your legs for twenty minutes and then try to walk across the room. Please don't run.

My Mum used to say that this numbness happens because the blood has stopped flowing properly. Poor circulation is just one of a number of reasons why this happens, but regardless of the cause, we all acknowledge that something of our *life* isn't present in the limb; hence why it's often nicknamed a *dead* arm.

The arm is still a part of us—at least it still looks like it's a part of us—our *life*, our blood is still made available to it, and yet our life has stopped finding its expression through it. It's biologically alive, but it has ceased to operate as it should.

That's what Humanity did in Eden. In reaching for *mine*, in ceasing to operate as we should, we also rejected the breath/Spirit being made available to us via the source of life, and so *living* stones reverted to *dead* stones. We refused to be an expression, a vehicle for the life of God within the creation temple. The Human mirror that should have been looking towards God and reflecting out into the world, instead curved in on itself, and things became distorted. Not only did humanity enslave itself, but (to borrow the Apostle Paul's words from Romans 8) creation also found itself in bondage; no longer having access to the life that should have been mediated to it through God's symbols on Earth.[28] Divine life stopped flowing through us and death began to reign.

To use a Jewish concept; prior to the rebellion of God's images, things existed in a state of *Shalom*—a harmonious, flourishing knitted togetherness. But afterwards, things began to unravel; things began to perish. Paradise—to use the title of Milton's famous poem—was lost. Some of what was was undone, and what should have been was stalled.

I know the story talks about humanity being removed from Eden, but in a sense, it was us who tried to oust God. It was *I* who usurped the creation. We tried to kick God out of his resting place. We wanted to fill the world with our image. We thought we could hold back chaos—a force that undoes creation—but instead, we perpetuated it.

## THE REFLECTION-LESS GOD

The Jewish and Christian worldview doesn't pretend that all is as it should be; it never has. It acknowledges that this temple of God doesn't radiate with the glory it was designed to house.

That's not to say that the material world is bad or evil, it's not. This is God's world, and it is both intrinsically good and beautiful. Creation is a breathtaking, wondrous space. So it's not the material world that we need rescuing from; in many ways, it needs rescuing from *us*.

But please don't misunderstand that either. I'm not asking for a planet devoid of humans, or condoning mass global genocide. At its core, humanity is not repulsive or depraved. Like creation, we too are intrinsically and inherently beautiful.

However, deep down in each of us, we recognise that something isn't as it should be. There appear to be flaws, blemishes and cracks within this Temple's structure. And then there's the terrible stuff that happens, the things we would identify as acts of evil, injustice and suffering. We switch on our TV sets or pick up the daily newspapers, and we shudder as we sense it.

Maybe it's only me, but I look at our world some days and I wonder *'Where is God?'*

I don't ask that because I claim to be religious. I asked that question a long time before I made any decision to follow Jesus. But since making that decision, the question's potency has hardly diminished. If anything, that question has been amplified; my whole being groans all the more loudly when I see the devastation of violence, greed, poverty, hunger, and disease across our globe.

I'm not naïve enough to believe I am the only one to sense this, either. I'm certain that when we all look across our world, and stare hard at all the wars, the oppression, the environmental damage, the injustice—all that we would intriguingly label as *inhumanity*—we all wonder,

   *'Where is God?'*

*'How can there be a God?'*

It's easy to see why people reject the concept of God. Deep down, I don't think it's anything at all to do with the sciences or philosophical questions about meaning (maybe these issues are the gloss over the deeper struggle?). Personally, I think we look at the world, the *inhumanity* of it all, and we don't see a God in any of it.

The irony is, I think God would agree with this atheistic perspective— God struggles to see himself in this kind of humanity as well. And this problem is one that crops up frequently within Scripture.

As well as expressing our age-old concerns about the apparent absence of God, the book of Psalms also poignantly echoes the Creator's search for self:

> The LORD looks down from heaven
> on the entire human race;
> he looks to see if there is even one with real understanding,
> one who seeks for God.
> But no, all have turned away from God;
> all have become corrupt.
> No one does good,
> Not even one![29]

Picture that: God searching over the temple of creation, looking for his reflection, his *image*, and not being able to see it. It's not a coincidence that the first question asked by God in Scripture is, 'Where are you?'[30] It's a question that can be heard echoing down the cavernous narratives of the canon.

Along with God, we find ourselves also involved in that search. We look for God, asking if God exists, but what we see isn't enough to convince us that God is there. We too struggle to see God's *image* in the world.

Can you see the circular nature of the problem?

## FALLING SHORT

The Apostle Paul wrote, 'All have sinned; all fall short of God's glorious standard.'[31] This isn't a matter of behaviour, per se, or of merely keeping rules. This *falling short of God's standard* is speaking of the absence of God's *image* reflected through our life. The Greek that is used in this verse carries the thought of missing the mark, like an archer missing a target. But as I've said, this is not a moral target as such, but an *imaging* target; we neglected our vocation of making God visible.

Of course, this is a hard truth to swallow. So instead, we blame the apparent "absence" of God, on God. Either, a) God is angry at us and is actively punishing us through the hardships of life; or b) God is apathetic towards human affairs and has abandoned us altogether; or c) there is no God anyway, and there never has been.

Like a dog chasing its tail, we suspect that there's a culprit at the end of this riddle. But we fail to acknowledge that it's us and that there's still another option: d) we were meant to make God visible, to be the bearers of divine life, to be stewards of this world, but we turned our backs on the calling and instead we degraded, defiled and distorted the authentic image we were supposed to transmit (again, we'll come back to this later in Part 6).

The crazy thing is, that in those moments when our humanity is at its very best—which is most days, I think—when we are shown love, or kindness, or compassion, or mercy and tenderness; those days when someone invests in us or comes alongside us in our hardest struggles; when we feel cared for and valued and wanted; when we're creative, or we pull together in some great humanitarian project to solve a crisis or bring about the end of injustice; or when we feel "at one" with nature, or experience art or a symphony or a concert; or when we hear a child's infectious giggle… on *those* days, we catch a glimmer of something. Something within us is aroused to the potential for a divine presence in the midst of our reality. But it's never enough to convince us of God. At best, we say things like, 'my faith in humanity has been restored…'

Which says it all, really.

Even at our human best, we cannot repair the *image*. Why? Because what made us image bearers in the first place didn't come from anything we naturally possessed as humans. This for me is the difference between an atheistic humanitarianism and a Christian one. It's not about us solely being good, just and ethical humans (though this is great); it's being an earthy humanity saturated in the Spirit of God. It's about us being jars of clay, earthen vessels filled with divine glory. After all, an *image* placed in a temple without the essence of the divine remains *dead*, raw matter and not *living* stone.

The solution can never be found in humanity trying to pull itself up by its own bootstraps; it will never be enough. This can never be merely a matter of self-help. We need rescue, not just self-discovery. We need repair and not only self-realisation. We need to be reconciled (reunited) with the one whose image we're to reflect, and this reconciliation is what the story of Jesus is all about.

# 1.6 | RELATE

When it comes to life as we know it, relationships are essential.

From what we currently understand of our universe, and how it functions, there are four fundamental forces that mix the galactic ingredients together. Those forces (energies) are Gravity, the Electromagnetic force, and the Strong and Weak nuclear forces. The nuclear forces are what keep the smallest, sub-atomic, building blocks of matter talking to each other: quarks, which interact with each other to form neutrons and protons. As the conversation of this nuclear relationship is enlarged to involve a cloud of electrons or even a sole electron, Atoms are formed. And when these Atoms interact with each other, a wide variety of molecules bloom into existence, forming the building blocks for every substance within our universe.

The simplest element birthed from this quantum conversation is a Hydrogen Atom, which comes into being when one proton connects with a single electron. Apparently, to find a single isolated Hydrogen Atom in the "wild" is a pretty rare thing. Hydrogen atoms are nature's most philandering relationship-builders, they're "wired" to connect. One of the unique relationships that Hydrogen forms is with another atom called Oxygen. When two hydrogen atoms buddy up with a single Oxygen atom, the product of this party is Water ($H_2O$).

Water is what makes life as we know it possible on our planet. And our planet is awash with the stuff; seventy-one percent of the Earth's surface is covered in the liquid result of this fertile trio of Hydrogen and Oxygen, making our world unique within our Solar System.

Now there's a nice term, *Solar System*. Here's a phrase that neatly encapsulates the large-scale relationship that is taking place between the mass-communal, atomic conversation called Earth, that we live on, and the other mass atomic conversations that are drifting near to us. Our planet, our solar system, our galaxy is one huge melodic chorus involving billions, upon billions, upon billions of atomic voices.

But back to water.

As our planet dances—orbits and spins—as it follows its pathway through our solar system, this huge body of water shifts to the rhythm of the waltz. Not only does the tempo of our own planet affect this relationship, but the momentum of our oceans and seas is also stimulated by other interstellar objects. The moon's gravity pulls on our oceans, causing them to ebb and flow in a way that alters their interactions with the solid material of Earth. The Sun showers billions of photons upon us daily, causing this water to heat up in its presence and cool in its absence. This heating and cooling also brings about changes in water's chemical relationship to itself; this, in turn, affects the rhythm of conversation between every trio of $H_2O$. Not enough photons and the water cools down, the movements of the molecules slow, and it freezes to a solid. Too many photons and the water heats up, the molecules speed up and evaporate into our atmosphere as a gas.

How this liaison of Hydrogen and Oxygen relates to all this pushing and pulling, ebbing and flowing, heating and cooling is what generates our planet's weather patterns.

*Patterns*, that's another nice relational word.

How these weather patterns, in turn, combine, collude and converse with the elements that form our planet is what is responsible for the immense diversity of landscapes we find here on Earth. Our world has been sculpted and moulded through its embrace with wet and dry, and hot and cold. Take rain, for example. As rain hits the ground, its movements channel and shape the foundations and ceilings of our world. Not only do streams and rivers help define the contours of our planet, but in their midst, a diversity of life arises.

We use the term Ecosystems to describe the connected and interdependent web of relationships that exist between a vast array of animal and plant life within geographical regions. They thrive because of the relationship that is integral between them and water. The Amazon rainforest alone is home to a kaleidoscopic nexus of thousands of entwined relationships; with its flora being responsible for producing over twenty percent of the world's oxygen. This one network of life finds itself plugged into the greater network of our planet. The air you're breathing right now is part Amazonian (it's probably best not to ask what the rest is made of).

Pause for a moment, and take a deep breath.

Inhale.

Exhale.

Feel what is happening. You breathe in—which is an action that is only possible due to a fragile combination of biological relationships—and as you do so, a whole network of other biological and chemical reactions are triggered in your body. *Body*, another word that disguises a multitude of finite connections.

Our capacity to build relationships and influence the world around us depends upon our body's ability to gather and process the oxygen that we inhale, along with many other nutrients, minerals and chemicals that we take in and discharge. We reap and we sow, from this vast network around us. We are entangled in existence. And yet, being human—being an individual, being an organism—is a whole physiological relationship in itself, a relationship that involves an immense organisation of cells, proteins, tendons, bone and plasma. Each of us is a microcosm, a world within a world.

You're a walking ecosystem. Your body is the natural habitat for a hundred trillion (that's one hundred followed by twelve zeros) microorganisms.[32] I thought I would slip that in, in case you're feeling lonely right now. But without this microbiological zoo, there would be processes that our bodies wouldn't be able to perform; these are the very processes that gather the nutrients and minerals we need from the world around us. We need the zoo we carry, and they need us. It's a symbiotic relationship, one which is reflective of our own symbiotic relationship to the vast world around us.

Chemically speaking, we're sixty-six to seventy percent $H_2O$ dialoguing with Calcium and other molecules, caught up in an ongoing conversation of quantum and cosmic proportions. However, being alive is more than the material and energy of which we consist in this passing moment. On a cellular level, the building blocks of our material existence are dying and being replaced all the time. The substance that formed you last year has long passed away and the energy you used to get from then to now has dissipated, and yet *you* haven't. Our awareness of ourselves and our culture isn't shed with our dead cells. Within humanity, relationship not only produces substance, but it surpasses it, too. It becomes immaterial, moving into constructs and ideas, dreams and memory, love and hate.

Yes, we are caught in a web of space and time, of cause and consequence, of sensations and feelings, but we're not merely a product of the molecular reactions happening within us or the laws of nature acting upon us. We don't only behave, but as human beings, we also *act*, both corporately and individually. We too have become our own force of nature. As humans, we can override the fundamental forces, destabilise the internal relationships of an atom and subsequently destabilise the course of world history.

*Everything* is relationship.

Everything, from Atoms, to the orbit and rotation of the planets; to the germination of a seed; to the sounds of musical notes and the sensations we experience when we hear those notes played in certain arrangements; to how blood is pumped around the sixty-thousand plus miles of vessels in our body; to the taste of a Sausage, Egg and Bacon sandwich (with a splash of brown sauce); to the movement of electricity; to the arrangement of our DNA; to the reading of the words on this page.

You could say, therefore, that to exist is to relate; to relate is to exist.

I relate, therefore I am.

We relate, therefore we are.

This brings us to the uniqueness of humanity within all of this entanglement. We recognise these relationships; we have the ability to discover and catalogue them. We can manipulate and manage them, creating relationships that are rarely encountered in the wilds of the universe. We even believe that once we understand how something functions, then we can also determine its meaning and destiny for being; including our own.

It's because of our ability to perceive these connections that we're also able to recognise when something is broken, or dysfunctional, or out of sync. And I'm not talking about crockery, air-conditioning units, or the track-listing on your iPhone.

Regardless of whether we label ourselves Atheists, Agnostics, Deists or Theists, we all talk about certain relationships as being dysfunctional or broken, especially when it comes to the bonds that exist between humanity and the world. We speak of global-warming, anti-social behaviour, human trafficking, unfair trade, the destruction of the rainforests, poverty, disease, war, corrupt and oppressive political regimes, etc. All of us use these terms, and when we do so, we know that something, somewhere, has gone wrong at a relational level.

On the other side of that, we also hope that if we can repair the relationship—address the imbalance or abuse, or remove the corruption, etc.—then we can ultimately fix the problem. Fundamentally, we know that for something to flourish as it should, the relationships need to be right.

All the issues mentioned above are crucial, and we'll discuss them more as we move through this book. For now, though, I want to stress that it is imperative that we work for justice, fight against the objectification of people, and learn to relate sustainably and responsibly to our environment. These relationships matter and are essential to the flourishing of life on Earth, and as such, our vocation as image bearers means that we cannot be neglectful of them.

However, the Bible speaks of another connection, one which is foundational to all the others; we were all made to relate to God. From a biblical perspective, our disharmony with the world around us is an echo of the breakdown in our relationship with our creator. The Old Testament prophets point to the lack of a relationship with God as being the source of social injustices, oppression, and the abuse of authority. The New Testament writers speak of the fruit of our breakdown being greed, envy, selfishness and hostility to one another. All of these things are symptoms of the bigger underlying issue. It's not that we lack good morality or ethics as such. The root of the problem is not so much the behavioural symptoms which emerge and spread; the root of the problem is in fact distance. The issues stem from a broken relationship, the distancing of ourselves from the Divine.

Relationships matter. But it's the *nature* of a relationship that is vital. Being distant from God is still, in a sense, a measure of relationship. But God wants much more. God wants us to be the image bearers of divine life to the world around us.

## SHALOM

Creation was God's masterpiece, God's Magnum Opus, God's pièce de résistance (which literally means, "a piece with staying power"). Creation was God's tapestry, and this tapestry was woven to be interconnected and interdependent.

*Woven* is a great analogy to use because it says something about the nature of the relationship. Woven isn't a description of a matted, jumbled, tangled random mess. Woven cloth consists of thousands, if not millions, of individual threads all purposely and carefully interlaced with each other. Each thread looping over and under, around and through its neighbours with a million points of contact.

It's this harmonious entwining of life that the Bible calls *Shalom*, which we often translate as *peace*. Shalom is not an absence of war per se, as we would think when using the word *peace*, but the absence of chaos, disorder and degradation. In Jewish thinking, Shalom is the difference between knotted and knitted. Shalom is the difference between a tangled ball of mess and the masterpiece of a tapestry. Shalom is relationship without knots. Shalom is where everything finds itself flourishing, within every dimension of reality, not at the expense of something else, but because all relationships are right and in balance. Everything flourishes as each part acts as one whole and, we could say, as it loves its neighbours.

The story of the Bible is the story of God pursuing a restoration of his relationship with humanity—his image bearers—in order that all life would exist in Shalom and flourish again. It's the story of God's continual faithfulness to us and the world. It is a story that culminates in God taking on flesh and dwelling amongst us, a God who loved the world so much, that he gave his own expression to it in order that it might cease to perish and unravel, and begin to thrive once more (to paraphrase the famous verse of John 3:16).

This is not the story of an angry Creator seeking to dispose of humanity because we quit our job and thus sabotaged the divine dream. As one voice in the book of Samuel says it, 'But God does not just sweep life away; instead, he devises ways to bring us back when we have been separated from him'.[33]

When God came in the flesh, we did not witness a destroyer, but a restorer. In Jesus, we see God knitting back together the fabric of creation. Jesus awakened the world to its inherent worth, beauty and vocation. His miracles (or at least most of them) were not about circumventing the laws of nature, but mending them. Jesus not only restored people's sight, speech and movement, but also their equality, dignity and connection to the wider community. When we observe the things that took place when Jesus walked the Earth, we witness creation flourishing and functioning as it should in response to the life of God being made available to it.

Most importantly, Jesus called us back to God. When Jesus spoke of humanity's relationship with God, he didn't talk about us being rejected or unwanted; he described us as *lost*. Which is a good way of saying 'out-of-place', 'dislocated', or 'distanced' from our vocation. Jesus diagnosed the problem as relational, and instead of waiting for us to close the distance, God, in Christ, moved toward us.

It's not that we loved God and sought the divine, but that God loved and sought us. God is the one who draws us back into relationship.

In sum, Jesus does for us, what we could not do for ourselves. Jesus does for Creation, what we could not do for it. Jesus is the reconciler, the one who has come to fix the broken mirrors of humanity, and the one who mirrors the divine in human form perfectly. Jesus is the source of God's life to an unravelling and perishing world. Through Christ, God breathes the Spirit over dead stones, making us into living stones and reconciling (reuniting) us to our divine vocation.

# 1.7 | REANIMATED

Paul the Apostle picks up on this same theme of reconciliation in another creation poem that occurs at the beginning of a New Testament letter called Colossians. A shortened version of this 'Christ Hymn' goes as follows:

Christ is the visible image of the invisible God […].


Everything was created through him and for him.
He existed before everything else,
    and he holds all creation together […].


For God in all his fullness was pleased to live in Christ,
    and through him God reconciled *everything* to himself.
He made peace [shalom] with everything in heaven and on earth
    by means of Christ's blood on the cross.[34]


Within this early church hymn that Paul quotes, Jesus is *the image* of God, for God's fullness dwelt in an earthy, human body. And through this *image*—through the life, death and resurrection of Jesus—God has and is repairing the broken image of humanity, making peace between the things of Heaven and Earth (how God has gone about this will be the implicit focus of the remainder of this book).

John's Gospel—his account of Jesus as the dwelling place of God on Earth—also purposely echoes the creation poem of Genesis with regards to these themes. John tells the story of God's new Temple (Christ) and how that temple gives life to the world. Within the first chapter of John alone, he alludes to Jesus being the *Word*, and the *Light*, and the *Glory* of God amongst us.[35] In parallel with the Genesis poem, John sees Jesus' work as a repeat of the acts of God in creation; Jesus, the Word made flesh, comes and splits the darkening chaos, bringing liberation from oppression. Jesus is life itself—real divine, flourishing, ordering life—which gives light and life to everything else; in Jesus, we behold the glory of God.

Both Paul and John, then, recognise that Jesus now becomes the source of divine life to creation. The vocation in which humanity failed, the incarnation of God now fulfils. Earlier than the poem above, Paul in his letter to the Colossians calls this the Good News, the Gospel: God has reconciled us to himself because through Jesus, the *perfect image* of the divine, we are liberated from our enslavement to the chaotic, oppressive forces of darkness and death, and reformed into image bearers.

There are a lot of big words that we use to describe this process (or different parts of this process, depending on which school of thought you subscribe to): Redemption, Salvation, Justification, Sanctification, and Atonement. But in short, to paraphrase Scot McKnight, what has taken place through the life, death and resurrection of Jesus is God's way of restoring the cracked images of humanity into glory-producing, life-bearing images as we participate in the perfect image, who is Jesus Christ.[36]

Or, as the Apostle Paul said it elsewhere, '[We] have had the veil removed so that we can be mirrors that brightly reflect the glory of the Lord. And as the Spirit of the Lord works within us, we become more and more like him and reflect his glory even more.'[37]

Or, in another place, 'He died for everyone so that those who receive his new life will no longer live to please themselves. Instead, they will live to please Christ, who died and was raised for them [...]. What this means is that those who are [in Christ become new creations]. They are not the same anymore, for the old life is gone. A new life has begun!'[38]

Or, again, 'For we are God's masterpiece. He has created us anew in Christ Jesus, so that we can do the good things he planned for us long ago.'[39]

We need to soak this in. What Jesus has done through his life, is not help rescue *me* from terra firma, or commission *me* to fill the world with my fulfilled dreams. That would only perpetuate our plight. No, what Jesus has done is a recommissioning of the plans that God had in store for us long ago, the plans mentioned in Genesis One and Two. As the Apostle Peter describes in 1 Peter 2:5, in Christ, we are remade to be *living* stones; anointed lumps of earthy matter that are to be transmitters of the sacred into God's creation, as we form ourselves around Jesus, who is the chief cornerstone of God's renovation project.

Like the original breath in the creation story, this Divine life is a gift that God freely offers to us; we don't earn it, we don't pay it back and it doesn't originate from our earthly works. However, like the blood flowing back into a numb arm, this life will revolutionise us and reanimate us in our image-bearing vocation. It turns us away from seeking to glorify ourselves, and towards seeking the glory of God.

I can't stress this enough, but the purpose of salvation is not about the quality of our post-mortem existence. In fact, it's not about death at all; it's about life, in the here and now, and in the resurrection life that follows after "life-after-death". God's plan of rescue is not some Jesus-led prison breakout from a Colditz version of creation. It's we who need rescue from ourselves and the consequences of *our mining*. God, in Jesus, has acted to save the world by repairing his image bearers.

And yet, it's so easy for us to strip all the global implications out of God's work of reconciliation and reduce it to being solely about *me*. Despite the creation-spanning overtures exhibited in the Christ Hymn quoted by Paul and in John's introduction to his gospel, God's salvation also gets regularly *mined*.

For some, following Jesus looks like getting to the end of the day, reviewing our personal sins and checking if "me and God" are still on speaking terms. But because we exist within an entangled web of existence, this privatised idea of religion is a delusion and a distraction from what we are called to. Even if we haven't "personally sinned" (whatever that means), we still have to ask whether we've been perpetuating and participating in the systems of oppression, consumerism and inequality etc. around us, *or* have we manifested God's desire for humanity and creation instead?

Maybe I'm alone in this and I'm out of line to suggest these things, but I find myself wrestling deeply with these issues. Questions that have revolved around "me and God" have stepped into the background, and questions about "us and God"—with topics like fair trade, inequality, and sustainability—appear to have amped up.

The bottom line is that there's a holistic, corporate humanity, God wishes to reform. It's *we* who are called to be like Christ. The Incarnation demonstrates what humanity should be like; to walk in sync with God and to walk in love with each other. God's saving work wishes to erode those stark disparities that have appeared across creation's landscapes as a result of our *mining* operations and our pyramid building. As such, salvation is not to be reduced to merely being a panacea to our "personal", "private" sins. Systemic sin is also in view—oppression, injustice, greed, inequality, war and poverty.

At its core, 'being in Christ' is the renewing, restoring, redeeming, reforging, reconciling, resurrecting and recommissioning of humanity to be the image bearers of the Divine within creation. God's saving work in Christ is not about us one day eternally escaping God's Temple, or about us avoiding our corporate responsibility within that Temple. The purpose of divine life is to restore us to our position within God's temple.

All of this is just the starting point, by the way; reconciliation is not the end goal. We've been reinstated with the purpose of us doing the good works that God had in mind for us from the start; to be partakers and partners in developing God's dream for this world. So instead of *mining* what we would want to perceive as *natural* resources, we must learn to *worship* with what are really *sacred* resources. This has to stop being about ripping, slashing, and throwing dice over the garment of God, and move towards us sharing in God's mission and adopting God's methods of making peace between Heaven and Earth.

For in Christ the fullness of God lives in a human body, and you are complete through your union with Christ.

-Colossians 2:9-10a (NLT)

# PART 02 | A TALE OF TWO TREES

The gods are on the side of the stronger.
– Gaius Julius Civilis [40]

The essence of every great lie is that it closely
parallels the truth.
– Shades [41]

The knowledge of the cross brings a conflict of
interest between the God who has become man
and the man who wishes to become God.
– Jürgen Moltmann [42]

The cross has been transformed into a harmless,
non-offensive ornament that Christians wear
around their necks. Rather than reminding us of
the "cost of discipleship", it has become a form
of "cheap grace", an easy way to salvation that
doesn't force us to confront the power of Christ's
message and mission.
– James H. Cone [43]

# 2.1 | OF DICE AND MEN

Of all the scenes in the Bible, there's one that strikes me as the most poignant and telling.

Jesus has been stripped naked and nailed to a cross, condemned to die under the torturous process of Roman crucifixion. His beaten and scourged body finds itself under tremendous pressure as it hangs suspended from its upper limbs, making each and every breath agonising and traumatic.

It was an excruciating way to die (*excruciating* derives its meaning from crucifixion) and it can't have been at all pleasant to watch. And yet, Jesus' crucifixion has drawn a crowd of spectators. There's a mixed ensemble of friend and foe, mourner and troll, gathering around the suffering saviour of Golgotha. The execution's atmosphere is saturated in a cacophony of tears and jeers. Sounds of heartfelt lament find themselves being discordantly enmeshed into the scorning, abusive tones of those who wish to get in the last word whilst Jesus struggles to grab what little breath he can.

However, it's not only the activities of human weeping and jeering that are being expressed at the cross. Even here, at the place of torture and death, profiteering (*mining*) flourishes.

The gospel accounts of Matthew, Mark, Luke and John all mention the story of the soldiers, who crucified Jesus, casting lots for his clothes.[44] Jesus' garments find themselves being distributed between the four of them in some silent, mutual compromise until they come to his robe. Woven in one seamless piece, this robe was too good to be torn into pieces and shared, or so the accounts tell us.

Which makes me think: if the robe was too good to be torn, does that mean that the rest of Jesus' garments were shared by ripping or slashing them apart into equal slices of scrap material?

If so, then this had been a violent division of the things of Jesus—a powerful metaphor of how we have divided the garment of creation. But the robe of Christ adds a prophetic tension into this so-called amicable division of the spoils of war and colonialism. The robe is worth keeping;

such quality shouldn't be subjected to violence. So, as a means of keeping the peace—ironically, in the bloodstained shadow of Rome's symbol of peace—the soldiers decide to cast lots, to throw dice.

To us, this seems like a nice, nonviolent, fair means of selection; like tossing a coin or drawing the short straw. But not everything is what it appears to be on the surface. There's something subtle being suggested in this act.

When we throw dice today, we understand that the outcome is strictly down to chance. If you roll a pair of dice one hundred times, percentages should play out and you'll eventually roll a double six. Or maybe not. It's likely, but never certain. For us, dice is a game of probability. No one controls the results, and therefore it's fair (unless someone plays with loaded dice).

But this is not what is going on within the ancient mindset of the first-century citizen. To them, casting lots or throwing dice wasn't the means of making a random decision, but the means of invoking a god's preference. Superstition highly nuances this game, and so what results isn't perceived to be chance or luck, but divine ordination. God controls the outcome, ergo, what transpires is more than fair, it's *decreed*. Fairness doesn't come into it.[45]

Apparently, in this ancient game—and in some ideas that are still prevalent today—it's God who chooses who rises and falls, who succeeds and fails; it's God who draws the lines between "us" and "them"; it's God who blesses and sponsors the competitive instinct for material progress. God, in this thinking, sides with the winners, not the loser, deciding who'll receive the material award. The divine intervenes and, in this scenario, the victor will walk away with a seamless robe.

What a contrast.

As four Roman soldiers roll dice, invoking the divine to choose who should be the worthy owner of a fine robe, God hangs bleeding and choking for breath on a cross mere feet away from them. In the shadow of the cross, all this so-called "divine ordination" is exposed for what it is, and what it has always been; men using god as a convenient way to sanction their schemes and dreams.

The cross unveils the truth. God is not the one blessing and legitimizing the human activity of ripping or gambling over his garment. God is not the one advocating a "winner takes all" philosophy, or defining "us" from "them", or prospering his favourites by giving them what they desire. God is not the one deciding who has, and who has not. God's hands are pierced, and he hangs naked, unclothed before the world, giving himself for the healing of the nations.

At the cross, the tree of life for all humanity, mankind is revealed to be grasping for the power to coerce and control. At the cross, four individuals, undeterred by the surrounding audible mixture of grieving and raucous voices, toss dice over divine property using a twisted concept of divine privilege.

And yet over this act, through what must have been a weakening and spluttering voice, piercing the atmosphere of dissonance, Jesus cries out with what little breath he has remaining, 'Father, forgive these people, because they don't know what they are doing.'[46]

Like the creation story, God speaks his loving and liberating oration into a world caught in the oppressive grip of chaos and darkness.

But I wonder, how many in the swarm around him gave any credence to these words?

It's a powerful scene; a moment in history that highlighted the difference between God and men. The crucifixion of Jesus provided a sobering contrast between human and divine acts, distinguishing the differences between what *we* think God wants and does, and what God actually wants and does.

## 2.2 | A CATHOLIC CROSSROAD

A few years back, whilst writing my first book, I had an overnight stay in a monastery. I wasn't part of a group, or there to take part in a planned retreat. I was intentionally on my own, seeking twenty-four hours of contemplation and prayer away from the bustle of life and technological distractions. And trust me when I say that there's nothing like a Catholic monastery for peace and quiet.

That may shock some of my Pentecostal kin, but I can't deny that there was a powerful and tangible sense of being with God while I was there. And it didn't require noise, shouting, dancing, utterances, or someone playing nice keyboard harmonies in the background. In what was a formative time for me, it was silence—a divine silence—that punctured the hard-to-reach recesses of my heart.

To be clear from the start; I'm not a participant in the Christian *Hunger Games*. I'm not anti-Catholic or anti any other denomination or movement that doesn't subscribe to "my gang's" fundamentals and style. I personally think we Christians are prone to being far too tribal; we insist on trying to *convert* other Christian traditions instead of *conversing* with them. We can be suspicious of one another because of an arrogant ignorance that leads us to assume '*we* know the truth' and '*they* don't'. If unchecked, a tendency to eliminate or silence other expressions of the faith, in the hope of being the last, theologically-vindicated movement standing, can emerge. And sadly, world history has witnessed far too many of these in-house Battle Royales and borne many of the scars. But as far as I'm concerned, we need each other. We need to stand together. There's something each branch of the church brings to the table. I'm not saying there are many Christianities; rather, there's one Christ and we're all in conversation about him and with him.

Maybe such thinking is naïve of me. But my view of Christ has been deeply enriched, and continues to be so, by the teaching of Anabaptists, Catholics, Anglicans, Lutherans, Methodists, Mennonites and others of both liberal and conservative perspective. I'm thankful for their voices, and I don't want to win any of them to my views by assassinating their own; I simply want to view more of Christ. Sure, there's Catholic teaching that doesn't resonate with me. But there's heaps of theology that thrives within Pentecostal circles (such as Rapture theology, Tithing, Moralism, Biblical literalism, Prosperity teaching and certain ways the gifts of the Spirit are exercised and thought about) that I'm much more uncomfortable with.

Which brings me back to the monastery.

It contained a chapel, a square room, of modest size, with chairs arranged down three of the sides. And there, hanging on the remaining wall, overlooking everything in the chapel, was a large cross. I'm not sure whether the room was too small, or the cross was too big, but this symbol seemed disproportionate to everything else. Like, twice as big as it needed to be. You certainly couldn't miss it; the room was overshadowed by its scale and your gaze was automatically drawn towards it.

But it wasn't only the size of this cross that caught my attention. This cross was different from what I was accustomed to. This wasn't some vacant, whitewashed cross, but one that was occupied by a bloodstained image of Christ. This was a crucifix, and its corpus was a baptism to my senses. Sitting there in its presence was profound and disturbing, in a soul-stirring, revolutionary way. So much so, that I spent hours in its shade. I wanted to be there; I wanted to bear witness to this scene for as long as possible before having to return to the disarray of life.

Saying that I wasn't used to being exposed to such imagery may sound odd. Don't get me wrong, I had seen icons, ornaments, and jewellery displaying this crucified form. But I had never been exposed to this image in a religious atmosphere for such a prolonged period of time, and especially to one of such size. Why? Because within many churches of the Protestant and Evangelical tradition, it's usually the Empty Cross that is displayed (if any cross is displayed at all). The reasoning for this varies.

For some evangelicals, there's a theological thrust to their refusal to have a crucifix on display: Christ has been raised and therefore the cross is empty. Although they see the cross as a great victory to celebrate and a moment that has altered the course of history, it's still considered a done thing, a bridge crossed, an instant confined to the diary pages of Jesus' life that fails to fully capture, and which pales in comparison to, the true beauty of his current glorious, reigning splendour. As such, the cross can be demeaned and viewed as something that God *stooped* to; it's a caged God that we encounter there and not God's full, undisclosed glory. Diametrically opposed to this, however, is the empty cross; it speaks of God breaking free from these shackles and humiliating the cross—as well as the death it dealt—with resurrection life. And so the resurrection is also demeaned and seen as God's big Houdini-like 'Aha' moment; as the Divine laughs at our stupidity for thinking that we had God nailed. Not all evangelicals think this way, of course. But for those who do, the resurrection is repeatedly pitted against the cross as we argue over which was the more accurate portrait of God.

I don't buy it, though. The empty cross and the crucifix don't speak at cross purposes. As we'll see in this part of the book, the cross is not where God's nature was diminished, but where it was revealed. And the resurrection is not God's flourishing finish—like a magician's prestige, that reassures us that the reality we thought we witnessed was nothing more than an illusion—but where this cruciform image of God is vindicated as the genuine article. As a reversal of the consequences of humanity's choice in Eden, the resurrection proves that death cannot claim and hold onto the divine likeness.

But it's not only certain theology that struggles with a crucifix. For some leaders in my tradition, there's also a worry that it borders on idolatry; a pastoral anxiety that people will be encouraged and drawn into praying to such images.

I don't buy into this either, and I'm also suspicious that this concern is bordering on paranoia. It's not images that lead people to worship idols; it's bad teaching and wrong concepts that turn symbols into gods. The use of images does not equate to idolatry. After all, it's possible to worship idols without having any concrete imagery by merely possessing abstract ideology alone. Moreover, the use of symbols has helped focus people devotionally for centuries within the church.

If anything, maybe it's the fact that we lack a cross of any sort within our sanctuaries, and especially one bearing Christ, that has contributed to a whole tide of bad teaching? Maybe not contemplating the crucified saviour has allowed us to make an idol out of God, and strap wrong ideologies onto the Divine?

## CROSS PURPOSES

Paul the Apostle wrote, *post-resurrection*, that '[W]e preach Christ crucified, to the Jews a stumbling block and to the Greeks foolishness, but to those who are called, both Jews and Greeks, Christ the power of God and the wisdom of God.'[47] Christ was risen, but the cross was far from redundant, and much more than a footnote in history.

Within the early church, highlighted throughout the writing of the New Testament, the crucifixion was both the key revelation concerning the nature of God and a pattern for the life of discipleship. The early church, through the lens of the resurrection, came to see the crucifixion as a place of divine victory and revelation as opposed to a place of defeat, shame, and crushed hopes. The cross of Christ was the epicentre from which God's commonwealth launched itself into the midst of a self-absorbed human society; it was the ultimate confrontation between the dream of God and the dice-throwing, mining dreams of men, and the moment when the reigning powers of death and darkness had their grip on creation shattered. Or to put that another way, using the words of St Athanasius:

> By man, death has gained its power over men;
> by the Word made Man, death has been destroyed and life raised up anew.[48]

Of course, the incarnation as a whole did this. I'm a firm believer that the whole of Jesus' life and ministry, along with his death and resurrection, demonstrated and inaugurated the Kingdom of God. When we look at Jesus, we see God—what God is like, what God wants, how God comes to reign, and what God does with the power that humanity desires. But although the entire life of Jesus exhibited this, the cross drew all this together and revealed it in high definition, sharply contrasting it with the way in which human empires establish and maintain their rule.

You can't miss the disparity between the kingdoms of God and men when you observe the body of God being broken by the rule of men. You can't miss the juxtaposition between those who grasp at power and the God who empties himself of power. While the world of man continues to engage in its violent competition for material progress and transcendence—as it scapegoats, victimises and oppresses—the God made man exhales forgiveness over the world. Not as consent, but as a call to cease. The crucified God is the antithesis of the human proclivity to play dice over the possessions of others and build empires.

I know some of us worry about having an image of the crucified Christ hanging in our churches; we're more "at ease" with an empty cross. And I know that this *ease* is often a worry with regards to having idols. But I have to ask, maybe the cross isn't meant to put us at ease? Maybe the crucified form of God disturbs us because it destroys our idols, obliterating our preconceived ideas of God?

Don't get me wrong, I don't want idol-worship either. And yet, I can't help but wonder if it is precisely because of the absence of this central image in our churches, that other ideals and idolatries have blended into modern church orthodoxy and orthopraxy in its place? Let's be honest, the following list of ideologies is no stranger to certain church trends: Worship of Self; Consumerism; Exhibitionism; Individualistic tendencies; Materialism; Self-Help; Self-Righteousness? And then there is the biggest idol of all: a pursuit of both physical and spiritual euphoria.

It's remarkable to note how often the modern Charismatic trend roots an experience of God only within an exciting, sensually stimulating experience. Ergo lament, silence, liturgy, sacrament and contemplation—along with anything else that seems to deny human arousal—gets scornfully relegated to the status of 'empty practice' or 'man-made religion' (although, isn't the opposite as likely to be true?).

All this stimulation may help to explain why many of us struggle with prayer and contemplation in the privacy of our homes, and why many of us struggle to sense God during our own periods of suffering. We're told on Sundays that we can experience God anywhere, anytime. But the stimulant-saturated experience of the weekend service strips us of the ability to detect God without a show, or deludes into thinking that "God moments" ought to be hyperactive and adrenaline-fuelled. We've been weaned on the idea that 'if I don't feel God, God must be absent'.

The truth, however, is that God's at home in the stillness; we're the ones who get restless. God doesn't have to be attracted through noise, lights, smells, bells and whistles. God is *always* present. Always. There's a holiness that permeates the normal humdrum routine of daily living which is sacred; a normality that doesn't need to be transcended or escaped from.

Hey, I'm saying this as a Charismatic and not as someone from an "enemy" camp. I'm not saying there is no value in euphoric moments or anthem-led praise, or that liberty in God's Spirit shouldn't lead to an experience of well-being, joy and human delight.

Amen to all of that.

However, our overemphasis on party-themes, concerts, 'this Sunday is going to be the best Sunday ever' goals, and "life-hack" preaching, all reek with the stench of throwing dice in the presence of the crucified saviour.

That's harsh, I admit. Maybe too harsh. But when we gather together, what is it we're seeking? What are we really hoping to walk away with?

Please don't misunderstand the point I'm making. I am not asking for services filled with an emphasis on sackcloth and ashes, or a return to a holiness-style of preaching which leaves everyone feeling rotten, filthy and unloved. That would be a step in the wrong direction altogether. The Gospel of the cross is still *good* news.

You are loved.

Incredibly.

Unconditionally.

Divinely Loved.

However, God's love led to the giving of self, and not self-interest.

Surely then, the denial of self is more cross-like, more Christ-like, than us throwing spiritually-loaded dice in order to get what we want, whilst thinking that this is what God is about. And if we strip all of the cross-symbols, cross-talk and cross-patterns out of the church, what are we left with that communicates this? Without the cross, following Jesus is merchandised as the road to health, wealth and everything else. But running counter to this, the cross exhibits a God who is no stranger to pain, isolation or forsakenness. The cross demonstrates a God who lays down all power and identifies with us in co-suffering love.

Instead of offering the world a genie God, a 'name it claim it' religion or a Houdini-like God who escapes peril and provides escape, a God who suffers—a God who has faced anguish and who identifies with us in our pain and difficulty—might be the most vital piece of theology we have to offer our society. Our world needs to witness the crucified God.

## COUNTER IMAGERY

Of course, not everyone will agree with me. Admittedly, you would be right to argue that the cross has not always been the symbol of Christianity, in the sense that it has not always been brandished around necklines or displayed on altars. But during the first century, a symbolic cross would have been surplus to requirement. The early church existed in an era where real Roman crosses lined roads and highways, and some of the early Christians found their lives being ended on such crosses. The cross was a daily reality for them, and being prepared to carry your cross as a follower of Jesus wasn't a metaphor. So although those first-century believers didn't generally adorn their houses or meeting places with a physical cross, or make the symbol of a cross to identify themselves to each other, the cross was still a central symbol of living the faith.

In contrast, maybe we in the modern, Western church do need reminding of this with concrete imagery?

Again, we may be wary of having a crucified Christ, or any symbol, on show in our church halls; we're worried about what connotations people will attach to such imagery. But let's not be so ignorant and naïve; our modern mega-church sanctuaries already possess powerful counter-imagery to which people subconsciously attach notions. In my mind's eye, when I picture the architectural layout of most modern mega-churches (tapping into and subliminally fuelling the ideologies of individualism, exhibitionism, self-gratification etc.), the most central and potent symbol on display is a *stage*.

Don't brush that off and dismiss it as unimportant—you need to dwell on that for a moment and let it shock you to the core.

I'm no expert on church architecture and interior design; I am nought but a humble and despised structural engineer in comparison to those who practise such magnificent professions.[49] However, I do know that there's a huge difference between the way in which the layouts of temples and cathedrals used to be designed, and how modern sanctuaries are currently set up. Temples and cathedrals were purposely infused with symbolism that would draw the senses of the congregations towards God; they strove to connect Earth and Heaven through columns, vaulted ceilings and naturally-illuminated stained-glass windows. Whereas today, we prefer to switch off the lights, blackout creation (including the congregation), and spotlight the microphone.

Which makes me think—and I say this with some trepidation—but maybe the growth of the modern church in some quarters over the past twenty to thirty years isn't down to God at all. Maybe it draws people in because instead of offering something counter-cultural, it merely mimics and endorses the narcissistic, self-centred, "selfie-saturated" stream that exists in our culture today?

Do our meetings promote self-interest more than self-denial? Even though we may not literally throw dice during our gatherings, are we there for the furthering of God's dream, or our own devices and desires?

Somehow, there has to be a truce between the Empty Cross and the Crucifix in our thinking and in our symbolism. I'm not on about trivializing the cross by reducing it to jewellery, or treating it like a brand logo, or decorating it as a floodlit stage ornament. But beholding Jesus on a cross somehow arrested me in a way that was against my egocentric disposition, and I believe it can do that for others.

The cross is a catholic crossroad, an appeal from God of universal magnitude that intersects and disrupts the self-centred inclination of humanity. This bloodstained cross of Christ, not a whitewashed one which is then backlit with LED luminescence, is where God demonstrated his cruciform, self-emptying nature. It's this cross which provides a pattern for what humanity, as the bearers of the divine image, is supposed to display; we must not be self-fulfilling, but self-emptying.

But as with some of the Jews and Greeks of Paul's era, maybe this sounds too ridiculous to our modern Western ears? After all, we often share in their thinking: God's surely with the one who's holding the winning dice; God can't be with the one who's dying and losing in the world's eyes.

I suppose, when we boil it all down, the cross is a challenge because, through it, God poses the question, 'Who do you say I am?' And our response to this question defines what it means for us to be disciples and image bearers of the Divine.

# 2.3 | THE WAY OF THE CROSS

Jesus is on his way to Jerusalem for the Passover festival. This is a week that will culminate with the crucifixion, a week that we now call the Passion Week or Holy Week.

As always, Jesus' disciples are travelling along with him, and as they set off on their journey, Jesus asks them a question: 'Who do people say I am?'[50]

The disciples respond by riffing off the people's views of Jesus: some say he's a prophet, others say he's the Old Testament prophet Elijah come back from the dead, while others think he's the recently beheaded, wilderness-dweller John the Baptist.

Jesus neither affirms nor denies any of these rumours. He doesn't even acknowledge that his disciples have replied. Instead, he turns to them and asks, 'Who do *you* say I am?'

Of course, they could give the typical Sunday-school answer of 'Jesus'. And they'd be right, Jesus is Jesus. But Jesus isn't asking for a name; he's not experiencing a mild form of amnesia. Even the crowd's views on Jesus aren't about 'names' per se, but about mission. The focus of Jesus' question and the opinions of the people is the nature of what Jesus is undertaking. Jesus wants to know if his disciples understand what he's been up to and what they think the motive is behind what he's been doing.

At this point, Jesus' disciple Simon Peter takes his opportunity to shine, declaring, 'You are the Messiah!' (I like to imagine Peter saying this with lots of gusto and pride).

But then something odd happens, at least in Mark's version of the events. Immediately following Peter's declaration, Jesus tells them to keep shtum. Peter was probably expecting a gold star, or a pat on the back, or a 'Well done, my good and faithful servant'. But all Peter and the rest of the twelve receive is a warning: 'Don't tell anyone that!' And then Jesus goes on to explain what will happen at the climax of their journey to Jerusalem: Jesus will be rejected and killed. This same conversation then moves into the famous scene where Jesus calls Peter 'Satan' and culminates with Jesus saying:

> If anyone is ashamed of me and my message [...] the Son of Man will be ashamed of that person when he returns in the glory of his Father [...]. I tell you the truth, some standing here right now will not die before they see the Kingdom of God [God's rule and commonwealth] arrive in great power![51]

In most Bibles, all these little pieces of conversation between Jesus' initial question (in Mark 8:27) and his closing words above (in Mark 9:1) are broken into neat paragraphs, but it's important to see this conversation as one linear episode.

I've heard many interpretations of this episode, some of which were spiritually abusive—especially regarding the part about denying and being ashamed of Jesus. I can't have been the only one who was told, by others using this passage, that if you don't tell people about your conversion to faith then the whole salvation deal isn't sealed. But that's a terrible interpretation of these events. Think about it: how can Jesus claim that God will deny any part of his Kingdom to his disciples if they're ashamed of talking about Jesus (if talking about Jesus is what we think this is about), when Jesus has just *warned* his disciples not to say a word about who he is? That's a bit unfair, don't you think?

To understand this passage better, let's step back to Peter's answer, because his declaration of 'Messiah' is the catalyst to this moment, giving Jesus the opportunity to say something that he needs to get into his disciples' heads.

When Peter yells 'Messiah', he's not doing so into a political or theological vacuum. Nor is Peter spiritualising this title to mean someone who saves our *souls* from sin, as many today would understand it. For a Jew like Peter, sin wasn't unimportant, but the effects of sin had led to the real-world oppression of his people via the domination of Rome (the latest oppressor in a five-hundred-year-long period in which Israel had been ruled by one foreign power after another). Thinking within a framework similar to the one found in the Old Testament books of Judges, Samuel and Kings (along with the Apocryphal stories of the Maccabees), Peter is culturally saturated with the idea of a Saviour who would come and liberate God's people from the oppression they were experiencing at enemy hands.

*Messiah* was a politically loaded word, and many expected this Messiah to be the earthly example of how God would rule the world if God was physically king. Which is true. But there's a lie, which closely parallels the truth, that's affecting the human ideas of what this Messiah would be like.

In some minds, how God would rule and how God would ascend to the throne of a global empire would be akin to how the Roman Empire, and most other empires, had done so; God would rule by military force and an oppressive, totalitarian regime. In the hopes of some of the Jewish people, then, this Messiah would be an undefeatable personality; the dice would always roll in their favour because God's power, will and authority would be channelled through them. Rome wouldn't have a chance.

This Messiah, after defeating Rome and re-establishing Israel's political identity, would then restore the nation of Israel back to its covenant worship to God. The salvation this Messiah would bring wasn't some otherworldly, disembodied hope centred on souls. It was a *this-world* hope. Peter's mind, along with the minds of the other disciples' (and of anyone else who heard any of this) would have been full of these hopes and ideas of how God would do what needed to be done.

It should come as no surprise that Jesus, knowing that these militant messianic ideas would be floating around in his followers' heads, tries to explain to them that this isn't how God's Kingdom will come. This isn't the only time that he attempts to do so, either. The journey to Jerusalem will see Jesus try to reshape his disciples' thinking on two further occasions (Mark 9:31 and Mark 10:32-34).

According to Jesus, God's Kingdom was at hand; already within reach (see Mark 1:15). This had been Jesus' message since the beginning of his public ministry. But it wasn't coming through an armed campaign against Israel's enemies. Its arrival would not reflect the militaristic hopes that others held about the Messiah. This is probably why Jesus never refers to himself using the term *Messiah* within the gospels, and why he tells his disciples not to tell anyone he's the Messiah; he's uncomfortable with the violent ideology that has become attached to the term and purposely distances himself from this definition. As Jesus tries to tell his followers, God's kingdom will be installed because God's man, the actual Messiah, is, paradoxically, going to be betrayed, rejected, beaten and killed! But then, three days later, he will rise again.

Jesus also promises his disciples that some of them will not die until they see this Kingdom arrive with great power (Mark 9:1). This isn't a reference to some future event which is set to occur at the second-coming, but an allusion to the fact that some of the disciples standing before him will witness both his death and resurrection.

Jesus is challenging his disciples' mental pictures of how God works and what God is like. He wants them to see that the answer to his question, 'Who do you say I am?' is not framed by their preconceptions, but by the crucifixion. God will come to rule, not through an act of domination, but through the act of radical, self-emptying love and life-giving, resurrection power. Counter-intuitively to our ideas of reigning, God doesn't grasp at power, but lays all power down. This is what God looks like, according to Jesus: a suffering servant, not a warlord.

And all God's people said, Amen?

Definitely, and defiantly, no.

## A QUIET WORD

Jesus' words clash against Peter's ideas in a huge way. When Peter declares Jesus to be the Messiah, he's laying onto Jesus the entire mantle of his expectations and dreams. And Peter is deeply offended that Jesus has refused to don the robe of a military leader.

So Peter pulls Jesus aside—away from the others and from the crowds that are usually around Jesus—and he begins to tell Jesus that he's saying all the wrong things. Or as some translations put, he begins to *correct* Jesus' theology and political vision.

This pulling aside is crucial! Don't miss what is happening here. Missing this is what leads many, in my opinion, to misunderstand why Jesus connects denying him with being ashamed of him later on in verse 37. You see, Peter pulls Jesus to one side, hoping not to embarrass Jesus in front of the others, but what it reveals, in a Freudian-slip kind of way, is that Peter himself is ashamed of this idea of a suffering God. A suffering God isn't a great nationalistic image. And a call to follow a Messiah who is willingly going to be tortured and killed is hardly an inspiring call to arms in the struggle for independence.

But as Peter attempts to straighten out Jesus' theology, Jesus gives him a stern and brutal rebuke, 'Get away from me, Satan!' (we'll come to this in a moment). Jesus continues, 'No Peter, *you're* the one who's got it wrong. Your problem is that you think God is like a man, and that God should rule in the way that humans' use power, but God isn't like that' (my paraphrase).

Jesus' rebuke doesn't stop there, either. Peter wanted this to be a 'private chit-chat', out of earshot of anybody else. Usually, as seen in other gospel episodes, Jesus is pretty respectful of people who want to talk to him alone. But not this time; Jesus isn't letting this go unnoticed.

So Jesus calls the rest of the disciples over, and says to all of them, 'If you want to follow God's way, then you, too, need to put aside your selfish ambition and carry your cross, and follow me! If you try using force to keep or advance your life, you'll lose it. But if you pour out your life for God's agenda, you'll find life'.

I know we want to over-spiritualise these words. But let's not forget the context here. Jesus is challenging the disciples' ideas on how God's way is advanced and achieved. They think it's through violent force, and so if they want to be the top dogs, to have liberation and take-hold of a life of independence, they believe it will come through violent revolution. But that isn't the case. Life is lost that way; death begets more death; killing leads to more killing; violence does not end violence. As Jesus says, what's the point of gaining the whole world, but losing your life in the process?

The disciples are expecting a call to pick up their nation's flag, or to pick up their swords. But Jesus doesn't give them this call to arms. Instead, Jesus calls his disciples to put aside their *selfish ambition* (which isn't just a private ambition, but in this context also a nationalistic one), shoulder their cross and follow his way. Can you see the contrast Jesus is making?

The Roman cross was a symbol of power domination. Everyone who lived at that time would have known the horrors of this excruciating and humiliating way to die. If there was ever a symbol of how human power and authority perversely manifest themselves, then crucifixion is it. This is how human empires maintain control, and how those oppressed by that control generally seek to overthrow it—through violence.

Some of us may still believe the old lie that violence will save the world and make it a better and safer place to live in. But as far as track records go, violent manipulation, coercion and force have proved themselves impotent in stopping violent manipulation, coercion and force; they breed more of their kind, in a historically repeating cycle. As nonviolence advocate Walter Wink says, 'Violence simply is not radical enough, since it generally changes only the rulers but not the rules.'[52]

Violence is not the way of God. God's way is marked by radical self-emptying love. So as imitators of God's way, we carry crosses, we don't hang people on them. We are more willing to be the crucified, than to kill, regardless of whether the context is the making of our personal dreams into reality or if it's a nationalistic dream. Don't get me wrong, as Christians we are not to be *death-seekers*. However—and this is paramount—we are not *death-dealers*, either. We do not seek to have *our* way and *our* dreams through violently overpowering, oppressing and crushing others. We do not tear, or rip, or throw dice in order to grasp power over creation.

Sadly, we live in a world where some people will use force to get their way—be it physical or psychological. But that is not to be us. We are to die to that way, and be alive to God's way of changing and saving the world.

God's way is cruciform; God brings order to the world through laying down his power, and not through taking the lives of others. As we saw in the first part of this book, in the creation story, God liberates his creation from its enslavement to chaos and disorder, not by imitating those things, but through speaking life into it and giving order to it.

We too, are to bear, to manifest this image of God. And it's not the case that this cruciform image is a new image that Jesus gives to us—although Jesus' life certainly clarifies it. God has always, right from the beginning, laid down power, and humanity has always been called to reflect this.

In other words, God's Kingdom way has always been at hand, if we'd only be willing to pick up our cross.

# 2.4 | THE TREE OF SELF-RULE

We certainly haven't finished with the episode between Jesus and Peter; it will weave its way into this present section. However, for the discerning reader, it may seem like we've jumped a big gap in the biblical narrative between the first and second parts of this book. One moment we were talking about the creation story of Genesis One, and the next we're at the Crucifixion.

So let's step back a moment and explore the next part of Genesis, because this helps to emphasise the point with which I finished the last section.

There's that strange story within Genesis chapters two and three, about a man and woman being placed in a garden that they are to cultivate, tend to, and extend (there will be more on this in Part 3). It's also worth noting, that in the same way that God dispels the chaos and brings order to creation through naming (separating, assigning function)  and blessing the differing elements of the cosmos, God also gives humanity the task of naming and separating; as seen in Genesis Two, where Adam names the animals. So where Genesis One gives humanity the mandate to rule over creation as image bearers, Genesis Two provides a glimpse of how this rule is to be exercised. Like God, humanity is not to collude with chaos and oppression by imitating them, but they are to imitate God's way of liberation. Human rule was not to be oppressive, repressive or exploitative, but an extension of divine life. We were to reflect God's wise and benevolent rule.

To aid with this extension, there are two special trees placed within the garden along with humanity: the 'Tree of Life' and the 'Tree of the Knowledge of Good and Evil'. I'm uncertain that we're to understand every aspect of this scene as literal, or as historically accurate. As other commentators have said, it could be parabolic, or symbolic of real events (feel free to dig into the *Further Reading* section at the back). So the decision as to whether we see these trees as actual living flora, or merely symbolic of some kind of divine mechanism at work in creation, is up to you. And as to whether you want to imagine a real talking serpent, well, that's another conversation altogether.

Either way, regardless of whether we see this story as myth, or as historical, or as a metaphorisation of history, let's not be dismissive of what these two trees represent, or demean their importance to human beings flourishing as image bearers.[53] By being present in this account, both of these trees are imperative to humanity's task of imaging God and extending God's sacred space.

The 'Tree of Life' is easier to understand than the other—this is the mechanism through which the life of God is made available to humanity. Through eating of this tree, humanity transcends its mortal, dust form, and is made immortal; they will avoid experiencing death as long as they have access to its fruit. But this immortality is not a disembodied immortality; it's eternal life upon terra firma.

The second tree, on the other hand, has always caused something of a stir as to what it was for. What does this knowledge of good and evil represent? Wouldn't Adam and Eve have figured out the distinction between good and evil over time? Also, doesn't the Bible itself, through such books as Proverbs and Ecclesiastes, encourage us to seek and discern the difference between good and evil so that we can walk in a righteous way? Furthermore, for many, it always seemed to be an odd addition to this garden, in that, if we are to take the story as it is given, things might have turned out much better if it had just been left out.

It feels like God did something stupid with this tree. God tells humanity that they can eat from any tree in the garden—including the Tree of Life—whenever they want to, and as much as they want to. But they can't eat from the Tree of the Knowledge of Good and Evil. If they do, then the life of God which is being made available to them, and which should be liberating creation, will cease to be available and death will reign instead. In other words, instead of God's creation moving forward, things will begin to unravel and chaos will gain the upper hand. And this choice between life and death, oppression and liberation—a pattern frequently echoed in

Scripture—is entirely at the whim of humanity. Not only does having this tree seem surplus to requirement, but it's also dangerous, and God, in his wisdom, has just pointed it out to humanity! Which hardly switches off our curiosity.

Like the famous red button on the dash-board in those spy films, it appears that God knowingly plants a self-destruct button in the midst of this beautiful creation, and then leaves us in charge of it.

We know how this story goes. Even if the book of Genesis had stopped at this point, we would have easily envisaged how this was going to play out. This is like leaving an open paint can next to a toddler. Surely God must have known what was going to transpire?

But as I said, there must be something about this mechanism which is essential to humanity's imaging of God. This tree can't be surplus to requirement, so why would God put it there?

Let's think of it one way. In providing this mechanism—in providing the means to have all of his endeavours and plans thwarted—it's as if God surrenders and lays aside his power to rule through domination. It's as if God is saying, 'You can go against the call. You can take over if you want to; if you want to usurp my place as the centre and source of all this, you can. The means of doing so is right there. The Kingdom of Self is at hand.'

God's not giving his consent to this, of course, but he's not controlling the situation either. The God we believe is in control chooses not to control. God's giving humanity freedom of choice. There's the Tree of Life, or the Tree of Self-Rule. This choice is imperative to the calling of bearing God's likeness.

Humanity wants to be as powerful as God; they want to be in God's position. But what does God do with his power and position in this story? He surrenders it the form of a tree and places it within the grasp of humanity.

In the Genesis story, Adam and Eve eat of the fruit, believing that as they do so they will become like God. And yes, there is a connection between this fruit and the power of God, but the lie they believe is that grasping the fruit will grant them power and autonomy. But in reality, it's only as they *refuse* to grasp at this power that they really image the power of God and have liberty.

This is why the Tree of Self-Rule is needed. We cannot display God's likeness without it because the image that accurately displays what God is like is that of power laid down. It's only as we refuse to grasp at the Kingdom of Self, that we express the Kingdom of God.

For Adam and Eve, they bear God's image as long as they refrain from grasping at power because God doesn't grasp at power. Or as the Apostle Paul would later write about Jesus, 'Though he was God, he did not demand and cling to his rights as God.'[54] But both Adam and Eve, acting out of selfish ambition, in seeking to control and dominate, in trying to forcefully take hold of their idea of life and liberation, lose their lives (remember Jesus words to his disciples?) and the whole thing begins to unravel. They gain the world but forfeit their souls. The garment of creation that God entrusted to them begins to fray and tear.

Paradoxically, though, ousting God and taking control doesn't satisfy; it generates an unquenchable thirst and paranoia to be in control. It's not enough. What they thought would lead to life and liberty ensnares them instead. This grasping, this tearing, this rolling the dice for supremacy, develops into an ingrained pattern, and the story of humanity from this scene forward is one which is marred by division and power struggles (as we'll see in Part 3).

I find it interesting to note that everything that results after the fall is a domination issue; someone wishing to be on top, with someone else being objectified, enslaved, or scapegoated as a result. But this is the fruit of the Tree of Self-Rule: death dominates and chaos ensues. Instead of imaging God's modus operandi, we mimic chaos. Instead of peacefully consecrating and blessing, we tend to cleave and label, divide and conquer, tear and toss dice.

Selfish ambition always leads us toward seeking to dominate and consume others, instead of learning to control and deny ourselves. The

New Testament writer James hits this point right on the head when he says, 'For wherever there is jealousy and *selfish ambition*, there you find disorder [chaos] and every kind of evil.'[55] James describes this motive as 'devilish'—i.e. opposed to God's way (think of Jesus' rebuke to Peter)—and goes on to say that Heaven's way is peace loving, gentle at all times, and *willing to yield*.[56] This way is exactly what God models in the garden, what Jesus exhibits on the cross, and what Jesus is trying to get into to his disciples' heads as they travel to Jerusalem.

## DEVILISH

All this brings us back to the road towards Jerusalem.

It's this same *selfish* ambition that Jesus tells his disciples to put aside. It's not ambition per se; Jesus himself has a goal, a mission, a drive. But it's this selfish grasping at power, this jealousy, this desire to enforce our will, this wanting our way over others. All of this creates anti-life and perpetuates chaos.

Selfish ambition will scapegoat, demonise, cause hate to proliferate, normalise greed, grasp at inequality, and spread fear. Selfish ambition builds fences and walls, along with tanks and guns to defend those walls. Selfish ambition builds crosses and nails people to them in order to "keep the peace".

But in Christ, we are called to become cross-carriers—carriers of our own cross—and not crucifiers. In other words, we are more willing to lay aside our power than to use it to destroy or dominate others.

It's this selfish ambition that grabs at Peter as he pulls Jesus aside. Peter is looking for a Messiah who will come and use power to militantly take control. In Peter's mind, that is what God is like and therefore, that's what God's Messiah should do. Peter's correction of Jesus is tainted by the idea that God is with the world's idea of the strong.

I can picture Peter trying to motivate Jesus; 'You can't talk like that, Jesus. That's not how victories are won. That's not how winners speak. You're not going to die in Jerusalem, but our enemies will. God is with you;

you're going to win!' But these ideologies are as bitter to Jesus as the wine they try to offer him while he's being crucified. And so Jesus spits them out. Jesus resists the lie to which Adam and Eve, and many of us since, have fallen victim. He rebukes Peter: 'Get behind me, Satan!' Jesus isn't saying that Peter is *the* devil, but his thinking, to use the Apostle James' words from earlier, is *devilish* because Peter's self-serving, self-preserving, self-glorifying, self-exalting thinking is in opposition to, and in conflict with, the character and the way of the God who empties himself.

Knowing this is having the knowledge of good and evil.

But Peter is possessed by these ideals. He's consumed with self and, worse than this, a militant nationalism. Peter's seeing things totally from a human perspective of how to ascend, and how to rule. He's blind to God's perspective. Jesus' way doesn't look like winning; it looks like losing, and it's *embarrassing* and *shameful* in Peter's thinking.

I can't help but wonder, if Jesus came into the Western church today—to those streams which pulsate with exhibitionism and self-interest—and suggested that the way in which God was going to do something significant is through humiliation, ridicule, suffering and maybe dying, how many of us, like Peter, would pull Jesus aside and say, 'Don't speak like that. God's got great things in store for you! Speak with faith, man; everything's going to be awesome. In fact, Jesus, stop confessing and professing all that "death and suffering" stuff over your life. Rebuke it; don't accept it!'?

I'll be honest, as much as I mentally understand Jesus' message of, 'If you give up your life…you'll find life', believing that the exchange rate runs in that direction is a lot harder. My own self-preserving, self-promoting nature bucks against that idea and labels it as an embarrassing way to live.

This is why Jesus, as he talks about what is going to unfold at Jerusalem and as he challenges his disciples to pick up their cross, also mentions being ashamed of him. It is not about being too embarrassed to say 'I'm a Christian' to our friends and family. It's the shame of professing that God's way is cross-shaped, self-emptying, and the shame of exhibiting that same way. This is foolishness to many, to repeat the Apostle Paul's words.[57] And yet, Jesus' message, mission and Kingdom agenda, and how that Kingdom operates, were beautifully demonstrated through his willingness to die a shameful death on a cross.

'God has become King; his coronation was his crucifixion, and his crown is made of thorns. Sacrificially dying on a cross is how God rules.' This is an embarrassing thing to declare, but this is how God works. God lays power down. This clashes against our own ideas of how we attain our dreams. It always will. Self-ambition, self-seeking, self-righteousness and self-preservation are always threatened, or are shamed, when exposed to the idea and the reality of radical self-emptying love.

# 2.5 | LIFE 'N' DEATH

It may sound like an odd, depressing way to talk about ourselves, but the New Testament writers talked a lot about being dead in Christ, or dying in Christ.[58] It's strange, then, that despite how common this theme is within the New Testament, it's not nearly as popular a topic for sermon series, or a common subject matter of any top-selling Christian books, or the inspiration behind more worship lyrics.

A Christianity from which the cross is absent—a watered-down version which allows me to have it my way—is way more appealing to my taste buds than the notion of dying to self. I think most us prefer the idea of throwing dice in the presence of the crucified saviour, in order to get what we want; it's more comfortable than following the pattern of cruciform love presented to us.

But whether I like it or not, there's a part of *me* that needs to be operated on, straightened out, untwisted, or that possibly has to die. And maybe I'm only speaking on behalf of myself, but anything that normally clashes with my desires, and goes against my grain, or confronts my wrong opinions, prejudices and world view, or instructs me that I must love my enemies, usually isn't pleasant.

I'm reminded of a scene within C. S. Lewis' *The Voyage of the Dawn Treader*. In this particular scene, the snotty-nosed, greedy cousin of the Pevensie children, Eustace, gets transformed into a dragon by some cursed gold. Despite the drastic change in his appearance, this conversion is no more than an outward manifestation of Eustace's internal, beastly nature. A nature he has adamantly refused to acknowledge, but is now traumatically caused to confront.

When Eustace finally comes to the point where he accepts his true self and is ready to shed it, it is then that he encounters the lion Aslan; who instructs Eustace to rid himself of his serpent-like nature and to bathe. But no matter how much Eustace tries, he is incapable of scraping off his scaly character. Self-help doesn't work for him. With every piece of skin he removes, more grows back in its place; thicker and more calloused. The more he trusts in ego, the more hardened he becomes to real change. So, as an admission of his inability to transform himself, Eustace surrenders himself to the claws of Aslan. This isn't easy either. Aslan's claws are painful as they tear away at the dragon's hide, but Eustace understands this suffering to be essential to his redemption, as the lion's touch releases the real Eustace from his entombment. It's not the claws which are inflicting suffering on him, but his dying to a former self that is riddled with selfishness and arrogance.

In a similar way, it's not the claws of God that are painful (I would even suggest that God doesn't use claws on us at all). It's the removal of our self-centeredness, as it is peeled from us, that is intense. In this sense, there's a kind of "dying" that helps us to live; it is a death which activates the release of this resurrection life in us—a life that reflects the character of our creator. For me, as I suspect for most of us who set out to stumble in the footsteps of Christ, there's no skirting this process. This is a daily process of dying and living, and dying and living, and dying and…

Except, this is hard to swallow if all we want is 'have it your way' Christianity. We want the dice, and we're often happier to follow the teachings and rituals of anything that promises to convince God to make our dice throws roll 'snake-eyes'. But the crazy thing is that, in addition to the centrality of the Cross, church tradition has been full of 'death' symbols and patterns that should have countered our taste buds.

Fasting is one of these symbols. However, within some circles, fasting has been spun as a certified way of getting our way with God. Apparently, fasting helps us to push God's proverbial arm further up his proverbial back. It's moronic then, to call this *fasting*; it sounds more like haggling and trading. '*If I do X, will you furnish me with Y*'.

Biblical fasting, however, at its truest expression, was about going *without*. To fast is to *deny* self, to put aside any cultural anaesthetic and to encounter reality and our mortality as they are. Fasting nurtured grief and expressed lament, but it also fertilised hope. Fasting was a *modelled death*, a posture that signalled dependency upon divine life and divine rescue. The traditional church practice of Lent grasps this, as the commencing of the forty-day fasting period begins with Ash Wednesday, a service which encourages and commissions us to recall that we are but dust (mortal) and in need of redemption; we are in need of the mercy and life of God.

Baptism is another potent symbol of this dying process. Also nicknamed the water-grave, baptism means being submerged, dunked, saturated and enclosed within the identity of Jesus. It pictorially expresses how an old pattern in life has come to an end, and how a new way has emerged in the life of Christ. What baptism invokes isn't a one-time event; it's a ceremonial representation of what daily life is now going to look like for the believer: dying with Christ and being raised with him. Speaking on the symbol of baptism, Rachel Held Evans describes this iterating process as follows:

> Baptism reminds us that there's no ladder to holiness to climb, no self-improvement plan to follow. It's just death and resurrection, over and over again, day after day, as God reaches down into our deepest graves and with the same power that raised Jesus from the dead wrests us from our pride, our apathy, our fear, our prejudice, our anger, our hurt and our despair.[59]

To paraphrase that, God has to rescue us from the scaly dragon-hides that our serpent-like self-centeredness has entombed us in and that also often seeks to entomb others.

It's not through our self-improvement and self-preservation plans that we transform ourselves or the world, but by letting go of our hold on self entirely, through death, and resurrection. This is what participating in God's mission and means to save the world looks like in our lives. To rephrase the Apostle Paul, 'As *I* am being crucified, Jesus' life expresses itself through me.'[60]

Please don't misunderstand what I am suggesting here. Please understand that Paul is not endorsing—and neither am I—that we should seek death or look to harm ourselves. Nor is this about us being corpses for Jesus by becoming emotionally, mentally and physically detached from our world.

Being dead in Christ means living and exercising influence in a way that is both antithetical and counter-cultural to the way in which human empires, such as Rome, have exercised and continue to exercise power when seeking their dreams. We are *dead* to employing oppressive force, manipulation, and strong-arm bullying to attain power and maintain control. In fact, we don't want power, in any of that sense, at all. In Christ, we are dead to *that* way. In Christ, we are *alive* to a whole other way of being human.

Dying to self is the only avenue through which the world thrives.

## CHOOSE LIFE?

Personally, I find myself conflicted. I want to believe that the way of the cross, the cruciform life, the way of self-emptying works, but it sounds impotent to me in the face of the world's dilemmas. It's hard to look back at the bloody, broken body on a cross and say 'That's how God saves the world'. It is embarrassing to say, and shameful to write, but it's true.

It's hard to believe because the serpent-spun perspective has seeped into me, via cultural and generational osmosis. I think that playing God means holding the dice, or being the one who uses a hammer to drive in the nails. But what God actually does is to hold his palms wide open to receive the world's pain and anguish.

I would love to shout out with Paul that I have been crucified with Christ, but it's a daily challenge to die to self-rule, to refrain from grasping at power, and to die to selfish ambition. It's too tempting for me to play at my idea of God. It's difficult to believe that it's the laying down of power that is the wellspring of life. And yet that's what the cross is. The cross of Christ is the place from where divine life and forgiveness flows, as all power is laid down.

When we behold the cross, we realise that God saves the world by pouring divine life into it, and not through killing and controlling others. It appears that God doesn't contribute to history's division of 'winners' and 'losers' by deciding who lives in which camp, but puts this way of thinking to shame by giving up his life. Which makes me wonder, maybe God's best for me, for us, comes to pass not through making all of our dice roll a double six, but by calling us into this self-emptying lifestyle?

I therefore have a choice to make, as I look at the crucified form of my saviour;

Imitate or ignore.
Behold and worship, or toss dice.

It's foolishness, I know, but I'm devoting myself to picking up my cross.

As for me, God forbid that I should boast about anything except the cross of our Lord Jesus Christ. Because of that cross, my interest in this world died long ago, and the world's interest in me is also long dead.

-Galatians 6:14 (NLT)

# PART 03 | GLORY SEEKERS

And God blessed them, and God said to them,
'Be fruitful and multiply, and fill the earth and
subdue it; and have dominion over the fish of the
sea and over the birds of the air and over every
living thing that moves upon the earth.'
– Genesis[61]


I hate the word *ruin.* Especially when it's a verb.
– Corban Sherwin[62]


The Christian resolution to find the world ugly
and bad has made the world ugly and bad.
– Friedrich Nietzsche[63]

# 3.1 | STINKING APES

In the original 1968 version of *Planet of the Apes*, astronaut George Taylor, played by the legendary Charlton Heston, finds his spacecraft sucked through a cosmic anomaly, spat out into uncharted space and then crash-landing onto the surface of a remote planet.

As Taylor emerges from his wreck and slowly begins to explore this foreign, yet strangely familiar environment, he discovers that the planet is dominated by bipedal, talking apes. He explores a terrain in which wise Orangutans, curious Chimpanzees, and ruthless militant Gorillas have evolved to become the top of the food chain. These are Apes that talk, and farm, and read and write and build, and sadly, also oppress.

In this alternate world, humans still exist, but they're herded like cattle, or hunted, or used for slave labour; only existing as a resource for the Ape society to develop and expand. To keep humans from thinking above their station and to prevent any compassionate Ape from believing that humans have greater potential, a deeply entrenched prejudice prevails which perceives the humans as vermin; they are nothing more than wild animals, incapable of any thought and action above their carnal drives and beastly, base nature. At best, the human animal can be tamed, and maybe house-trained, but they can never be educated and they will never be equal. For generations this view of humanity has triumphed, allowing the status quo to remain unchallenged. Until Charlton Heston steps onto the scene, that is, and his famous cry of, 'Take your stinkin' paws off me, you damn dirty ape!' threatens to bring the current hierarchy crashing to the ground. And thus begins the story of Taylor's revolution for human dignity and liberation.

If you've only ever seen the original film (forgetting the sequels— although *Beneath the Planet of the Apes* wasn't so bad), then like me, when I first watched it, you'll be highly sympathetic towards the human plight. You may see the Apes as the problem, and interpret the film's story as a power-struggle between victimised humans and villainous, sapient Simians. Down with the dirty Apes!

However, as the film comes to an end—here comes a 50-year-old spoiler alert—we discover that this planet isn't some distant, alien world after all, but the future destiny of Earth. In the powerful, metaphorical imagery of the movie's closing scene, we recognize that the screenwriters are presenting to us their idea of the self-induced, dystopian demise of humanity's dominance. This is the world of our making, we realise, as Heston's character witnesses the crumbling remains of the Statue of Liberty and falls to his knees, prophetically crying, 'What have we done?'

I loved *Planet of the Apes*—and it still remains one of my all-time favourites, what I would call 'a classic'. But then a new trilogy of films came along; *Rise of* (2011), *Dawn of* (2014) and *War for the Planet of Apes* (2017), which added their own take into this franchise with regards to the beginnings of the simian revolution.[64] I found myself loving these films, too.

In these films, we discover that the apes are in fact the victims, and that it's we humans who are the villains. In this "new" take on the films, it is the apes that have been exploited for the sake of mankind's society; they are the ones who have been oppressed, subjected to tests, and robbed of their freedom. When watching the new films, instead of standing with the humans, I couldn't help but emphasise with the ape's leader, Caesar (voiced by the talented Andy Serkis), as he fights for the right to be accepted and not exploited or exterminated. Caesar's commanding, 'No!' in *'Rise of'* was as powerful to me as Heston's retort in the original.

At first, to the hard-core fan of the original series, this new movie's trajectory feels like a ridiculous departure from the message conveyed in the original Heston movie. But it is the exact same message—the real story of the films—being transmitted in a different way, from a different angle.

If you have only seen the 1968 original, or if, sadly, you have only seen the latest franchise, then you may be prone to jump to one of two extremes: either you'll be on the side of the humans, or on the side of the apes. Maybe you're so in love with what you believe the story is about, that you've inevitably become blinded to the real intent of the *Planet of the Apes* franchise.

However, if you've seen both, or if you're one of those clever and discerning viewers of the original film, you'll come to realise that these films are telling a tale that is much more profound than a narrative about a crash-landed human or a lab-tested chimp. You'll see that this story isn't about humans versus apes, or even apes versus humans; it's about injustice, inhumanity and inequality, and how those things play out in our interactions with each other. Although the films make use of the idea of one species versus another to aid in conveying its message, the reality is that they are exposing the violence of a single species (humanity) and its internal segregation. When you begin to grasp this, then it stops being a film, or just a story to listen to, and instead, it becomes a challenge. It should be apparent that the *Planet of the Apes* is not a story which promotes an 'us versus them' world view, but one which exposes the disastrous consequences of this 'us versus them' way of living. This tale is not a sci-fi epic, but a prophetic parable; a retelling of human history. This story should make us all take a good, long look at the world and at each other and ask, as Heston's character did, 'What have *we* done?'

For some though, the film will always remain an entertaining story of one astronaut against an army of apes. They'll not see the original intent behind the film. The approach that the latest films employ to amplify the clarion call of the original movie will be lost on them, because accepting the actual message of the story means allowing their warped and ingrained interpretations of the old story to die.

## LOSING THE PLOT

I can't help but wonder that some stories we Christians tell each other are also a departure from the original message of the Bible. We've made this into something it was never intended to be: a story of human transcendence, or going to Heaven forever, or God seeking to destroy the world. We've told the story of a God who is *out there* and who must be reached before he gets here, because if we fail to make it—if we fail to escape, or fail to submit to divine subjugation before he arrives—then there will be hell to pay. Literally.

At the heart of this skewed version of the story is a transcendence of self *beyond* or *above* the material world. In both ways, creation is treated as an "extra" in the story of our soul's ascension—a restriction on the divinely given role we have to play. As such, the world is often portrayed as evil and irreparably corrupt; it's seen as something from which we must be delivered. And the only way of keeping it in better order, until its eventual destruction, is through the use of coercive power; power practised through dominance, oppression and elitist control.

'We're just passing through this world and on to the next' is something I've heard said time and time again. This is a lie which, sadly, allows some Christians to foster apathy towards anything they deem not 'spiritual' or of any eternal value. And I'm not only talking about the mere existence of an apathy towards entertainment, technology, science or popular culture—which is sad in itself—but frighteningly such apathy also promotes a disengagement with the environment, solving the problem of poverty, and speaking against injustice. 'It's a corrupt world', they say, 'which can't be changed. All we need to do is make it through with our souls intact.'

Ironically—in what should be an obviously apparent contradiction to all of this—adherents of the prosperity versions of the gospel continue to seek material promotion, worldly gain and the 'best life ever' as they pass through this world that they also believe to be fleeting, perverse and set on a course for eternal damnation. So as well as encouraging a reticence towards saving the physical world, they also help to normalise greed, individualism, and consumerism, as believers seek, like locust, to strip the material world of life and resources.

Adopting such views makes us no different from those who loot shops in the midst of a riot, and this 'smash-and-grab Christianity' is a far departure from the message shared by Jesus, and the example he gave.

It also makes idolatrous claims about God; it presents God as someone who is apathetic towards the material creation and its current state, because it promotes the image of a deity who is absolutely besotted with the promotion of the non-material soul.

But this isn't the story of the Jewish and Christian Scriptures at all. How did we get here? How have we made this about escaping or empire-building? How has this withered into getting to Heaven after we die, so that the world can go to hell? Of course, there is a theological-historical story to account for the way in which all this has developed over the past seventeen to fifteen hundred years. But I'll leave that for you to explore through better writers than I.

For now, though, I feel the need to pull us back into Scripture's story. Because the original plot and hope of this story—the story which Jesus steps into and realigns—isn't the ascent of humanity from an evil world, but the salvation of the world and the descent of God.

The truth is—and has always been— that God is not *out there*, but that God is *here*. God is not watching us, God is with us. And there's a whole cosmos of difference between those two viewpoints, a lot of space between *there* and *here*.

# 3.2 | REST, SACRED SPACE, FLOODS, AND BABEL

The climax of Genesis' creation account is not the forming of mankind, but the repose of God within his creation temple. Despite the crescendo of God's 'very good' over all that was done in the creator's six days of work, it's only the seventh day, the day when God comes to fill his temple and rest within it, that receives the accolade of 'Holy'.

This resting on the seventh day isn't God putting his feet up, grabbing forty winks and doing nothing with the rest of eternity. It's symbolic of God ceasing from his work of ordering the cosmos, and speaks of God now coming to reign within it. In other words, God stops establishing the functions of the creation and now begins to run it and inhabit it. It's a difference between arranging and sustaining. It's a transition from one kind of work to another, not a ceasing of all work per se.

The idea of God's rest being equivalent to God's reign is alluded to in various ways throughout the Bible's imagery. In particular, there's the reference to Heaven being God's throne and the Earth being his footstool.[65] This terminology isn't a derogatory euphemism for Earth being some sort of divine doormat. On the contrary, it sees creation as a place of God's rest and where God's rule, which is sourced at his throne, finds its expression.

Jesus also reminds us of this rest/reign dynamic in the gospels. At one point during his ministry, whilst defending his own work on the Sabbath day, Jesus controversially points out to the teachers of religious law that God never stops working; God never ceases in his work of restoring creation.[66]

Having said all that, although Genesis climaxes with God resting after the completion of a certain set of tasks, the project of ordering creation isn't quite complete. In Genesis chapter two, we're given a scene in which God plants a garden in a land called Eden—a word which means delightful.[67] Within the land of delight, there also flows a river which waters God's garden, nourishing the plants and trees that grow there. And in this garden are also the two trees that we looked at in the previous chapter.

Now I'm English—and a modern generation of that—so I bring all sorts of British ideas to what a garden represents and what it is supposed to be used for. It's for BBQs, trampolines, swings and grazing space for our two pet rabbits. But regardless of how cute and fluffy our bunny rabbits are, this isn't the type of garden that Genesis has in mind.

In Middle Eastern thinking, within temples and palaces, gardens are deeply symbolic of sacred space—a place where Heaven and Earth are married together. They're multisensory environments, where every taste, aroma and sound testifies to the presence of something divine. Gardens are places of ordered beauty, places where the barrier between Heaven and Earth is so thin that they become indistinguishable.

It seems then, that although God had previously ordered the cosmos, via defining the functions of land and water, night and day etc., God still had some ordering to do. Planting this garden is the next phase in the divine dream. But although God begins this gardening task, God doesn't complete it. God passes this responsibility onto someone else.

So within this garden, God places humankind with the purpose that they should *tend* it and *care* for it.[68] This task involves more than pruning, raking up leaves and manuring the roses, though. When God gave his human images, his priests, the command to multiply and fill the Earth, population growth wasn't the only growth intended. Through the spread of human culture, not only was the original garden to be maintained, but it was to be expanded to universal proportions. We were, as the divine image, to multiply and fill the world with the knowledge of the glory of the God who had already made his dwelling within it.[69] The world was to become a garden; a holistic 'thin' place in which the ordered Earth is suffused with the perceivable fragrance of heavenly delight. To evoke the words of the prophet, there is still to come a day when the world will be full of the *knowledge* of the glory of God.[70]

Are you with me so far?

The mission for humanity was this-worldly, right from the start. This wasn't a vision for escape or transcendence. It wasn't some platform for divine promotion. This was all about getting our hands dirty with Earth.

We've already hinted at this so far in this book—we were made to be images in God's creation temple. And as Divine images, we were to reign and rule creation in the way that reflected God's reign and rule. This was not to be a reign of terror or tyranny, nor one of destructive power; we were not to rule in an exploitative or repressive way. We were to be an eternal echo of God's *liberating oration* in the original creation poem. We were to rule by laying power down, serving and not controlling, and by refusing to collude with the oppressive ways of chaos and darkness. If we were concerned about the call in Genesis 1:28 to *subdue* the Earth and how that looks in practice, Genesis 2:15 reminds us that this subduing—bringing it to order—was to be practised through tenderness and compassion. This subduing was to resemble 'Capability' Brown and Monty Don, not Genghis Khan.[71]

However, instead of spreading sacred space—space where both humanity and creation flourished and the Kingdom of God was made manifest—the biblical story is one of mankind spreading violence. In the place of gardens, we cultivated territory. Humanity imitated chaos and filled the world with its likeness and knowledge instead of God's. And within the chapters which follow Genesis Three, humanity's violence towards humanity continues to accelerate at an exponential rate.

It's not all bad, though. As humanity flourishes so does human art, and musicianship and technology—all good things, all things that further God's ordering of the world. But entwined within these ordering activities is also a dark taint. Not only are musical instruments fashioned at the hands of skilled artisans, but also weapons. Tribal communities, differing cultures, and languages all beautifully emerge, but so do empires and oppression, revenge and war.

We shouldn't miss this important plot point. When it comes to defining *sin*, we have a knack of breaking sin down into a host of differing activities. But Genesis' focus on sin indicates that its ultimate manifestation and symptom is human violence: violence towards each other and towards God's creation. As an antithesis of the gardening vocation we were called to, sin is the activity of making God's presence unperceivable. Sin is the failure to worship God, as we destroy the image of God in each other and ransack, desecrate and abuse God's temple. It's the inclination to exile God from his own creation; to tear and shred the shalom of the world as we work at divorcing Heaven from Earth.

It's telling to note that within the creation account, God separates, names, blesses and commissions all manner of things as he orders the creation. God also calls mankind to share this mission, following the same divine methodology. However, never in the creation account does God separate Heaven and Earth; we are the ones who do that. God's intent was for a fusion of the two; Earth was to be the dwelling of God, but Scripture presents us with a tale of rebelling images, who seek to take ownership for themselves and give no honour or tribute to the creator God.[72]

The increase of this violence gets so bad that by the time we reach the story of Noah (in Genesis 6), God is said to have reached the end of his proverbial rope. And in what is a rather disturbing event, God allows the world to be flooded; destroying this exponential spread of the plague of violence by destroying its carrier. All of humanity, with the exception of Noah and his kin, perishes in this watery catastrophe.

## WHEN THE ROOF CAVES IN

Putting aside questions of whether this flood was a local one, or one of global proportions (which is a conversation that misses the point of this story, because, as we do with the accounts of creation, we bring twenty-first-century questions to a story which isn't responding to us), this episode alone appears to contradict the idea of a God who doesn't use oppressive and militant power. The flood makes God look like a violent, genocidal maniac, does it not? And it wouldn't be alone in the corpus of Scripture; there are other stories which suggest that God is quite disposed to use and condone violence. We'll come back to this idea of a violent God later, in Part Six.

What we need to focus on now though, is what this flood was, or more importantly, what it was seen to represent. In this episode, it's the waters *above* and the waters *below* which collapse in on themselves. Going back to our creation story of Genesis, this isn't seen as torrential rain and groundwater; but the collapse of the divinely ordered cosmos. Remember the ancient arrangement of the world: in the beginning, God parts the primordial water of chaos, separating it above and below. In the flood account, God is understood to have allowed this holding back to cease, and for the world to once again be consumed and revert back to its original disordered state.

Like the creation story, this flood account is also—and remarkably in a way that should get us thinking—echoed in the story of Israel's exodus from Egypt. The whole scene of the parting of the Red Sea, which subsequently collapses upon the imperialistic, oppressive forces of Pharaoh's army as they attempt to thwart God's plan of blessing the nations, can't help but come to mind.[73] The two tales overlap in allegory and scenes where the violent, image bearers of Chaos are consumed and the image bearers of God are liberated.

Could this flood story also be symbolic?

If so, that doesn't mean that a flood never happened in history. There are numerous ancient texts which appear to describe a huge deluge, and the overlap between the stories seems to suggest a historical event (although they all derive different meanings from that event). It wouldn't be difficult to imagine those who witnessed this flood placing the blame for this at Heaven's door either; after all, God rules the cosmos. However, could this account also be read as God consenting to humanity having what it wants? If humanity wants to fill the world with chaos, through its violence and inhumanity, then, lo and behold, the primordial Chaos that humanity has chosen to imitate and fill the world with, once again comes and engulfs the world.

It's easy to see the survivors filling this epic flooding with such cosmological meaning. Like the imagery of the fallen, crumbling head of the Statue of Liberty at the end of *Planet of the Apes*, this story speaks of the world humanity has built imploding on itself. Perpetuating chaos is always self-destructive; it will lead in a direction opposite to the ordering and flourishing God has intended for the world.

Maybe—and I might be going out on a limb here—there's only so much chaos that the world can take?

As the world spins on, we consume, spend and use the environment in an unsustainable way, until it all hits the tipping-point and we find our world collapsing in, unable to support our greed, oppression, violence and exploitation of the environment any longer. It's a little like the giant bucket at the indoor water-park that we take our kids to; the bucket keeps filling and filling, until it unbalances and the deluge spills over a crowd of happy and delighted children. Except that in our case, when the world order we're accustomed to collapses, it's not delightful or enjoyable. It's devastating, economically, culturally and physically. Sometimes it's a man-versus-man bloodbath, a red tide of violent, foaming erosion akin to Charles Dickens' sea in his classic *A Tale of Two Cities*. History certainly testifies to this pattern; The French Revolution, the burning of Rome, or the American Civil War, and many more such events, echo something of how much oppression, greed, exploitation and human tyrannical dominance the world is capable of containing before something, or someone, pushes back and declares that enough is enough.

In Noah's day, something snaps. The world tips on its head, and it isn't pleasant. We need to see that this is certainly not a story of God's glory filling the world, but a story of chaos swamping the world. The flood is a horrible scene; a disaster of great proportions. In no way is this a great moment in world history, or something that should be celebrated or thought of as a divine victory. It doesn't make a great bedtime story, either.

The unedited reality of this event is as nightmarish as the Holocaust. It's a baptism of death. Through human mediators, chaos takes a grip of the world; plunging it into liquescent darkness.

But God doesn't call it a day with creation or people.

The story starts over again, as if from the very beginning. Echoing Genesis once more, God steps into the void and confusion and sends a wind—symbolic of divine breath and Spirit—which moves across the flooded land, separating the waters.[74] And then, at the beginning of Genesis chapter nine, God calls Noah and his family and gives them the same commissioning that was given to humanity originally: 'Multiply and fill'.

What's important for us to note here is that the Earth has not been destroyed in the deluge; instead, the Earth is cleansed from the current violent world order of mankind. Neither is Noah saved from the flood for a heavenly destination; Noah and his family are saved for Earth. And like mankind in Genesis One, Noah and his kin are given the same commissioning: to fill the world with the knowledge of the glory of God. Their mandate again is a this-worldly one to extend sacred space. Interestingly, this command to 'multiply and fill' does differ from the original call in one respect; it's coupled with a prohibition against sin's expression through violence: 'Do not murder'.[75]

And from that day forth, everyone lived happily ever after.

No. No, they did not.

## THE TOWER OF BLANDNESS

Once more the violence spreads, as the continuing books of the Bible unfold. However, the next major disruption we meet within the Genesis narrative may not appear to be a story of violence on the surface, but it's still a story of human resistance.

God had commissioned humanity to *go* and fill the world, but in chapter eleven of Genesis, humanity instead involves itself in a huge construction project, a great tower that reaches to the skies. This construction site becomes known as *Babel,* which coincidentally means confusion and chaos.[76] Not only do humans intend to build this as a monument to their own greatness, but Genesis also says that their motivation is to prevent them from being scattered all over the world.

Did you notice that?

God says 'Go!', but they don't want to go and fill the Earth. They wish to remain in one place, not spreading sacred space, not filling the world with the knowledge of the glory of God. This fits with what we've seen so far, in that humanity seems intent on perpetuating chaos and thwarting God's purpose of ordering creation. To make matters worse, the people in this story wish to build a monument to their own glory, and one that will ascend to the heavens. In other words, they're seeking human transcendence instead of manifesting the immanence of God.[77]

Without seeing this, the story of God confusing the languages of the people, in order to bring their construction project to a halt, may seem a tad callous. But there's something spectacular, life-affirming and redemptive about this judgement; God is legitimising diversity and humanity's this-worldly vocation. To see this, we only need to look closer.

A literal reading of the Tower of Babel often leaves people thinking that this story marks the moment when different languages first showed up in human history. However, you only need to jump back one chapter, to Genesis Ten, and you'll see those differing languages had already developed.

In Genesis Ten, we read about the sons of Noah and their wives, who 'multiplied and filled the earth' after the flood. The nations of the world apparently originated from these three human pairs, and in each of the three passages regarding their descendants (one each for Japheth, Ham and Shem) we read concluding statements about the diverse, ethnic groups that arose: each had its own identity, lands and *language*.

If you want to check that out, read Genesis 10:4, 20 and 32.

Therefore, God's disruption in Genesis Eleven isn't about new sounds at all, but about the prevention of cultural genocide: God is *restoring* the diversity that already existed. It's not that God is objecting to the building of a tower, but to the way it is being built.

In some sense, then, we could say that the story of the Tower of Babel is focused on the dawn of human empires, and that within this story (or prior to this story—see the note at the end of this section), an imperialistic, world super-power has emerged that is forcing other ethnic groups to build on its behalf and to adopt its culture; this also includes adopting its language as a 'common-tongue'.[78] Such an interpretation wouldn't be a stretch of the imagination, to say the least. Imperialism has always sought to eradicate one form of culture and replace it with its own as it seeks to mould the world into what it perceives to be the perfect image of humanity. Colonial conquests throughout history testify to the removal of tribal traditions, rites and, in particular, languages. The Assyrian Empire forced its subject peoples to learn its own tongue. The Greek Empire, under Alexander the Great, spread its culture and language over most of the known world. And the British Empire used the exact same tactic. Some would also argue that through the dynasty of Hollywood, Americanisms are also currently becoming prevalent. Empires have always been built by coercing uniformity to generate a faux impression of unity.

In sum, the Tower of Babel was a monumental strike at, and inversion of God's global, kaleidoscopic dream for the Kingdom of Heaven on Earth, where things are reconciled to each other in their distinction, and not forced together through oppression and violence.

God wants diversity in the creation temple, a mosaic of diverse cultures, colours, styles and sounds. This medley of beauty is one way in which the magnificent glory of God is displayed in the human race. After all, gardens aren't meant to be bland. However, human empires have a knack of resisting this dream by making things monotone, despite the fact that no single colour, or language, or tribe on its own can ever testify to the abundance and greatness of the Divine. There's to be no sacred language and no sacred culture, and so God thwarts Babel's attempt to ruin the world's magnificence by confusing the people's language. Again, this act is restorative; God restores the human mixture of culture, colour and tongues that forceful human imperialism sought to standardise.

This narrative, then, is also a story of redemption. God, in confusing the languages, is overturning the damage and blandness caused by violent domination, and restoring humanity to their vocation to diversify, to multiply, to fill. It's also telling to note that God doesn't bring this about through a violent act. Once again, as in the original creation account of Genesis One, God uses words. As in the flood account, God rhythmically breathes, undoing the effects of the chaotic taint that is being spread by humanity; thus God performs an act of creativity, an act of sanctified separation and setting apart.[79]

Most importantly, we need to notice God's this-worldly purpose in disrupting Babel's construction. God's scattering of humanity commissions them to go back into the wilds of the world to act as agents in cultivating sacred space.

Surely if all God wanted was for people to reach Heaven, if that's what the biblical story is about, then instead of confusing their language, God would have pointed out the stupidity of their thinking that Heaven is in the sky. In the place of tongues, God could have given them better directions. But in a way, I suppose God *does* give them better directions to Paradise: God calls them to this world, to display the Creator's nature through compassionate stewardship and diversity. God wants the divine image bearers to fill the creation Temple with the knowledge of the glory of God. God wants a marriage of Heaven and Earth. God wants humanity to grasp what Belinda Carlisle stumbled upon in the 80s: Heaven is a place on Earth.

# 3.3 | THE SECTION WITH THE MOST ENDNOTES

Hopefully so far—and we're still only within the first part of Scripture's story—we should already be seeing a recurring theme in this dream of God's: it's about the expansion of sacred space on Earth. This is not the story of a God who is apathetic towards the world and who is only interested in the non-material soul of individuals. This is the story of God's descent into creation and not our escape from it.

God has a dream: Heaven on Earth.

Except there's always something that gets in the way of this dream's fruition: humanity. So for God to restore the mission for creation, God first has to launch a mission to restore fallen humanity; a mission that involves calling some of humanity to be priests to the rest of humanity, priests charged with the mandate of calling them back as a whole into being the image of God within creation. Or, to put that another way, God calls a people to be an image of God for those who have forgotten what the image of God is meant to look like.

That mission starts with the call of a man called Abram in Genesis chapter twelve, and a covenant agreement with him to father a nation which would be a *blessing to* the nations. Again, it's a *this*-world mission. But even then, this dream within a dream takes further twists and turns throughout the remaining narrative of Scripture, leading God to employ another dream within a dream, within a dream. God must manifest himself to the people who were called to manifest him to the global population who were originally called to image God.

Still with me?

They'll be more of that story to come. But again, we must realise that this isn't a call for humanity to leave the Earth and go to Heaven, but for humanity to embrace Heaven on Earth.

## ECLECTIC DREAMS

I remember the first time I read through the entire Old Testament. Even at the tender age of eighteen, it struck me how little the people of the Old Testament expressed their hope as being in a future, blissful, disembodied state. Come to think of it, none of them did so. Their hope was always this-worldly, a hope that looked for a restoration of all things.

What follows is a quick whistle-stop tour:

The Prophet Isaiah spoke of the day when God would finally reign in all the Earth. In that finalising of the ages, God will be the one who settles all international disputes, as all nations will be called to beat their swords into ploughshares and their spears into pruning hooks (we will come back to this in a moment, when we look at Micah). When God reigns, according to Isaiah, all wars will cease and all military training will become redundant. Isaiah is so consumed with this vision that he calls the people of Israel to walk in the light of this future; he wants Israel to embody this future hope in the midst of her present world order.[80] In another place, Isaiah envisions God's dream coming to pass as a global feast, a great festival in which all the nations of the world will be invited to celebrate God's reign. In that day, God will remove the shadow of death that hangs over the Earth. Death will be swallowed up forever and all tears and sorrow will be wiped away.[81] Isaiah also poetically pictures God destroying the great dragon of the sea, Leviathan, who, in ancient writing, is an idiomatic anthropomorphism (a non-literal personification) of the chaotic forces.[82] Isaiah even goes as far to state that the ultimate hope, which must come to pass when God finally defeats the power of death and disorder in the world, is that all which death and disorder have tainted and stolen must be restored; including those who have died. Isaiah, then, sees a this-worldly hope which looks for the renewal of all things and the resurrection of those that have died.[83] Isaiah's not looking to go Heaven, but stating that Heaven's rule will be fully realised on Earth.

Isaiah isn't alone.

The Prophet Ezekiel—who was a charismatic and peculiar personality—envisions a restored Temple. We haven't focused much on the physical Temple here. But for our current purposes, it's worth noting that the Temple wasn't treated as a place to practise religion (after all, life is the arena where religion is practised), but as the place where Heaven and Earth were married to one another.

The Temple was seen as *sacred space*, a place filled with the fullness of God *and* the knowledge of that fullness, a microcosm of the intent for the whole Creation Temple. And as sacred space, the temple was purposely filled with Garden imagery; stone columns adorned with pomegranates represented trees and spoke of the natural environment which God had ordered, ordained and made into his dwelling. In Ezekiel's hope, this sacred space, this garden space—the temple space—is seen to be enlarged in comparison to the original Jerusalem Temple which had been destroyed by the Neo-Babylonian Empire under the command of Nebuchadnezzar. This envisioned expansion echoes God's commission to humanity in Eden: to spread sacred space. Ezekiel's visionary Temple (unlike Jerusalem's but like the Garden of Eden) also has a river flowing from its altar which brings healing to the land and the sea and to whatever dwells in both; 'wherever this river flows, everything will live'. Ezekiel's eschatology clearly employs hope for this world's restoration, and he consistently employs language which contains echoes of the Eden of Genesis.[84]

Micah is one of my favourites. This prophet shares the same hope as Isaiah: God will rule the world, not a brand new one, but this present one. The word *world*, in the biblical languages, is often used as a shorthand way of describing the political and social systems of the world and not necessarily the creation itself. So when the prophets do mention a 'new' world, they aren't speaking of the material structure, but the functional one; they are seeking the establishment of a new world order. This is what Micah and Isaiah look toward to when they prophetically imagine the day when God will settle all international disputes and when all the nations of the world will re-forge their weapons of mass destruction into farming equipment.[85] There's something symbolic here that we shouldn't miss. Yes, this clearly means world peace (Yay!), but notice that the tools for war become tools for husbandry, i.e. gardening. In the end, according to Micah, humanity will stop warring over creation as a secular resource and will return to its original vocation of tending to the earth as sacred space by filling it with the knowledge of the glory of the God who dwells in it. It's a repentance in which people turn from being vassals of violence to curators of compassion.

There are many more Old Testament references to such a this-worldly, future hope. And I have purposely picked a few passages which speak of this ultimate conclusion. But if we broadened this scan to cover all of Israel's own national hopes and promises, we would also see there a hope which is earthy, this-worldly, as they seek to be restored to the land of promise, never to be uprooted from it again.[86] Never does anyone wish for a disembodied state. In all these passages—and the ones to follow—the solution to the problem is not a better afterlife. That's still another version of *death*, and death is never hoped for because death is the problem. Death, in all its permeations of violence, oppression, famine, disease and so on, is the ultimate enemy. The perishing that has been perpetuated and mediated through human vassals is what people long for liberation from. Not life itself, but freedom from oppression, inequality, hunger, war, corrupt tyrannical leaders, and so forth.

Has anything changed in our own hopes for today? How many of us long for death? And if and when we do find ourselves longing for it, isn't it because we do long for a better life, but, believing such a thing to be impossible, we then long for death as a release? This too, is what we see in the Old Testament. When people wished for death in the Scriptures, they did so in the hopes of a release from oppression. In their minds, it was better not to exist at all than to experience life in its current state. Sadly, in their view, death seemed a better option than life. Of course, this wasn't God's intent at all for life. God's idea was for people to choose life, not death, but life for some had become bitter and abrasive. Some Old

Testament writers expressed the hope that God could bring them back from the dead, rescuing them from Hades for a better Earth-based life to come, whilst others spoke of the futility of life, or the irony of calling life '*life*' within the present, corrupted world order.[87]

## THE INBETWEENERS

As we move into the period between the Old and the New Testaments, the hope remains the same. For the sake of brevity, I'll keep this survey to the writing contained in what we now call the Apocrypha.

The writer of the Wisdom of Solomon speaks against inviting or perpetuating death, as God created things to be good, stating:

> Do not invite death by the error of your life,
>> or bring on destruction by the works of your hands;
> because God did not make death,
>> and he does not delight in the death of the living.
> For he created all things so that they might exist;
>> the generative forces of the world are wholesome,
>> and there is no destructive poison in them,
>> and the dominion of Hades is not on earth.
> For righteousness is immortal.[88]

Notice the connection between death and its domain; Hades cannot rule over the Earth, because only righteousness is immortal. There's an implication in this verse that the Earth itself is the territory over which death and life are battling. But death will not win—death cannot win—and righteousness (God's way) will continue to reign. Where will God's way continue to reign? On Earth. In another passage, after speaking of the fate of the righteous and the ungodly, Solomon also cryptically speaks of God equipping creation to repel its enemies in the last days.[89] Creation itself will shake off its bonds. In other words, this current creation will be liberated from all that holds it in bondage to corruption and decay. It will not be destroyed or left to rot. Nor is it seen as transient.

In the book of 2 Esdras, despite speaking of the torments to come, the writer still envisions the ultimate pursuit of God to be the renewal and restoration of the material world.[90] These torments, like the flood, seem to be understood as a purging, cleansing action removing the then functional world order which has tainted and infected the material world. Heaven will then occupy the Earth, along with a restored humanity.

Of course, not all the intertestamental writers are so optimistic about humanity. Jesus, son of Sirach, in the book called Ecclesiasticus (aka Sirach) didn't foresee any hope beyond death at all for humanity. There was no hope for the continuance of a soul in a blissful disembodied state, or of a possible future bodily resurrection. However, despite his post-mortem pessimism, the Son of Sirach's hope was still earthy; this-worldly life mattered and was of great, divinely imbued value. Earth was where humanity fulfilled its God-given vocation. Creation rolled on forever, in Sirach's view, whilst humans were born and returned to the dust. But living with wisdom and acquiring a good reputation was still of eternal importance because these were the things that the future generations would remember you by.[91] For Sirach, creation was not a temporary and passing thing—God had made sure of that—whereas humanity was. In a strange twist from today's way of thinking, then, Sirach saw creation as inheriting Heaven, while mankind returned to the Earth as dust.

## REDEMPTION SONGS

Moving into the New Testament—I will again keep things as brief as possible whilst making the same point—Luke's Gospel opens up with the births of John the Baptist and Jesus. Their arrival is enveloped in songs which express hope in God's redemptive action. And all of these redemptive hopes are this-worldly hopes.

Mary's song of praise (also known as the *Magnificat*) parallels the Old Testament dreams of Hannah.[92] Mary speaks of the news of her child Jesus as being the turning point in world history, the moment when God will turn the tables—society's hierarchical tables—upside down. Jesus' arrival signals the inauguration of the time when God will scatter the proud, lift up the lowly and satisfy the impoverished. It's not the world that is destroyed at Jesus' arrival, but the present world order, the chaos, oppression and disarray that have been perpetuated through mankind's abusive grasping for power and control. Through her son, God's kingdom—world order, commonwealth, intent for creation—would arrive.

Zechariah, at the birth of his son John, speaks of this Baptizer as being the forerunner to God's salvation.[93] And God's salvation, in Zechariah's prayer, is not seen as an escape from planet Earth, but as a release from enemies and fear, and the end of exile. This salvation is liberation from darkness and the shadow of death. This salvation will direct humanity to the way of peace-making (Shalom-making) and away from their violent ripping and tearing pursuits. As Zechariah puts it, also invoking the symbols of the Genesis creation poem (and echoing Isaiah 9:2):

> Because of God's tender mercy,
>> the Light from heaven is about to break upon us,
>> to give light to those who sit in darkness and in the shadow
>> of death,
>> and guide us to the path of peace.[94]

Simeon, a devout Jew who happened to be present at Jesus' circumcision and dedication, declared in prayer that this child would be the one to reveal God's glorious light to the nations.[95] This child, Simeon says, is a 'Saviour to all nations', not an escape vehicle that saves us from a material existence or who saves us from an angry God, but, as Matthew's gospel eruditely puts it, 'who will save his people from their sin'.[96]

I know this is a lot to read through and take in, but again and again, we see a hope for this world. All those words at Jesus' birth, and not a single person mentions a child who has come to give us a better, five-star accommodation, version of death. This child was about life, this-worldly life.

Jesus himself—to sadly whittle this down to a small number of his words—declared that he had come to give *life* in all its fullness, not to take, or steal, or destroy.[97] Many have noted that the word *life* here is not the Greek word *Bios* (βιος, as in Biology) but *Zōé* (ζωή, which is seen as spiritual life, or the energy that animates the *Bios* life). But although this verse is not speaking of biological life, it doesn't mean it's referring to a disembodied life in some after-death state, either. In fact, if we think back to Part One of this book, this is the divine life which makes us into image bearers; it's not a life that results or emerges from our biology but is a gift of the Divine (as 1 Peter 2:23 and John 1:13, 3:6, clearly express). It may not be a life which finds its source in this world, but it is the life that animates this world. *Zōé* life is not in opposition to *Bios* life, but it is what *Bios* life was meant to be the container for and transmitter of.

This being the case, there is still a this-world ethical thrust to this life that Jesus has come to give. This is life to its fullest intent, magnitude, depth and dimension. This is garden life. Ordered life. Life free from oppression and decay. This life, understood in a Jewish framework of hope, wouldn't make sense in a bodiless condition without taste, touch and breath. Going back to the prayers noted above in Luke, humanity, and in particular Israel, already had *biological* life—they could breathe and talk, and eat and reproduce—but they still felt 'dead in their sin' because of the exile, oppression and ordering of the world around them.

Jesus sees his purpose as one of liberating human life from its bondage so that it could continue in its original commission to be once again what God had always intended it to be: a divine reflection into creation. He did not come to provide the escape vehicle from creation. Jesus has come to breathe divinity upon the human clay. Moreover, Jesus spoke of himself as being 'the Resurrection and the Life', promising that those who believe in him, although they will die, they will live again.[98] Notice the contrast is not between one version of death and another, better version of death, but between death and life itself.

Of course, one of the most famous verses of all says the same thing:

> For God so loved the world that he gave his only Son, so that everyone who believes in him will not perish but have eternal life. God did not send his Son into the world to condemn it, but to save it.[99]

But because we've lost the plot, and made this about God saving souls for Heaven, we read this verse in the wrong way (often highlighted by the way people frequently stop Jesus' words mid-sentence, missing out verse seventeen). As N. T. Wright has succinctly noted in many places, but more recently in his excellent book *The Day the Revolution Began*, this verse gets mistakenly read as God hating the world and killing his son, in order to vent his hatred, leaving him then able to help a number of people escape from it. But God, in Jesus, gives himself to the world (the cosmos) in order to stop the perishing of creation and humanity. God doesn't add to the decay. God doesn't add to the chaos, the despair and the darkness. God doesn't kill his Son; it's humanity who does that. I believe in a creator who became skin and sinew, and who allowed the very fabric of his being to be torn as an act of love towards the world. God, on the cross, uses his own death as the means of defeating the powers of death and sin, and overthrows their reign with eternal, resurrection, divine life.

Moving on from the Gospels, it is important to notice what the remainder of the New Testament has to say on this theme.

Paul, in his letter to the Ephesians, writes that God's plan—what has always been God's plan—is to bring everything together, everything in Earth and Heaven, under the authority of Jesus.[100] God doesn't do away with the Earth and keep Heaven alone, but in Christ, both are remarried together to form one realm. In another place, Paul also writes that the whole of creation is groaning in anticipation of the day of its liberation, when the image bearers of God will finally resume their vocation and the bondage of death and decay, which currently enslaves it, will be no more.[101] This is a far cry from the idea of God destroying the planet.

In the book of the Acts of the Apostles, the accounts of the early church in the wake of Jesus' resurrection and ascension are given. Not only does the praxis of the church reflect an ethical concern for life in this world and a community which is counter-imperial, via the sharing of possessions and the meeting of each other's needs, but the preaching of the Apostles also reflects an ultimate hope for this world and not a hope for a better afterlife.[102] On the Day of Pentecost, as the conclusion to his great sermon, Peter encourages his fellow Jews by saying that if they would turn back to God and be baptised in Jesus' name (into Jesus' way of living), *then* they would receive the Holy Spirit.[103] *Not,* then they would go to Heaven when they died. For Peter, salvation was the presence of God being embodied in an earthly humanity. In accepting Jesus, they would once again receive the Spirit of God and become bearers of divine life.

In Peter's next sermon, prompted by the healing of a crippled man, he once again urges his people to turn from their sins and turn back to God, saying that the result would be as follows:

> Then wonderful times of refreshment will come from the presence of the Lord, and he will send Jesus your Messiah to you again. For he must remain in heaven until the time for the final *restoration* of *all things*, as God promised long ago through his prophets.[104]

It should be obvious that Peter's not preaching a 'save your souls' message, but an 'embodying God's image' message which looks towards the day when this world will be restored and not abandoned. Wherever you look in the preaching of Acts, the Gospel has a *this-worldly* message, reflective of the Jewish hope and not the modern escapist one. The focus is the forgiveness of sins and the receiving of the Spirit of God; the recommissioning of humanity as image bearers (starting with Israel, and then moving out into the other nations of the world).[105]

One of the most beautiful pictures, however, comes from the book of Revelation. In its closing chapters, it, like the passage in Ezekiel's Temple, envisions a heavenly city coming down to Earth, heralded with the proclamation, 'Look, the home of God is now among his people! He will live with them, and they will be his people. God himself will be with them.'[106] God in this vision, echoing the hopes of Isaiah and Micah, will remove all sorrow and there will be no more pain, or death, or suffering. And all this happens, not in some new creation, but in *this* creation. God announces: 'Look, I am making all things new!' not, 'I am making all new things!'[107]

The scale of Revelation's heavenly city is also important; it's gigantic. Ezekiel prophetically imagined a sacred space larger than the original temple; within his temple, the Holy of Holies is thirty-five feet square, only sixteen percent larger than the original. But Revelation's city is much larger than that, measuring a whopping 1,400 miles long by 1,400 miles wide—that's 211,200 times larger than Ezekiel's—and furthermore, this entire city is the Holy of Holies; all of it is sacred space.[108] Of course, this geometry is not to be taken literally, but figuratively as the expansion of the sacred. Revelation 21:22 speaks of there being no need of a Temple in this city, or lights, for the glory of God illuminates it all and the nations of the world walk in its light. Like the Eden of old, this sacred sphere also has living water flowing from it; a river of life, where, upon each bank, there grows a Tree of Life, the leaves of which are used as a balm for the healing of this world's nations.

Revelation speaks of a time when sacred space will cover the entire Earth and, fulfilling the prophetic emphasis of Habakkuk and Isaiah, all the people of the Earth will be aware of the presence of the glory of God.[109] This is when God's dream comes true.

# 3.4 | THE SKY IS *NOT* FALLING

That was intense, I know. So take a quick breath, and rest awhile. But I won't apologise for the excursion, since it was more than necessary—and, I assure you, it was a brief journey through a large story.

What I want us to grasp is the *this*-world emphasis and hope that are put forward throughout the grand narrative of the Bible. Holding to this trajectory as a framework enables us to then see how each episode of Scripture fits within it. But if we refuse to hold to this, and if we instead bring our own ingrained preconceptions of what we think this story is about, we risk turning a story of God saving the world and reigning in it into a tale of God helping our souls escape from a material prison.

Speaking of stories, let's consider a childhood favourite.

## RUN RABBIT

I'm sure you'll be familiar with Beatrix Potter's famous *Tale of Peter Rabbit*.

Peter's not very good at following the rules, unlike his sisters Flopsy, Mopsy and Cottontail. So despite being told by his mother not to go into the garden of Mr McGregor, Peter does so anyway, and binges on a forbidden buffet of lettuce, beans and radishes. But it's not long before a rage-filled Mr McGregor spots him, and the mad pursuit, which dominates most of Potter's wonderful tale, begins. Peter walks into the garden on two legs, but he ends up fleeing on all fours, losing his shoes and his beautiful blue coat in the process.

From a certain perspective, you could argue that the more Peter runs away from Mr McGregor, the wilder he becomes; losing his human-like attributes and exhibiting the animal more and more. And on that basis, it may be tempting to see a parallel there with what I've said in the book so far. But please don't.

Peter has an excellent reason to run. Mr McGregor's angry cry of 'Stop! Thief!' as he pursues Peter brandishing a garden fork, shouldn't be heard as a call to repentance. If Peter stops, he'll be slain, flayed and fricasseed.

I don't want you reading what we've said so far and thinking that God is now engaged in a rage-filled pursuit crying 'Stop! Thief!' because of the damage we have done to God's garden paradise. Sure, God's not happy with this, and yes, God is in pursuit of humanity. But the Creator is not out to destroy us; God is seeking to liberate us from all that is destroying us. It's not God who punishes us, but the wages of our own sin: death. Death and despair are what pursue us and pull us on a downward spiral away from all we were created for.[110] God, on the other hand, runs after us with forgiveness and life pouring out of every movement.

When we look at the story and see what transpires when God arrives in the flesh, it should shock us to discover how uncondemning, forgiving, loving and merciful this God is. Even God's final words on the cross, as people mock and reject him, are not words of accusation, or bitterness, or judgement of mankind. They are instead a plea for us to stop running from God and receive the gracious divine forgiveness that he extends towards us.

It turns out that God is not like Mr McGregor, brandishing death and hunting us down in his wrath. Neither is God like other literary enforcers, such as George Orwell's *Big Brother*, apathetically monitoring and controlling us from afar. God desires to dwell with us. This God, who is perfectly exhibited in the serving and suffering flesh of Jesus, is inviting the whole of humanity to resign from the business of spreading chaos and come into the family business of gardening.

## THE GARDENER

There's a great sequence at the end of John's gospel, where he describes Mary Magdalene being the first disciple to encounter the resurrected Jesus.[111]

After discovering the empty tomb in the early hours of a Sunday morning, tears of anguish well in Mary's eyes as she understandably believes that someone has moved Jesus' body to another burial plot within this *garden* cemetery. But as the tears begin to flow, Jesus appears and consoles her. John tells us that Mary doesn't recognise Jesus at first, but instead mistakes him for someone else. Who? The local gardener.

I think John is purposely playing with us here by using this literary motif. This is John, after all. John, who throughout his gospel, has purposely echoed the creation account of Genesis. John, by creating these echoes of the Jewish story and its symbols, has been trying to get us to see that Jesus is God's Temple on Earth. Jesus is the dwelling place of God and the image of God. Jesus is the Edenic water of life. Jesus is the light and life that overcomes darkness and death. Jesus is the sacred dream of God manifested among humanity.

So although Mary is wrong, she's also right to believe that the one consoling her is the gardener. Jesus is the one who extends the sacred and beautifies the world through his life, death and resurrection. And in the same fashion that Jesus commissions Mary, the first apostle to the other apostles, to tell of this sacred extension that has been launched through the resurrection, Jesus has also commissioned us to spread the seed of this garden.

Jesus sends *us* back out into the world, *for* the world. We are to take this new Eden's water and bring healing and life to the nations, creating gardens where there are currently wildernesses.

Except, this doesn't look like the message we spread with what is normally categorised as evangelism. Again, demonstrating our unfamiliarity with the plot of Scripture—regardless of how many verses we can segregate and quote—the version often espoused sounds more like Chicken Licken's news that *'The Sky is falling'*. Like Licken, there are those who proclaim that the material world is falling to pieces and that we need to escape before it collapses in on us all.

But the sky is not falling. God has made sure of this. In Christ, God has acted to renew the fraying shalom of the material creation, and to repair his image bearers. God is not asking us to abandon planet Earth, but summoning us to put aside our inclination to disrupt the Shalom of creation, to put aside our oppressive systems, our war-making machinery, our inequality, our greed and our exploitative stewardship of our planet's ecology.

This is not a call to 'smash and grab' what we can as we pass through the collapsing rubble. It's a call to put back. It's a call to take responsibility. It's a call to paint the world beautiful, a call to exhibit God's faithfulness; a call, echoing the multiple calls of God throughout Scripture, to do justice, practise mercy and express love.[112] The way of Christ is not escaping the world, but lovingly embracing the world and bringing it into the knowledge of God's glory.

As Friedrich Nietzsche noted, certain versions of the Christian message have been determined to see the world as bad and ugly. And therefore, through their practice and endorsement of 'smash and grab as we pass through' spiritually, they haven't sought to stop and stem what genuinely is bad and ugly. Sadly, there have been things done and said under the banner of Jesus that have perpetuated the corruption. Instead of gardening, we have also aided in the spread of the wilderness.

We have contributed to the hate and scapegoating. We have jostled for control and militantly defended our hold on power. We too have empowered oppressive regimes, used death, stigmatised victims and colluded with corrupt political regimes, all for the sake of gaining a place of prestige or to protect our political privilege. We should have spoken more truth to power. We should have aligned ourselves more with the disenfranchised, the foreigner, the orphan and the widow. We should have fed, lifted up and spoken for the powerless, instead of courting the powerful and being their viceroys.

A Christianity which images Christ is marked by beauty. And, I must add, there are many beautifying projects that the church at large is involved in; including working with the destitute, tackling slavery, and delivering humanitarian aid. So my criticism above isn't levelled at the whole of the church, through all of time. It is, however, directed at those groups and individuals who have been induced or seduced by the self-absorbed, prosperity and escapist distortions of the gospel.

To those people, I say this: the message of God's presence, and the hope of it being fully manifested here on Earth, should motivate us towards ending war, poverty, injustice and greed. Generosity should expel our consumerism. Equality should seek to extinguish patriarchy, racism, slavery and xenophobia. A sacred view of creation should inspire us to tend it and care for it in a sustainable way, free from exploitation and irreparable damage. Our desire for Justice should cause us to rethink our economy so that the poor, the immigrant and the bereaved are not oppressed, left behind, or deprived of opportunity whilst the wealthy pay themselves six-figure bonuses. In other words, our call is not to seek escape, or personal glory, fortune or the fulfilment of our desires. Our call is to benevolent stewardship of each other and our environment.

'[Shalom] I leave with you, My [shalom] I give to you.'[113] This shalom—translated as peace—is what Jesus has called us to. And this peace isn't some private, spiritual contentment that permits us to ignore the plight of the world around us. It's a call to contribute towards shalom in the world, to follow the re-braiding pattern that Jesus has initiated. It's a call to garden sacred space. After all, as Jesus also said elsewhere, 'God blesses those who work for [shalom], for *they* will be called the children of God.'[114]

# 3.5 | HUNTING THE IMMANENT

For nearly twelve months now, I've been a searcher of the unseen, a participant in capturing the invisible, a hunter of the unreal within the real world around me.

No, I'm sadly not describing some mystical experience involving some sort of spiritual awakening.

Yes—as you've probably guessed—I've been playing Pokémon Go. With the kids, of course.

To be clear, prior to playing the game, I knew nothing about Pokémon. But with the help of a couple of workmates, and the eager and experienced mentoring of our two sons, I've started to come to terms with Lures, Ultra-Balls, Incense and the need to Evolve. I can now distinguish a Weedle from a Caterpie. I can storm and decimate an opponent's gym with the greatest of ease. And I've even been known to capture a 'Razz Berry' intoxicated Dragonair in a single, 'excellent rated' throw!

All very useful life skills, I'm sure you'll agree.

That's not to say that any of this is normal to me; it still feels strange.

I assure you, as a guy in his late thirties, I don't habitually wander the streets to capture rare, animated, imaginary creatures. To repeat myself, I've only downloaded the game because of the kids.

Although, even when my sons aren't with me, I've still found myself being sucked into this crazy hunt. What was once a strange practice for me is becoming increasingly normal. The past few months alone have seen me dutifully devoting my lunch-breaks to meandering the streets near work, seeking the invisible.

I think—if I am entirely truthful—that I may have an addiction (Steph would certainly say I have). I'm addicted to looking. And all of this searching feels familiar, as if it's a human trait that is latent within me; sometimes it's passive, whilst at other times it's actively, hungrily roaming.

Aren't we all searching for something? And I wonder, in most cases, is what we're searching for something 'other'; something that is not of this material world, but that can still be found within it? Call it a search for meaning or purpose, if you like. For some of us, though, we discover ourselves not only hunting the reason for our being, but also seeking the origin of that reason. Whose intent and action are we a product of?

In the Jewish and Christian traditions, God is said to be everywhere: permeating the material reality around us, an invisible resident. The fragrance, the presence and the glory of the Creator are entwined within the fabric of our surroundings. The cosmos is steeped within the divine reality and sustained by a divine faithfulness to it.

That isn't to say that God and the cosmos are one and the same (which is the claim of pantheism). It means that the God who transcends (exists outside of it, other than it) is also immanent within it, near at hand, a hair's breadth away. So close that an inaudible human whisper arrests God's attention. The mystics amongst us would say that the world is full of 'thin places', moments and locations where the sacred becomes tangible, where the veil between what is unseen and seen becomes non-existent. We may find ourselves in the middle of a natural wilderness, or in the car on the way to work, when suddenly we find ourselves stumbling into the garden oasis of the Divine's presence.

Like the menagerie of Pokémon Go, God is a being that can be sought and discovered, even in the murkiest of circumstances and locations. Unlike the game though, this quest doesn't require a mobile and a GPS location. All that's required for this hunt is our humanness. All we need to do is keep our senses open and expectant.

However, sometimes it feels as if God doesn't want to be tracked down. The divine presence appears elusive and unobvious. And in a world that is often abrasive, full of conflict and fractured, it feels like we're running thin on the 'thin places'.

But the testimony of the Scriptures is that God is always present, always near. The kingdom is at hand. And when the storms do come and the fierce chaotic winds buffet us, it's in those moments that I find our searching intensifies, and our sensitivity to divine movement heightens.

As we've discussed so far in this book, to be human is to bear the divine image; we are to disclose the immanency of the transcendent God who is always here, especially within those wilderness moments that lack order and calm. It's in those places that we're called to garden and cultivate; it's then that we are to contribute to increasing the thin, sacred vales. To an extent, we are to embody those thin places for others, to become a font for God's living water. As I said in my previous book, with regards to expressing love through worship, we are called to perceive God and make God perceivable. This is the quintessence of worship.

Jesus fleshed out the sacred perfectly. When we watch Jesus, we see God. God amongst the weary, the broken and the sidelined of this world. God challenging corruption, hierarchy, patriarchy and elitism. God challenging our addiction to violent power. God bringing life and hope to the hopeless, faith to the disenfranchised, and unconditional love to humanity. God exhibiting a humanity that bears his image, a humanity that is as it should be.

I wonder, what if the farthest you had to look for the sacred was the person next to you? What if the farthest they had to look, was you?

So go forth and multiply. Hunt down the sacred. Go and be a Spirit-infused 'thin place' in the world. Because if we don't, and if all we do is seek our own glory instead of expressing God's, aren't we then building Babel? Aren't we then just building walls?

Until at last the Spirit is poured down upon us from
Heaven.

Then the wilderness will become a fertile field,

>            And the fertile field will become a lush and
>            fertile forest.

Justice will rule in the wilderness and righteousness in
the fertile field.

And this righteousness will bring peace.

Quietness and confidence will fill the land forever.

>                                   -Isaiah 32:15-17 (NLT)

# PART 04 | GARDEN WALLS

[C]ommunity cannot feed for long on itself; it can
only flourish where always the boundaries are
giving way to the coming of others from beyond
them – unknown and undiscovered brothers.
– Howard Thurman[115]


Where is your brother?
– God (Genesis)[116]


All generalizations are dangerous, even this one.
– Alexandre Dumas[117]

# 4.1 | BEDROOMS AND BORDERS

The sound of slamming doors, followed by the loud cry of 'Get out of my room!' is becoming a semi-regular occurrence in our home.

Our two boys have the modern luxury of separate bedrooms (something my five brothers and I never had as children). Most of the time, they're both more than willing to operate an open-door policy. But on certain occasions, one brother will get shoved out, a door gets slammed (and then wedged shut via body weight), and a siege commences.

Now and then, Steph and I will intervene.

Sometimes we'll take up the cause of the room's occupant; especially when the invader has ruined his sibling's peace and quiet by leaping on to his unsuspecting back. More often than not though, it's the door slammer who gets it.

'Open that door and let your brother in, now!' is the usual way in which we commence the "negotiation period". And if agreements can't be made, they usually come to an abrupt end with something like this: 'It's not *your* room; it's *our* room, in *our* house!'

I'll defend our kids' rights to privacy; that's important. But for some reason, instead of seeing their rooms as places of welcome, they only perceive territory. It's never *just* a bedroom to them; it's their land, their own little micro-kingdom. Their door frames, at the point where the colour of the carpet changes from hallway-brown to bedroom-blue, have become borders.

Two extra borders, in a world that is already overstocked with borders.

I often wonder what it would be like to live in a world without any borders. But it's difficult to envision a world without territory, without margins, without conflict and imperial strife.

The thing is, the majority of the world's borders don't exist on a map. More often, they're etched, using a more enduring ink, within human memories and human hearts.

Borders on a map are nothing more than lines, and with the exception of the odd natural feature—such as a sea, a river, or a mountain range—nearly all of these lines have no real tangible presence. A map's lines are nothing more than a virtual representation of where one country's jurisdiction and governance ends and another one begins. Lines of this kind don't hurt or separate people.

However, this changes dramatically depending upon how we adopt those lines within our attitudes and identity; when what are *only* intangible, geographical divisions start to be fleshed out and fragmented further with our own smaller partitions. And when, in the place of ink, we begin to draw the lines using xenophobia,

> and racism,
>
> and sexism,
>
> and ageism,
>
> and ableism,
>
> and elitism,
>
> and so on, and so forth…

These lines run deep. So deep, that in some instances, those who practise them often fail to notice them. They've become so ingrained, having been handed down as an inheritance or adopted through cultural osmosis, that they're second nature.

These lines, motivated by history, or vengeance, or bitterness, or twisted stereotypes and warped ideologies, carry the toxic aroma of a permanent marker. They're the strong opinions which refuse to come out in the wash. And similar to the results of moving a pen back and forth over the same point, they've been drawn in over and over again into our cultures, deepening the indentation and tearing the pages of history through a repetitive cycle of arrogance, unforgiveness and irresponsibility.

Lines made up of ink don't hurt. But when we take distinctions like gender, or colour, or social status, or ethnicity, or sexuality, or film tastes, or fashion sense, or hair colour, or our favourite sports team, or accent, or the district we grew up in etc., and begin to use them as borders, and patrol them, and wrap them in twisted philosophical barbed-wire, then that's where the real pain and the torment erupt. It's these kinds of lines that start wars. These human-drawn lines cause oppression and poverty and abuse. It's these types of lines that are the hardest borders in our world to cross, and there is no passport or official document to aid you in the crossing. These lines make or break the very fabric of our human relationships, forming the basis of the distinction between who is our neighbour and who is our enemy.

I can't help but think that the key difference between a neighbour and an enemy is the kind of line that we have drawn.

There's still a line.

There's always a line.

But our neighbour's line is faint and broken and drawn in pencil, whereas an enemy's line is usually dark, thick, solid and permanent. And our world is full of enemy lines, lines we refuse to allow anyone to cross.

The startling thing is that when you view our planet from space, it doesn't look like an atlas or a road map. And yet somehow, humanity has managed to take this vast, beautiful, open world and split it into a million pieces. We are meticulous in dividing up this world we share. We treat variance like a dot-to-dot puzzle, drawing a line wherever we're able. It should never cease to amaze us and shame us when we realise the scale and extent to which we can go in achieving this. Even in a small room full of people, there potentially exist more lines than those on an ordinance survey map of a large town.

We've populated creation with everybody's own micro-kingdom; the world—God's world—has become a place full of human bedrooms. And when lines become walls, the garden dream of God is not being manifested. When we image borders, we fail in imaging God.

# 4.2 | WHERE THE STREETS HAVE NO NAME

As the book of Genesis unfolds, human life becomes extremely territorial.

The story says that it begins as a division between Adam and Eve. A power struggle for dominance will develop between male and female, a battle of the sexes, a fight for control over one another. This is important to note; Patriarchy is a wall that was not built by God, but by men. It may flavour passages and scenes within the narrative of the Bible, due to its cultural presence, but we're to see this as a darkening, chaotic taint that is working against the garden paradise God intended. Instead of humanity working together to tend and care for the garden, those destined to be partners and co-heirs begin to jostle for rank.

By the next chapter, in the story of Cain and Abel, we see that the power struggle has quickly ascended into brother versus brother. Cain, full of anger and dejection, and disregarding God's warning to be wary of the Sin which is out to assault and destroy him, manifests the chaos by attacking and destroying his own kin.

Abel's brutal death is no mere footnote. Sibling rivalry is a big thing in the story of Genesis. You could even say that it's the major theme of the entire book. What starts with Cain and Abel is also echoed in the stories of Isaac and Ishmael, Jacob and Esau, Rachel and Leah, and Joseph and his brothers (which we'll come to in the next chapter). To paraphrase a summary of Genesis by Rabbi Lord Jonathan Sacks, in his book *Not In God's Name*, Genesis makes forming a universe look simple, but trying to get humans to relate well with each other is another, more complex procedure altogether.[118]

Maybe one way to think of these sibling narratives would be as stories of the stronger seeking to oppress or eliminate the weaker. Or as stories of competition and jealousy. Or as stories of skewed favouritism, and the friction which builds up between the privileged and the rejected. Sadly, these are all still recurring themes in world history.

After the Cain and Abel episode, the divisions continue to spin rapidly out of control. The world begins to be cut into slices. Micro-kingdoms, some bigger than others, start to emerge and grow. Some dominate, enslaving others and consuming resources. Soon, what should have been a peaceful home to both humanity and God begins to resemble a chessboard, with the divisions often being drawn with subjugation and blood.

But God has a plan to fix this. Echoing the this-world commission of Adam and Eve, and Noah and his family, God calls another human pair, Abram and Sarai, from out of a human micro-kingdom (Ur) and into a life of wandering. Abram and Sarai are called into a life *without borders* and are led into a search for a 'heavenly land'—a city with eternal foundations, a commonwealth, a human society designed and built by God.[119] God calls Abram and Sarai with the sole purpose of using this human pair, and their descendants, as a vehicle of God's blessing to this broken and fractured world—a blessing that would undo the consequences of the fall and demolish the barriers that had been drawn between God and humankind, and between humans themselves.[120]

This single pair eventually develops into a nation: Israel. But over the course of the Bible's narrative, Israel also becomes obsessed with maintaining borders rather than dismantling them. As many of the Old Testament Prophets attest, instead of being an example to the world of the image and blessing of God, many of their leaders perpetuated the chaos around them and exhibited the traits of the false gods they worshipped.[121] Instead of erasing the lines of oppression, greed, poverty and violence, they drew them in as well. Instead of gardening, they too imitated the border-building exercise of the world.

By the time of the New Testament, this nation of Israel found itself being oppressed at the hands of a stronger nation: Rome. And some of its citizens were desperate to do anything it took to re-draw their own borders back in—even if that meant drawing them in with the blood of their own enemies. For some, the lines could only be drawn in this way.

But this doesn't stop God in his plan. God himself comes as a human into this nation and proclaims that the Kingdom had arrived. That heavenly city, which Abram had set off in search of, had come. According to the prophet Isaiah, this Kingdom would be an 'ever-expanding, peaceful government' that would never end; an intensifying sacred place.[122] This world order not only has eternal foundations, but it would also be eternally spacious. In other words, this is a kingdom without borders; edges and fringes are not a part of its make-up.

## THE PROPHETIC MIC DROP

On one occasion, at the start of this Kingdom's proclamation, God the man—Jesus—enters into a synagogue in Nazareth and announces the liberating words of the prophet Isaiah:

> [Jesus] unrolled the scroll to the place where it says:
> *"The Spirit of the Lord is upon me,*
> > *for he has anointed me to bring Good News to the poor.*
> *He has sent me to proclaim*
> > *that captives will be released,*
> > *that the blind will see,*
> > *that the downtrodden will be freed from their oppressors,*
> > *and that the time of the Lord's favor has come."*
> He rolled up the scroll, handed it back to the attendant, and sat down. Everyone in the synagogue stared at him intently.[123]

To paraphrase, 'The Spirit of the Lord is upon me. I've come to dismantle the lines that humanity has drawn with its greed, its oppression and its ignorance.'

At this point, the writer of this account states that every eye was fixed upon Jesus as he takes a seat. Why?

It wasn't because he was super attractive, or because he has sat in some special reserved seating (as some commentators might add). They're fixated because Jesus finished too soon; Jesus had performed the ancient equivalent of a 'mic drop'.

Jesus places a full stop in Isaiah's prose where there wasn't one, effectively censoring the climax of Isaiah's visionary statement. His audience have spotted this and are wondering why he has sat down mid-reading. If you like, imagine how you would feel listening to some important news, or a doctor, or a lecturer giving a talk, only for them to suddenly cut off part way through the main headline, or diagnosis, or stop short in the middle of their talk and then stare at you. That's what is happening here. Silence lingers in the synagogue as Jesus' audience awkwardly wait for him to continue.

In time, Jesus' lips move, uttering words that intensify the atmospheric tension he's created, *'This Scripture has come true today before your very eyes!'*[124] Except, these aren't the words the crowd were looking for; those aren't the missing words of Isaiah.

What was the bit Jesus censored?

Well, Isaiah's version concludes with, '... *the Lord's favor has come,* (comma—pause for effect, take a breath, and then...) *and with it, the day of God's anger against their enemies.'*[125]

That's some climax that Jesus cuts off, almost as if he disagrees with Isaiah's depiction of how God's intent will be concluded. In other words, Jesus is editorially questioning the words of one of Scripture's most famous prophets. And the idea of this prophecy coming to pass without the climax, which Jesus deleted, causes a buzz of conversation amongst the excitable onlookers.

*'How'* some of them would have been thinking, *'can this prophecy of God's favour be fulfilled whilst Rome is still in charge? Surely,'* they say, echoing the same Messianic ideas of Peter, *'if God's Kingdom has come, why haven't our enemies been eliminated and our lines been redrawn?'*

But for God, it's these lines—the thick, bold, permanent lines of competition, violence and dominance—which are the problem in the first place. God's favour has come to erase the human lines of oppression, greed and ignorance, etc., not merely to draw them back in with a different colour ink.

They want lines.

We want lines.

God doesn't.

You see, this Kingdom—this divine intent for humanity—operates in a way which is upside-down compared to the dividing ways of a world that often seeks to remove enemies. This Kingdom's manifesto—its constitution, its cultural foundation—is centred on the love of enemies, and loving them with the intent of removing these dark, thick, solid borders.

One of the primary distinctions of the life of Jesus, one that has inspired activists such as Mohandas Gandhi and Martin Luther King Jr, is his consistent ethical thrust to erase the lines of division. And Jesus' method of removing these lines wasn't by seeking to erase the enemy through some militaristic, 'death-dealing' campaign—such action only contributes to drawing more lines. Jesus sought to remove the lines through his practical demonstration of loving his enemies, and loving those that his culture would have told him to keep at a distance.

Jesus' ministry was one that consistently ignored and overcame the borders drawn by humanity. Instead of building walls, Jesus made space at the table for everyone on the social spectrum. He reached out to and shared food with the marginalised, the prostitute, and the tax-collector, the Jewish leaders and their Roman oppressors. His compassion, love, wisdom and healing power were available to all who wanted it. All of Jesus' parables, miracles, and prophetic utterances demonstrated his mandate of not only bringing good news to the poor and the oppressed, *but also* to those who inflicted poverty of the poor in the first place, and to those who did the oppressing. In other words, his ministry sought to restore and generate community between a fragmented humanity, to remove the lines, extend the sacred and bring peace on Earth.

## DISRUPTIVE INFLUENCE

Someone may wish to quote Luke 12:51-52 at me here, where Jesus states that he didn't come to bring peace on Earth. Some have therefore taken from this that Jesus had come with the express purpose of spreading division, disunity, and upset. But this statement from Jesus shouldn't be understood this way.

When Jesus states that he hasn't come to bring peace (shalom) on Earth, he isn't admitting to being an antagonist against shalom. Jesus is not saying, 'I am the bringer of war, violence, disunity, hatred, and bigotry'. It would be hypocritical of Jesus to teach that 'God blesses those who work for peace (shalom), for they will be called the children of God' (Matthew 5:9), and then for him to adopt a mission statement and practice that is opposite to this. Jesus knows his mission to dismantle the walls that are defiling the sacred garden intent of God will be met with hostility from those who a) don't want it that way; and b), are trying to bring about God's intent through non-peace-making methods.

If we take into account the social and political predicament of Israel at this time, and the nationalistic and militant Messianic hopes held by some of his followers and crowds, Jesus could be hinting here that he has not come to bring peace as they think peace is brought. In other words, Jesus hadn't come to lead a military campaign against Rome, because forced peace—peace attained by violence—isn't peace and neither is it a viable solution to the violent inclination that has divided God's world in the first place. Jesus also knows that if Israel tries to raise an armed revolt against Rome, then they will be crushed (as ultimately happens in AD 70).

This also makes better sense of what Jesus says in the passage immediately after the above verse, with regard to the signs of the times and making peace with your accuser before it's too late.[126] In this passage, Jesus is clear that he hasn't come to bring a call to arms, but rather a call to be reconciled. Jesus is calling those around him to love their enemy (Rome) and to seek peace and justice in a nonviolent way, not through military action.

Of course, Jesus' message of reconciliation wasn't a popular one in his time (it still isn't in our time). As Jesus said, even family relationships would be divided because of people's opinions of him and his praxis.[127] And this tension does lead to violent action. However, it's not Jesus who brings the tide of violence, but the violence is brought upon Jesus via his scourging and crucifixion.[128]

So although Jesus understood that his mission to erase the lines would cause social tension, retaliation and friction—as it highlighted the world's self-interested desire to segregate and divide—he never advocated the drawing of lines. Jesus never added to the cultural or political rhetoric of hate. And, in a way that shouldn't surprise us, people hated this. To such an extent that it was Jesus' refusal to scapegoat, demonise or exclude that contributed to Jesus being scapegoated, demonised and excluded.

It should strike us then—especially in our own uber-nationalistic age—that Jesus never used racial, xenophobic, sexist, or ageist bigotry to draw people around him and his cause. Unlike some world leaders, Jesus never once exploited or propagated people's paranoia of 'the other' to manipulate any decision or action. Jesus never used hate to increase his opinion polls. Instead, Jesus called people to love one another; to love *all* others.

This should make us think about what it means to follow Jesus Christ in the twenty-first century. Especially when it is all too easy to jump onto whatever social-media platform we use and perpetuate the ongoing demonising, scapegoating chaos.

We are called to practise a life of peace-making, justice, mercy, generosity, grace, forgiveness, speaking truth to power, and love. Practising such ways will cause disruption to the greedy, oppressive, prejudiced and maligned systems in our world. To some, we're a fragrance of life and liberation; to others, we stink of death, to paraphrase the Apostle Paul.[129] But either way, both these aromas emanate from our work of healing the divisions of this world, not perpetuating them. As St. Francis of Assisi put it:

> Since you speak of peace, all the more so must you have it in your hearts. Let none be provoked to anger or scandal by you, but rather may they be drawn to peace and goodwill, to benignity and concord through your gentleness. We have been called to heal wounds, to unite what has fallen apart, and to bring home those who have lost their way.[130]

## COPY GOD

In another place, a few scenes after the above synagogue scene, Jesus adds further nuance to his message:

> But to you who are willing to listen, I say, love your enemies! Do good to those who hate you. Bless those who curse you. Pray for those who hurt you. If someone slaps you on one cheek, offer the other cheek also. If someone demands your coat, offer your shirt also. Give to anyone who asks; and when things are taken away from you, don't try to get them back. Do to others as you would like them to do to you.
>
> If you love only those who love you, why should you get credit for that? Even sinners love those who love them! And if you do good only to those who do good to you, why should you get credit? Even sinners do that much! And if you lend money only to those who can repay you, why should you get credit? Even sinners will lend to other sinners for a full return.
>
> Love your enemies! Do good to them. Lend to them without expecting to be repaid. Then your reward from heaven will be very great, and you will truly be acting as children of the Most High, *for*

*he is kind to those who are unthankful and wicked. You must be compassionate, just as your Father is compassionate.*[131]

Jesus highlights a shocking thing here about God's character—a trait that we are told to imitate as divine image bearers; *'for he is kind to those who are unthankful and wicked. You must be compassionate, just as your Father is compassionate'.*

Now, if you thought what Jesus did to Isaiah's sentence was a shocking edit to the Scriptures, then what Jesus has just said in this verse is radical.

If you've ever read the book of Psalms you'll notice that what Jesus says in this verse goes against some of the things that the Psalmists petition God to do. The Psalms are full of references to 'God destroying the wicked' and requests for God to avenge his people by spilling their enemies' blood.[132] This idea of God is also prevalent in the same prophets who said that God longs for justice and mercy and compassion. The same prophets who critiqued Israel's inability to manifest God's benevolent rule, also seem quick to add, or think, that God, acting like some human ruler, is also out for enemy blood; and typically, Israel's enemies' blood. But like what he does with Isaiah, Jesus challenges this perception and says that these things are not God's way at all.[133]

I know this messes with how some of us understand Scripture and how it should be read, but Jesus—God's ultimate revelation of the divine nature and example of divine imaging in humanity—tells us in this short verse and shows us through his life and ministry a God who doesn't hate the wicked and who doesn't want to see enemies slaughtered.

God is *kind* to the unthankful and the wicked.

God is compassionate to everyone.

But Jesus doesn't stop there.

Straight after these words, Jesus then starts teaching, 'Stop judging others… Stop condemning others… Start forgiving… Be generous'[134]

I've often heard it said, and I've often read, that what Jesus is teaching in this passage is that if *we* judge others, *God* will judge us. Strangely though, you'll notice that Jesus doesn't mention God in connection with any of these things. All he says is don't judge and you won't be judged, but Jesus doesn't state that it is God who's doing the judging.

Odd, yes?

The reason for this is that Jesus, between verses twenty-seven and thirty-seven of Luke 6, hasn't changed topic. It's easy to think that way because of how Bible translators have dissected Jesus words and inserted subtitles between them. It's easy, if you pull these two passages apart from one another, to think that Jesus is the kind of teacher who can never stay on point, who is always going off on tangents and jumping all over the place. But within the *Stop Judging* paragraph, Jesus continues his discourse on how it looks in practical terms for us to love our enemies.

So this 'forgiving, judging, condemning' is *not* about our relationship with God at all, but about our relationship with our enemies. After all, hasn't God already forgiven us? Hasn't God already been generous? Hasn't God already been merciful? In other words, this isn't God condemning us or withholding forgiveness from us, but our enemies doing so because we also withhold forgiveness and mercy from them.

If all we do is deal with our enemies in the same way that they deal with us—if all we do is return enemy fire, and keep throwing out judgement, and keep on withholding compassion—then this cycle of division and oppression will keep spinning on and on. But Jesus hasn't come to allow that wheel to spin endlessly, or to give us new terms to justify spinning it. Jesus came to break the wheel entirely.

'Love your enemies,' Jesus tells us in Luke 6:27-36.

'Well, how do we do that?' is our cynical response.

'Stop making them your enemies through your prejudices, your condemning self-righteous attitudes, your grudges and your greed!' is the thrust of his reply in Luke 6:37-38 (and beyond).

Throughout the entire passage that calls us to do good to our enemies, to bless them, to lend to them, to stop judging and to start forgiving, Jesus is saying, '*Stop drawing enemy lines!*'

The truth is that we're often quick to cast ourselves as the heroes, the good guys, but slow to admit that we're also our enemy's enemy. We seldom admit, especially in international disputes, that we have contributed towards our enemies' retaliation—and maybe even that we have coerced, terrorised and taunted them into taking this step. Seldom do we ask, 'Why do they see us as the enemy?'

Of course, we could all sit back and say, 'I'll stop being an enemy when they do.' But Jesus says we're not to wait for the initiative of those who live on the other side of the lines. Our example is to be taken from God's action, God's initiative; 'for [God]', Jesus tells us, 'is kind to the unthankful and to those who are wicked. You must be compassionate, just as your Father is compassionate'.

Jesus' advice when we come against enemy lines or are tempted to draw them, is to do what God actually does, and not what we think that God should do: We are to live as if the lines don't exist

## RADICAL COMPASSION

God is not into lines.

God is big on welcomes.

And so I firmly believe that when the Kingdom of God has fully manifested itself—when God's dream becomes reality and when the trajectory of world history has reached its destination—it will be a world without borders, whether that be geographical, social, economic, political or national. In the heavenly city, the streets have no names. In that day, there'll be no more Ghettos or Condos, Hamptons or Hoods, slums or exclusive suburbs. It will be a world of lasting equality, human dignity and glory to God, because all grudges and greed will have come to an end. It will still be a world full of beautiful national diversity, distinctive cultures and a variety of tongues, but humanity's micro-kingdoms will no longer exist because they will all be engulfed by an eternal commonwealth of justice and mercy, peace and love.

So to follow Jesus is not an easy thing, as it requires us to open doors and not to build walls; to spread mercy and not oppressive mortar. As images of God's compassionate reign, we become Peacemakers, in the proper sense of what that means, because we live a life of love that refuses to see, and refuses to be confined by the enemies' lines. We are more than conquerors, precisely because we are *not* conquerors at all.

Therefore, to return once more to the words of Howard Thurman:

> Let us now go forth to save the land of our birth from the plague that first drove us into the 'will to quarantine' and to separate ourselves behind self-imposed walls. For this is why we were born: Men, all men belong to each other, and he who shuts himself away diminishes himself, and he who shuts another away from him destroys himself.[135]

Sadly, this hasn't always been true of the church. We've drawn our fair share of the lines that have existed and still exist today. And to help us do this, we've baptised these line-drawing activities in a twisted idea of divine favour.

# 4.3 | "US" AND "THEM"

One of my favourite subjects in school was Art. And I can still remember the important lessons instilled into us during those first few weeks of secondary school.

At the end of one period, our teacher, Mr Rostrom, had some well-aimed constructive criticism to throw at the work we'd all been producing. His main gripe was with our insistence on drawing or painting things which didn't exist. He wasn't giving us a lecture on impressionism versus realism, but exposing the bad habit we had of drawing lines.

Outlines, to be precise.

We'd paint still-life objects—like plants or a collection of musical instruments—and each object would find itself being enclosed in a thick boundary of colour. The drawing of another student's facial features would end up banded in charcoal. And even actual lines—when they did occur on cereal box designs or brand logos—ended up with extra outlines.

We couldn't help it. We drew outlines around everything without giving it a second thought. Our childhood method of drawing things like houses, cars, and laser-toting dinosaurs—all of which could then be coloured in— had entrenched this habit deep into our innocent subconscious. We struggled to put away these childish things. 'How,' we wondered, 'are we to distinguish one thing from another without drawing lines?'

It drove our art teacher crazy, and his repetitive summons to repent of this practice drove most of us crazy too. The call to stop drawing lines would be reissued to us acne-faced tweens nearly every week for the first year of 'big school': first, at the start of the class, as paper was placed and paint was readied; second, during the class, as Mr Rostrom toured the tables looking over every budding artist's shoulder; and finally, at the end of class, when someone's wet portrait would be held up as a visual example of what 'not to do' while its tearing paint flowed with shame.

Eventually, we caught onto his vision and learnt to stop seeing things that weren't there. We came to understand that for every object that exists, there are surfaces accented by shadow and tinted with light, but no lines.

There. Are. No. Lines.

## LIFE IN STEREO

Sometimes, it's not a matter of learning to see, but learning to un-see. We need to look closer, examine the detail, and learn not to be afraid to suspend our opinions and become part of the muddled-middle. Sometimes we have to be brave enough to admit that we are wrong, or at least ill-informed. It takes time to perceive the intricate complexity of life and the issues which develop under that heading. It takes courage to embrace learning and questioning with a humility that accepts that life is more dynamic and all-encompassing than our own individual experience of it. We need to see the accented surfaces, and not allow the world view we have learnt by nurture, or through cultural osmosis, or apathy, or half-of-the-story teaching, tempt us into drawing bold outlines where none exist. After all, perceptions that are built on over-generalisations, stereotypes and hearsay are not perceptive, they're perverse.

Stereotypes are especially dangerous and lethal in this regard, and our media-saturated world thrives on creating and distributing caricatures that whitewash over our shared uniqueness and commonality with uninformed inferences and clichés. The thing is, they're hard to resist because of how "easy" they appear to make things. Stereotypes, by placing crude outlines around *them*, provide an oversimplified pattern of our world, one that helps *us* find significance. The more we can shove others into clustered groupings, the less complex the world appears. Our anxiety is reduced by "knowing" who is who. For instance, who can be trusted? Who are the baddies? Who needs help? Who needs shunning? And the more we can tether these definitions to distinctions like skin colour, or language, or a particular neighbourhood, the easier we feel it is to navigate the world around us safely. But it's all a game of deception.

Sure, if you look hard enough, you can always find a person who'll confirm your stereotype; the prime example of a warped imagination. However, finding them is like looking for Wally (or his American counterpart, Waldo) within a sea of faces. You'll only see them when you ignore all the other information. And this ignorance is a dangerous thing, because our prejudices seduce us into believing that we are seeing the world as it really is, when in reality we are blind to it.

Stereotypes—or labels, or outlines—blind us to the *us* in *them* and the *them* in *us*. And as Jesus goes on to say, following his entreaty to love our enemies and to stop judging each other, blind people—people blinded by prejudice, hate, remorse, discrimination—cannot help others to see. People who see only outlines will help others to see only outlines, which inevitably leads others into the same cycle of dehumanising and objectifying violence towards one another. Or, to use Jesus' words, 'What good is it for one blind person to lead another? The first one will fall into a ditch and pull the other down also.'[136]

We need to see that there are no outlines in God's vision for the world. No inequality. And yet, despite the claim that they are committed to God's vision, this habit of drawing outlines is entrenched within the behaviour of religious people.

One of the most potent outlines used in Christian circles is drawn through a misunderstanding of God's *favour*, which perceives lines around ourselves and around others that privilege *us* whilst disempowering *them*. 'Equal, but separate', is how some may even describe it. Like the outcome of a game of dice, some believe that these outlines have been bestowed by God. 'God is with *us,* not *them*', they declare, redacting all the global implications out of what that means. But in the Life of Jesus—the manifest activity of the Kingdom of God, the gardener of the sacred—we witness a prophetic posture that names and shames *all* the divisions made by hierarchies and empires; even the ones that have been built using a twisted conception of God's *favour*. And if we looked closer at this divine posture, we would see that Jesus is not on *our* side.[137]

## BACK TO THE SYNAGOGUE

Going back to the synagogue at Nazareth (where Jesus quotes, and cuts short, the Isaiah passage that we looked at in the previous section), Jesus clearly speaks of his arrival as being the inauguration of the *Lord's favour*. The hallmark of this season, as he purposely spelled out in how he quoted Isaiah, is not bloodshed and death, but mercy and liberation. This favour of God is exhibited through the blind seeing, the lame dancing and the oppressed being released.

At the time of Jesus, a few of his fellow Jews (like the disciple Peter) had understood *favour* as an outline being drawn around them; a line of distinction, which qualified them to be in a place of supremacy above others. And although they currently found themselves oppressed by a foreign state, one day, they believed, God would overturn the tables and put them in charge.

However, Jesus, in this address at his hometown, counters this idea and calls his people to once again pick up their vocation of being God's vehicle of blessing *to* the nations of the world, instead of desiring to be *over* the nations of the world. Yes, the year of the Lord's favour had indeed come, but Jesus had come to release the oppressed, not to enslave others. His challenge to them, and his mission, is to see his people reshaped and liberated into being a nation that will seek to manifest God's dream on planet Earth and to lay down their own nationalistic dream. But will they see this?

The synagogue is already in a buzz about Jesus' identity and audacious claims—an excitement that is laced with nationalist fervour and that is also suspicious of Jesus' intent for this fervour. They want to know *how* Isaiah's prophecy has apparently come to pass 'before their very eyes', especially when he has removed the climax of their enemies being overthrown.

Jesus knows they've caught on. He senses their frustration and confusion. So after giving the synagogue a moment to soak in his declaration that Isaiah's words have been fulfilled, Jesus continues his synagogue teaching. But instead of reassuring them and, in turn, quenching their passions, Jesus does something that enrages them, sending them into a frenzy for blood. By the end of Jesus' speech, they're no longer transfixed by his gracious words but desiring to kill him.

What is it Jesus says that angers the crowd?

Jesus calls out their wrong ideas of favouritism by reminding them of two of Israel's finest and most dramatic prophets, Elijah and Elisha, and the mighty miracles they performed for non-Israelites.[138]

Other prophets, such as Jeremiah, Isaiah and Ezekiel, spoke their oracles and had their words transcribed. But Elijah and Elisha were prophets that others wrote about. Their stories are full of excitement, action and the miraculous. Even Chuck Norris would be jealous of what these two could do!

Isaiah, Jeremiah, and the other prophetic texts of the Bible, have a nice balance between the self-criticism of their own people and the pronunciation of judgement on other nations. But Elijah and Elisha mostly challenged Israel's own corrupt monarchy, condemning the tyrannical systems of greed and power which had perpetuated injustice, poverty and oppression. Like the other prophets, they saw Israel's failure in her vocation of being a blessing to the other nations. They not only critiqued this, though, but they also practised the alternative—as all good prophets should. As such, their miraculous acts weren't reserved for those who shared their nationality; their most powerful miracles were for foreigners.

Both Elijah and Elisha manifested the vocation of Israel; to bless those beyond their own territorial lines. Their identity as children of Israel, and as members of God's chosen nation, didn't lead them to nationalism or elitism. But they ministered, healed, served and blessed those of other nations. They didn't see God's favour as a call to exclude, but rather a call to extend. It wasn't seen as an outline to self, or a promotion to ethnic domination, but as a privilege to administer the Kingdom of God, the Kingdom of mercy, justice and forgiveness, to the world around them.

Jesus picks these two heroes of faith purposely as the climax of the not-so-subtle point he is trying to get across to the synagogue in his hometown of Nazareth. By using Elijah and Elisha (and specifically their healing ministry to *non*-Israelites), Jesus is contrasting them with the violent climax he's omitted from Isaiah, whilst also showing how Elijah and Elisha exemplified the words of Isaiah that were not omitted. Jesus is effectively saying to his audience, 'In the days of Elijah and Elisha, God didn't show his favour by using them to liberate the people of Israel; God demonstrated his favour by sending them to those across the borders'.

Jesus has already told them implicitly, through his edit of Isaiah, that God is not here to redraw their idea of borders. And now, Jesus explicitly shows them that the Lord's favour isn't here for them alone, but also for those they want to exclude from it.

Unsurprisingly, this drives Jesus' listeners crazy, and a group of worshippers happily becomes a group of would-be murderers. Luke's gospel tells us their reaction: 'Jumping up, they mobbed [Jesus] and forced him to the edge of the hill on which the town was built. They intended to push [Jesus] over the cliff, but he passed right through the crowd and went on his way.'[139]

A challenge to their *us* and *them* thinking caused this violent reaction. It seems to me, that those who wish to do violence, or who are led by a mob-mentality to defend their tribalism, will always let the way of peace pass through their midst. Sometimes, when life is viewed through so-called "God-given" outlines, people can mistakenly believe that doing violence in order to protect these lines can also be an act of worship—as we'll see in the next section.

We too have also been apt at misinterpreting *favour* to mean *favouritism*, thinking that God has outlined us out of preference; outlining and highlighting *us* against the dull background of *them*. But this is wrong. We have been outlined, we have been commissioned; but not as an endorsement of '*us* or *them*' living, or '*us* over *them*' control. Like the call of Abram and Sarai, like the call of Israel as a whole, our call is '*us for* them'.

Paul, a Jew who once thought that God's purpose for his life was to violently patrol the borders of Israel's covenant with God, writes in the New Testament letter to the Ephesians, 'But God is so rich in mercy, and he loved us so very much, that even while we were dead because of our sins, he gave us life when he raised Christ from the dead. [...] And so God can always point to us as examples of the incredible wealth of his favour and kindness toward us, as shown in all he had done for us through Christ Jesus.'[140]

Did you catch that?

    We are *examples*,

    to *others*,

    of *God's...*

Personal preferences? Favourite gender? Colour? Nationality? Style? Social class? No.

We are examples of *God's incredible kindness.*

No matter how you read that, it isn't an endorsement of you or me. It is not God picking us because we're the best of the bunch, or the ones that showed the most potential to be faithful. And we weren't picked because of our gifts or talents either. We are not examples of ourselves. We demonstrate to the world how crazy, zealous and passionately boundless the favour of God is. We are examples of the ridiculous depths to which God's love, mercy and kindness can plunge.

Knowing this should cause us to cast down all our faux diadems of supremacy, privilege, status and accomplishment at the foot of our own cross, instead of casting our dice at the feet of others' crosses.

We are not God's favourites and we did not initiate the grace and favour of God towards us; we are merely invited to inhale it, and then breathe it freely back out into the life of the world.

# 4.4 | BAPTISMS OF FIRE

Jesus doesn't upset only his local synagogue. His disciples also struggled to grasp this idea of favour, as they journeyed with him along the ancient byways of Israel. Luke's account of Jesus tells us of one particular conversation which takes place as they travelled together.[141]

Jesus is on his way to Jerusalem, with his disciples in tow. He's already had a run-in with Peter's ideas of what a Messiah is meant to be like and how God's Kingdom—God's dream—is supposed to come on Earth. And as we've seen, Jesus pulled all the disciples into what Peter wanted to keep as a private chat. You would have thought this "pep talk" would have straightened out the disciples' thinking. But like many of us today, their ideologies have a high inertia; they find it difficult to change their expectations of Jesus, even when they continually encounter the opposite.

So as the disciples travel on the road towards Jerusalem, we find Jesus continually attempting to correct their ideas of the kind of Messiah he is. In this particular scene (which occurs only several verses after Jesus rebukes Peter), Jesus has just descended the 'Mount of Transfiguration' and cast a demon out of a child. And whilst the crowds marvel at how amazing this all is (in other words, whilst the crowd's expectations and excitement amp up by several notches), Jesus pulls his disciples aside for another team talk.[142] He reminds them for the second time of the climax to their journey to Jerusalem. It won't look like the Transfiguration or the miraculous liberation of a child; instead, the climax will be a crucifixion.

The significance of Jesus' words is lost on them though. They still can't grasp it. Their brains are too engrossed with other things. After witnessing Jesus exorcize a foreign, oppressive influence from a young boy, their imaginations are probably running wild with dreams of the glorious liberation of Israel from the foreign oppression of Rome.

As their journey continues these nationalistic dreams of glory keep slipping out in the disciples' conversations, and it's not long before these fantasies find expression in the form of an argument over which of them will be the greatest in the kingdom to come. They're arguing about rank and favour; the honours that will be bestowed upon them on the basis of whose military acts helped to restore God's Kingdom in their imagined repossession of Jerusalem from the Romans. Whose exploits will prove that they are most favoured by God? Whose dice will win?

Helping to fuel this argument are also their past exploits and experiences. A few episodes before this, Jesus gave them the power to work miracles and sent them to demonstrate the Kingdom of God to the villages on the way to Jerusalem. For all twelve of them, the memories of those events are still fresh. They can still vividly recall how they cast out demons and healed the sick as they advanced the Kingdom. *They* too repaired what was broken. *They* too can cast out unwanted forces.

Imagine what that would do to your ego.

The disciples are drunk on this feeling of power. And although Jesus had them serving bread and fish to the masses immediately after their miracle-working field-trip, they still appear ignorant of the notion that this divine power isn't about dominating others. They fail to see that this is a function-restoring, creation-repairing, serving power—it casts out oppression, it heals the consequences of chaos, it proclaims and exhibits the commonwealth of God's dream for the world.

Like Jesus' talk of being crucified, this use of power is lost on them. They're too focused on boasting of what *they* did, and what *they'll* come to do in the battle for Jerusalem. They feel God has granted them the authority to widen the gaps and heighten the walls between *us* and *them*; even between *us* and *us*.

Adding to the in-house tensions, three of them are still swooning from the extraordinary mountaintop experience they've had with Jesus. Peter, James and John all had a front-row seat at the Transfiguration. Out of The Twelve, this trio are 'The Three'. If they originally saw themselves as being within the inner circle of Jesus' entourage of crowds, they'll now think they are on the 'inside' of the 'inside'; seeing themselves as the favourites of the favourites because they've had an 'access all areas' pass to the spectacular.

And although Jesus had told them to keep this transfiguration moment to themselves, in the midst of a bunch of over-inflated egos, this secret knowledge is bound to prompt a pompous feeling that 'we know something you don't know'.

Drunk on power, drunk on knowledge, drunk on ideas of status, and heroic deeds, the twelve turn on each other and start to fight. It's a drunken brawl.

So Jesus, after hearing enough of the boasting and witnessing the in-house punch-up, stops walking. He faces down his followers and turns the tables on their thinking by placing a child amongst them, saying, 'Anyone who *welcomes* a little child like this on my behalf welcomes me, and anyone who welcomes me welcomes my Father who sent me. Whoever is the *least* among you is the greatest'.[143] This may seem cryptic, but by doing this, Jesus is telling them that honouring his way is not done through conquests, exploits or division, but through service and welcome offered to the least and the littlest. In other words, it's not acts of war that will manifest God's Kingdom, but acts of compassionate service and welcome to others.

This only gets the disciples thinking though, and, unsurprisingly, one of them throws out a feeler question to see how far this welcome and compassion has to extend.

John, testing the limits, asks Jesus about someone they saw exorcising demons in Jesus' name, someone he and the others must have seen when they'd been sent to preach the Kingdom of God. 'We tried to stop him, Jesus, because he wasn't part of *our* group', John announces, obviously seeking approval for his excluding actions.

Tellingly, John's a little coy in offering up any information about *how* they attempted to get this other to stop. With a nickname like 'Son of Thunder', I struggle to envision John asking in a calm, well-mannered way. Moreover, if the disciples are prone to fight amongst themselves, how will they treat someone outside of their group? I can't help but wonder; what did John's (possibly aggressive) eagerness to exclude communicate to this stranger about the Kingdom of God?

It's quite shocking really; this other person was inspired by Jesus and sought to participate in God's dream for humanity. But because he wasn't seen by John as a 'team Jesus' badge-holder, John tells him he can't be a part. John was originally sent out by Jesus to extend the sacred dream of God, to invite people into God's commonwealth, but instead, he slams the door in somebody's face.

John's confession to Jesus is conveyed in a tone that implies the question: 'Wasn't I right to do that?' John has protected the outline of favour that he's perceived to be around Jesus' group, and he now hopes Jesus will draw a special outline around him so he can stand out within the group.

But John's dreams explode in his face. Jesus isn't pleased with this turn of events. Exclusion wasn't what he sent his disciples out for. If people rejected them, fine. But Jesus commissioned his disciples to model the welcome of God, not rejection and barriers. So Jesus' response to John is as stern as his earlier rebuke of Peter, 'Don't stop him! Anyone who is not against you is for you.'[144]

This couldn't be any clearer, could it?

But hang on a minute, because there appears to be a space for wiggle-room in that answer. What about those who *aren't* for us, can we reject them? Is this Kingdom still open to those who shut *us* out? I can imagine this grey area looming large in the minds of the disciples. And in the next scene, we see this grey area producing its fruit.

## BURNING AMBITION

Jesus starts walking again towards Jerusalem. Luke tells us he resolutely sets out; Jesus wants to get to Jerusalem for the Passover, as there are things which must be done and said before his time of suffering is to begin. But his determination to get to Jerusalem isn't embraced by all. Jesus sends a message to a Samaritan village up ahead, and they *refuse* welcome to him. They shut Jesus out.

Things had always been tense between Jews and Samaritans; each group had their prejudicial views of the other. However, Jesus' prior sojourn with them (in John 4) had been positive; they liked Jesus, and they liked what he said about the Kingdom of God. This time around, though, they're not so keen. Because of the tenacity with which he is going to Jerusalem, they want nothing to do with him. They *reject* him, and in doing so, they are also rejecting his entourage.

This is where that grey area shows up.

Because it's at this point in the story, when Jesus hears of the Samaritans' refusal of hospitality and welcome, that John (the same John who's recently been chastised by Jesus) and his brother James come and whisper into Jesus' ear a rather sinister prayer request.

Purposely trying to exploit the grey area, they ask Jesus if they can go ahead and call down fire from Heaven to destroy the village and its inhabitants. James and John are praying for genocide, for a massacre, and they're asking God to bless and endorse this by honouring their request.

Wow! Now that's insane. Imagine followers of Jesus not only fighting among themselves, but also seeking the destruction of people who aren't of shared ethnicity, who aren't part of their group, who aren't willing to welcome them. And imagine that request coming from hearts that believe that this is in the service of God's dream because it flows out of a warped sense of God's favour. Surely this should be difficult to picture.

Oh, wait. History testifies of this, too.

There are two things worth noting with James and John's request. First, it's *they* who will call down the fire. They are asking for consent, not an endowment. They feel that they have this power in their grasp already. Again, reflective of the motivation behind their boasting, they've misunderstood the goal of divine power. Again and again, Jesus has tried to make them see that God's Kingdom is characterised by liberty, healing, and restoration. But in all these prior examples (or so the grey area in their thinking will lead them to believe) this liberation was for their own people—for *us*. This occasion, though, is no longer about *us*, but *them*.

James and John believe this scenario is the exception to the rule—these Samaritans are not part of *us* and have clearly shown that they're also not *for us*. Surely then, this is when we can refuse welcome, and, going further than that, this is when we can seek destruction? Their idea of favour has warped into favouritism, and their request of how this elimination will transpire speaks clearly of their twisted sense of what God's Kingdom is like and how it operates.

Which brings us to the second thing to notice about their request. The means by which this annihilation will take place instantly sparks a biblical plot point. It's impossible to read this request for 'fire from Heaven' without it evoking the story of Sodom and Gomorrah.[145] This is a Freudian slip of great proportions. This remark exposes James and John's nationalistic views and demonstrates their low opinion of the Samaritans (and revealingly, this story is still used today by some to describe their opinions of others). The venomous, prejudiced, xenophobic tendency to subjugate or remove others is dripping from their tongues as they bring this request to Jesus' ear. Unlike their forefather, Abraham, in the original story, they don't even try to spare some of the people. They refuse to believe that anything righteous and loved by God could be found amongst *those* kind of people. As far as they're concerned, these Samaritans are fit only for destruction.

Of course, the above implies a desire to see the world purged of the people they view as infectious and unholy. But could there be another perspective behind this request, one which sees the Samaritans as a sacrifice, a gift to God and the extension of his rule? If so, then there's another story of 'fire from Heaven' which springs to mind. It's found in the book of 1 Kings, chapter 18, and it involves the prophet Elijah (whom we briefly looked at in the previous section) as he challenges the false civil religion that controlled Israel in his day.[146]

Elijah's challenge takes place on Mount Carmel, and involves a divine contest, a play-off between the real God and the false god, Baal, between the real ruler and those who had usurped the stage. Two huge sacrificial mounds are prepared, and a bull's carcass is placed on top of each. All that needs to happen is to call on a divine power to send down *fire from Heaven* and set the sacrifice aflame. Whichever deity lights up their offering first, is the real one. Not only then would the real God be vindicated, but, as an added bonus, so would the faithfulness of the real God's followers.

If it is this story that is in the thoughts of James and John, especially as they travel towards Jerusalem, then maybe they see the inhabitants of the Samaritan village as a sacrifice on the altar of contest between the oppression of Rome and its civil religion, on the one side, and the true worship of God, on the other. Because they still think that Jesus is about to remove the Roman stranglehold on their culture, maybe they're seeing this as an opportunity to give Rome a demonstration of what happens to those who get in the way of the worship of the one true God.

If this is the case, then they are seeing this as a means of vindicating not only God, but also themselves. The light from this sacrificial pyre would illuminate those who are "favoured", highlighting *us* in distinction from *them*. In other words, in order to prove their self-righteousness, they are willing to incinerate those they consider as garbage.

Whether it be Sodom or Carmel that is behind their request, the inhospitable Samaritan village, John and James believe, is where the door to the Kingdom must close. This is where the welcome runs out. *Us*, yes. *Them*, no. And remember, they're asking this thinking that it is in line with the Kingdom's vision. They're asking to do this so that God's glory may be revealed, so that God's name may be honoured, vindicated—feared, even.

These guys had missed it. By a long way. Their theology is skewed. Their picture of God's power, God's Spirit, God's authority is perverted and tainted by their nationalism, their xenophobia and their twisted concept of favour.

They're not alone. Their request has found its way out of many lips over the centuries. Our own intercessions and prayers (as well as our open conversations and Facebook posts, etc.) testify of our feelings towards those we see as threats to us and ours. We too can be scalding in our judgements. We too can hold to beliefs which lead us to feel that some people deserve elimination.

Especially in recent days.

The idea of a God who heals a fractured and broken world by smiting all those who seek to break it through their terrorising methods is appealing. In my own anger, shock and despair, I find James and John's sentiments being on the tip of the tongue, trying to fly out of my mouth. But death is incapable of bearing life. Violence will never breed peace. Hate, to quote the Reverend Martin Luther King Jr, can never drive out hate.

Thankfully, Jesus doesn't answer all our prayers with 'yes'. Thankfully, asking in God's name is not a guarantee that you'll get what you desire. Giving them the same fierce response he gave to Peter's anti-Christ thinking, Jesus rebukes them both. To paraphrase the verse that some gospel manuscripts add to this rebuke, 'You have no idea of how dark and malign your desires are! God's dream does not include the destruction of people; God's dream involves saving them!'

## BURNING HEARTS

Now fast-forward a couple of months after this event, and we find ourselves in a scene where James and John get their request granted. Thankfully, it's in a remixed fashion.

It's the feast of Pentecost, and the Sons of Thunder can be seen together with the other disciples praying and waiting upon God. When all of a sudden, to use the words of Acts 2:

> [T]here was a sound from heaven like the roaring of a mighty windstorm in the skies above them, and it filled the house where they were meeting. Then, what looked like flames or tongues of fire appeared and settled on each of [the disciples].[147]

This *fire from Heaven* doesn't reduce them to charred ashes, nor does it brand them with the power to maim their enemies. This fire falls in order to empower them to preach and to practise the Good News of the Kingdom of God to all nations.

God's fire falls, but it doesn't come to destroy life, it comes to ignite divine life and diversity within humanity. Like the Babel story, this tongue-induced disruption of God causes a manifestation of global variance and beauty to emerge. The disciples are like tapers—enflamed to touch the world with love and light. *All* the world, not just the bits they like.

It's this commissioning experience that would later lead the disciple John to write, 'Let us continue to love one another; for love comes from God. Anyone who loves is born of God and knows God.'[148] The heat of the Holy Spirit had obviously melted the hard places in John's violent, thunderous nature. Boundaries dissolve under the passion of the Holy Spirit. The same John who once prayed for the horrifying death of others now encourages us to be led by the Spirit towards love for others. This same John would also record Jesus telling us that love, at its pinnacle, is exhibited in the act of laying your own life down on the sacrificial altar, not someone else's.[149]

It's an extraordinary story of conversion. Those who once bickered and argued, who excluded and sought to eliminate, are now prepared to lay their lives down in order to demonstrate the ridiculous generosity and grace of God.

Such an account, on top of everything else I've said so far in this chapter, should cause us to root out the perversions in our theology. If we, even for one moment, begin to believe that Jesus would endorse our walls and our way of policing those walls, then maybe we aren't for Jesus or his Kingdom. I wonder, if we genuinely heard the heart of God for others, would we also hear Jesus saying to us, 'You have no idea of how dark and malign your desires are'?

Do our hearts contain the desire to control who's in or out? Do we find ourselves having arguments (real or imagined) with others over who's the greatest, who's better than others, who are closer and more faithful to God? Have we ever desired to see others erased, thinking they are beyond the grace of God's Kingdom?

We are in desperate need of the breath of God. The Holy Spirit consumes our hatred, our bitterness, our desire for vengeance. When the Spirit falls, I discover that it's my prejudices, preferences, stereotypes and twisted sense of justice which God seeks to annihilate.

I need to hear this right now, especially in the midst of a country affected by acts of terrorism and fear. I need a baptism in God's agenda. I need empowerment from above to practise the ethic of God's Kingdom, because it's certainly not going to come from within me.

So to God I pray, 'Burn them all! Burn up my hate, my blood lust, my paranoia, my ability to demonise and scapegoat. Burn up anything that leads me away from love.'

Hopefully, this isn't only my prayer! As Spirit-filled people, we are called to unite what is broken and heal what is hurting. We're to cultivate sacred gardens in barren wastelands, thereby bringing life, not death. The focus of Pentecost is not on sensationalism, but on generating an authentic, loving, Spirit-soaked, earthy, human community which bears the hallmarks of the self-emptying, benevolent God.

Maybe—and I could be speaking to myself here—following Jesus is impossible without us hearing the Spirit challenge our cravings for supremacy, privilege and exclusivity?

And yet, despite our claims to be Spirit-filled (and all the charismatic doctrines we have used to support those claims), we are still the stuff of lines, instead of being the stuff of dreams.

We still believe God has preferences and favourites. For some, perpetuating the tension between Adam and Eve, we believe God has a preference for men over women. Instead of tearing this wall down and recognising that this wasn't God's dream for humanity, we've reinforced it by baptising patriarchal dominance, thereby deepening the wounds that have been inflicted on women across the world.

You would think that by the time we reached the 21st century that this wall would have been long gone, but it remains. It remains through people expending huge amounts of energy to maintain their grasp on power, even if it means holding onto archaic and unsubstantiated science about the sacredness of testosterone. As I said in a review for Elaine Storkey's phenomenal *Scars Across Humanity: Understanding and Overcoming Violence Against Women*, 'the violence against women has perpetuated for far too long'. Horrors such as female genital mutilation, selective infanticide, rape (and the insidious blame culture that goes with it), trafficking, domestic abuse and discrimination in the workplace need to come to a long, overdue end. But a church which endorses a class system based on gender will never be fully able to speak or act effectively concerning these issues. As long as women are objectified, degraded, treated as 'second best' or made the subject matter of 'locker room' talk, then God's dream is not being manifested. Instead of gardening, we're spreading the weeds of the fall.

And then there's colour. Here's a line that has a deep history. Sadly, this line still has a deep present. Recently I finished reading Claudia Rankine's *Citizen: An American Lyric*, in which her prose poetry exposes the lines which continue to be drawn as racial barriers. In one place she poignantly writes:

because white men can't

police their imagination

black men are dying.[150]

Rankine's poetry hits the mark every time in this biographical description of a world in which she finds her blackness being simultaneously made invisible and stigmatised. But I found the imagery within the book also arresting to my senses, especially one particular image that can be found on page 91 of her book.

On that page, there's a photograph taken from 1930. It is night time, and a crowd of faces find themselves in the shade of a tree. Noticeably, all of the visible faces are white. Some of them are even looking at the camera, acknowledging their participation in the memory of the moment. On the left-hand side of the photo, a couple are holding hands and smiling, as young lovers do in some picturesque romantic scene. Along with them, most of the other faces in the crowd also display a calm countenance, as if it's a normal summer evening beneath the stars. But to the right of the centre, just below the tree, there's a stern-faced man, pointing at something hanging in the darkness of the boughs above. You can't see what's hanging there though; the photograph's contrast has been purposely manipulated to make invisible the person that your imagination knows is there.

This 1930s image is not of an innocent, summer evening. It's a photograph of a public lynching. And the barbaric brutality of what has happened to a black man has been hidden in a sea of white serenity.

I couldn't take my eyes off this photograph, and I found myself hating the unhidden faces which stared back at me. How could these people be so calm, as if this were normal? What rubbish ideology had they been indoctrinated with that made them think that this was right? Did any of them, I wondered, suspect, even in the slightest, that what they were involved in was grotesque and inhumane?

I tried to imagine what sort of conversations they would be having beneath those trees and afterwards as they travelled home. What prayers would they be saying that night—what would they be perversely thanking God for? The more I looked into the unsympathetic eyes of the stern-faced man, the more I found myself being disgusted at being white. My skin has a history. And then, when I think further, so does my language and my religion.

Like patriarchy, racism has also found itself being endorsed by the idol that people have made of God. The ground cries out about the horrific ways in which part of humanity has dominated and oppressed those of different tones, and done so in the name of God. Some have insisted that God is on the side of the white, whilst being incredibly ignorant of the historical fact that the saviour they worshipped was a non-white, Middle-Easterner who was also lynched by a mob. As with patriarchy, you would have hoped that we would have gotten past this by now. But this disease of the human condition is still at large. You would think we would have learned the lesson of Cain versus Abel, but white supremacy continues to perpetuate this hideous crime against our brothers and sisters. Thankfully, there have been many who have seen this, and have stood against the tide of discrimination. But there still remains a lot of work to be done.

## BLOWIN' IN THE WIND

Racism and patriarchy are only two out of the many walls that a warped sense of favour has constructed and defended. It's heartbreaking when I think about it all. Like the giant-hearted John Coffey, in Stephen King's novel *The Green Mile*, I'm tired of people being ugly to each other. And I know I'm not alone in this. Many of us are tired of supremacy-induced myopia and fear-mongering tribalism. We're tired of the Pilate-like handwashing which is just another way of repeating Cain's question to God: 'Am I my brother's keeper?'

More of us need to hear the complaint of God to Cain ('What have you done? Listen—your brother's blood cries out to me from the ground!') and repent of our contribution to and collusion with the systemic evils that continue to turn paradise into a prison for many.[151] It's time we started being more enthusiastic about searching out the image of God in those around us, instead of being so passionate about seeking out enemies.

Racism, xenophobia, misogyny, hatred, classism, greed, scapegoating, elitism, moralism, and supremacy are only some of the many things which are incompatible with the Kingdom of God. They all run counter to the dream of God's Heaven on Earth, and they all stem from a root that believes some of us are better positioned than the rest and that only some of us are the chosen few. But as Jesus said, it's the all-encompassing *many* that are called, but very few are ever chosen.[152]

Again, favour is not to be confused with favouritism. God is not on *our* side. Favour is not God drawing an outline around *us*, whilst hiding *them* in the shadows. God's favour, in Jesus' words, is the release of captives, freedom for the oppressed, and good news to the poor, etc. In this sense, then, the year of the Lord's favour is simultaneously the unveiling of all human dignity.

God's favour is the eraser to our lines, and our calling is to be involved in this process. We need to silence the stereotypes, lay down our arms, release the grip on our egos, and once more pick up the tools of husbandry and recommit ourselves to the vocation God has given to us.

My message for the church in our era would be this: Stop adding to the spread and contamination of hatred, fear, paranoia and "us versus them" thinking. Be an expression of the divine economy; extend love, justice, mercy and forgiveness. See the Imago Dei in everyone you meet. Seek to be like Christ towards everyone you meet. Be image bearers. Be gardeners. Tear down the walls which are despoiling the view. Give life, and stem the tide of death.

This isn't easy though. Letting go of our categories requires us to rip up those crooked foundations that we've built our understanding of self upon. And maybe we're too afraid of who we'll become when we can't tell *us* from *them*. Our outlines exert an addictive influence upon how we define who we are. Especially when those self-drawn outlines are the only way in which we derive any sense of self-worth or meaning in life; when our identity emerges solely as the product of competitively striving with our siblings; when we feel that there's something intrinsically attractive about us that makes us our parents' favourite. But we're treading on dangerous ground whenever we feel there's something unique to us that functions as the tether to God's favour.

We are loved. But there's nothing bespoke that you possess that has attracted God's unconditional love to you. Don't ever believe the lie that God would choose you to the exclusion of anybody else. God has no favourites.

That's not to say you aren't unique, or special in any way. You are. There has never been anybody like you, and there never will be again. So celebrate your uniqueness. But also be humbled by it. Never forget that the world is full of another seven billion unique individuals. Celebrate them also. Don't let an obsession with your uniqueness lead you to arrogance, but let it lead you to discover the unique in those around you. Let it lead you to bless others.

I suppose one of the places that best encapsulates the heart of what I've been trying to say is a Christmas carol, *It Came Upon a Midnight Clear* (penned by the Unitarian minister Edmund Sears in 1849). Most people will know the first verse of the song, which retells the angelic host's anthem before the bewildered shepherds: 'Glory to God in the highest, and on earth peace, goodwill toward men'.[153] But it's the two central stanzas of the carol that I find personally sobering:

> Still through the cloven skies they come
> With peaceful wings unfurled
> And still their heavenly music floats
> O'er all the weary world;
> Above its sad and lowly plains
> They bend on hovering wing.
> And ever o'er its Babel sounds
> The blessed angels sing.

> Yet with the woes of sin and strife
>
> The world hath suffered long;
>
> Beneath the angel-strain have rolled
>
> Two thousand years of wrong;
>
> And man, at war with man, hears not
>
> The love song which they bring:
>
> O hush the noise, ye men of strife,
>
> And hear the angels sing.

We need to hear the love song of Heaven and the lament of God over this garden, over this Temple. The midnight chorus has been sung and the darkness is now fading into light. The Resurrection has brought with it the dawning of a new world order. The Spirit of Pentecost has descended already, and the mighty wind of God—the breath of God—continues to sweep across our landscapes of discrimination, straining to turn our chaos into beauty. The answer to our pain, the call to participate in God's dream, is blowin' in the wind, to use Bob Dylan's line. So, let's 'hush the noise, ye men of strife, and hear the angels sing'.

Then Jesus told them [...] 'And when I am lifted up from the earth, I will draw *everyone* to myself.'

-John 12:30-32 (NLT, 2015 ed.) [italics mine].

[Christ] has broken down the wall of hostility that used to separate us. [...] His purpose was to make peace between Jews and Gentiles by creating in himself one new person from the two groups. Together as one body, Christ reconciled both groups to God by means of his death, and our hostility toward each other was put to death.

[So] now you Gentiles *are no longer strangers and foreigners*. You are *citizens* [...]. You are *members* [...]. *We* are his house, built on the foundation of the apostles and the prophets. And the cornerstone is Christ Jesus himself. We who believe are carefully joined together, becoming a holy temple (a sacred space) for the Lord.

-Ephesians 2:14b-21 (NLT) [italics mine].

# PART 05 | A CLASH OF DREAMS

Nessun dorma, nessun dorma.
– Puccini[154]

He must become greater and greater, and I must
become less and less.
– John the Baptist[155]

If thou therefore wilt worship me, all shall be
thine.
– Luke 4:7 (KJV)

The greatest happiness of life is the conviction
that we are loved—loved for ourselves, or rather,
loved in spite of ourselves.
– Victor Hugo[156]

# 5.1 | MIRROR, MIRROR, ON THE WALL...

As I write this chapter, I do so with a bruised ego.

This isn't unusual for me. My depression, insecurity and low self-confidence, along with my natural introversion, often struggles under such feelings. But this time around, it's quite a personal wound, and my head is swimming with a hazardous concoction of emotions.

What it boils down to is a lack of recognition. I feel that I should have been honoured in a certain way. I feel as if I've been disowned and disregarded. If I could be entirely honest with myself, the offence was nothing—I am, when I view this from a more rational frame of mind, massively overreacting. But I've allowed the oversight to ferment in my imagination, and mixed into it all sorts of other slights and opinions; this has then gone on to produce an intoxicating, potent mix of internal anger and resentment. All of which is then topped off with a much deeper and darker layer of depression, which in turn sends my paranoia spiralling further and further downward.

It's a vicious cycle of descent. And—to a large extent—it's self-inflicted.

When I was younger, I always thought I'd grow up to be the hero, the one who would have some incredible inner strength, making me capable of carrying those around me. The roads of life have taken other turns, though, and I find myself being dependent and in need of help. I find myself, through my depression and inability to cope with stress, doing more leaning than carrying.

It's soul-crushing. I'm not the man I dreamt I'd be as a boy. I'm not even the man I dreamt I'd be as an adult.

So when *I* get overlooked, in *my* opinion, it stings all the more. Much, much more than it should. I take it very personally indeed, which causes my head to dip all the more deeply into the fathomless sea of self.

But surely there's no shame in admitting my need of others, my dependence on others, is there? And I know I'm not the only person who senses this dichotomy in the midst of the endless, mass-produced pulp of therapies, advice and mantras which seek to prefix everything in life with *self*.

So I'll go first, and hopefully begin the twilight bark against this terrible labelling: Hi, my name is Tristan, and I need help. I'm not self-made. I'm not self-sustaining. I can't make it alone. Without Steph, without one or two close friends, without my faith—I would crumble to pieces; this life would be too crushing to endure.

And yet, despite how much I insist that there's no shame in not being self-made or being bankrupt when it comes to inner strength, I still carry this awful sense of failure. I'm conflicted and embarrassed. I switch on social media, or the television, or observe the covers of magazines filled with 'B-list-celebs', or listen to some garbage prosperity preaching or motivational speaker, and I feel that I've missed the mark. That I've failed in being all that society and my whims tell me *I* could have been.

I'm a product of my time, you see. I live in a society that is becoming increasingly self-consumed. The atmosphere of our age is saturated with subversive messages that goad us into pursuing the "best life ever" by sowing seeds of dissatisfaction into the lives we have now. But instead of life getting fuller and more satisfying, as they promised, following their voices has stripped life of all its innate beauty and simplicity, making it seem more emaciated and sour. Every day, it gets easier to identify what *I* lack and how insignificant *I* am. It's non-stop. Twenty-four seven, our "Feudal Brandlords" sell their wares, advising us on how to look, how to live, how to be happy, to progress and transcend, through the flitting trends of the day which dictate what to own, what to do and what to desire.[157] We're stuck in this restless, self-help era that is spellbound by the siren calls to achieve, acquire, accumulate, ascend… and then repeat.

No matter how I try to look at it, I still arrive at the same conclusion: today's world consistently calls us to dream, but we're seldom allowed to sleep. 'Nessun dorma (No one sleeps)', to quote Puccini. Like Calaf's teasing question in Puccini's famous opera, *Turandot*, Western culture has us running ragged in search of a secret it has no desire to unveil.

It's exhausting. And try as I have to resist this, it's still possessed me to an extent. I've marinated in this culture of distraction, illusion, celebritism and entertainment for far too long for it not to have seeped into me. This self-grown, self-plucked, self-squeezed lifestyle, despite being delusional, is addictive. It feels good to live for self, to seek satisfaction, to do anything and everything that gratifies the hunger and insatiable thirsts of *I*.

Even my rebellion against the self-seeking trends of today is partially fuelled by a greater insistence on *my* self-satisfaction being *my own* independent endeavour. After all, who else really cares about *me*? Who else sees *my* humanity as some*one* and not some*thing*? To the brands and fashion logos of the world, we're just consumers. To our governments, we're data and votes. And to our workplaces, we're either profiteers or overheads. Even the airlines that carry us on vacations have ceased to see us as passengers and have instead labelled us as SLCs (self-loading cargo). If I'm going to be self-grown, I don't want to be riding in on their coat-tails as a product of their regimes. And so *I'm* prone to affirming anything that affirms me. My interest is peaked by the things I find interesting. People who are like me, and people who like me, are, strangely enough, nearly always the people I consider as being nice people. Odd coincidence? Probably not.

What I think of as "God's voice" and "God's will" also appear to be easier to discern when they align with the things I like to do and the things I want to be. I've often made an idol out of God. *GOD*, in this sense, then, becomes a word which is synonymous with gaining and winning, and the antonym of giving and losing. With this god, I feel called to practise the prosthetic life and not a prophetic one. This god becomes the receptacle of my dreams, a mirror to self. With this god, *I* become more, not less. And my prayers to this god, stained with a consumer mindset, sound more like a bartering system: I offer my life, my all, as long I get what I want at the end of it. In many ways, the motivation behind my prayers echoes the Devil's proposition to Jesus, 'I will give it all to you… if you only kneel down and worship *me*'.[158]

Like so many illusory, shallow-looking lakes and ponds that I've walked around, this thinking should be signposted, 'Danger! Deep Water!' Self-realisation and self-discovery appear to be a calming, cleansing and refreshing oasis in life. They display a safe countenance and promise pleasure and satisfaction. But are we becoming increasingly naïve about how deceptively deep and perilous the currents of this sea of self can be?

There's an old myth you may know about a man called Narcissus. As this ancient story goes, Narcissus is cursed by the goddess Nemesis because of his conceitedness, vanity and hard-heartedness toward others. Leading him to a pool of water one day, Nemesis causes Narcissus to fall in love with the vision of his own handsome reflection. It probably didn't take too much effort on Nemesis' part, because it's not long before the narcissist finds himself besotted and rooted to the side the pool, seeking to win the love of the water's echo of self. Gradually, through a consistent lack of food and drink, Narcissus slowly wastes away to nothing by that mirror's edge, pining away for his reflection to reciprocate his love.

In more modern literature, Harry Potter, during his first year at Hogwarts School of Witchcraft and Wizardry, finds himself also pining away before the Mirror of Erised—a mirror that reflects the deepest desires of those who look into it.[159] For his best friend Ron, the mirror displays a desire for recognition and glory, as Ron beholds himself as a Quidditch champion. For Harry's headmaster, the highly esteemed Professor Albus Percival Wulfric Brian Dumbledore, the mirror merely reflects him receiving the gift of a new pair of socks. But for Harry, the mirror tells of other, deeper human desires: the parents who were killed whilst he was still too young to know them. For days on end, Harry finds himself staring into Erised's version of reality, gazing fondly at the reflection of him reunited with his deceased parents, as he wonders whether it could ever become real. The days pass until Professor Dumbledore finally has to pull Harry away from the mirror, warning him that men, like the mythological Narcissus, have wasted away or gone mad as they stared continually into the mirror, wanting to know if the visions they perceived were possible. Dumbledore's advice to Harry is that it isn't wise to dwell on dreams and forget to live.

Great advice! But what else are we to expect from the wise and learned Dumbledore?

However, what happens when society tells us that we can do both? What happens when living is enmeshed with our dreams becoming reality? What happens when the quality of life is made tantamount with wish fulfilment? What happens when the value of a life is measured by the ladder of success?

## PERCENTAGES

We all have a way of gauging our lives to see if they are successful. There's a lens we look through that allows us to view our progress in order to decide whether we are going in the right direction; are we flying, or falling?

For some, the difference between soaring or sinking is a measure of the good days outweighing the bad ones. More victories than injuries. More smiles than tears. Provision more than poverty. Less sickness, more health. It's a game of percentages; Life is good when there's a low percentage of whatever we each consider as bad.

But such a measure isn't always possible. Some tragedies send their tremors rippling across time, tainting the good days ahead. So if we're counting the good versus the bad, what happens when something takes place that causes the rest of our life to move down a course we never intended or desired? A course, that regardless of the amount of "good" things which take place along it, forever remains a path we never wanted to walk? Some people say that we should just make the best of it. These same people say that life is full of choices; choices we can all make to turn our circumstances around. But I'm finding that life is full of happenings, and that those "choices"—that people seem to speak of so frequently—aren't as equally or as abundantly dispersed as some folk assume they are.

Counting the percentages doesn't work. Maybe we shouldn't be counting at all? But 'counting percentages' is alarmingly widespread.

In some circles, the measure of a successful life has a direct correlation to wish fulfilment. A successful life is one that reaches its own desired destination. In these circles, it's constantly pushed that it's crucial for you to have a purpose in life, that you have some goal, that you must have some dream which is above and beyond the daily cycle of normalcy. The advocates of this message are keen to encourage people to never settle for the mediocre or the ordinary. And their definition of *mediocre* neglects to consider the good life we have as part of the world's top two percent; instead, it's infected by their wrong definition of success, which involves correctly answering the question: 'Are you living your dream or not?' Millions of people within the prosperous, Western hemisphere, motivated by a false sense of dissatisfaction, are giving all they can in order to live the dream.

Who can blame them though? Especially as we're all spun the lie that we have settled for a half-life in comparison to all that we could be and all that we could have; or that we're falling behind the rest of the crowd; or that our "fifteen minutes of fame" has a sell-by date that expires at a faster rate the older you get. Not only are these external rumours enough to contend with, but our internal drives also begin to collude with this deception as we throw off the shackles of our mediocrity and begin to pursue a life of "greater significance". It feels good to pursue a dream. There's an addictive rush of endorphins that comes as you rush after all you desire to have and become; it all sends an exotic judder of excitement down our sense of self. And when you get there, at that moment when it all falls into place, boom! The climatic rush of satisfaction is so high it makes you dizzy. Nothing beats the feeling of winning, or achieving, or reaching our desired destination.

Well, for a short time, anyway, because we find ourselves needing something else, as the taste of what we've achieved becomes a bitter memory of glory once held. As George R. R. Martin's King Robert Baratheon (first of his name) confesses to the honourable Lord Eddard Stark, he had never felt as alive whilst chasing the crown and killing those who stood in his way of getting it. But now that he has it, he's never felt so dead.[160]

Sadly, there's the bitter side to the tale of chasing dreams. There's a squalid underside which is exposed when what we desire is beyond our reach; or when all we're promised or teased with by the siren calls of society's whims is like a carrot dangling from an ever-elongating stick; or when someone beats us to our own intended goal, or steals it from us; or when it dawns on us that we do have real limits. It all stings, with a jealous, poisonous pang. When our dreams are aborted or stillborn, or stolen or shown to be an illusion, the pain is crushing. It tastes like death. It is death.

It's death because we're told that our dreams are the reason for our existence. So what is left of us when our dreams rot and our visions fade? Is there still a *self* when we stop seeking self-improvement, or when self-fulfilment is denied to us? It's much more of a death blow when our Christian faith has been kindled and sustained by the idea of a God who is all about *me* achieving *my* dream.

What happens, for example, as we speedily approach the age of thirty and end up having a midlife crisis because we realise we're nowhere close to achieving our dreams—the same dreams that we feel God had given to us and endorsed? Because our idea of life's quality has become so wrapped up in our dreams, when this happens, we collapse. Our idea of life falls to pieces, and our mirror-based faith shatters into a billion shards of hope deferred.

We've all seen it, all witnessed it. Some of us have experienced the fallout of it, and have been left to gather up the pieces with not a single prosperity teacher or self-help coach around to help us do so or explain why this catastrophe has happened.

To be clear, I'm not against having dreams and goals or personal ambitions, or reaching our potential as humans. We all have dreams, myself included. But when our sense of self-worth and our perspective on life becomes tethered to their actualisation, we need to be careful.

Furthermore, I'm not speaking against dreams for freedom, or dignity, or justice. There are many who dream of acceptance and release. There are those who dream of provision, opportunity and equality. There are those who dream of being parents, or who dream of parenting those without families, or who dream of having parents. There are those who dream of a better world without walls and death and disease, those who long to feel community and love. And then there are those who dream of respite from the enclosing darkness that increases its grip with every hour that passes. These are all good dreams. These are dreams which share the ache of the Spirit of God as it broods over a creation tainted with chaos.

But there are those of us in the West—the prosperous West—whose dreams are fuelled by self-ambition, consumerism, fashionable whims, material progress and exhibitionism. This absurd self-absorption, instead of leading us towards our potential, is drowning all we could be and damming up the blessing we should be to the wider world around us.

## HACKED TO PIECES

As I've said, this isn't an exclusively secular issue. It's penetrated the church, becoming increasingly prevalent because it appeals to our individualism and craving for gratification. Some churches have become specialists in this field; they know their craft and they practise it in a way that is world-class. Marketing has replaced discipleship, omnipresent branding has usurped symbolism, entertainment has taken the place of the Table, and, as I mentioned in an earlier part of this book, the stage has become the focus of our contemplation.

An endless stream of 'baptised' life hacks, which are totally unbiblical, but which have been bolted on to any preaching that supposedly aims to be relevant, is being served up in a good number of church services. Sermons are structured around self-help advice, with Jesus making an occasional appearance like a mascot to endorse the product's message. It's not the best advice to build your life around either. It's advice which sows anxiety, not peace; it doesn't inspire faith, but becomes a wet-nurse preparing us for consumerism and competition:

> If you don't build your dream, someone will hire you to help them build theirs.

> Be stubborn about pursuing your dream, but be flexible in your methods.

> Keep moving forward. Stay away from still people: still moaning; still losing; still lazing; still broken.

> Respond to rejection by being more you, not less you.[161]

> Too many of us are not living our dreams, because we would rather live in our fears.

> The size of your dreams is a measure of how big you think God is.

Yes, that set of quotes is sickening. And if it's not twisting your stomach right now, then please pray. That last one is the most gut-wrenching for me, though, as it's laced with a guilt-inducing toxin; you're apparently demeaning God, and what God is for, if you don't desire more. Using this scale, Jesus' God must have been microscopic.

And then there's one of my all-time favourite life-hacks:

> Spend time on those that love you unconditionally. Don't waste it on those that only love you when the conditions are right for them.

Think on it a little while, and you'll soon realise how illogical and oxymoronic that statement is, and how the praxis it encourages is totally unlike the praxis Jesus lived out and calls his followers to adopt. If everyone put this advice into practice, the world would be a much lonelier place, void of all authentic love. Unmasked, this mantra is a call to become like Narcissus and devote ourselves to those who only reflect us—which is a minuscule number of people (one, if you want to do a head count). Seriously, if the only people we ever love and show empathy towards are those who are like us, then aren't we more in love with ourselves than with God's image?

But despite how ludicrous and non-Christ-like such talk is, we continue to lap this junk up as if our lives depended on it. In turn, this creates a million-dollar global enterprise for those who peddle false diagnoses and remedies to our felt sense that something in this world is out of sync. Instead of being called to let go of our obsession with self, they call us to search deeper into ourselves because the answers we seek and the wellspring of life are apparently hidden within us, waiting for the chance to flow forth freely—or so we're told. So the human mirror that should have been angled towards God and out into the world turns more and more inward upon itself.

Again, this is the message of some churches, not the world 'out-there' (which is often found to be much more wary of garbage like this). And God—whenever the Divine's name drops into this sort of conversation—instead of being held up as the image we should bear, is idolised and held up as a mirror to our own nature and the reflection of our desires; like Rowling's Mirror of Erised.

With all this talk of winning, achieving, desiring, it makes you think that Christianity, in some quarters, has become a religion for the winners, and not for the losers. Is there any room left in these churches for the have-nots, the broken, the fatigued, the lost, the hurt, the failures and the disillusioned? Can such churches be emphatic towards those on the margins, without sounding arrogant and patronising, and without assigning blame to those who find themselves marginalized? Can a church which imitates the systems of a success-seeking world prophetically challenge the amount of poverty, stress and dehumanisation those very systems leave in their wake? Is there a gospel that still speaks of us being loved unconditionally with a love that is independent of our worldly status and accomplishments?

Sadly, there seems to be no end to the insipid tide of advice which is labelled as discipleship and which is packaged into sermons with titles like: 'Seven Biblical Reasons to Chase Your Dreams'; 'Are You Dreaming BIG enough?'; 'Scriptural Incentives that Keep us Dreaming Big'... And the way in which Bible verses are ripped and raped out of context to endorse these messages is mind-blowing.

Jeremiah's famous declaration of, 'For I know the plans I have for you… they are plans for good and not for disaster, to give you a future and a hope', is probably the most popular, and over-abused verse of all time.[162]

Sure, it's a great promise. And in light of this book's topic and God's dream for this world, it's a promise we can all cling to. However, to use this as a 'name it, claim it' mantra or as a promise that God will endeavour to fulfil our personal goals in life is a long way off base.

This great promise wasn't addressed to a singular *you*, for a start. In its original context, this promise was given to the community of Israel who'd been carried away into exile to Babylon. It was given to inspire hope in those held in captivity, those who had been torn from their land, those whose lives had taken a drastic turn from all that they considered as normal, ordinary and mediocre (let alone all they had dreamed). These words were given to slaves, to the oppressed, to the disinherited, to the distraught, to the victims of those who dreamed of global domination. Jeremiah is giving these words as a postscript to telling his own people that the abrasive season of exile ahead of them isn't going to be a flash in a pan; there are still seventy years of captivity ahead. So Jeremiah wants them not to lose hope; he needs them to know that this exile is not going to be forever. God will turn this around. And yet, many of those on the receiving end of these words knew that they wouldn't survive past seventy years. They would never see this captivity end. They would die in their captivity. They could only believe that this promise was meant for the generations which followed; they would have to pass this hope on. This promise was never an assurance of personal wish-fulfilment, but it was rather the assurance that God had not abandoned his people.

Jeremiah 29:11 wasn't written to modern Westerners who already have freedom, food, and futures, but to the underdogs, the despised, and the trampled on. This verse isn't addressed to the likes of a consumer, ogling the latest fad and hoping for fame; but to the third-world, sweatshop worker who earns next-to-nothing making the latest fads in depravation whilst longing for human dignity. Admittedly, there are those in the West who do find themselves in bondage, deprived of human dignity, deeply distraught, and the victims of another's self-obsessed dreams. So by all means, cling to this verse if that is you and know that God hasn't walked out on you. But for those of us who are ignorant of the freedom, wealth and opportunity we already possess, and who still use this verse in an insatiable desire for more, please stop.

Please.

Stop.

Maybe we need God to show us how much we already have?

If we looked at the mirror image of God—the incarnation in Christ—we would see God calling us to a different set of desires altogether. So to help us to see this image, and to help us glimpse the eternal foundations of God's dream, we're going to dip our toes into a story that has been hijacked by prosperity teachers for far too long.

# 5.2 | HEY JOE!

The story of Joseph gets trawled all over the place whenever a church decides to do a series on dreams.

Joseph's story is an epic one, occupying a huge chunk of the page space in the book of Genesis.[163] As the great-grandson of Abram and Sarai, whom we briefly looked at in Part four, Joseph is the hero of a story which is probably one of the most famous Bible tales. It's even got its own stage musical—with an award-winning score!

As the story goes, Joseph has a dream. And by the end of the story, after enduring great tribulation and trials, the perseverance of Joseph pays off and he gets what he dreamed of.

Or so goes the lesson that is taught by many preachers who advocate self-help and self-actualisation.

The truth, however, is much more sinister.

Firstly, although the end of Joseph's story sees a dramatic turn in circumstances, his life could hardly be called living the dream. It's more of a living nightmare. He's betrayed by his brothers and thrown into a pit, where he is almost killed, but then sold into slavery by those same brothers. He is lied about, imprisoned, and then forgotten. Joseph's story is accented by experiences of treachery, pain, isolation and abandonment. And not in brief periods either, but in long, drawn-out, desolated years. Despite the fact that Joseph has a dream (which we'll come to in a moment), Joseph's heart longs for a different road, one that leads him back to his home, his father and his brother Benjamin.

Here is a journey marred by tragedy. If we counted the percentages, in order to measure its success, Joseph's life would fall at the bottom end of the scale. Regardless of how many "good" things transpire along this trail that Joseph finds himself thrown onto, it remains the oppressive pit of servitude into which his brothers first threw him; a road with little freedom of choice, a thoroughfare with no exits, a life without liberty. Yes, he ultimately finds himself becoming prime minister of Egypt, but he's still a lapdog, a glorified slave, for someone else. He can't even go and bury his own father without getting consent.[164] Which reminds me, that when Joseph is finally reunited with his father near the end of the tale, their final years together are extremely brief; this offers Joseph little recompense for the time stolen from him.

I assure you, none of us would want this dream.

Secondly, as much as we're encouraged to have a personal goal above the monotony of normalcy, Joseph wasn't seeking such a thing. As far as we know, prior to being thrown into a pit of subservience, Joseph enjoyed those Canaan days. And the dream he had one night—an actual dream experienced during sleep, not a personal ambition—wasn't something he conjured up or strategized for, but something of the future that God had allowed Joseph to glimpse. From the way in which Joseph responds to having this dream, it's fairly obvious that he doesn't understand what it fully means or what impact it should have on his daily living. As such, Joseph doesn't wake up the next morning and enrol in leadership college. In fact, the opposite happens; he continues to follow his father's instructions and dutifully looks after sheep.

This second point is crucial for understanding Joseph's story. This *isn't* a story about Joseph's personal aspirations, hopes and desires (of which we see little mention in his tale), but rather the dream of God. Knowing this makes a huge difference in how we read Joseph's tale, because through this lens we see how Joseph—the progeny and vehicle of God's dream— becomes the victim of the egocentric dreams of those around him. Joseph's life is a clash of dreams.

Think about it. In Joseph's story, everyone is seeking to live their dream through him. His father, Jacob, shows excessive favouritism towards him— much to his brothers' irritation—because he reflects the woman that Jacob once loved and now memorialises in him. Joseph's brothers try to achieve their dreams by having Joseph eliminated from the scene, maybe in the hope that without him around life will be easier and their father will love them more. Potiphar's dreams are realised when he finds a trusted person to manage his household, thus avoiding the necessity of worrying about it and allowing him to give himself to his other pursuits. Potiphar's wife's desires exhibit themselves in her sexual craving for Joseph, and after her attempt at seduction is rejected, she protects herself and gets her revenge by scapegoating Joseph and having him thrown in prison.

And on and on it goes… Joseph is the puppet, the constant scapegoat of everyone else's whimsical desires; the victim of people wishing to advance. Sadly, a world full of people all striving to be successful in the world's eyes, is also a world full of victims; these are people who have been robbed, cheated, assassinated, lied about and oppressed—people who have had their humanity and dignity torn from them by others trying to gain, or take what they desire.

Joseph's story *is* about dreams. But it's the opposite of how the prosperity teachers spin it. It's not a story encouraging us to build our dreams before others use us to build theirs. It's a story which calls us (as Jesus did to Peter) to repent of our selfish ambition for power and control. Instead of calling us to realise our egocentric personal aspirations, this story is a warning about how those sorts of dreams are perversely played out.

It is God's dream, not Joseph's, that is assaulted, rejected, ridiculed and killed—and yet, it's God's dream that saves humanity in a time of disaster, not mankind's schemes. It is God's purpose that brings life and light out of the grip of chaos. It is God's vision that preserves life at a time of famine, a time when the world had ceased to flourish and function as God had originally intended it to do. As in the creation poem and the narrative of the Crucifixion, it is God's liberating *telos* that overcomes the powers of death and darkness which are exhibited through the dreams and schemes of dice-throwing humanity.[165]

I hope you can see the link here with this book and the other stories of Genesis that we have explored? The whole thrust of Joseph's tale weaves itself beautifully into the theme of Scripture that we saw in Part Three. In its own microscopic way, Joseph's saga retells the story of how God's dream for creation is thwarted by selfish ambition, but how God then turns all of that selfish intent around and still manages to steer the conclusion towards his world-saving purposes. This is a story that gives real hope and value to human life, because God's dream of a redeemed creation temple cannot be sabotaged, despite how much we try.

As Joseph himself comments at the end of his tale, as he looks back and reviews all that has happened to him—how others have abused him to get to where they wanted to be—he defines God's sovereignty as taking what people intended for evil and turning it toward good.[166] For Joseph, God's sovereignty wasn't the cause of his heartache, pain and suffering—Joseph, like most of us, certainly knew the real source of all this. But for Joseph, God's sovereign power was able to turn all of this turmoil around and still arrive at the intended destination for humanity, a flourishing end, a beautiful end.

Jesus' story too, is a clash of dreams.

When Jesus walked this Earth, he preached and manifested God's dream for the world. When we watch Jesus we see what it means to bear God's image. It's not a less-than-human life, but a more fully human life that practises the nature of God; a life which challenges our Babel-building and our refusal to display the immanence of God through our communal, peace-loving stewardship of each other and our ecology. Jesus spoke against injustice and violence and greed. His practice of compassion and humility went against the grain of the national, religious, imperialistic, and individualistic dreams of those around him.

It's no surprise then that Jesus, like Joseph, also found himself victimised, betrayed, traded for money, lied about and stripped of human dignity. People got increasingly frustrated in their failed attempts to make him align with their own desires, and they got deeply aggravated when Jesus purposely acted against those desires. Especially those desires that they thought reflected God's intent.

His story culminates with the ultimate vent of human ambition: the death of someone who is a threat to all we long for, the removal of someone who is getting in our dream's way. Those who were jealous of Jesus' popularity, those whose hold on power was threatened by Jesus' open commensality and empowerment of the powerless, those whose Babel walls crumbled before his re-creative and liberating authority, have him crucified. But as in Joseph's story, God also takes up this intent for evil and turns it towards the intended goal.

Joseph's brothers planned to thwart the dreams he had by throwing him into a pit and selling him into slavery. But their act of violence, through the sovereignty of God, becomes a crucial step in the chain of events that births the dream into reality. God takes the brothers' plan of slavery and makes it the germinating ground for his plan to save the world from famine. In the same way, those who crucified Jesus, hoping to humiliate and derail his ministry, unknowingly provide the platform God would use to vindicate and establish it forever, as his own death on the cross becomes the means to launch liberating resurrection life into a world gripped in a famine of death and oppression.

In both cases, it's God's skill that takes what was meant for evil and turns it to good. It's God's dream that leads to a flourishing world.

There are important lessons for us all to learn from this. Neither Joseph's nor Jesus' stories endorse the idea of God being a mirror to our desires, but they reveal the truth that our self-absorbed mirrors are blinding us to a much better reality for all.

The self-help versions of the gospel want you to believe that it is the distance between our present selves and our future/potential selves which is of the greatest importance in life, and that our progress and maturity is a matter of closing the distance between the two. The gospel, then, in this context, is distorted and seen as God endorsing and helping *us* on a journey of self-discovery and self-fulfilment. Ergo, our dream is all that matters to God, and nothing and *no-one* is going to stand in the way.

However, in the gospel Jesus taught, it's the present distance between ourselves and our neighbour, and ourselves and our enemy, which is of greater importance. Real growth and maturity are shown in our love for one another. It is through our proximity to each other that Christ is made visible, and God's dream for us (corporately) is thereby made manifest in the world. Ergo, God's dream for the whole of creation—which includes us—is all that matters to God, and no individual's egocentric dream is going to get in the way of this and prevent its eventual fulfilment. As the Apostle Paul reminds us, nothing—not life or death, demons or angels, fear, doubt, time and space, or the hell-bent, malignant powers which are striving to thwart God's plan—can ever separate us from the conclusion of God's faithful love for us and creation.[167]

Why? Because neither the megalomaniac dreams of mankind, or the pursuit of fortune and glory, can bring salvation and worth to humanity. But the life, death and resurrection of the dreamer of God, does.

Maybe then, there are some dreams God might need us to let go of, because not all of our dreams are compatible with the vision of God for this world. But we wouldn't be the first people in the world to think that our personal dreams are merely an extension of God's will. We're certainly not the first generation to imagine God as mirroring our desires. Even in Jesus' time, people tried to retain a piece of the 'Real-Estate of Self' in God's Kingdom.

Jesus is on his way to Jerusalem. It's a long journey, one which the gospel writers fill with interruption and conversation.

One time—sometime after Jesus has had a certain discussion with James and John for confusing their own malignant desires with God's—Jesus is approached by a Rich Young Man.[169]

The Young Man asks Jesus what he must do to have eternal life. Please understand, he's not asking about disembodied life in Heaven after death; that's a modern Christian way to read what is meant by life eternal. In a way which is more in line with what we discovered in Part Three, this man is asking how he can be a part of God's Kingdom, God's commonwealth as it comes on Earth. In other words, he is asking, 'Jesus, how can I be a part of God's plan for this world?'

Jesus can never resist such a question, so he tells him honestly how to be a part of God's vision for the world; all he need do is follow the commandments. The Young Man wants to be pretty certain with his stake, though. So he asks in reply, 'Which ones?' Let's face it, there are an awful lot of commandments in the Law of Moses—Jewish tradition holds that there are 613 in total—so his question is a valid one.

So Jesus boils it down for the man by listing out the Ten Commandments:

'Do not murder…

Do not commit adultery…

Do not steal…

Do not testify falsely…

Honour your mother and father…

…and love your neighbour as yourself.'

The Young Man replies to this by saying that he has followed all of these laws his whole life. Full stars, well done! And then, without commenting any further on what Jesus had said, he boldly asks what *else* is required. Boy, this guy is desperate.

We'll pause the story there for a moment, because there are a few things we need to take note of at this point.

Firstly, I hope you can see that practising the life Jesus emphasised by listing the commandments would generate a garden-like world. Doing these things doesn't build walls, nor does it perpetuate chaos and violence. A society which refrains from murdering and stealing and so forth makes the world a better and safer place for everyone. I'm sure we'd all agree.

Secondly, did you notice what Jesus did in this list of commandments? You may want to check out the original Ten Commandments (also known as the Decalogue) written in Moses' Law, so you can compare and contrast.[170] Because if this was a test on 'What are the Ten Commandments?', Jesus would have failed.

There are two things Jesus does; he *omits* and he *amends*. A simple count tells you that Jesus doesn't list all ten. Count them, if you don't believe me, and you'll soon see that Jesus takes ten and makes it into six. Not quite as miraculous as turning water into wine, I admit, but important nonetheless.

What instantly stands out is that Jesus omits the first three commandments. These three are all primarily focused on proper worship of God: Don't worship other gods; don't make idols; don't misuse God's name. Jesus also omits commandment number four, which concerns the keeping of the Sabbath—I've written on this before, so I won't take up too much space here. What I would say, though, is that many commentators see the fourth commandment as the turning point in this list between our worship of God (dealt with in the first three) and our relationship with fellow humanity (the remaining six).

Again, Jesus doesn't mention any of these at all. He skips straight into the final six which deal with us and others. I find this peculiar—Jesus fixes the basis of this man's participation in God's Kingdom not on whether or not he has idols, whether or not he has blasphemed, if he worships other gods, or if he keeps the Sabbath. But apparently, Jesus sets the criteria solely on his commitment to his fellow humans.

This may appear odd, but I like this, because it should stop us from adopting an attitude which seeks to escape or ignore the world by embracing private religious notions. According to such notions, all that matters is 'going to Heaven', a feat accomplished by loving God alone. But Jewish theology doesn't embrace this attitude at all; this Rich Young Man and Jesus both see God's Kingdom as a this-world social-political reality—a divinely aligned human organism—not some private, individual religious hope for a disembodied, post-mortem state of bliss. If all that mattered was the observance of the first three commandments, we could all curl up in a ball or stick our heads in the sand and ignore the world until Kingdom come. But we are called to practise the ethical thrusts of this Kingdom now, to work it out within the community surrounding us. We're called to image the God we claim to worship in commandments one to three by the practice of commandments four to ten.

Jesus doesn't omit the first three commandments because he sees them as non-essentials. Jesus knows that the true practice of worshipping God is expressed through our human relationships with each other. To murder is to blaspheme and desecrate the image of God; to steal and to dishonour others is to worship other gods. Our theology—what we believe about God—will always be expressed in our interactions with others. Not killing, not coveting, not stealing and not treating each other as objects, etc., is a big part of how we display the immanence of God; it's how we live as citizens of the Kingdom; it's how we exhibit the marriage between Heaven and Earth.

So don't be worried about Jesus cutting this down to six commandments from ten. It makes sense; especially as we move through this story. But this reduction isn't the omission or amendment I wanted us to see; there's something else here that Jesus does with the remaining six that is linguistically akin to a magician's sleight of hand. Did you see what *that* was?

Jesus purposely omits the final commandment. Sure, he lists murder and adultery and stealing… but Jesus fails to mention, 'Do not covet', and in its place, Jesus slips in, 'Love your neighbour as yourself'.

Why does Jesus make this switch? Well, I'll come back to that soon. What's important is that you notice it, because the Young Man seems to have missed it altogether.

Maybe he could be forgiven? After all, we can miss this too, and we have it written down in front of us. But hang on a moment, Luke's version of this account tells us that this Young Man isn't just any young man; he's a *religious* leader. So he should have spotted this.

What also stands out is that this Young Religious Man thought that, like all the others, he had kept this commandment his whole life. Maybe he gets so used to hearing a repetitive call of 'do not' that he also hears the final statement as a prohibition. Or maybe he still hears 'do not covet' play over in his head, because he's memorised these laws, and so he doesn't spot Jesus' switch. Either way, he hears this list of commands as a task list on refraining and somehow perceives it to be complete. Finished. Passed. Requiring no further action. This would explain why he asks for more things to do.

How does he make such an assessment? How can he be sure that all is completed? And could it be that Jesus' purposeful edit of the final commandment is his way of sensitively highlighting to the Young Man how ridiculous such ideas of completion are?

You see, unlike the previous five items on Jesus' list, loving your neighbour doesn't begin with a 'Do Not'. It is implicitly loaded with a call to continually 'do'. There is no possible way of scratching this off the list.

Also—and here's Jesus' possible reason for the replacement—unlike 'Do not covet', the call to practise loving your neighbour addresses the coveting problem from the other side of the economic fence. Otherwise, people could believe that possessing everything you can is a viable means for meeting the requirements of this particular commandment. After all, what does a person who has many possessions covet?

And as someone who had many possessions, the Rich Young Man probably doesn't covet what those around him have, because his neighbours own nothing he wants or needs. The poor and the oppressed in his society, those who beg on street corners, plagued with prejudice and disease, possess precisely everything this Young Man doesn't want: poverty. So instead of urging the Young Man not to covet—because Jesus knows this young lad doesn't covet—Jesus instead, through his tweak, calls him to address the imbalance and to change the predicament of his neighbour; which was the intent behind the original law anyway.

But after hearing five 'do nots' in a row, the Young Man is still hearing Jesus' adjustment as a 'do not', and thus fails to acknowledge that he has, in his abundance, what others need. He believes he has acted in love, because he doesn't covet, but he is blind to what he has withheld from his neighbours that would have changed their world dramatically. As such, he has not acted in love towards them.

As I said, I don't think the Young Man picks up on this change from 'not doing' (which he already excels in) to 'doing'. Which is why, after he asks Jesus what *else* he can do, Jesus then repeats the meaning of his last commandment more explicitly, telling him to 'sell what he has, and give the proceeds to the poor'. Jesus isn't assigning the Young Man an extra task to do here. Jesus is clarifying what 'do not covet' involves within this man's context. This Young Man lives in wealth while some of his countrymen live in poverty; if he really wants to participate meaningfully in God's plan for humanity, then he cannot ignore that inequality any longer.

As the story goes, it's at this point that the Young Man finally gets it— the penny drops—and he walks away, saddened because he has many possessions.

It turns out that the Young Man does covet after all. If Jesus had kept the list unedited, this would never have been brought to the surface. But the way in which Jesus sensitively directs the conversation exposes the Young Man's desire to grasp by revealing his inability to let go. He takes pride in his ability to 'do not'. But when Jesus calls him to let go, it proves too much for him. He would rather have what others haven't, than see others have what he has. The desire to take and the desire to withhold are two faces of the same coveting coin.

Like the Rich Young Religious Man, I also find it easier to excel in the 'do nots' of life. I have kept many rules which prescribe that I do nothing. I'm an expert in religious laws of procrastination. To prove it, I've kept at least five of Jesus' six 'do nots' (if I read them all as 'do nots'). That's a score of eighty-three percent, which would have gotten me a distinction on my college coursework. I should be proud. But to read the Ten Commandments as the negation of various actions is to misunderstand the life that they want us to exhibit.

The Decalogue is not to be seen as a list of prohibitions. Instead of seeing the Ten Commandments as telling us not to covet—which is easy if we're living the dream and are content in life—we need to hear them as a call to be generous. We're not supposed to read these and examine our consciences to see what we have *abstained from* inflicting on others, but instead to reflect on what we have *done for* the benefit of others and not only for ourselves. We may *not* have killed, or stolen, or coveted, but have we *done* justice, mercy and love? In other words, these laws are not calling us to look at ourselves, but to view the distance between ourselves and those around us.

Jesus' call to us hasn't changed. It's not that Jesus is calling us to sell all we own as he does in the case of the Young Man, but in our contexts we are all called to be spreaders of the sacred garden. To have eternal life means to practise an alternative way (a Kingdom way) of living in the midst of a culture in which people seek to seize and cling on to what they desire and crave through whatever means possible.

What has all this got to do with personal dreams, selfish ambition, and the sea of self we discussed earlier? Absolutely everything! This is a perfect example of how Jesus's manifestation of God's dream clashed with humanity's self-absorbed dreams. And it's worth noting that this isn't a clash of dreams between God and those who hated Jesus and wanted to see him removed (although there are plenty of examples of such conflicts in the gospels). This is a clash with someone who appeared to be *for* Jesus;

someone who also believed Jesus to be the Messiah, someone who would happily have hailed him as lord.

someone who also believed Jesus to be the Messiah, someone who would happily have hailed him as lord.

# 5.4 | EQUALITY? REALLY?

Remember that Jesus is on his way to Jerusalem when he is asked this question. Like the disciples, this Young Man envisages Jesus' road trip culminating in the Romans being booted out of Jerusalem and Jesus being enthroned. So while he's got the chance, this man comes to Jesus, in advance of his coronation, in order to guarantee himself a place in Jesus' world order afterwards.

This helps us to see that there is something of a selfish motive to this man's request. He's got plenty of assets, and he wants to know that they'll be protected in whatever political reconstruction is ahead; 'Is there still place for *me* and *mine* in the world order to come?'

This man says he wants to be part of the Kingdom of God and he believes Jesus to be the protagonist of that Kingdom. But at the same time, he wants to maintain the status quo. He's happy to have Jesus as King, but, at the very least, he also wants to keep what he has gained from the societal hierarchy that he senses is about to be reconfigured under Jesus' change in regime. I suppose we could say that he's happy to embrace God's dream, as long as it protects his own dream's investments and all he has accumulated. Sound familiar?

If we're not careful, then like this Young Man, we too may wrongly perceive Jesus as being the extender, defender, and maintainer of *our* way of life, when he is really calling us to a whole other way of being human.

The Young Man wants to keep the inequality that he has benefited from. We may also want this. But Jesus' world order will turn everything on its head. God's dream is a dream for real equality in the world. One without *I*'s. The Kingdom of God is not an investment bank for us to deposit our assets into or which will allow acquisitive exploitation to continue. The Kingdom is not some guarded citadel, like the one in Edgar Allan Poe's *Masque of Red Death*; where all that we have achieved and hoarded to ourselves is immune to the radical changes happening in the world, whilst we dance, sing and celebrate in our quarantined opulent arrogance. God will not sponsor inequality.

I know we all talk about equality, but true equality—if that's what we want—would mean the death of *me*.

Yes, that should send a shudder down the spine of our culture which is so infatuated with self-fulfilment and self-gratification. For those who dream of being great in the world's eyes, it's a big knock on the head. Even Jesus' disciples got worried about this. As they watch the Young Man walking away, they become anxious about their *place* and *status* in the Kingdom—especially as they had given up and invested so much. But Jesus assures them that those who have given up anything for the Kingdom will get back so much more. This isn't Jesus stating that the Kingdom runs on stocks and shares with guaranteed gains, by the way. What Jesus is stating here is that in a world order where all things belong to everyone—a world order without a huge gulf between rich and poor, a world with equality—no one is going to be without.

Jesus also promises his disciples that in the regeneration—when God's global dream comes into full fruition—there won't be 'first' and 'last', or 'least' and 'greatest'. These terms will drop out of our vocabulary because the extremes they label will no longer exist. We'll all be equal in status, with no divisions, no walls, no pyramids, no elite, no rich, no poor, and even, dare I add, no celebrities.

This hits us today in the West, because there are a torrent of individualistic dreams which drive us to be on top and which make us desire worldly success. Most of our dreams—dreams fuelled by the media excess and consumerist drivel that is fed to us from corporate brands—are *private* ones, which see us exclusively rising from the dust to become stars. Dreams of *I* uniquely standing out from the *we*. Dreams of success, admiration, accumulation and distinction. There's a stream of people in our world, both irreligious and religious, who desire the status level and perks of a Kardashian lifestyle.

I should add here, I have nothing personally against the Kardashian family. I'm only taking them as an example of the lifestyle people crave, and which is paraded on countless television shows as the yardstick of success. Heck, even I find myself sometimes craving their world; which proves that I fail at the coveting commandment too (my score's now dropped to sixty-six percent).

But in a truly equal society, there can't be Kardashians. There isn't any star status, or those who have excess.

That's not to say that there'll be no actors, writers, artists or poets in the regeneration. But the distance between rich and poor, no-one and someone, celebrated and despised must be erased.

I hope this is coming across right. Please do not go out there and start taking what others have or kidnapping celebs. Seriously, don't! But God's dream for a fairer world entails no seats of status, no VIPs.

At first, all this sounds great. But it's death to our individualism. It's death to the 'limelight'. It's death to dreams in which 'the world revolves around me'. It's death to privilege. It's death to a system that supports an uneven distribution of choice and opportunity. It's death to million-dollar bonuses and the introduction of a maximum wage. It may even be death to monetary systems altogether. It's death to positions of privilege, an end to social ranking, and the downfall of exclusive access to the best that the world has to offer in healthcare, education and housing.

We say we want equality—and I'm sure we do—but many of us also hold on to dreams of one day becoming unequal to others. We have two value systems at war within us: we cheer for the death of stupid banker's bonuses and celebrity pay-packets, but some of us also dream of the day when we will inherit or win or earn a ridiculous sum of money. We applaud the idea of an even distribution of choice and opportunity, but something in us still recoils from the idea of an economy where my effort, my ability, my hard work doesn't lead to extra bonus perks and exclusive doors.

We say 'Let your Kingdom come', but we, like the Rich Young 'Religious' Man, still want our piece of prime real-estate within it. We want

God to protect our dreams and our assets whilst God's dream comes to pass.

Which is an oxymoron if ever there was one.

No seats of status—could you live with that? A world where no one is celebrated, but where everyone is celebrated? A place where everyone is unique but where we all live as equals, because none of us are superior and all of us are exceptional?

I know that I'm at risk of sounding like Syndrome from Pixar's *The Incredibles*; in that, if everyone is super or exceptional, then no one is. But the fact remains that our world is astonishingly biased in whom it celebrates and whom it disdains. There are people who get large sums of money (which we are becoming increasingly desensitised to) which are insanely disproportionate to the contribution they make to wider society. Wouldn't it be great to celebrate teachers, nurses, street cleaners, stay-at-home parents, students, janitors, and single mothers as much as we celebrate Justin Bieber?[171]

But we don't. We give socialites primetime television shows and pay footballers million-dollar contracts, whilst our media and press simultaneously take pains to shame those on benefits and blame the poor and the foreigner for deepening the nation's deficit. And as this goes on, thousands of people load up their credit cards, getting ever further into debt, in a futile effort to grasp the lifestyle which is freely given to those who have already. But this is the nature of the inequality of human empires.[172]

The thing is, we all recognise how lopsided the world is. We all think it's stupid. We all know that it's disproportionately ridiculous to pay footballers what we do, whilst our nurses have to beg for more. However, if someone put a clamp on this, we would go crazy. There would be outcries of, 'Who are you to put a limit on what I can have?'

Again, we say we want the Kingdom of God, but do we really want it if it means that our dreams need to have boundaries?

I'm for equality. I know you are too. But would we want it?

Equality doesn't mean that we must all lose our distinctions and differences, our idiosyncrasies, our personalities or our talents. It doesn't mean that some of us won't be better at certain things than others, whilst others will be better at other things than we are. But it does mean that none of us are better people, people of more worth and value than anyone else and who therefore deserve more credit and applause and reward.

We all long for unity. But unity cannot grow where our idea of an ideal society is one which allows for, celebrates, and purposely develops and maintains hierarchical peaks and troughs. For unity to exist, hierarchy must flatline.

I know this is a tough call, but what if living the dream required us to let go of some of our dreams, or the motives behind them? Are we willing to surrender our kingdoms for God's? Or, like the Rich Young Ruler, do we walk away, dejected, because we would rather have our vision for the world, a vision where we come first?

This may come as a shock, but Jesus didn't die so that our dreams could come true. He gave his life for the dream of God. This doesn't mean we are unloved, the opposite is true; we are loved more than we can imagine.

# 5.5 | STAINED BY LOVE

My youngest son has a stuffed toy called Sweaky.

Sweaky is a mouse. Although, if you ever saw it, you'd be right to point out that it looks more like a rat. But please don't do that around my son; he'd be quick to put you right on the matter and highly offended at your inability to classify stuffed animals.

The thing is though, despite resembling a rat, this mouse doesn't look like it used to.

When we first brought Sweaky home, it was bright white and its stuffing was proportioned evenly throughout its body. Now, however, its head is permanently cocked to one side due to consistent cuddles and squeezes. And although Sweaky has had to go through the pain of two or three major re-stuffing surgeries, his innards are once again finding themselves squeezed into all the wrong places; he's slimmer round his waist (almost empty of stuffing), swollen in his head, and is plump in his front legs and derrière.

As for Sweaky's white coat, it's now worn and dappled in different tones of grey. There's no longer a single trace of white fur to be seen. The daily contact with my son's skin, sweat, tears and saliva has stained this mouse forever. Sweaky's appearance will never be the same again.

But this is the kind of staining that I don't want to wash away with detergent and mask beneath a fragrance of lavender. For us, these stains are sacred.

He's covered with the odour of affection, dyed with love, baptised in relationship. As a result, when I pick Sweaky up, he smells like my son; my boy is present in his material.

This stuffed toy entered our home as a clone, a manufactured replication that resembled all the others formed by mass production. Now, though, this toy is one in a million and irreplaceable. I would even say that it's priceless!

And yet, Sweaky's pricelessness isn't located in, or dependent upon anything that he contributes or possesses. If you saw this mouse lying around, you wouldn't spot anything valuable with your eyes. You would be tempted to pick him up and throw him in the trash. His value, worth and "esteem" find their sole source in the heart of my seven-year-old son.

All Sweaky does—the only thing a stuffed animal can do—is display my son's love. And I assure you, Sweaky looks loved. Sweaky stinks of love.

Like my little boy's stuffed mouse, our worth isn't found in ourselves either. We can follow all the mass-produced advice we like in becoming unique, but we'll only end up being far from unique and a part of the factory line. We may try to do things to get people to like us and love us, but maybe this thinking is backwards?

The idea of *self* has become something of an idol in our modern culture. It's where we seek for hope and redemption. Maybe we've become too obsessed with discovering ourselves and revealing our "real self" to the world, feeling that we don't exist if we cannot answer the question 'Who am I?' in some deep and meaningful way that finds its source in ourselves first and in others second (or last, or even never)?

We expend time and energy trying to unearth our inner beauty, and maybe trying to paint ourselves beautiful. But we can only truly discover who we are in communion with others. Our worth can never be found within ourselves, because the source of our belovedness will always be located in the one who loves us. We can only find *self* in another.

This is true of human relationships, and it's true also of our relationship with God.

What if our primary pursuit in life isn't to discover who we are in some individualist, isolated exploration of our self? What if our pursuit should instead be focussed on revealing the one who already loves us?

As a Christian, I believe that our worth and our identity find their source in the heart of an extraordinary creator God who already loves us, who has given himself for us, and who longs for us to carry the fragrance and flavour of divine love. This is a love given by grace, a love that is entirely independent of whatever we bring. A love so pure that it isn't strengthened by our contribution—it just is. This is the love we've all been looking for.

And yet, even we Christians can wrestle against this love. It's like our desire for self-sought self-awareness pollutes our ability to embrace something we feel we haven't earned. We seek to make ourselves *someone* in order to be *something* to someone else. This objectification of ourselves causes us to reject real unconditional love.

If we're not careful, the meaning of our faith can be warped if our Christianity becomes an exercise in discovering ourselves through our own efforts. If all we ever learn at church, or in our private devotions are "life-hacks" and "tips for getting closer to God", then maybe we've missed the whole story of Scripture, a story that isn't about mankind's pursuit of God, but about God's pursuit of humanity whilst mankind was fixated on itself.

Unlike us, my son's stuffed toy isn't self-aware, of course. It doesn't ponder its meaning or psychoanalyse itself in order to figure out who or what it is. It's a stuffed toy, an inanimate object, an unconscious collection of fabric. But, in our house, Sweaky is still very much an identity; he'll always be *someone* and not just *something* to my son. Sweaky is animated by the imaginative love of my child.

Sweaky is, because my son loves.

We are, because God loves.

And when we begin to explore the divine source of our belovedness instead of trying to beautify ourselves, then our self begins to melt into and meld with the identity of the one who loves us. Like Sweaky, we become alive in this love and begin to carry the image, the presence of God. God seeps into us, and our earthy material becomes permeated with the incense of divine delight. We become sacred objects, not through self-improvement, but through surrender.

Like my son's stuffed toy, we are to look loved. We are to be dappled with the beauty of God, stained by divine affection. We are to carry the aroma of God's dream for all humanity.

Or, to paraphrase the New Testament writer John, we manifest love, because we are loved.[173]

These stains are sacred precisely because they speak of the one who loves us, and not of ourselves.

And so we're blessed, not because we meet the world's unattainable and ever-shifting standard of success, but because we are caught up in a love and a dream that is more than the productivity of *I* could ever attain. Although we must let go of our fetishisation of self, we are not to abandon our sense of self, but allow ourselves to be receptacles of a more sacred, holistic, flourishing vision for the world beyond *I*, a world full of eternal life.

---

Search me, O God, and know my heart;

test me and know my anxious thoughts.

Point out anything in me that offends you,

and lead me along the path of everlasting life.

-Psalm 139:23-24 (NLT)

---

# PART o6 | THE BASTARDISATION OF GOD

I AM WHO I AM
– God (Exodus)[174]

Accursed creator! Why did you form a monster
so hideous that even *you* turned away from me
in disgust?
– Frankenstein's Creation[175]

Everyone takes the limits of his own field of
vision for the limits of the world.
– Arthur Schopenhauer[176]

Concepts create idols; only wonder comprehends
anything.
People kill over idols.
Wonder makes us fall to our knees.
– St Gregory of Nyssa[177]

But the crowd shouted louder and louder for
Jesus' death, and their voices prevailed. [. . .]
Jesus said, "Father, forgive these people, because
they don't know what they are doing."
– Luke's Gospel[178]

# 6.1 | ROCKY REVELATIONS

I want you to imagine that you're holding a rock, a stone or a pebble.

Better still, if there's one nearby, pick it up. Examine it closely. Feel its texture. Get a sense of its weight. Observe its colour, shape and size. Notice the surface deviations and the way the light plays on them, accenting and changing its appearance as you turn it over in your hand.

You could ask a lot of questions about that rock. And while it's true that you can't get blood from a stone, there's nothing stopping us, because of our intellectual superiority, from extracting every ounce of what we can get from it. We could cut it open. Slice it. Crush it. Grind it. We could heat it till it melts, or freeze it till it cracks apart. We could interrogate it under a microscope, viewing it on smaller and smaller levels of complexity, observing and exposing all that it is made of atomically. Sure, it won't resemble a rock when we're finished with it, but we will know all there is to know, leaving no stone unturned, as they say.

But that's a rock, and you possess a far greater mind than it does. So let's go up a number of tiers and try something on your own scale.

Take another human being—another sentient, animate part of our material world—and see what you could find out about the person.

Let's start with a total stranger; someone unknown to you. Go and find one.

Only joking. But pretend with me that you have.

We could also treat our imaginary human like an object, throw him/her into a laboratory, and perform a careful and thorough dissection. Remember, this is only a thought experiment. Please don't try this at home!

Theoretically speaking, though, we could discover everything about the person's biological and chemical nature through our imaginary autopsy, to the depths of the human genome and beyond. Unlike our rock, there is a lot of literal blood to be had from another human being. But if we didn't want that kind of information, then we could insert this individual into an MRI scanner and discover how our subject functions while it remains as a conscious, non-dissected whole. Alternatively, we could stick the person on a running machine and monitor their heartbeat, or get a urine sample, or put them on some scales.

Of course, we don't have to stop there, either. We could observe our human subject in ordinary life; no monitoring equipment would be required for this beyond our own nosey scrutiny. We could watch how they interact, where they work, and what they like to eat. We could also search through emails and social media accounts, or do the work of a historian and uncover every skeleton hiding in their family's closet.

Because our subject is like us—and unlike the rock that we should have put down by now—we can discover a lot about our stranger by merely interpreting their humanity through our own experience of being human. We don't only have the tools of the biological, chemical and physical sciences at our disposal, we can also interrogate with sociology and psychology.

These processes alone could keep us researching our stranger for years, and the information printout would have more pages than the Encyclopaedia Britannica. However, even after we've scrutinised our subject socially and performed a dissection in a lab, could we really say that we *know* him/her? With all of our invasive and non-invasive examinations, would they have stopped being a stranger?

The answer to that is *no*, by the way.

Despite all the tests you could inflict upon your stranger, they will still remain just that—a stranger. They will still contain secrets. Occasionally, even a person we've known for a whole lifetime can turn out to be someone we never knew. As Charles Dickens eloquently said it:

> A wonderful fact to reflect upon, that every human creature is constituted to be that profound secret and mystery to every other.[179]

The startling reality is that the only real way of seeing somebody, is if they choose to let you in; if *they* choose to open the door and *reveal* themselves to you. In other words, what's required is revelation.

## REVELATION

*Revelation* is often dismissed as a religious form of knowledge, a spiritual way in which information is attained. But on a peer to peer, physical level, we find ourselves reliant upon others to reveal (communicate) themselves to us in order to know anything about anybody.

Hopefully, we can all admit, communication is an arduous thing. And great communication—the precise transmission of yourself and your thoughts to another via words or expression—requires four phases going entirely to plan:

First, you have to know what you intend to say.

Second, you then have the uphill task of articulating precisely what you intended.

Thirdly, your audience needs to be hearing you.

And finally, your audience has to correctly understand and interpret what *they've* heard you express.

Even when you're talking to somebody right next to you, this process is challenging. It is more difficult than we give it credit for, despite how often we ourselves have experienced this process going terribly wrong.

The first transition, the move between stage one and two, is a nightmare. At least, it is for me. I know we believe that we think in words, but we also think emotionally. Or, to put that more clearly, I *feel*. I sense. And often those impressions, or ideas, or images are difficult to put into words. Trust me; I've faced it with every page of this book so far. It's hard to take the abstract and then find the right words, or analogy, or tone, to articulate that feeling into something tangible that can be sensed by another.

In many ways, words can be inept at taking what's on the inside and putting it out there. When I'm hurt, or full of ache, all I can do is scream or cry, and this may—because you have also screamed and cried—develop some level of empathy between the two of us. But it hardly translates my feelings into yours. I can never know the ache that makes you cry or the anguish that is tormenting you on the inside, and vice versa.

Even those who excel at communicating struggle to bare the very depths of their being. It's a minefield. One wrong turn of phrase, one wrong adjective or adverb, an unintended tone of voice, a pause in the wrong place, and our whole intent goes up in smoke.

Writing it down doesn't make it any less prone to error. Sure, the written word is not as spontaneous as a conversation, because you have the privilege of editing and rearranging your execution. That said, I've been playing with these paragraphs for hours now, and I'm still unconvinced that they are saying what I want them to say.

But let's pretend you're the best communicator in town, and you're able to execute the transition from stage one to stage two perfectly; you know what you want to say and you know how to say it. Not only would I want your help for the next book (if there is one), but now your perfectly verbalised, exposed self finds itself completely at the mercy of another's interpretation.

Stage three—what was heard—comes prepacked with problems. Did I hear you right? Did you ask for four candles or fork handles? Mix into this the distractions, abstractions, and tangents of thought breaking out in your listener's head, and it becomes increasingly easier to miss the finer detail of your verbalised self. Take it further still by mixing in some colloquialisms, body language, idioms, satire, sarcasm or irony, and I could be totally lost in what you're intending to say.

But let's say that I heard you right and I pass stage three. Hearing is one thing, but understanding what you meant is something completely different, and meanings are slippery things to grasp.

You may have expressed yourself clearly, enabling me to tangibly encounter what you've conveyed. But it's now my senses that are tasting and touching what you've made concrete, in order for me to move it back into the abstract recesses of my own self. On a certain level, I must make your expression my own, if I'm to feel and comprehend your meaning as easily as you do. So my own frames of reference—my knowledge, reasoning skills, emotions, memory and culture—will creep across everything you've said, converting it into something I can absorb.

It's far from foolproof. This process of understanding what *I've* heard you say has been proved more than capable of taking what has been revealed and making it fit whatever size we fancy. We could use the same words and believe we're saying the same things, when the reality is that we could be on totally different wavelengths.

Of course, context helps. If we share the same time and space and world view, then the communication of the self is less prone to error, though certainly not altogether immune from it. But separate you and me by a few millennia, and place one of us in a foreign, ancient culture, and the difficulty rating has increased exponentially. For example, in a thousand years, will anyone know what a 'zig-a-zig-ah' is? I'm not convinced that we knew two decades ago.[180] Even in the year of writing the draft of this book, many of us have been perplexed over 'covfefe'.

On top of all of the above, even if we executed every stage of this transference of consciousness perfectly, all these stages have helped us to do is encounter the 'other' for a single moment. But there were a billion moments preceding this and there will be a billion more to follow.

In short, I can know everything there is to know about a rock, but getting to grips with another human, even with the means of revelation at our disposal, is a tough task, maybe even an impossible one.

So let's go up another tier again and consider God.

## AS ABOVE, SO BELOW?

Is it possible to know everything about God, as I can do with a rock? Or, if God is more complicated than a fellow human being, which must be at least one of the qualifications for being God, is it possible to know anything at all about God? And what if this God is more than my limited five senses can handle; what if God is more than my sensory range can detect?

If there is a God, a being unformed by our universe and outside of it all, then, unlike the rock and my fellow human, I cannot perform an autopsy on this being to see what it is made of. I can objectify a stone and I can objectify (wrongly) another human being in my pursuit of knowledge, but I can never objectify God. Just as when I am relating to my peers, I am entirely reliant upon revelation; I must wait for that being to reveal itself to me. But unlike relating to my peers, who I can talk *across* to and empathise with, this being is *above* us and must communicate *down* to us. I'm not talking about physical directions here, but like the rock in our own hands, we are comparatively nothing to this something's superior intellect and perspective. We are the rock at the mercy of divine fingers. And so this being, if it wants us to grasp something of its nature, must accommodate to our limited perspective.

However, despite our shortcomings, we humans have proved ourselves rather adept at wrestling with things we don't understand by thinking of them in terms of what we can understand. Just because we haven't seen, or touched, or tasted something, hasn't stopped us from employing our imaginations, taking educated guesses and then testing our hypotheses. We compare and contrast all the time. We liken things to other things. We apply rules of symmetry by projecting smaller facts upon larger mysteries of knowledge, and by casting larger realities down upon the hidden details.

Philosophy has done this for millennia, and scientific textbooks do this all time, if only to help us grasp what we currently haven't got a frame of reference for. For example, when scientists describe how electrons move around in an atom—something we will never see with our naked eye—they talk about the model of our solar system and how the planets orbit the sun, and describe an electron's movement around an atom's nucleus as being something similar. And although this isn't an accurate picture of what's happening either, it does furnish us with a mental foothold and a good starting place from which we can explore reality more deeply. Pick up any good science writer, and you'll find their works full of analogies and "lies to children" (as some call them) that enable us to grapple with the complex layers of reality in bite-sized chunks.

Writers of science fiction also play the same game; if they really wrote about an alien culture on an alien world, we wouldn't be able to picture it. Most science fiction isn't alien to us. Nearly all of the extraterrestrials we meet in fiction share an uncanny resemblance to creatures we have seen, and they behave in ways that aren't too dissimilar to how we or other earthy things behave. When you think about it, fictional alien civilisations aren't that alien at all; they just have blue milk (to use a Star Wars reference).

Whether it's through the writers of fact or fiction, we have glimpsed the stars by being pointed to life on Earth. In order to help us grasp the unseen or incomprehensible, these authors have had to describe the unseen and incomprehensible in relation to something we have experienced, and then, once some common ground has been established, they've moved us forward from there.

Theology—speaking of God—is no different.

All theological language is metaphor; it is the grasping of our consciousness to understand a reality and sentience that is beyond us, *other* than us, and *more* than us. As Franciscan priest, Fr. Richard Rohr describes it:

> Our speaking of God is a search for similes, analogies, and metaphors. All theological language is an approximation, offered tentatively in holy awe. That's the best human language can achieve. We can say, *"It's like—it's similar to…,"* but we can never say, *"It is…"* because we are in the realm of beyond, of transcendence, of mystery. And we must—absolutely must— maintain a fundamental humility before the Great Mystery. If we do not, religion always worships itself and its formulations and never God.[181]

Whenever we talk about God—something totally beyond us—we still begin at home. We lean on human traits and characteristics, a technique known as *anthropomorphism*, to describe what God is like. In simpler terms, we ascribe to God human tendencies, anatomy, gender and reason. We give God our features and motives. We say that God sees, God hears, God was saddened… or that 'we are the rock at the mercy of divine fingers'. We do all this because it's easier to imagine what something is like if we can liken it to ourselves and to our pre-existing experiences. And if no one does this for us—no theologian, philosopher, scientist, or God—we'll only do it for ourselves anyway. It's a natural human tendency that we all possess.

This should get us thinking. Because even though we're reliant upon revelation to know anything about God, we will still interpret what has been revealed through what we currently understand. And if the Divine doesn't reveal itself, it won't prevent those who believe there is something or someone "up there" from fantasising about what that someone is like, or stop them from thinking that they live "up there" in the first place.

When God does reveal himself/herself/itself, the divine isn't doing so into a vacuum. When we convert to a religion or find ourselves adopting one for the first time, we certainly don't come as a blank page, with no images of what God is like and how God behaves yet sketched in our minds. Our culture is permeated with ideas about the creator(s), leaving us with no short supply of divine images to choose from or reject. This is so even within Christianity! As much as we like to ask whether we Christians worship the same God as the Muslims do, I sometimes find myself asking whether we worship the same God as each other.

Even when we encounter something of God that differs from our convictions and theories, it can take a while for that encounter to be treated without suspicion. Until we are willing to embrace that new, foreign experience, it remains in our mind's quarantine zone. And when that idea is released to run and play with the other ideas in our mental playground, it does so on the proviso that it should cause little disturbance to all that we profess to "understand".

Seriously, none of us—the religious and irreligious—like having our ideas of God messed with. Although—and I'm jumping ahead of myself here—I think God wants to mess with our ideas of who God is. If we are supposed to image God, as I've been saying in this book, then God needs to. But until God does, we remain spoilt for choice; finding ourselves either rejecting many of the options given to us, or rejecting all them.

It's not that this problem is a new one, either, because we currently stand at the summit of the human epoch with a million hand-me-down projections of the Divine to choose from. The ancient world also articulated various concepts of God into their surrounding cultures. Archaeologists and historians have uncovered a smorgasbord of mythologies, architecture and rituals, which are laden with theological musings, as proof of the ancient world's attempt to tether everything from 'Why are we here?' to 'Why are they in power?' to some divine reference point.

In a nutshell, we may be dependent upon divine revelation, but this certainly hasn't stopped us from trying to figure God out, or prevented us from plastering our interpretations onto the Creator whenever it has chosen to reveal itself. So when God communicates the divine identity in a way that we can hear, the question is: do we really listen and comprehend? Regardless of how infallible God is (putting aside how we came to figure out that God had this attribute anyway) human reasoning simply isn't.

I suppose what I'm trying to say is this: even when God perfectly executes stages one and two in revealing something to us, what God reveals still remains at the mercy of our whimsical handling of stages three and four.

# 6.2 | THE IDOLATRY OF GOD

Why I am saying all this, and why did I give this chapter such a horrendous title?

Well, at the back end of 2016 I read an excellent book by Oxford University's current Simonyi Chair for the Public Understanding of Science: Professor Marcus Du Sautoy. The book's called *What We Cannot Know*, and within it, Du Sautoy skilfully explores whether there are any corners of reality that will forever remain beyond our comprehension. Inevitably, then, packaged into the category of things on the other side of our universe and beyond, God comes under regular discussion (notably, our inability to fully comprehend our neighbour never does).

Near the end of the book, Du Sautoy shares his reasons for choosing to be an atheist. And, to be honest, I could relate to them. The idea of a being that could be scaled down to be comprehended by us, but still be called God, seems odd and, to use Du Sautoy's own terminology 'impoverished'. Although I don't go all the way with Du Sautoy in thinking that God must remain an unknown, a complete mystery, to be thought of as God (as I've said, I believe the Divine can reveal itself to us proverbial rocks), I can empathise with what he means when he feels that the picture of God has been bastardized to become a tainted, warped, distorted, and hijacked human projection.

I think this is the scriptural story we are exploring, too; it is the problem to begin with. At one point in his book, I think Du Sautoy hits the biblical problem on the head without realising it, when he says:

> The trouble with most religions is that the God that is served up has so many properties that are nothing to do with the definition. It's as if we are working backwards, focussing on the strange properties conjured up over generations *without really understanding what the original definition was.*[182]

Of course, I could have misunderstood what Du Sautoy was trying to say with my own reasoning (to keep with this section's theme). But this problem, I believe, is at the heart of Scripture. Those called to be the image of God laid that image down, and then overlooked it or twisted it to their own ends. We have forgotten what the original was like, either purposely or through other means. Meaning that when God speaks, we are drawn into a wrestling match between the voice we are hearing on one side, and the projections of God that we have made sacred, on the other.

The Bible is the story of God redeeming and reconciling his image. Not in the sense of saving individuals from their private, "personal sins"—as has commonly been thought—but rather in the sense of helping us to see what image we're supposed to reflect, in order that we might turn away from *the Sin* of believing in, testifying to and exhibiting lies about God. It's this problem that is the source of all our systemic illnesses of greed, oppression and violence towards each other. It's this problem that has prevented humanity from exhibiting God's dream.

Idolatry is a trend which has never gone out of fashion. Behind every bad thing that has happened in history, there has always been an idea, an image, or an idol. Sadly, God's image has often been twisted to suit our own agenda. Many have endorsed the imbalances in our world by invoking the nature of God. Many reject God because of what they have been shown about God. God has been touted as the champion of our crusades, our patriarchy, our racism, and our greed.

Within Scripture, we witness this scapegoating of God firsthand, as well as God's rejection of these false portrayals. And when we think about it, it all started with a lie in the first place.

## THE CREATION OF A MONSTER

Way back in the story of the Garden of Eden, we find the Bible disclosing the roots of our problem. It's not that we ate some parabolic, proverbial fruit, when we shouldn't have. It's not that we broke some rule. It's not a moral problem that then creates more moral problems. The story speaks of

God's image-bearing humanity buying into a lie, a lie which they swallowed and then passed on. Or, to use the metaphor of a fruit, a deception that they bit into, digested and regurgitated.

In the story of Genesis 3, a serpent tells Adam and Eve that God can't be trusted. They can't eat the fruit from the Tree of the Knowledge of Good and Evil because in doing so, they will become gods themselves. They're told the 'threat of death' that God waved over them for eating the fruit (which wasn't a threat of punishment at all), is nothing more than a scare tactic employed by God to cover his paranoia of being usurped. When we read this story, we notice the obvious irony in what the serpent is saying: humanity was already made in God's likeness and given the vocation to exhibit God's benevolent rule in the world. But the serpent's twist on the truth poisons their thinking and discolours their perception of reality by getting them to suspect that God is being protective of his status; God is being untruthful; God is repressive and self-serving. God, according to the lie, is a dictator who wields power through the threat of death, and not someone who lays all power down.

We could put it this way: the serpent makes a counterfeit image of God and, in turn, a counterfeit definition of what it means to be God-like. Thus, idolatry kicks in. Not in the sense that Adam and Eve made a physical statue of God, but in the sense that they masked the reality of God with their own polluted notions. Idolatry isn't just a matter of worshipping statues or false deities. Idolatry is also about holding on to wrong ideas of God.

It's this lie—this alternative projection of God—that then cleaves the no-holds-barred intimacy between God and humanity. Within the story, when God comes in the evening to be with Adam and Eve, we find them cowering away from God—hiding behind creation, the trees of the Garden, in order to avoid their expectations and ideas of the creator. *'I heard you in the garden, and I was afraid because I was naked, so I hid'.*[183] This is the man's explanation of why he ran and hid from God. Fear and shame had warped Adam and Eve's idea of God's receptivity to them.

The mood here is on par with the emotions of Frankenstein's creation, as it speaks of its own rejection at the hands of its maker in Mary Shelley's famous novel. Adam and Eve both *feel* that God is disgusted with them. They don't know this of course; they merely suspect it—they are leaning on their own understanding. They can't trust God's intentions anymore. Not because God was untrustworthy, but because they *believe* God is. They believe God had come to punish them, and punish them for being human. In this sense, their situation is the inverse of the dilemma faced by Dr Frankenstein's creation; they portray God as the monster and then turned away from God in disgust.

They were called to communion with the Divine, called to rule with God. But to do so entails trust (belief), and this trust has been severed. Moreover, when pressed by God to explain what has happened, Adam blames Eve (and God), and Eve blames the serpent (part of creation). The chaos, which poisoned mankind's view of God, now seeps further into their view of each other and their environment.

And the lie didn't stop there. When we move into the story of Adam and Eve's offspring, the lies about God also appear to have been passed on.

When their son, Cain, finds his harvest offering being refused, he interprets this as being personally rejected by God. And yet it is God who ends up personally comforting and conversing with Cain after this supposed "rejection", rather than with his brother Abel (whose offering was accepted).

In other words, Cain believes that God is distant and apathetic. However, God acts to counter Cain's theological distortion with a revelation of the true divine nature, and draws near to the dejected Cain. It's this revealing of the divine self that exposes the false theology and gives room for Cain to turn away from it. But Cain refuses to take notice of this revelation and instead leans on his own ideas of God—an absent God who appears to have favourites—as the fuel for his jealousy and eventual murder of his brother, Abel. Even after this horrendous affair, God puts forth mercy again by drawing close to Cain. But still, the lies spin on and spill over into the generations that follow.

Lamech, a descendant of Cain (and an instigator of the systemic blight known as patriarchy), also casts his own vision of God. After Lamech kills a youth, he infects the revelation of God's mercy to Cain with his own ideology. Lamech believes that God will kill anyone who now seeks revenge for the violent crime he's committed. Lamech forms God into his own personal bodyguard and hitman. Lamech's God is defined by violent revenge and is extremely if favour of Lamech's desires and world view: God's enemies are coincidentally Lamech's enemies, and this God is also a silent endorser of Lamech's objectifying view of women. Lamech might have not crafted a literal idol of stone or wood, but his idolatry was manifested in ways that tangibly affected this world.

As the Apostle Paul would later write; 'They traded the truth about God for a lie.'[184] Or to use Du Sautoy's terminology, they laid aside the original, authentic definition of God, and instead, subscribed to a bastardized, made-man image.

Sin, as we see in these episodes with Adam and Eve, Cain, and Lamech, does not change how God looks at us, but how we look at God. Sin contorts how we perceive, interpret and respond to God's acts; it's a relational thing. Which is why Sin can't be beaten from us or moralised away; both techniques merely reinforce our twisted ideas of what God is like and how God works. Only mercy—an exposure to God's likeness, to God's compassionate grace, tender kindness and unconditional love—is powerful enough to slay the beast we've envisioned and cast out the demons we've entertained. Only the mercy put forth by God is able to renew our thinking and release us from the bondage we've put ourselves under. Only truth can break the lie and set us free.

Already we see how God provides the solution to our bastardisation: God doesn't move away from humanity, but reveals the divine nature all the more to counter their notions. We've just witnessed this in Cain's episode, but this same pattern is at work within the story of Genesis 3.

*Adam and Eve believe* God can't be trusted, but it's God who clothes them in their nakedness, God who shows concern for their well-being and who loves them. *They think* God will be angry at them, or that God is going to kill them, and so they hide, but it's God who calls them out from behind the bush-shaped obstruction to their vision and who calls them back into relationship, speaking to them gently. God is never angry with humanity in the story of Adam and Eve.[185] God never conforms to their delusions, but presents them with an image that is counter to their belief. They expect to die suddenly (and probably at God's proverbial hands) after eating the fruit of the Tree. But, acting in a way that must have been strange to their expectations, God does what he repeatedly does; he commissions them and sends them out into the world.

Remember what we looked at in Part Three, where God commissions humanity to spread the garden? Well, in Genesis 3:23, although it speaks of banishment from the Garden of Eden, it also speaks of God calling humanity back into its original vocation; '[God] sent [humanity] out to *cultivate the ground* from which he had been made.'[186] God doesn't give up on humanity, or the dream for the world. As much as we might believe, like Frankenstein's Monster, that God has turned away from us in disgust and condemned us to the mess we've made or been born into, this simply isn't the thrust of the Bible's story. The story we read isn't the story of an apathetic creator, but the story of a God who sets out to defeat the lie which is enslaving humanity, and does so by making the divine character visible.

Already at the beginning of Scripture, we see the narratives speaking of three things: God revealing himself, wrong human interpretation/projection, and God countering these false images through revelation.

## THE STUFF OF NIGHTMARES

When we read the Bible, it feels as if God has many faces. There are some that are nice, and others which are downright ugly and twisted. But this is the wrestle between the lies we have told and the truth God wants us to see. Within the Scripture's unfolding story, there's this continual tension between human portrayal and divine revelation. Sometimes it shows this explicitly and at other times, subversively. And often, we have to take a broad scan of all its passages, especially its contradictions, and discern this trajectory for ourselves. But overall, the Bible—a journal of multiple accounts of humanity wrestling with the image of God—reveals to us a growing, developing understanding of who God really is; this revelation culminates in the face of Jesus.

Because of our own capacity to cast God into an image of our own design, this conversation is paramount to looking at this divine dream of Heaven on Earth. Paradise was lost when humanity believed a lie, and as I've said, idolatry hasn't gone out of fashion. We're still prone to understanding God as being akin to a genie, or the cosmic law enforcer, or a xenophobic megalomaniac. God is often described as being the one who helps us towards our success and accumulation of wealth; the hand behind our rolling dice, or the mascot to our nationalism and the cheerleader to our vision of world order. Our personal dreams can infect how we see God, making God the stuff of our "enemy's" or "competitor's" nightmares. And to endorse these images—in order to endorse our own destructive, brutal and evil endeavours—we've employed every violent, genocidal Bible verse we could get our hands on. Our preconceived ideas have more influence on our theology and interpretation of Scripture than we'd be willing to admit.

Or to put the problem another way, if God is OK with using violence to achieve what God wants, and we are supposed to image God, then why can't we use violence to achieve what we believe God wants? Or so some people will reason. If God is for elitist hierarchies—where some are favoured and others rejected—then what's the point in challenging inequality, especially if we find ourselves on the "blessed" and "divinely ordained" side of the equation? In a disturbing way, we don't have to look too far back in history to see these so-called "biblical" understandings of God being used to endorse warfare, exploitation, segregation and greed. But this, I feel, is where we've missed the tensions of Scripture, and the struggle between human projections and divine reality.

Of course, all this raises a rather obvious question. If, as I've said so far in this book, God wants us to turn away from our violence, greed and wall building, and if God wants us to exhibit love, justice and mercy and to become gardeners of the sacred, because that is what God is like and therefore the image we should bear, then what are we to do with all those Bible stories that present the image of a violent and destructive God? What do we do with the God who also appears to cultivate chaos and inequality instead of benevolent, liberating, creation-flourishing order? What about the God who is grotesque and not beautiful?

Are these stories true, or are they lies? Or to be more precise, can we trust these stories as being infallible accounts of an encounter with God? Or are these a mingling of actual encounters and human projection, a hash of infallible divine revelation and fallible human interpretation? Could the Bible, by telling these stories, be authoritatively exposing to us this human struggle to comprehend God, and also calling us into this divine fray?

To get us thinking, let's look at a famous story of idolatry and its fruit: the story of the Golden Calf. A story which, as it turns out, may not be about the Golden Calf at all.

Moses—an ex-prince of Egypt, a murderer, then a runaway, a stranger in a foreign land, and now the unexpected, (and unwilling) geriatric, stammering voice of God's liberation—has had a crazy number of weeks. The sort of weeks that most people in his age-band wouldn't wish for.

He's found himself having to convince his own people, who have been enslaved for four hundred years, to trust him that things are about to change as he's had a word from God and because he's got a big stick. He's found himself—an eighty-year-old nobody—brandishing that same stick at a Pharaoh, the most powerful man in the world, and challenging him to release the slave-labour force that he feels is vital for Egypt's growth. And then, because of this Pharaoh's unwillingness to yield, Moses has had to be the conduit for God in a plague-filled contest against the divine pantheon of Egypt. To top it all off, after just recently escaping the bondage of Egypt via the sprinkling of a lamb's blood and by passing through the baptismal waters of the Red Sea, Moses now finds himself face to face with the God of his ancestors, the God who had revealed himself to Moses many months earlier from a burning bush using the cryptic words, 'I AM, WHO I AM'.

Far from where he imagined life would throw him, Moses stands on top of Mount Sinai, with the newly freed Hebrew nation waiting in the valley below, as he receives God's commandments on how this nation of ex-slaves is to leave the ideologies of Egypt behind and begin a new, anti-imperial experiment in being human.

This hasn't been like nipping next door for a cup of tea, though. Moses has been away from his people for an awfully long time—in his defence, there are a lot of commandments to go through. But due to the length of this unusual sojourn, the Hebrews in the valley are getting anxious, believing that Moses has "disappeared" (or worse). Moses had gone up to meet with God, and then would come down to communicate God's will to them. But with Moses gone, who will show them what God wants? Who will lead them to the Promised Land? So Aaron, Moses' older brother, in response to the peoples' request, crafts an *image* of God to quell the rising crisis of faith.[187]

Remember that images (idols, ikons) in temples were perceived to relay the life and will of the gods they represented. Maybe then, Aaron was thinking that if God had a statue, then God could breathe on it, imbuing it with the divine Spirit, so that through the image they would be able to discern God's will? It's important to see that there's nothing odd about this; it was a common Ancient Middle Eastern practice. More so, if you've come from Egypt, where you've lived all your life, and where your ancestors have lived for a few centuries in servitude, and where the gods were displayed through statues. Aaron's plan isn't a bad one—he's just a man of his times.

I know that before this story happens the Ten Commandments are given, and that these same commandments forbid making any images (for reasons I've already expressed in a previous chapter), but maybe Aaron hasn't quite figured out what this means. After all, the law literally says not to make idols of *other* gods to worship, but is it strictly saying no to statues of *the* one true God? It's not like Aaron could ask Moses for some interpretative clarity on the matter at hand either; Moses has "disappeared", remember? Of course, he could ask God. But, in Aaron's head, how would you go about doing that without some mediator between yourself and God. Without Moses, or without some statue, God, according to Aaron's faculties, is on mute.

Aaron's plan, to some extent, is pure genius; he's attempting to give God a mouth to speak from. And in order to achieve this goal, Aaron calls the people together and asks them for donations of gold earrings, from which he forms the infamous Golden Calf.

This may seem insulting. Aaron represents God as a grass-eating calf. But again, this is nothing unusual for the time. And although it may seem demeaning to make God resemble an animal, there could be good intentions behind this, too.

Remember the concept of anthropomorphism we looked at, which means ascribing to God human traits and characteristics in order to understand God? Well, there's a problem with that; it can cause us to conceptually reduce God to being exactly like us. So to counter this, most ancients practised a kind of *zoomorphism*; i.e., they ascribed non-human traits to deities—animal attributes, to be precise. But I don't think they did so to demean God or reduce God's divinity. In a way, their nonhuman, animal-shaped statues forced them to remember that the divine nature wasn't human. It was different. It was 'other'. It was Holy. So, Aaron making God look like a bull isn't a slur on God's character at all. It could be seen as a compliment, an acknowledgement that God is not like us.

I need to say this for two reasons. Firstly, in what is about to take place, God's displeasure is not aroused because Aaron made his statue wrong. If Aaron had made a Golden Human, we would be having the same conversation (actually, if Aaron had made a human statue, things could have been potentially worse). Secondly, to stress what we've already said, Aaron and the Hebrew Nation are only acting on what they know. They're making God in their preconceived image. And this statue, regardless of its outward appearance, makes no character statements regarding the divine nature, per se. Divine nature—what God is like, how God behaves, what God wants—is usually projected onto idols by those worshipping them. It's we who bring idols to 'life'—as it were—with our own pre-existing ideas of God and with our desires about how we want God to perform.

Knowing this helps us to appreciate the nature of God's frustration and complaint against the Hebrews and their golden image; it's *not only* that they have made an image, but *they are ascribing to that image the glory and honour that is due to God*. Additionally, *how* they're ascribing that glory and honour (their worship) to the statue involves 'pagan revelry', to use the term found in Exodus 32:6. We can't be certain of what that involved exactly, but if we look at later parts of Scripture, where the Israelites also involved themselves in the sacrificial rituals of other nations, it could be anything from child sacrifice to the sexual objectification of others. The bottom line is that their wrong view of God leads them into objectifying and oppressive acts towards others in the name of God.

So it's not the Golden Calf that's the big issue—though, yes, that was wrong. But it's the honour given to this preconceived image of God and how that honour is then manifested by the people through their exploitation and violence.

I'm doing a lot to save Aaron's rep here, I know. But I do think we usually give him far more grief than he rightly deserves. His intentions weren't wrong, and, like many of us, he's acting on the projections of God he already knows or has deduced by interpretation from his experiences. In many ways, he has far less information to act on than we do. So maybe, we should get off his case.

It's Moses I want us to take a look at. Because whilst he is up on the mountaintop, God sees what is happening below: the people he has rescued are worshipping and sacrificing to a golden image saying, 'Behold the God who delivered you, O Israel'. I need you to note that it is God who sees this, *not* Moses. Moses won't see what is happening until he reaches the end of his descent, and he's only aware of what is happening in the Hebrew camp because God has told him.

And God is not happy. Not one bit.

So much so, that we then encounter one of the strangest conversations in the Bible. God expresses to Moses his wish to destroy the Hebrew people because they have become corrupt. Shocking, I know. Moses then gets involved in a debate with God—a debate which revolves around what message such an act would send to the world at large about God's nature. It's crucial to see the motivation and direction of this whole debate: it starts with a false image of God that the people are worshipping and it ends with Moses appealing to God to think about the image God will display. To paraphrase Moses, 'You'll look like a devious reprobate, who lures people in with false promises in order to destroy them. What will the Egyptians think about you then?' So compelling is Moses' defence and appeal to God's character that God defers to Moses' wisdom and decides instead to be merciful. Apparently, God changes his mind and decides not to destroy the people.

Note that and underline it. Not so much the changing mind thing (we'll touch on that in a moment or so). But I want you to notice that God says he is *not* going to destroy the infant Israelite nation, and does so *because* of the *image* it would portray. God doesn't enforce the wrong images that the people hold to of a God who is exploitative and oppressive, but as in the stories of Adam and Eve, and Cain, God counters it with the truth about himself. Mercy prevails, and as the text tells us, 'the LORD *withdrew* his threat and *did not* bring his people the disaster he had threatened.'[188]

There's some strange wording at play in that verse. Why tell us that God *didn't* bring his people disaster? Why does the narrative tell us this now, before we move on? Ask yourself, if you didn't have the rest of the story, what would you be expecting to happen in the next scene? There was a threat of violence to purge the corruption, but now we are expectant of something other than violence to heal these broken people.

Maybe this whole conversation was a test for Moses? Maybe God wanted to see what Moses thought about God by confronting Moses' own ideas of how a deity is supposed to act (using an approach similar to how many understand the Abraham and Isaac scene in Genesis 22)? Or maybe this whole conversation is a literary device employed by the storyteller in order to present us with this internal tug-of-war between differing views of God's nature and how God should deal with sin: should it be through violence, or mercy? Whichever it is, we finish the conversation between God and Moses expecting Moses to demonstrate God's mercy.

However, what we expect isn't what we get. We're promised mercy, but what follows is death. And, as we'll see, it's Moses, the one who changed God's mind, who decrees the violence.

After "persuading" God to turn from violence, Moses then descends the hill of the LORD. And as he nears the bottom, the noises from the orgy below begin to meet his senses. But it's only as Moses arrives at the camp that he finally sees what is going on.

And Moses isn't happy. Not one bit.

So much so, that Moses takes the two stone tablets, inscribed by God with the Commandments, and smashes them on the ground. This act is symbolic of how Moses now feels about his people and God. Moments before, he happily pleaded for their lives. But now, acting on his own (not God's) rage-filled perspective, he feels that these people aren't entitled to God's words anymore, even though God—and I can't stress this enough—put mercy forward whilst knowing full well what was taking place. As far as Moses is concerned, they are no longer worthy of the revelation of God's benevolent nature.

Moses can pacify the anger of God, apparently, but he's unable to control his own temper. Which seems unbalanced, does it not?

Moses storms into the camp. He takes their gold statue, grinds it to dust and then spoon-feeds it to the people as punishment. But this isn't punitive enough for Moses; this won't purge Israel of their crimes. So Moses does something shocking; he stands up before the people and shouts, 'All of you who are on the LORD's side, come over here and join me [...]. This is what the LORD, the God of Israel, says: Strap on your swords! Go back and forth from one end of the camp to the other, killing even your brothers, friends and neighbours.'[189] According to this story, those who zealously volunteered to pick up their swords, slaughtered three thousand people.

Three thousand! That's a hideous amount of blood.

Yes, you should be shocked. You may also wish to speculate on how many of those wielding a sword previously frolicked before the statue. Seems to me like the perfect opportunity to scapegoat someone else and save your own skin.

But are you shocked for the same reason I am?

Let's do a quick recap. God sees what is going on. God says he's going to kill. Moses "changes" God's mind. God puts forth mercy. Moses then leaves God's presence. Moses sees for himself what's going on. Moses then says that God said to kill. And then three thousand people are massacred—in God's name!

Is it just me, or is there a looming inconsistency here? Either we've been excluded from some private and quick conversation between Moses and God or someone's not telling the truth.

God put forth mercy. But Moses, even though he has heard God's decision of not to kill, decides to kill anyway, saying that God said so.[190]

Now *that's* idolatry.

Poor Aaron. Aaron's name is dirt, and his character is made disreputable whenever his example is pulled out in Bible studies and Sunday School classes. Bible commentaries have been trolling and scapegoating Aaron for centuries because of his artistic license. Translators even stuck a label on this story and called it 'the Golden Calf', drawing attention to Aaron's huge error. But Moses' error—the real elephant in the room—remains oblivious to many.

All Aaron does is make an image of God—following the conventions of his time—and he does so with good intent, I believe. A golden, *silent* statue, I should add, which can only have ideas of God projected onto it. But Moses' act certainly makes statements about the character of God; claims which counter the mercy and forgiveness that Moses had just heard from the lips of God. The Calf is merely the sound of a starting-pistol, commencing the events that are going to unfold and culminate in Moses' own idolatry; instead of one bad expression of God being replaced with an authentic expression of God's likeness (as we see in the Garden account), it's distorted further by another bastardisation.

This is a story of two idols, not one. One is conceptual, the other visual. And we often find ourselves condemning the visual one. Maybe this is why the Ten Commandments speak not only of making statues, but also of misusing God's name; the two go hand-in-hand. Blasphemy, in other words, isn't merely using God's name as a swear-word, but about the things we do in the name of God; the actions, the ordinances, the motivations that we attribute to God. Moses' act *speaks* volumes about God in comparison to a mute, golden statue.

## SIGNS AND WONDER

Of course, we could ask why the Bible doesn't condemn Moses, why it doesn't have some qualifying statement at the end saying that Moses got it wrong.

But the Bible does condemn this action, doesn't it? Maybe not explicitly like the crafting of Aaron's Calf, but the story certainly makes no attempts to hide what has happened. It did tell us about the conversation that Moses had with God; it did tell us of God's decision; it did tell us about what Moses chose not to express. Its layout is clear. It doesn't need to give some 'concluding' thought or moral summary like the ones we're used to in our devotionals. It's all there to see. But if we're looking for clear signals, we may miss it.

To give an analogy: I remember learning to drive. One of the most important lessons I had was the one on road signs (especially after I botched my third driving exam because I failed to notice a speed limit sign). My driving instructor once told me that when you're driving on some roads, you don't need signs. You will, if you're travelling at forty, fifty or seventy miles per hour and you go into a different speed zone. But most of the time the speed limit signs aren't there, and if they are, then they're surplus to requirement. He would say, (and I need you to imagine some wise, Gandalf-like voice here), 'Tristan, the road layout itself tells you it's a thirty zone: the footpaths; the height of the street lights; the distance of the houses from the roadside; the crossing points, local shops and conveniences. You don't need a sign-post. You need to read the road.'

As many Jewish commentators and Midrashim show, the Scriptures often leave us to read the road and discern it for ourselves; it calls us to wonder; it calls us to, 'look closer.' In other words, Scripture doesn't explicitly say that Moses is in the wrong, but the way the account is laid out should cause us to say, 'Hang on Moses, that's not what God said to do!'

When we look closer, we can see that Exodus 32 is not only about a Golden Calf; which is all we are summoned to see when Bible translators put their inorganic section titles into the text. The story is clearly telling the account of one man's failure to mediate God's likeness, and that one man isn't Aaron. There's an irony here too: Moses is the one man that should be better positioned to get this right. Moses has been meeting with God face to face. Yet even Moses struggles to act on the fresh (and authentic) revelation of God and not fall back onto his old preconceptions.

As it stands, the writing is on the wall, so to speak, that Moses didn't act on God's mercy as instructed. And as discerning readers, we are to take this evidence into account as we form our verdict.

## TWO STRIKES AND YOU'RE OUT?

In case you think I'm being harsh on Moses here, I need to point out that this wouldn't be the only time that Moses would get this transmission wrong. There's a more famous story of Moses' faults; a story that involves a rock, in Numbers 20:1-13.

The years have passed and Moses and the people find themselves wandering around in the Sinai wilderness. They are thirsty, and so are their cattle, so they cry out (complain) to Moses (and God) about this absence of life's most vital element. God hears his people and tells Moses to *speak* to a rock, which will then miraculously produce life-giving water. But Moses doesn't speak to the rock; instead, he *hits* it twice with his staff. He fails to transmit God's image again. Unlike the incident with the Golden Calf, this story explicitly points out God's displeasure with his action, and this time God decides to bar Moses from entering the Promised Land as punishment.

Which always seemed harsh, especially for a single mistake, and for merely hitting a rock!

But what if this isn't a one time offence? What if this story is underlining a repetitive character trait of Moses, and not the impatient reaction of God?

There's another story which is important in bringing this all this together, which also involves Moses getting water from a rock. It takes place many years before the scene in Numbers 20, and the Golden Calf incident, and can be found in Exodus 17:1-7. In this account, the people are also crying out for water, and this time God does instruct Moses to hit the rock, but *only once*. Moses does so, and lo and behold, life-giving water emerges.

But in the later event of Numbers 20—maybe as a means of developing his understanding of God's nature—Moses is told *not* to strike; all he has to do is *speak* (communicate and reveal God) to the rock. Moses can abandon the violence because God doesn't need to employ violence to provide for his people; as in the creation accounts, God can speak to the void and bring forth life. Again, maybe God is trying to show the people something in order to move their notions of the divine nature along? But, as with the Golden Calf incident, will Moses pass this revelation on through his actions towards the rock?

Sadly, as we've seen, Moses, instead of speaking, vents his own personal anger again at the people and strikes the rock, not once but *twice*. God desires to move away from the violence, or, should I say that God wants to move his people away from the violence-endorsing image of God. But Moses escalates the violence and entrenches the image deeper. Instead of heeding God's fresh revelation of his nature by speaking to the rock, Moses leans on his former experience of God and beats it instead.

To see this clearer, God's condemnation of Moses' rock-beating shenanigans is profound, and doesn't only relate to the rock incident, but to Moses' overall leadership for the past forty years. 'Because you *did not trust me enough to demonstrate my holiness to the people* of Israel, you will not lead them into the land I am giving them!'[191] Moses did not demonstrate God's holiness, God's otherness. Why? Well, God says it was a lack of *trust*—a lack of *belief* in what Moses was beginning to discern of God's nature. This condemnation is not solely because Moses hit a rock; it's because Moses failed to take the people forward in their understanding of the real nature of God. His failing was to demonstrate God's *otherness* over and against the ideas that the people already held.

So this story, too, is emphasising explicitly what the Golden Calf story tells us subversively. Not only does Moses seem to have a predisposition to use brute force to get what he wants (Moses' own personal exile from Egypt started because of his inclination to bring liberation through violence—he killed an Egyptian soldier who was beating a Hebrew slave), but Moses thinks that God has a predisposition towards violence as well.

God is trying to get Moses and the people to grasp the reality of the divine image. God must succeed, if they're to exhibit that divine likeness in the Promised Land. Step by step, God is not only leading them out of geographical Egypt, but also out of theological Egypt. In other words, God is moving them out of a domineering culture that was endorsed by, and reflective of, the restless and forceful gods that Egypt professed belief in, and into a way of being human that is restful and that is reflective of a God of peace. But regardless of the endeavours of God to show them this, Moses always leans back on his former understandings of a violent God, instead of trusting in and demonstrating the fresh revelation of a God who puts forth mercy.

The foundation of all of this is God's initial revelation to Moses. God reveals the divine identity as, 'I AM, WHO AM'. It's not 'I am what you want me to be', or even 'I am what you think I am'. At the heart of this revelation is the summons to leave behind our preconceptions and discover the truth for what it is, a reminder that our assumptions don't always take us in the right direction.

As I said earlier in this chapter, the Bible is the story of God redeeming the divine image. It's not just revealing what God has said, but also what *we* have said God has said. Scripture reveals how we have misunderstood God and reflected images that are counter to the divine nature and dream. It lifts the cover on us, revealing how we have used God to endorse our own understanding.

If we're prepared to read the road, we'll see that Scripture has a subversive way of telling us that not everything done in the name of God is from God. Like 'all that glisters is not gold', not all that is called God, is God.

# 6.4 | THE SOLILOQUY OF GOD

I've always loved dinosaurs and Steven Spielberg movies. So when the Hollywood maestro brought *Jurassic Park* to the big screen in the early nineties, I was very excited, to say the least. The film still remains one of my all-time favourites. And to this day, the movement of ripples in any vessel of water, be it a glass or the puddle in our street's pothole, instantaneously sends my mind back to the second most epic chase sequence in cinematic history (the chariot race in the original *Ben Hur* being the first).

Fast forward to over twenty years later, and there I am, with Steph and our two boys, sitting in a cinema, awaiting the darkness to fall over the audience once more and for *Jurassic World* to fill the screen.

Our youngest, Eaden, was only seven at the time, but with the exception of creepy-crawlies, darkness, and the idea of creepy-crawlies in the darkness, he's not scared of much. So we figured he'd be fine watching this film. As it turned out, he was. He loved it and was possibly the most laid-back person in the theatre that evening. And just in case you're wondering, he slept great that night, too.

The lady sitting to my right, however, jumped out of her seat more times than I could count. Especially whenever the genetically engineered Idominus Rex would smash everything in its path to get at some tasty human morsels.

I can't lie; I found it highly entertaining watching my fellow audience member react. Each time the 'Iddy Rex' appeared on screen, her hands would grip the armrest tightly in terror. Whereas Eaden, on my left, would be sat there with a huge grin on his face, eating his sweets. The only time my son did shift in his seat was during the final showdown. And that wasn't to shrink away, but to move to the edge of his seat for a closer look.

If you've never seen this great prehistoric biopic, be warned, as I'm putting out a spoiler. At the end of the film, when the park's technology and operational guidelines have once again failed to cage the carnal ferocity of nature, we find the surviving humans huddled together, hoping to make a break for freedom and safety. But preventing them from doing so is the formidable 'Iddy', a foe that even their team of semi-compliant Velociraptors struggle to bring down. With their chances of survival looking slim, the park's manager, played by Bryce Dallas Howard, decides that what they need is more teeth, more claws and more prehistoric muscle on their side. So she does what most rational thinking people would do in her situation; she goes and releases a Tyrannosaurus Rex, and, using herself as running bait, leads it back to the fray, hoping that the 'Iddy' will be distracted by an equal-sized threat.

By the way, Dallas Howard is impressive in this feat. In the original nineties blockbuster, actors Sam Neill and Jeff Goldblum struggled to outrun a nine-ton T-Rex running at full speed; and they were driving a 4x4. But Howard manages her Olympian-like sprint whilst wearing high heels.

High heels, people!

But I digress. Without spoiling the ending for you, because I guess you're now itching to watch this film, their plan succeeds. The T-Rex steps into the ring for them and fights off their attacker, giving them the time needed to escape the island. Hooray.

Film ends.

Credits roll.

Lights go up.

I could feel the tension in my female neighbour release itself as the theatre was once more bathed in light. But when I looked to the left, I discovered Eaden sat there with a perplexed look on his face, a look that prompted me to catch his eye and ask, 'Are you OK?' In response to my concern, Eaden then asked the greatest question I've ever heard: 'Daddy, was the T-Rex a good guy?'

It's a fair question. And to be honest, it's one I've asked a lot when reading the Bible.

No. Not in regards to a Tyrannosaur (remember, they weren't allowed on Noah's boat!).

But I have asked it in regards to God. There are portions of Scripture where I can't help but ask, 'Is God the good guy?' And unlike my son, who asked it because the T-Rex seemed to display an unusual sense of self-sacrifice and altruism, I'm asking because, in some scenes, God seems more carnal than the dinosaur should have been.

It's there, in black and white. And rightly, critics of the Bible, like Richard Dawkins, are erudite in pulling out the example of a mean, tyrant, genocidal God as proof of why belief in this kind of God is dangerous. And, I should add, it is dangerous. But is that what the Bible is saying? Are these stories true, or as Moses' Calf scene exhibits, are people putting words in the mouth of God?

The scene in the last section about Moses and the Golden Calf is an easy example to pick out. As I said then, the layout of the story clearly highlights the difference between what God said and how Moses acted. But what of those other stories, where God is said to have decreed slaughter and murder? Scenes of plagues, earthquakes, fire and death? Sometimes, when God enters a scene in the Bible, I'm not calm; my hand tightly grips the arm of the chair, just like my neighbour in the cinema.

Not in all stories, though. When compared to the amount of text in the Old and New Testaments, these scenes of horror take up a small proportion of the total page count. And in both the Old and New, there are a greater number of stories about God's grace, compassion and mercy, God's identification with the slave and the oppressed, and God's condemnation of repressive and violent regimes.[192] But that small proportion of horror still represents more than I would want there to be.

I'm going to be blunt. I not convinced that we should be taking these stories at face value as telling the truth about God's actions or decrees. That doesn't mean we should throw them away, or cherry-pick them either; definitely not. These stories have something valuable to teach us. Neither does it mean that the Bible isn't telling us the truth about what people thought and believed. But we do need to be careful with how we understand these stories and Scripture as a whole.

How do we do this?

Well, we could just read the Bible in a 'Simon Says' fashion. We could assume that when it says 'God said', it's absolutely God, and wherever it doesn't explicitly say 'God said', it's not. But that's a dangerously oversimplified approach. Not only that, but such a methodology wouldn't have worked with the Golden Calf, either; in that story, God apparently says many, contradictory things.

But our desire for such an approach does reveal something about us: we want it simple—and that's the problem. We want something that we can pick up and that explicitly tells us what to believe and how to behave without having to immerse and engage our minds in the literary, cultural, and historical context. We want a format that doesn't need to be interpreted, and that can be understood in an ad hoc, 'plain text', 'flat' way, as we have within textbooks, reference manuals, and codes of practice. However (and thankfully), the Bible doesn't give us doctrines and instructions in the format of simple statements that need only to be memorised and regurgitated; it gives us narratives. And if we're willing to traverse the complex topography that exists within and between these narratives, then we may find ourselves going down roads that our flat, 'Simon says' way of reading never lead us down. As we saw in the previous section, the structure of the Bible's stories—its figurative speech, the multi-vocal perspectives of its authors, even its contradictions—are all road markings nudging us to look again and consider more carefully.

## SUBVERSIVE MIRROR

For example, in his excellent book *Not in God's Name*, Rabbi Lord Jonathan Sacks addresses how the Hebrew Bible (the Christian Old Testament) is wrongly used as a means of endorsing violence that's done in God's name. For some, the words of the Bible are clear about God having a preference for certain people over others, and this, they believe, endorses the idea that we should live out our "blessed" domination over others. But by taking us deeper into the 'Sibling rivalry' tales of Genesis that are often used to support such views—the stories of Ishmael and Isaac (via Hagar and Sarah), Jacob and Esau, Leah and Rachel, and Joseph and his brothers—Lord Sacks shows how the Bible speaks against the conclusions that our flat, 'Simon says' approach produces.

Instead of sanctioning the man-made image of a God who sponsors hierarchy, these stories, through their narrative structure and their use of wordplay in the original Hebrew language, again and again, speak of a God who identifies and empathises with the outcast, the rejected and the downtrodden. They speak of a God who blesses all, and who seeks to bless all, and not of a God who blesses the few to the detriment of the many. And as such, the book of Genesis (and the remaining Torah), through its account of these sibling rivalries, subversively overturns our ideas of a God who encourages and exemplifies violence, and exposes *our* desire to struggle against one another in God's name for God's blessings.

As Rabbi Sacks puts it, 'What if the Hebrew Bible understood, as did [Sigmund] Freud and [René] Girard, as did Greek and Roman myth, that sibling rivalry is the most primal form of violence? And what if, rather than endorsing it, it set out to undermine it, subvert it, challenge it, and eventually replace it with another, quite different way of understanding our relationship with God and with the human Other? What if Genesis is a more profound, multi-levelled, transformative text than we have taken it to be? What if it turned out to be God's way of saying to us what he said to Cain: that violence in a sacred cause is not holy but an act of desecration? What if God were saying: *Not in My Name?*'[193]

To summarise, instead of reading the Bible as if everything it says should be taken as our prime example of how humanity is supposed to look, we need to discern what it's describing about the inclinations of mankind. In other words, appreciating the contours of its narratives should help us to see that the Bible is not always being *prescriptive* of moral practice or theological belief, but *descriptive*. It's reporting events, not dictating a creed. Sometimes, its writers are subversively exposing the oppressive practices and twisted ideologies that we have made normative.

The writer of the New Testament letter Hebrews also makes this same point:

> For the word of God is full of living power. It is sharper than the sharpest knife, cutting deep into our innermost thoughts and desires. It *exposes us* for what we really are.[194]

The Bible is exposing *us*, not only revealing God, the writer of Hebrews says. Like Rabbi Lord Sacks, they encourage us to read Scripture as a critique of humanity, and not just as a list of rules, examples or theological statements that we should unquestioningly follow.

To borrow a term that I read in Margaret Atwood's introduction to *The Handmaid's Tale*, maybe we could describe Scripture as a *literature of witness*.[195] As such, the Bible, in clearly presenting our inhumanity and idolatry, subverts it. It does so in the same way that Charles Dickens exposes our malignant treatment and oppression of the poor in, well, every book he's ever written. And like the way in which Franz Kafka reveals our apathetic neglect of those we deem dysfunctional and of no benefit to us in his story *The Metamorphosis*. Or, to keep modern, the way in which George R. R. Martin's *Song of Ice and Fire* series lifts the lid on the tyranny of the elite, the obsession with power, the patriarchal objectification of women, the inhumanity of slavery, and the indiscriminate, futile, blight of war. We're not to read these stories, and many others, as if the authors are saying, 'This is OK and acceptable; therefore, go and do likewise'. Most of these writings, especially Kafka's, don't give us "road signs" either; they require immersion and critique to filter out what they are pointing us towards. These tales call us to take a long, hard look at ourselves in the mirror, and then repent and change.

As we read the Bible, we see the human tendency to project lies about God. Often, God is cast as the culprit; God is the source of the genocides, land theft, scapegoating and horror. But is the Bible agreeing that God is to blame, or is it highlighting to us *our* tendency to pin the blame on God?

An anthropomorphic understanding of God (one in which we ascribe human traits to God) consistently attempts to understand the Divine with reference to ourselves. But the limitation of this way of thinking (especially if we have forgotten what the original definition of God was), and the damaging fruit it produces, is that how God rules, how God behaves, how God judges and deals with disorder, often resembles the ways a fallen humanity that is blind to the true image of God deals with disorder. As I said earlier, even when God does reveal his/her/its nature into our milieu of divine notions, we're still likely to interpret this in the light of the world view we already possess.

What we're presented with in the unfolding story of Scripture is God's consistent attempts to help humanity 'get it'. We see God's unswerving struggle against anthropomorphism, which culminates in the final and the truest revelation of God, in Jesus. God becomes flesh to give us a clear anthropomorphic description of the Divine, and not one which is based on our self-idolising inclinations. Jesus, God incarnate, kills the lie(s) we have believed and told about God.

It's not that Jesus came to forgive our sins; God forgave sins in the Old Testament, and Jesus did this before his crucifixion. But God comes in the flesh to deal with the *root* of Sin—our idolatry: the false images we hold of God, which lead us either to misrepresent God or to reject God. In the 'God made flesh' we see that God doesn't look like us at all; God looks like Jesus, and God calls us to believe in (to trust and to give allegiance to) and to be conformed to this real image.

The gospel writer John, sums up this human plight and its solution when he writes:

> But although the world was made through him, the world didn't recognise him [...]. So the Word became human and lived here on earth among us. He was full of unfailing love and faithfulness. [...] No one has ever seen God. But his only Son, who is himself God [...] has told us about him.[196]

To paraphrase John's introductory words to his Gospel account: 'We rejected God, and were unable to recognise God, so God came and showed us what he was like.'

I'm jumping ahead of myself here, and we'll come back to John's words (and the importance of the Incarnation—God becoming flesh) shortly. At this point, what I'm trying to get across is that the Bible is the journal of humanity, over many generations, grappling with God—grappling with how to comprehend, how to describe and how to live out this experience of divine revelation. As this journey moves forward, we find that Scripture offers a self-critical window on itself, constantly refining and challenging its own views, knowing that with every fresh revelation and experience of God, there also comes the greater insight to be able to look back. As we'll see in this section, there's a progression of thought within the Bible. But saying that there is a shift in understanding doesn't necessarily imply that the Bible is therefore incorrect.

So please hear me here. I'm not saying the Bible cannot be trusted in what it is saying; it can. And I'm certainly not suggesting that we adopt the decision of that old Marcionite heresy to get rid of the Old Testament altogether. Not at all! I would never endorse any ideas that advocate removing the Old Testament or not trusting it for two reasons: Firstly, as we'll explore in the pages ahead, the Old Testament authoritatively presents this story of wrestling with God and guides us through its progressive revelation. Secondly, the story of Jesus only makes sense in the light of the Old Testament and the human problem it presents to us.[197]

The problems occur when we, the readers, stop at one moment in this journey of Scripture and forget that there is more to come. It's like reading *The Fellowship of the Ring,* and not reading the remaining two parts. It's like watching *The Sixth Sense,* but stopping it ten minutes from the end and missing that famous twist that changes your interpretation of everything that has happened so far in the film. It's like reading the Gospels, but stopping at the crucifixion.

The narrative of the Bible isn't stagnant. There's more of God to come; fresh revelation that feeds back into what has gone before, and that therefore helps us to separate the reality from the fiction, the face of God from the human projection.[198] We don't need to put down the Old Testament or throw it away out of suspicion. What we need to do is to pick it up and travel with it. Through these words, words I respect and cherish and hold as authoritative, the Spirit of God is trying to move us along in the right direction.[199]

## PROGRESSIVE REVELATION

In her excellent book *War in the Hebrew Bible*, Hebrew scholar Susan Niditch surveys the Old Testament's portrait of God's relationship to violence and war. Niditch's study highlights that there isn't just *one* singular view of God and war, but an overlapping of ideologies in some places and a clear conflict (pardon the pun) in others.

What Niditch identifies is a developing understanding of God and violence from the perspective of the writers. This progression originates from a pagan idea which sees the victims of war as sacrificial gifts to God (gifts requested by God, or needed to invoke God's blessing), but over hundreds of years, this notion is revised with the view of God's non-participation in war and a de-sacralisation of violent acts done in God's name. Overall, Niditch suggests, there is a growing discomfort within the Hebrew Bible of casting God as the instigator of violence, along with a growing awareness that maybe it's just us (humanity) looking for someone divine to blame as we kill for what *we* want and as we murder those *we* don't like.

Another great book that explores this idea of a growing awareness of God's non-violent nature is Raymund Schwager's *Must There Be Scapegoats?*, in which he applies René Girard's theories (found in *Violence and the Sacred*) to the Bible. Like Sacks and Niditch, Schwager demonstrates Scripture's subversive way of revealing that God neither calls for, nor endorses, violence. Rather, what the stories expose is the human tendency towards violent sacrifice—an exposure that culminates in God becoming humanity's scapegoat. The whole trajectory of the Bible's story, as Schwager proposes, is telling us that 'it is not God who must be appeased [through violence], but humans who must be delivered from their hatred', and that it is God's continual self-revelation of mercy which unmasks this latent violent nature within us.[200]

But it doesn't require scholars like Sacks, Niditch and Schwager to indicate this progression. If we're prepared to read the layout of the road, the Hebrew Bible does this by itself.

For example: Moses wrote that God punishes children for the sins of their parents, to the third and fourth generations. And in case you're wondering, this isn't some side comment, either. It's included in the Ten Commandments, the laws apparently spoken by God and carved in stone by God's proverbial finger.[201] However, the sacred status of these words doesn't stop the prophet Ezekiel, who is also claiming to speak on behalf of God, from coming along much later in the story and refuting this. According to Ezekiel, God doesn't make the child pay for the sins of their parents; instead, people are judged on an individual basis according to what they do (see Ezekiel 18:19). In short, Ezekiel revises Moses' statement about God. And he's not the only one.

Moses also wrote that eunuchs were prohibited from God's community (see Deuteronomy 23:1). But many centuries after Moses, the prophet Isaiah, speaking again on behalf of God, says that God's blessings are also for eunuchs. Through Isaiah, God also promises to give eunuchs an honour and legacy far greater than the one stolen from them when their testicles were removed (see Isaiah 56:3-5).

Of course, Moses' law may have originally been intended as a push against a normalised practise within his own culture, especially against those who saw castration as a means of becoming servants of god(s). Therefore, by banning those who were eunuchs from becoming priests, Moses would also have been desacralising violent images of God and pushing people towards a newer revelation.[202] But for those who would come along later in time and interpret Moses' law as excluding some people from God's community, Isaiah offers the corrective by repainting the idea of a God of compassion and not of brutality.

Many centuries after Isaiah's words, we read the story of an Ethiopian eunuch travelling along the road from Jerusalem to Gaza (see Acts 8:26-40). As he does, he avidly studies the words of Isaiah 53, which speak of God's Suffering Servant coming and implementing God's dream. The eunuch has a vested interest in this passage of Isaiah, and I can't help but think that this interest flows from what he's read after this passage about God's dream being inclusive of people like himself (i.e. the eunuch's of Isaiah 56). When the Evangelist Phillip shows up, this eunuch desperately wants to know whether Isaiah's words were self-referential or about someone else. This Suffering Servant is the cornerstone and instigator of what will come after, so the Ethiopian is eager to know whether this Suffering Servant has appeared or is still to come; his place as a part of the community of God depends on it. The text then tells us that Phillip points out that Isaiah wasn't talking about himself, but Jesus—who had indeed come and launched God's dream through his suffering. At that moment, they pass by a pool of water and the eunuch prods Phillip with the question, 'Can I be baptised?' In other words, because Jesus had come, the eunuch wants to claim Isaiah's promise and take his place in God's Kingdom—something which the words of the Mosaic Law had prohibited him from doing. Thankfully, Phillip doesn't revert to a plain-text reading of Moses' law, but following Isaiah's revision of Moses, and acting on the revelation and authority of Jesus, Phillip turns around and says, 'Absolutely!'

I bet the eunuch thanked God for progressive revelation.

As another example of progression, we could look at the sacrificial system. The Torah is full of the prescriptions for a system of Sin Offerings, Peace Offerings, Grain Offerings and Burnt Offerings etc. Again, most of these came from Moses and the Hebrew Nation's encounter with God at Mount Sinai. And yet, despite the abundance of these God-given ordinances, the prophet Jeremiah, again claiming to speak on behalf of

God, says: 'Away with your burnt offerings and sacrifices! Eat them yourselves! When I led your ancestors out of Egypt, it was not burnt offerings I wanted from them. *This is what I told them*: "Obey me, and I will be your God, and you will be my people. Only do as I say, and all will be well!"' (Jeremiah 7:21-23, NLT; italics mine).

According to Jeremiah, God never desired sacrifices. Jeremiah suggests that the *only* thing God desired was obedience. So maybe the sacrificial system itself, was a human projection of what God wanted because of the cultural norm of making sacrifices? It could be that God accommodated to the religious rites already held by the people, and that instead of dismantling the sacrificial system straightaway, God sought to reorient and 'refill' the existing symbolism of such acts.[203] Maybe the divine hope foresaw the people eventually understanding God better and realising that a sacrifice does not instigate the mercy of God, but that God, through his own faithfulness to the people, puts mercy forth anyway.[204]

Jeremiah certainly isn't alone in his sentiment on the sacrificial system. Centuries before Jeremiah, the Hebrew poets had already roused suspicions. The Psalmist (David) wrote to God saying:

> You take *no delight* in sacrifices or offerings.
> *Now that you have made me listen,* I *finally understand*—
> You *don't require* burnt offerings or sin offerings.[205]

Later, after acknowledging his own sins of adultery and murder, David speaks again of the impotence of violent sacrifice to atone for sin as he reflects on what God really desires:

> You would not be pleased with sacrifices, or I would bring them.
> If I brought you a burnt offering, you would not accept it.
> The sacrifice you want is a broken spirit.
> A broken and repentant heart, O God, you will not despise.[206]

In both cases, we see a progression of thought about God and sacrifices in line with that of Jeremiah. This same progression is further repeated by the prophet Hosea when he says, again speaking on behalf of God: 'I want you to be merciful; I don't want your sacrifices. I want you to *know God*; that's more important than burnt offerings.' This is a sentiment that Jesus would also echo during his own ministry.[207]

In each of the above, there's a sense of finally coming to terms with a fuller, more beautiful image of God, a God who doesn't require violence in order to heal, forgive and restore.[208] What God yearns for is obedience, for humanity to reflect the Divine's compassion and vision of justice.

As one final example of progression, King David's desire to build the Temple is also enlightening. Remember, a Temple is a microcosm of the sacred, garden intent of God for creation, a space where Heaven merges with Earth. But David is forbidden by God to build a Temple. According to the writer(s) of the book of Samuel, we're not given any reason for God's prohibition, except that God had chosen David's heir for the task. But a few centuries later, after the exile to Babylon, the writer(s) of Chronicles (the priesthood of the Ezra revival) shed fresh light on the matter: David was prohibited from building a sacred space because of his bloodstained hands.[209] Apparently, as we've seen throughout this book, the sacred and the violent are incompatible.

If we moved to the New Testament, we would see this same Old Testament practice of self-critique in action. Actually, we've already seen it in action within Part Four of this book, when Jesus purposely edited out Isaiah's prophetic conclusion of God killing the nation's enemies. We also saw this when Jesus corrects the expectations of the Psalmists, by saying that God is kind and merciful to the wicked. Neither of these things went down well with the crowds because they challenged their preconceived, "biblical" knowledge of God.

It's worth stating that these scenes are not examples of when Jesus merely challenged people's *interpretations* of the Scriptures (which he did do), but of when Jesus directly challenged the *words* of Scripture. We could also add to these scenes the Sermon on the Mount as Jesus repeatedly uses the formula, 'Moses said this, but I say […]' (or, 'The Torah said this, but I say […]').[210] To be clear, Jesus isn't doing anything new or revolutionary in challenging the words of Scripture—this is only what people before him, such as Isaiah, Jeremiah, David and Hosea had already done, as recorded in the biblical texts. Jesus, as it turns out, is following the great Hebrew prophetic tradition of 'faithfully questioning' Scripture's use to endorse violence, and did so to call out our distorted views of God (to use the author Derek Flood's terminology).[211] In other words, Jesus followed a Spirit-guided, *scriptural precedent* when he revised the theological views of Moses, Isaiah and the Psalmists.

Because of how some people choose to read the Bible, these clashes of opinion have been labelled contradictions and therefore problematic. However, these contradictions shouldn't be seen as problems, but as gifts. They show us a progression of experience in God's true likeness, and therefore they, and the texts they correct, should not be edited out.

## UNCERTAIN DEATH

All well and good, I hear you say (or not). But what about those laws that call for the death penalty, or those laws that seem regressive and dehumanising? Don't these laws put forward the idea of a God who demands violence?

Well, it could also be, as I have previously suggested in this chapter, that these laws expose something of our violent nature, not God's; i.e., that the violence within the commandments is a projection of our idolatry and the Ancient Near East's preconceived notions about what deities demand.[212]

But if you can't swallow that, and you want to see these laws as being an undiluted revelation of God's will (although, as we've just seen above, Ezekiel's, Isaiah's, Jeremiah's, and Jesus' stances would prove this problematic), then I think we would still need to do the hard work of reading these laws not against the backdrop of where we are today with our Human Rights laws, but against the backdrop of the Ancient Near East.

The Mosaic laws certainly are a 'mixed bag', to say the least, and some appear archaic to us looking back on them. But intermingled within this mixed bag, and giving rise to these commands, is the ethical thrust of loving our neighbour, loving the stranger, and having compassion for the oppressed, the poor and the slave. This empathy was there because Israel too, in its past bondage to Egypt, had experienced a life of slavery, impoverishment and alienation.[213] Because the Mosaic laws were fuelled by this ethic, it was progressive in comparison to the laws of the dominant cultures around them, as Bible scholars such as Christopher Wright and William Webb point out in their books (see the Further Reading section). To use Wright's hint, the idea behind Israel's slavery laws, for example, was that it should have been better to be a slave or foreigner in Israel than anywhere else.

But this doesn't mean we are to go back to the 'black and white' practice of these commands and bring back slavery. On the contrary, the opposite is true. These laws might not have been as progressive as we would have liked, but they did nudge humanity forward, and as Webb points out, we ought to see the *trajectory* of the redemptive work of God in these laws, against the backdrop of their own culture, and then follow that progression.

So if Moses' law led people towards placing a greater value on human equality and dignity, and according a more equal status to people of different gender and class in his day, to use some examples, then we should do the same. Reading these laws from today's position, then, we are not to see the ink and go back to ink, but we are to move forward in the direction and goal that the words aim towards. And that direction, I suggest, in line with the Hebrew prophets, is always towards doing justice, loving mercy and walking humbly.[214]

With regards to the death punishments, like many, I see these as spelling out the value of life and the seriousness of the offence.

For example, we see this in God's command to Noah after the flood when God recommissions humanity to go back out into the world. With this recommission comes a prohibition against violence: do not murder.

This makes a lot of sense, as it was violence that resulted in the world being engulfed by the watery grip of chaos. But with this prohibition, God also adds that those who murder should be put to death.[215]

Isn't this rather circular, though? After all, once the cycle of murdering a murderer starts, when does the killing stop?

Some translators have made this verse sound like God is demanding the blood of whoever takes a life. However, as the Complete Jewish Bible (CJB) and the New King James Version (NKJV) indicate, God is not demanding blood, but only pointing out the cyclical revenge pattern of violence. To paraphrase the CJB and NKJV: 'Whoever spills human blood, will find their blood being spilt.' In many ways, this is what Jesus taught when he said, 'Those who use the sword will be killed by the sword'.[216] These sayings aren't justifying violence, but pulling us away from violence by exposing its incapability to bring an end to violence.

After Noah, within the laws of Moses, we see the same thing; those who take a life must pay with a life. But again, this should be seen as a push towards valuing another's life as highly as our own, not as an endorsement to kill. This sacred view of others should act as a deterrent to violence in the first place. Moses is effectively saying to his culture, '*Their* life has the same value as *your* life'. God also says as much after the flood account, when he tells Noah that to kill others is wrong because they too are made to be the image of God; they too, have equal value.[217] What these commands do is prevent us from devaluing or demonising others in order to justify the reasons for our violence towards them.

It's also imperative to notice that God never abides by this rule of a life for a life. When Cain murders Abel, God does *not* kill Cain, nor does God tell someone else to kill him. Instead, God shows mercy once more and sends Cain out to wander with a mark of divine protection. Although Cain's exile should be seen as a penalty, within it is also the opportunity for Cain to once again pick up the vocation of being an image bearer and to go and cultivate sacred space.[218]

We don't have to look far for other examples of God breaking his own rules on the death penalty, either. The same could be said of the biblical murderers called Moses, David, and Saul (also known as the Apostle Paul). Their acts of murder should have resulted in their own deaths under the Mosaic law, but God consistently pursues them with the offer of life.

None of this is to say that God takes a light view of sin; the laws, again, spell out how serious it is to image violence and chaos instead of bearing God's image. Sin, the turning away from our vocation in order to image self or wrong images of God, matters to God and has direct repercussions on God's dream for the world. But God's way of dealing with sin is not to destroy those that are called to be image bearers, but to mercifully rescue them from the Sin (the idolatry) that is enslaving and destroying them.

## FISHY THEOLOGY

One of the biblical prophets who knew this best of all was Jonah.

Jonah receives a call from God to go to Nineveh, the Assyrian Empire's capital city, and preach a message from God which would call the then world-super-power to repentance. However, being no lover of the Assyrians (as they were an oppressive threat to Israel), Jonah doesn't want them to have the opportunity to change; he wants them dead, and he's awfully suspicious that God's kind nature doesn't want the same thing. Jonah's dream doesn't align with God's in this particular story; God certainly doesn't endorse or share Jonah's racist and xenophobic attitudes. Jonah knows this, and so instead of delivering God's liberating proclamation to the Assyrians, Jonah decides to run in the opposite direction.

After a series of unusual nautical twists and fishy turns—which you'll be familiar with—God eventually gets Jonah to Nineveh. And at Jonah's preaching, the nation goes into a state of lament and becomes open to receive God's mercy and forgiveness. But Jonah is ticked off by this and voices, what I believe, is one of the best complaints about God written in the whole of the Bible: 'LORD, was this not what I said when I was still in my country? Therefore I fled to Tarshish; for I know that you are a gracious and merciful God, slow to anger and abundant in loving kindness, *One who relents from doing harm.*'[219]

Please, don't read that as if Jonah is saying this in some worshipful tone of voice; he's not. Jonah has spat his dummy out and he's mad with rage at God—or, to be more specific, at a God who won't fall in line with what he wants God to be like.

I find this story fascinating, not only because of Jonah's reticence and suspicion of God's character, which is then proved true, but also because Jonah knows the power of God's mercy to transform the human heart. Jonah would have preferred God to deal with Assyria through some violent, punitive action instead of being merciful, and becomes angry at God *because God isn't violent.* Imagine that! Unlike many today who are embittered towards the Old Testament's "depiction" of a violent God, the *Old Testament* prophet Jonah is the exact opposite. He's bitter at God's benevolence. He's miffed with mercy. He's riled by God's unwillingness to abandon Assyria to her self-destructive fate. He wants God to turn His face away, but God flat out refuses.

I have to ask though, why did Jonah have such a suspicion? Where would he have conceived the idea of a God who always chooses mercy over violence? He could have construed such an idea only from Israel's own story and history; from Israel's own unfolding and enlarging vision of the nature of the Divine. Jonah, knowing God's tender faithfulness to his own people, has come to suspect that God has this disposition towards *all* people, *all* of the time. The same story-tradition that leads many today to see an angry tyrant of a God, had led Jonah to the opposite conclusion of seeing One who is abundant in loving kindness and who is unwilling to turn to violence. Richard Dawkins and Jonah have both read the same Hebrew Scriptures and formed completely opposing conclusions.

If Jonah had been around to hear Jesus speaking of a God who was kind and compassionate to the wicked—and who therefore calls us to reflect this same character—I can easily imagine Jonah saying 'Amen' (although it would have been said through gritted teeth).

In many ways, we have too low a view of Sin if we believe it can be 'beaten' away or plucked out like a weed. Sin has ensnared us, mingling in with all the inherent good that exists within us all. The only cure is God's powerful mercy. Like with Adam and Eve in the garden, it's only God showing us his true image and not conforming to our ideas, that causes us to emerge from behind the vision-blurring bush that we have buried ourselves in.

## THE TESTAMENT OF JESUS

In all of what has been seen so far—from the Golden Calf to the interpretations of the scholars and the prophets—there is a consensus that God, and those who are writing about God, are attempting to get humanity to understand that mercy is how God deals with Sin, not violence. God overcomes the reign of death through giving and generating life. As in the original Genesis creation poem, God didn't (and doesn't) collude with the forces of chaos and confusion; God subverts them, casting them and their methodologies aside.

Of course, there is so much more we could say; we are only touching the tip of how dynamic and complex the Bible is (and if we were to throw in the insights of Historical and Form criticism, things get even more interesting). What I want us to grasp, though, is that we cannot read Scripture lazily—we need to engage and discern.

Let's put it this way. When it comes to the story of David and Bathsheba, the story tells us that David's adultery and eventual murder of Uriah (Bathsheba's husband) are both wrong. But even if we read this story without such a summary, shouldn't we have been able to spot this for ourselves by knowing the Ten Commandments? Maybe then, in the same manner that we're able to spot murder for what it is, and coveting for what it is, and adultery for what it is, without having the biblical writers point it out or rebuke it, we should also be able to recognise when people are breaking the second and third commandments. Not only do we need to recognise when people are making God in their own image, but we also need to faithfully discern when people wrongly invoke God's name and character into an act.

Admittedly, golden calves are easy to spot, whereas wrong expectations, skewed anthropomorphisms, idolatrous concepts, moulding God in the form of another culture's gods, and putting words into God's mouth, are much harder to discern. But these things are not impossible to spot. As we've seen above, the prophets did it, and the scholars of the Hebrew Bible are able to do it. How much more so then, should we who follow Jesus be able to spot these things? Especially if we, like the Gospel writer John, believe that Jesus is the true revelation of God's nature.

We saw John's words earlier in this section. His statement that '*No one has ever seen God*' is bold and revolutionary.

John knows that the great Jewish patriarch Abraham was called a 'friend of God' (Isaiah 41:8; 2 Chronicles 20:7), a man who once welcomed God into his camp and served God food (Genesis 18). John also knows the story of the patriarch Jacob (Israel), the father of the Twelve Tribes. He knows that Jacob wrestled with God and had his hip wrenched out of his socket as a result. He knows that Jacob named the place of this wrestle, Peniel (meaning 'Face of God'), because he said, 'I have seen God face to face, yet my life has been spared' (Genesis 32:30). John's also not ignorant of the concluding words of the Torah. In Deuteronomy 34:10 it says, 'There has never been another prophet like Moses, whom the Lord knew *face to face*'.[220]

All these encounters with the Divine, plus many others, are the founding experiences of John's Jewish religion and theology. These people saw God and yet John is adamant that no one has ever seen God. However, John's statement is no accident. John's not dismissing the experiences of his founding fathers; he is not saying that they should no longer be held as sacred, nor is he saying that they didn't experience something. But John is saying that the something they experienced was only *something*, and not everything.

No one, John says, has ever seen God, except Jesus, who has shown us what God is really like. All the other encounters were glimmers in the half-light of human understanding, and must now be measured against the light of God's full self-disclosure in Christ. John, like Jeremiah, Ezekiel, the Psalmist and Jonah, is not rejecting the experiences recorded in Scripture, but holding them up and viewing them through a clearer revelation of God. For John, who makes a remarkable move for a Jew, what Jesus had to say of God trumps the Torah and the Prophets. For John, the story of Scripture must be viewed through the lens of Jesus.[221]

By taking Jesus as our lens, I believe that it will be much easier to spot wrong expectations, skewed anthropomorphisms, idolatrous concepts, or instances when words have been put into God's mouth. Jesus helps us see when people break the second and third commandments.

In Jesus, God deals with our bastardisations. The incarnation was the Creator's means of giving us a multisensory, no-holds-barred, tangible experience of the divine nature. God condescended to the limits of our means of knowing reality and truth. We struggle to put our flesh into words, but God's word—God's self-expression—became flesh and dwelled with us, for us.

This is nothing short of an act of love, an act of revelation, an act of transferring the fullness of one's self into a vulnerable form so that it can be felt by another. God chooses to step into the range of our grasp, allowing our awareness of the divine to move from abstract imagination to relational discovery.

Such a step certainly doesn't remove the mystery of who or what God is. Questions remain. But it does allow us to enter into that mystery with the whole of our beings. We don't have to stop being human to embrace the mystery of God. By God's invitation, we can poke our doubting and enquiring digits into the opened side of the incomprehensible made manifest. As we do so, we can know what God is like; God is like Jesus, and, to use Pastor Brian Zahnd's oft-quoted summary, God has *always* been like Jesus.

Let's have one final, short analogy before we move into the next section.

There's a device used in acting to help us know the true intentions or thoughts of a character. Occasionally, the character in question will turn aside from the onstage action and relay her inner feelings. When this happens, we, the audience, are not observing and then subsequently interpreting the external behaviour of the character during interactions with the other characters on the stage. Neither do we only see the other actors' responses to this character—which can also affect our view of the character. Instead, through this technique, we witness the character through who she says she is, and not through the filtering haze of everyone's exchanges with her.

This device is known as a *soliloquy*.

Taking everything I've said in this chapter so far, I want to suggest that Jesus is the soliloquy of God spoken into the dissonance of humanity's struggle to fully comprehend and relay their experience of God. God comes and does what we could not do by ourselves. His revelation liberates us from our Sin, our idolatry.

If we followed the Bible's own plotline, and we heard and saw the identity of God through Jesus, I believe we would come to see that God isn't the dinosaur we think God is. Maybe it's our ideas of a violent and vengeful God which are outdated and prehistoric. Maybe it's our violent scapegoating of God that put Christ to death.[222]

# 6.5 | THE FACE OF EVIL

Luke Skywalker finds himself in the green and murky swamps of the Dagobah System, trying to learn the ways of the Force from the reclusive and equally green Jedi Master, Yoda.

So far, Luke has made several rocks simultaneously rise from the ground, along with his faithful droid R2D2, whilst being in a one-armed handstand with Master Yoda balancing on top of his feet. He's learnt to be as agile as a Jedi, dodging, swinging and somersaulting through the dense, vine-entangled swamps of Dagobah with Master Yoda on his back. And, as some creative interpretations of this scene would have us believe, Luke has also learnt about the perils of seagulls.[223] But his trials are far from complete.

As Luke moves through the undergrowth like Tarzan, Master Yoda warns him that although the source of a Jedi's strength comes from the Force, a Jedi must also be careful of the Dark Side of the Force; he tells his apprentice how easy it is to give into to the seductive impulses of anger, aggression and fear. Luke must be a passive vessel for peace, Yoda instructs, as Jedi only use the force for knowledge and defence, not for attack.

As he takes a break from his exercises, a strange sound comes from the surrounding vegetation, making Luke detect a change in the atmosphere and causing him to notice the entrance of a cave that is polluted by the Dark Side of the Force; the entrance to a challenge he must face alone. Looking towards the cave, Luke asks Yoda what he will find within it. 'Only what you take with you', Yoda replies.

Before proceeding, Luke picks up his belt, which contains his holstered blaster-pistol and Lightsaber. And although Yoda tells Luke that he'll have no need for weapons in this encounter, Luke displays doubt in a weaponless confrontation with the Dark Side and proceeds anyway, ready for a fight.

With his senses alive, Luke carefully lowers himself into the cave and begins to move through the jungle of gnarled roots and thick air, seeking for what has aroused his curiosity. As he moves towards the heart of the darkness, Luke's nemesis, the evil Darth Vader, emerges from the swirling mist and moves towards him, dressed in his all-black regalia, with his shadowy robe trailing behind him and his distinctive, heavy, mechanical breathing echoing from out of his mask. Vader, the Lord of the tyrannical Empire, a harbinger of the Dark Side of the Force, the masked face of Death within the galaxy. Vader, Evil's emissary.

But this is where the perceptions become blurred, because it's not Vader who attacks. It's Luke who unsheathes and wields his blue Lightsaber first, taking a stance which summons Vader to a duel. It's Luke who is the aggressor as the short duel takes place, while Lord Vader deflects his blows and embodies a Jedi's defensive posture. And it's Luke who shows no hesitation in seizing an opportunity to strike at Vader's helmet, cleaving the Dark Lord's head from his shoulders, sending it tumbling to the floor. Vader's headless form slumps and drops to the ground, still clutching his red Lightsaber.

Luke, now finding himself breathing heavily and with his Lightsaber still readied, turns to glance at the decapitated head before him. As he does so, the front of the mask explodes, exposing the elusive identity enclosed. It's then that we are called to witness the face that lies behind the shattered illusion of the dark helm; as it rolls on its side, revealing the face of Luke Skywalker himself.

As Yoda later comments, Luke Skywalker failed this test in the cave of Dagobah. And there has been much debate by Star Wars fans over why and how he failed. But like the story of Moses and the Golden Calf, all the information is there in the story itself. Yoda doesn't need to tell us how and why Luke failed, because he had already laid the path before us. Luke was to resist the Dark Side by refusing to be led by aggression and anger. Luke was to be a calm vessel of peace, only seeking to defend and not to attack. But Luke, it turns out, becomes the one who is more prepared to strike down than to be struck down. Unlike his original mentor, Obi-Wan Kenobi, who was willing to sacrifice himself in order to defeat evil, Luke's actions display his willingness to collude with it. Within the cave of Dagobah, it is Luke who is the emissary of the Dark Side, not Vader.

Before this experience, Luke would have liked to believe that he was exclusively a force for good—don't we all? But it was Luke who brought the illusory presence of Vader to this cavern, and as the shattered mask reveals, he too must wrestle with the influence that the Dark Side has on him. Under the seductive, subtle allure of evil, Luke would rather kill than be killed.[224]

It's difficult to admit the evil that influences us until we come face to face with it in a reflection of ourselves.

## SCAPEGOAT

In the first-ever episode of the British television show *Black Mirror*, entitled 'The National Anthem', writer Charlie Brooker takes a dark look at society's unknown collusion with terrorism.

In the episode, a young member of the Royal family has been kidnapped and threatened with death, unless the U.K. Prime Minister meets the ransom demands. But it's not money that the terrorist asks for, or the removal of British armies from overseas. All this sole individual wants is for the PM to disgrace himself live on public television by having sex with a pig.

At first, the threat is treated like a large, twisted practical joke. And the public, who have been let in on this demand because the terrorist has posted it directly onto YouTube, are initially in favour of the PM's decision to refuse such terms (even though they all share this video through their social media feeds). But when a finger arrives in the post with the threat of more body parts to follow, the nation's opinions change abruptly. Again, the kidnapper shares this information publicly—posting a video on the internet which appears to show the princess' digit being hacked off. And the public, in their concern for the fate of the victim and in their willingness to air their own opinions on what the government should do, continue to virally spread the terrorist's messages through their own social media channels and public conversation. Soon, the whole country is awash with the sentiment that the PM is an idiot for refusing to indulge in this sexual perversion and he's tainted as someone who is more concerned with his own reputation than with the life of an innocent girl.

Finding himself on the receiving end of a barrage of hate, and with no options left, the PM has to swallow the reality of the predicament before him, along with a Viagra, and in a broken, humiliated mess, proceeds to do what needs to be done. As he does so, the vast majority of the U.K. gathers around television sets—in pubs, hospital wards, sitting rooms and on the street pavements outside of their local audiovisual stores—to spectate this live-feed spectacle.

Except that they aren't spectators; they've colluded with this act of terrorism. The general public could have refused to share the initial ransom video, but they don't, and maybe understandably so. But when it comes to the actual "performance", none of them has to meet the ransom demands. Despite the fact that it is being aired on live TV, none of them *has* to watch. They could switch off their TV sets and refuse to be seduced by the terrorist's sick game. They could stop 'hash-tagging' and sharing the terrorist's videos on their social media accounts, thus stemming the flow of the kidnapper's influence and power. But they don't. Instead, they become the audience in attendance, unaware that they're all complicit accomplices in this vulgar act of terrorism.

As I said, the episode's title is 'The National Anthem', and there's probably a purposeful play on words here by the scriptwriter(s). Because maybe a better label on this episode would be *The National Anathema*—the National *Abomination*, the *Nation's Scapegoating*.

Would any of the characters in this fictitious story have seen themselves as being under the influence of evil, or acting as a network of terrorists? Probably not. But when you watch this critically from the perspective of an outsider, it's easy to spot and name the malign stimulus they are all acting under.

Again, it's difficult to admit the evil that influences us until a mirror is lifted up in front of us, exposing our likeness.

Both these particular stories, *Star Wars* and *Black Mirror* 'The National Anthem', stress the same point. They both show us how elusive evil can be, how subtle its influence. Even though we feel that we could all put a face to evil, how many of us would put our own? It's easier to project evil onto others. It's easier to view another individual or people group as doing evil or as being the source of the violence. Even God is scapegoated in this regard. And yet, as we've discovered in the last section, Scripture takes us on the journey of lifting the lid on this idolatry. If the Old Testament didn't do enough in moving us forward in the revelation of God's real nature—a nature which puts forth mercy, a nature which lays down power, a nature which acts in liberating love—then the New Testament closes this loop for good. The Word made flesh, God incarnate, puts the nails into the coffin of our idolatry. Literally.

The crucifixion is the unveiling of our nature, the uncovering of our desire to scapegoat, the revelation of our bondage to Sin, to idolatry. We meet the darkness that lurks within ourselves at the cross of Christ, as we recognise that it is our face behind the mask.

## AGNUS DEI

Jesus has made it all the way to Jerusalem. And, as he had told his disciples many times en route, his journey there has culminated with his own crucifixion.

Stripped naked, Jesus hangs as a spectacle before a world of onlookers. The crowd's motivations for being there are various. Some are his followers, mourning this perceived end to the world-changing movement they had become a part of, mourning the death of the warrior Messiah that God had sent them. Others are there because they were behind the plot to execute this 'blasphemer'; motivated by their jealousy of his popularity and by a concern for their sacred position on God. Others gather because they are the ones who have nailed his hands and feet, following the ordinances of the "divinely appointed" Caesar they serve. And whilst they wait for the inevitable last breath of their empire's victim, they cast lots over his clothing in the hope that their ideas of God will bless them. Others, pulled in by the commotion, have come for the spectacle; with no allegiances to anybody, waiting to see what happens next.

There have been countless books discussing who was strictly to blame for killing Jesus. But Luke, in the book of Acts, quotes the Apostle Peter as saying, 'For Herod Antipas, Pontius Pilate the governor, the Gentiles, and the people of Israel were all united against Jesus…'[225]

This is a *universal anathema*—an act of humanity, as they scapegoat an innocent man in the name of their nationality, their empire's peace, or in the name of God.

Writing many centuries before the crucifixion of Jesus, the prophet Isaiah is said to have foreseen this event when he wrote these harrowing words about the LORD's suffering servant:

> People despised and avoided him,
>> a man of pains,
>> well acquainted with illness.
> Like someone from whom people turn their faces,
>> he was despised;
>> we did not value him.
>
> In fact, it was our disease he bore,
>> our pains from which he suffered;
> Yet we regarded him as punished,
>> stricken and afflicted by God.
> But he was wounded because of our crimes,
>> crushed because of our sins;
>> the disciplining that makes us whole fell on him,
>> and by his bruises we are healed.

We all, like sheep, went astray;

we turned, each one, to his own way;

Yet ADONAI laid on him the guilt of all of us.


Though mistreated, he was submissive

—he did not open his mouth.

Like a lamb led to be slaughtered,

like a sheep before its shearers,

he did not open his mouth.[226]


As this song makes clear, we have a knack of looking upon the crucified Jesus and believing that it is God who is punishing and forsaking him, but it's our crimes that are wounding him, our sins that are crushing him. It is humanity's Sin that Jesus bore, as humanity unloads and transfers its Sin upon him. *We* did *our* violence upon Jesus. We lynched Christ.

In other words, it's not that Christ *becomes* our sin on the cross, and then is rejected by God in our place, therefore making a way for us to be forgiven. But it is rather that Christ *bears* the image of our Sin; Jesus exposes *our* rejection of God's likeness, *our* rejection of God's Kingdom. Jesus' broken, marred and pierced frame holds a mirror before us, unmasking our transgression of the human vocation.

Jesus bore our idolatrous disease. It is our evil, our tendency towards violence and scapegoating that is revealed in the twisted features and broken body of Christ. We would like to pretend that we're the reasonable ones, that we're objective and peace-loving and benign, and that it is God who is cruel, vindictive and to blame for the world's sorrows. But as the prophet Isaiah foresaw, it is our Sin that puts purity and innocence to death.

To a certain degree, the crucifixion of Christ is history's most glorious act of Culture Jamming. God artfully uses the symbol of Rome's peace, a cross—human empire's violent means of enforcing itself—to demonstrate that God is not the violent one at all. We might have cast God as vindictive, malign, distant, angry, vengeful and brutally vicious, but at the cross we see this turned around. God is sharing in the suffering of the oppressed, and it's the human powers which are dealing out the brutality. God is being rejected and forsaken, but it's humanity that's the alienating force.[227] God is dying, and emptying himself sacrificially, but its mankind's leaders scapegoating God, whilst others toss dice in his presence. In the crucified incarnation, the Divine allows humankind to project itself upon him. Our Sin is made manifest in his wounds because, like Abel's blood after being murdered by his brother Cain, Christ's issue of blood attests to humanity's ability to be less than human. The old Latin proverb proves true, *Homo homini lupus est* (Man is wolf to man).[228] We are the wolves, and God's lamb-like posture exposes our hunger for desecration.

Through becoming the victim of mankind, God puts a face and a name to our evil scapegoating. God unmasks our collusion with the dark side. God becomes the black mirror. On the cross, we come face to face with the darkness within us.

The reformed theologian, T. F. Torrance would describe the crucifixion as having both a dark and a light side: the dark side is the shadow that this dastardly act casts upon on our inhumanity, but the light side is the glory of God in his unflinching embrace of mankind.[229] And so, all is not lost in this exposure. Even here, in this disclosure of our Sin, mercy is put forward because God's true likeness is also revealed. Yes, on the cross we witness the blood-spilling, destructive effects of our belief in lies, but we also witness the radical, self-emptying, loving nature of the Divine, as God (to once again echo Torrance), submits to humanity's outrage and bears it all in love.

Jesus' sacrifice is not trying to convince God to approach us, forgive us and heal us. It's not, as some have suggested, that Jesus's death pacifies a vengeful God, allowing God to get past his "problem with us". The Dying Deity is an echo of Eden's 'Where are you?'; it is God, through the body we have broken, pouring out his life in pursuit of us and calling us back into fellowship within the Divine. And so God calls us, as he did with Cain, to listen to the prophetic voice of the blood we have spilt so that we can turn away from our idolatry. Christ's blood, like Abel's blood, certainly testifies to our violence, but it also proclaims a far better verdict on us than Abel's blood does. As the writer of Hebrews reminds us, Jesus's blood does not call out for violent retribution. The blood of Christ speaks forgiveness.[230] And if we choose to listen to it, Jesus' sacrificial issue of blood provides the means for our exodus from the serpent's enslaving, death-dealing lies.

To add nuance to this thought, it's also worth noting what our violence *didn't* do to Christ. Jesus bears the image of our violence and sin, but Jesus doesn't become violent and sinful—Jesus keeps exposing us to the divine image. As the Orthodox Bishop, Kallistos Ware points out in his remarkable book, *The Orthodox Way*:

> At his Agony in the garden and at his Crucifixion the forces of darkness assail him with all their violence, but they cannot change his compassion into hatred; they cannot prevent his love continuing to be itself. His love is tested to the furthest point, but it is not overwhelmed [...]. We should not say that Christ has suffered "instead of us", but rather that he has suffered *on our behalf* [...]; not substitution, but saving companionship.[231]

At the cross, God's raw, life-giving, passion for his creation is exhibited; we see a détournement of our violent symbolism. The cross, an instrument of torture and victimisation, the diadem of human justice, becomes the judgement seat of Christ and the place where forgiveness is dispensed, mercy is put forth and our evil is absorbed. It's where the lies that have enslaved us are put to death, and divine life, love and liberty are made available to us. By his stripes, we are healed. In his wounds, peace (shalom) is extended to a broken world. The call to turn from self, now that we have seen our darkest self, is given and grace for the turning flows.

The cross makes everything clear. The cross kills the lie. God has not estranged himself from us. God is not vengeful. God is not violent. God is not demanding blood before forgiveness can flow. God is not for some, and against others. God is not a tyrant. God is not a Caesar. God is not a Trump. God is not a monster. God is not indifferent. God has not turned away from us in disgust.

God is love.

God is love.

God. Is. Love. [232]

I had only heard about you before,

but now I have seen you with my own eyes.

I take back everything I said,

and I sit in dust and ashes to show my repentance.

-Job 42:5 (NLT, 2015 ed.)

God is Love, and all who live in love live in God, and God lives in them [...].

Such love has no fear, because perfect love expels all fear. If we are afraid, it is for fear of punishment, and this shows that we have not fully experienced his perfect love.

-1 John 4:16b, 18 (NLT, 2015 ed.)

# PART 07 | THE BEGINNING IS NIGH

[W]hat's past is prologue [...].
– Shakespeare[233]

It is possible to believe that all the past is but the beginning of a beginning, and that all that is and has been is but the twilight of the dawn.
– H. G. Wells[234]

But all shall be well, and all manner of things shall be well.
– Julian of Norwich[235]

The end of days will be the end of fear, the end of war; idolatry will disappear, knowledge of God will prevail.
– Abraham Joshua Heschel[236]

# 7.1 | FAREWELL TO RAMBO

As folk legend goes, there was once an old lady who swallowed a fly. We're not sure why she swallowed the fly. Perhaps she'll die?

But then the old lady swallowed a spider—crazy! A spider which wriggled and wiggled and tickled inside her. Apparently, she swallowed the spider to catch the fly. But we're not sure why she swallowed the fly. Perhaps she'll die?

To make matters worse, she then swallowed a bird. A live bird: feathers, beak, talons and all—totally absurd! Rumour has it that she swallowed the bird to catch the spider, which she had swallowed to catch the fly. But none of us know why she swallowed the fly. Perhaps she'll die…

You know this tale, and how it concludes. It's a tale in which the absurdity keeps on growing. After the bird, there's a cat, then a dog, followed by a goat, a cow and finally a side-order of horse—which leads to the death of the old lady, of course.

It's a ludicrous tale, but as a child, I would listen over and over again to the version performed by the legendary Burl Ives. At such a young age, the song infected me with giggles. But when I grew up the laughing stopped, as I began to recognise the powerful allegory hidden within this folk parable. There comes a point when you realise that it's not about an old lady and her bad diet. Instead, it's the tragic story of someone suffering from a malign confusion, in which the perceived solution to her plight is no cure at all, but just a bigger version of the ailment.

When you see this, and then move your gaze away from the song and onto world events, you'll see the same confusion at work. How do we end wars? We have a war to *end* all wars. How do we deal with the threat of nuclear fallout? We build bigger nuclear weapons, and use the threat of those bigger weapons to tell those with the smaller ones to get rid of them. How do we deal with the ever-widening gap between the rich and poor, and between the developed and the developing countries? We continue to trust in and prop up the trickle-down economy that has perpetuated the crisis all the more. How do we deal with the ascending unemployment rate? We generate zero-hour contracts which don't resolve anything, but the reduction in the benefits payout, and the apparent surge in the number of those "employed" makes the world look like a better place (if you only ever look at it through the eyes of data).

How are we taught to deal with hate? We're told to hate the haters.

How do we quench our dissatisfaction with material goods? We're told to grasp for newer goods through lucid advertisements.

How do we aim to develop a more inclusive society? We seek to exclude those who aren't inclusive.

How do we solve our sense of longing for genuine, unconditional acceptance within community? We take to social media, where we shun those unlike us and cultivate an echo chamber for our convictions. Or maybe it's just me?

The list goes on and on…

In the UK we have a way of describing those we see putting this 'Old Lady' mentality in action; we say they're trying to dig themselves out of a hole. But digging is what humanity does best, believing that the cure resembles the cause.

We desire justice, which is a noble desire. Our world needs justice—not in the sense of returning tit-for-tat, but in the sense of things being put right. However, in a world where we swallow spiders in order to catch flies, we'll all eventually end up choking on horses. We can't level the ground by deepening the holes. Nor can we fix the world's problems by mimicking the problems.

Admittedly, there is a certain logic to this way of thinking. After all, this tactic works for snake bites. We use the same venom a victim has been bitten with to develop an *anti*-venom that can be injected as a cure. But, in this case, the cure is not the cause; it's not even the same substance. Anti-venom is an antibody which, though originally derived from exposure to the venom, works to neutralize the effects of the venom. It doesn't continue to dig the hole; instead, it blunts the spade by binding itself to the poison and chemically rendering it harmless. In this sense, anti-venom isn't passive activism; it's a nonviolent, redemptive revolution that plays by a different set of rules than the poison.

## '¡VIVA LA REVOLUCIÓN!'

I believe the Kingdom of God is a similar revolution. It has come to transform and heal the world, but it doesn't play by the same rules as empires or governments. The *Sermon on the Mount* is its manifesto, not the *Art of War*. Following the pattern of its King, the Kingdom flows through the practice of self-emptying, co-suffering, cruciform love.

Through the ministry, cross and resurrection of Jesus, God has launched a new beginning into the world, a new pattern for humanity that echoes the original, ancient vocation. The incarnation is the epicentre of a new way of being more human, a Spirit-filled life, a life based on Jesus' command to 'Love one another, just as I have loved you,' that shows the world that there is another path to follow.[237] And if we allow this Spirit-led way to bind to us, it will neutralize the venomous influences that the serpent's bite has induced.

The beginning is nigh; a new world order has dawned. But the presence of this beginning is also a prophetic witness to the terminus of the old world order. World orders built on greed, tyranny, objectification and dehumanisation will know their end. World systems which perpetuate chaos and death will be swallowed up in life. The man-built walls that have dissected God's sacred garden will crumble, and the false images (the idolatry) that have endorsed these walls and desecrated God's Temple will be unmasked and shown to be nothing but death in disguise. The hope of the prophets will come true; God will reign and dwell with humanity, the world will be full of the knowledge of God's glory, swords and spears will be beaten into ploughshares and scythes, and the world will know everlasting life and shalom. This beginning marks the end of all that ceases to allow creation and humanity to flourish in the life of their Creator.

*However*, although the incarnation launched the dream of God, we still find ourselves caught up in this tension between its birth and its culmination. Yes, God died on the cross, defeating the lies and the dark power that enslaved us. Yes, Jesus rose from the dead, launching a revolution of regeneration into the world. But the world is still fractured, chaos limps on, and things remain far from perfect.

It's within this tension that the church finds its vocation: to be a colony of humanity that announces and exemplifies the Kingdom come in the here and now. But how the church engages in this mission is reflective of how we believe God will bring about the end of the present world order. How we envision God putting the world right—or whether we believe God will destroy this planet and start anew—ultimately feeds back into our present-day ethics.

This topic is crucial to living the dream and will form the substance of the final part of this book, because, ultimately, we exhibit what we hope for. Or to put that another way: *how we wait for the future demonstrates our belief about the nature of the future.* So the question on our lips is: how will this flourishing reality come to full maturity?

The answer's simple—but far from easy to swallow: the *How* has already happened. Jesus' radical act of self-emptying love on the cross has already done it. And when the culmination of the Kingdom transpires, it won't be because God has used violence to conquer violence, or death to overthrow death. Unlike the Old Lady, God's remedy for the world's ailment isn't an attempt to heal it through more forceful and deadlier versions of the problem. God heals the world, God saves the world, God's dream wins the day—as it did in Joseph's time and as it did in the Song of Creation—not because God colludes with or echoes the methods of chaos, darkness and death, but because of the proclamation and creative power of God's unconditional, liberating love.

## COME AGAIN?

Except that some of us aren't excited by this idea. Some of us are not convinced that God is able to save this world we currently live in. I hope I've said enough within the previous parts of this book to get us to rethink our ideas of God scrapping this planet, so I won't go over this again. But sadly, how some Christians envisage God saving this world—putting the world right—reflects more of the Old Lady's practise than it does Jesus of Nazareth's.

I believe in what Christians for many years have called the Second Coming.[238] I place my hope in the Resurrection and in God making his home with his people. However, when some imagine Jesus at his Second Coming, he barely resembles the character he was in his first. Which is shocking, because, as I've laid out in the last chapter, Jesus is *the image of God*. In Christ, God smashes our idolatry by perfectly presenting to us the divine likeness in order that we can know and reflect it in our lives. Through Jesus, we see that God is not violent, but loving, forgiving and merciful.

Maybe this revelation is too much to handle, because some people aren't too keen on the nonviolent Jesus, and so they've reinterpreted Jesus' exhibition of the divine nature as God giving us a final warning before he comes back with the big guns. Some imagine Jesus saying 'I'll be back' like Schwarzenegger's Terminator, and picture the Second Coming as Jesus showing his true colours as he takes up the sword to slaughter those who have refused to fall in line.

In this portrayal of the returning Jesus, he hasn't come to save, but to condemn—a full reversal of his earthly ministry in the first century. But does the same Jesus who critiqued the malign desire of James and John to send fire from Heaven relent and send it, and not solely upon the village that had refused his welcome, but upon the whole world? Does the same Jesus who commands us to love our enemies bend the rules in his own favour and play the hypocrite card? I don't believe so.

Following the writer of Hebrews, I believe that Jesus is the same yesterday, today and forever.[239] In other words, he's not a merciful, forgiving and compassionate healer and life-giver at his First Coming who then transforms into some homicidal bringer of death and destruction in his second. He's either one or the other. And seeing as we have records of the character and missional ethic of his First Coming, I'm going to reject all the conjecture on the Second Coming which contradicts this. At his Second Coming—when the Kingdom dream of God culminates and when every knee will bow—Jesus will still display the humble character and countenance of the Nazarene, not John Rambo. As Jesus himself said, it's an enemy who comes to steal, kill and destroy, whereas he had come to bring life in all its vibrancy.[240]

To make matters worse, certain streams of Christianity, during the past two hundred years, have developed Rapture theology; which envisions scenes which would rival *A Nightmare on Elm Street*. In this theological framework, the Rapture is the moment when God whisks all of his people out of the world before sending great tribulations and violence upon it. It doesn't matter if you're driving a train full of commuters or flying a plane full of SLCs when this happens, either. When it's your time to go—as this mentality paints it—your passengers will be left to die in the wreckage of the aftermath. Such violent ends have inspired Hal Lindsey's *The Late, Great Planet Earth*, and, more recently, Tim Lahaye and Jerry B. Jenkins' best-selling *Left Behind* book series. The latter has even made it to Hollywood in recent years.

To be clear, I'm not into the idea of The Rapture at all. I feel that it's a distortion of the biblical texts and it makes statements about God which are in opposition to the character displayed by Jesus. It's also escapist in its ideology, permitting us to separate ourselves from the world's ailments instead of getting our hands dirty. And as Dr Barbara R. Rossing explains in her amazing book *The Rapture Exposed*:

Christians are not dealt a get-out-of-tribulation-free card to play in the face of the world's suffering and trials [...]. Jesus never asked of God to "Beam me up" from the earth, nor can we. It is the temptation we must resist—as Jesus did. Tribulation is something that has happened and is still happening today for many of God's people in the world. God saves us not by snatching us out of the world, but by *coming into the world to be with us*. This is the central message of Jesus' incarnation and of the Bible.[241]

You would think the Cross of Christ would have made this clear, and stopped us from imagining such savage fantasies, and yet many continue to ignore the revelation given to us and instead place their hope in violence-fuelled ideas of redemption. Personally, I'm going to continue to put my hope in the God shown to us through Jesus, and I refuse to believe that God saves the world by imitating the very problems which plague it.

The way of the Cross is the way of God. Radical, self-emptying love is the pattern through which the world is saved and reconciled. If we can't swallow this, if we can't believe this isn't up to the task at hand and that God needs to resort to violence and right-handed, coercive force to get the job done, then maybe, as we have seen in Part Two, it is we who are ashamed of the Cross of Christ.

God saving the world through violence isn't saving the world at all. It's condemning it to more of the same, for death would still reign in such an economy. But if we believe that God will realise his dream through violent acts, oppression and force, then such beliefs will inevitably feed back into our ethical praxis today. Sadly, the belief in a God who judges the world through violence has led some to exclude, dehumanise, oppress and bully others in an attempt to exemplify now what is to be expected then. Without a clear vision of God's holiness—God's otherness to the methods of mankind—we risk imitating the methods of history's empires. We risk finding ourselves following the Rambo-like methods of Caesar instead of the Lamb-like way of Jesus.

## THE BEAST

We're certainly not the first generation to dwell in this tension between the present world order and the one to come. We're simply the latest in a two-thousand-year-old legacy. The first generation of this legacy (the first-century church) also wrestled long and hard with this problem. So much so, in fact, that an elder within the church, known as John the Seer, felt led by the Spirit to write one of the most controversial letters of history, which we now call the Book of Revelation.

With all its violent imagery, scenes of natural disasters, plagues and a lake of fire, it's easy to read Revelation like an apocalyptic version of the Old Lady's eating habits. And yet, John the Seer isn't writing an ancient *Left Behind* story to scare people into bending the knee to God. John is writing a pastoral letter to encourage believers to remain faithful to the way of Christ in the midst of a world that is steeped in an imperial mindset. As such, the intent behind this letter is to furnish the church of the first-century with a revelation of Christ, not to provide the 21st century with a coded-script of end-time future events.[242]

Revelation is saturated with symbolism, and is a prime example of what some scholars would call an apocalyptic genre of writing that was popular in the Second Temple Period (586 BC – AD 135). You could say that apocalyptic writing is poetry with bite. *Apocalypse* means to reveal, and to doff my cap towards N. T. Wright's analysis, the writers of apocalyptic episodes used vivid cosmic imagery (like earthquakes and the sun turning red) to describe and expose the political and social upheavals of their time.[243] They may speak of the moon becoming darkened, stars falling from the sky, and mountains melting like wax, but these ancient poets weren't describing the end of the space-time universe or expecting mountains to literally melt. Cosmic analogies provided effective descriptions of the theological significance of the world-shattering events around them.

This use of symbolism is an important thing to grasp, because it isn't just the characters within this saga that are symbolic (like Dragons, the Prophet, or the Woman and her Child), but also the events. Knowing this should help us to deliteralise the violent scenes within Revelation and see them as being symbolic of something else. After all, it makes no sense to claim that the personalities are symbolic whilst maintaining that stars crashing to earth, or a lake of fire, are literal.

That's not to say that these symbols don't have real-world referents, though. John the Seer, following tradition, purposely borrows Old Testament apocalyptic imagery to critique the dominant, real-world, empire of *his* time: Rome (which Revelation consistently refers to as Babylon). And in the same way that the prophetic visions of the Old Testament relayed this-world historical events through otherworldly eyes, Revelation was a declaration of judgement on the way in which the current world order functioned. In other words, like his forebears, John is not describing post-mortem judgement events or giving a chronological script for the end of the world. John is describing *this-side-of-life* events that will unfold against the *this-world* powerhouses of humanity.

It takes guts to speak truth to power, and it takes people with allegiances to something greater than their own flag and ethnicity to expose the corruption of the system they currently live in. John the Seer was one of those. In his day, Rome hailed itself as the Saviour of the World, Caesars were worshipped, and progress appeared to take place. But John's not having any of it; his vision provides a divine rebuttal to the narrative that was being spun by Rome's PR team. John doesn't hail Rome as a saviour, but casts Rome as Babylon, a Violent Beast and a Whore. Behind her masks of peace and prosperity, Rome, like others before her and long after her, had risen to glory on the exploitation, subjugation and death of others.[244] John's violent depictions in the Book of Revelation are not literal descriptions of God's violent acts, but, like a literary crucifixion, they are God's unmasking of Rome.

Against the backdrop of its claims of being a glorious, eternal city, John foresees an end to the creation-staining ethos of Babylon (Rome). But what's true of the Roman Empire is true of any world order that perpetuates chaos. As in the story of the Tower of Babel, which we considered within Part Three of this book, Babylon is the inversion of God's kaleidoscopic dream of the Kingdom of Heaven on Earth; an oppressively dominant, wall-building, culturally-genocidal, aggressive human way of gaining and maintaining power. It's self-obsessed, self-deluded and self-worshipping, and has a continual need to accumulate and attain, whatever the cost. Babylon is a world order that is a far cry away from the compassionate, just and benevolent rule that God called humanity to exhibit in the garden.[245] But although such monopolies have no place in the dream of God, this has not prevented people from hailing such imperial methods as the answer to the world's evils. Redemptive violence is an over-subscribed myth.

The problem is that we don't often see how malign the empires we serve can be. There's an illusion and a PR masquerade that is pulled over our eyes; making the countries we belong to seem like glamourous oases for our dreams. Even in our own time, the masks of peace, prosperity and power the Western world, in particular, wears, hide a host of abominations. We appear to be the saviours of the world, but there are others around the globe who have felt the sting of our expansion through sweatshops, human trafficking, arms deals, deforestation and the growing plight of poverty. Even in our own lands, the number of people finding themselves in the margins (homeless, unemployed, and dependent upon a welfare state) increases every decade as those at the top seek to centralise and gather as much power and wealth as possible.

Our nations—or should that also be our corporations, as they seem to carry much of the power today?—are not the saviours of the world, despite all the good we do and appear to do. We often provide aid to the broken systems we have helped create. To stop us from seeing this, though, we are anaesthetised with entertainment and enticed with false hope. Empires love to distract. We may not have a Colosseum, as Rome did, but the promises of glory and spectacle are thrown at us twenty-four seven.

Please don't misunderstand me; I'm not against Entertainment per se—I certainly have my favourite TV shows, books and music. And I'm not blind to the benefits, liberties and stability of where I live in the world. But what does my relative freedom cost everyone else? What does it cost our planet? What *has* it cost? I read journalists like Naomi Klein, Danny Dorling, Chris Hedges and others who unmask our modern world, and I realise that the price tag is much, much higher than I could have imagined.

## THE LAMB

In his book *Reading Revelation Responsibly* (a book I would highly recommend), Professor Michael J. Gorman insists that Revelation should be read as a repetitive, poetic call to the church to be a colony of the Kingdom and not of Rome. The church is to renounce the myth of redemptive violence and trust in (*and* manifest) the way in which God saves and rules the world.

To help convey how this looks, John employs another piece of counter-imperial imagery. Instead of describing a Caesar-like conqueror who is enthroned, John describes the real King of Kings (Emperor) as being a bloodstained, sacrificial lamb. For John, it's Jesus, the Lamb who was slain, who is *the* legitimate ruler and saviour of the world. And all the honours and titles normally reserved for Caesar are given to Christ: it is Jesus who is the origin and terminus of the spectrum of world history, the Alpha and Omega, the Beginning and the End.[246]

Gorman reminds us that the central image of John's letter is not a revelation of a violent, vengeful God, but of a Lamb. God's rule is 'Lamb-like' and God's way of saving the world is cruciform and self-emptying, not domineering. The blood that soaks the White Rider's cloak, in Revelation 19, is his own sacrificial blood, not the blood of his enemies, and justice (putting the world right) is administered by the sword from his mouth (his creative, liberating oration), not through wielding a sword in his hand with a militaristic agenda. To echo the words of N. T. Wright, Jesus' Kingdom of peace, liberty and justice only comes about through means that correspond to its message.[247] The vision of Christ that is presented in Revelation is not at odds with the image of the suffering servant presented within the gospels; the Revelation of Jesus does not resemble John Rambo, but echoes the crucified Nazarene.

Again, John's reminding the church of this posture because he longs for them to exhibit this pattern. They defeat evil not through mimicking it, but through living in a way that testifies to the power of Christ's blood (Christ's loving sacrifice).[248] As Gorman writes:

> Christ conquers by cruciform faithful resistance: not by inflicting but by absorbing violence; not by actually killing but by speaking his powerful word. [...] Christian resistance to empire and idolatry conforms to the pattern of Jesus Christ [...]: faithful, true, courageous, just and nonviolent. It is not passive but active, consisting of the formation of communities and individuals who pledge allegiance to God alone, who live in nonviolent love toward friends and enemies alike [...] and who, by God's Spirit, create mini-cultures of life as alternatives to empire's culture of death.[249]

In other words, we are to be anti-venom in a world full of hate, pain, greed and revenge. We're not to pledge our allegiance to the myth of redemptive violence by swallowing spiders in order to catch flies. We are to witness to the power of redemptive love.

## CHOKING ON HORSES

As strange as it sounds, I'm reminded of a film called *Confessions of a Shopaholic*—an adaptation of the Sophie Kinsella novel of the same name. In the film, Rebecca Bloomwood (played by Isla Fischer), racks up insurmountable debts on her credit cards due to her out-of-control shopping addiction. At one point in the story, as she hits rock-bottom, Rebecca has an apocalypse, a revelation: her eyes are opened to the magnitude of her problem and she screams out her frustration with the stores which once wooed her. She feels cheated and betrayed because the same shops that now send her hate mail used to tell her repeatedly that she was a valued customer. The systems that once enticed her with promises of prosperity and who championed her personal identity and dreams, are exposed for what they are: vampires which thrive through another's demise.

It's this same message Revelation is putting before us; it wants us to see the reality behind our empire's illusions of prosperity and acceptance, and yet we've often read this letter as a divine threat of violence. Revelation is *not* to be seen as hate mail from a God who once loved us. The thrust of Revelation is not the threat of hellfire and damnation, but the hope-filled reminder that God's love endures forever, and that God's love will overcome the powers of Hell.[250]

Imperialism, racism, nationalism, sexism, consumerism, injustice and other such things cannot go on perpetually. At some point, the world orders fuelled by these things will choke on horses. And in Revelation's imagery, the horses we choke on are the self-induced consequences of War, Conquest, Famine, and Death. Evil will choke on itself, and God will save the world from being swallowed up in evil's self-destructive demise.

In chapter 18 of Revelation, John hears a messenger of God declare, 'Babylon is fallen' (echoing Isaiah 21:9 and Jeremiah 51:8).[251] God will liberate the world—both its substance and its people—from the malign, imprisoning dreams of Babylon. And although those who participated in and profited from Babylon's ethic will weep about it, we are encouraged to rejoice. Later on in this extraordinary letter, John will also paint the hope that we will see not only the end of Babylon, but also the end of evil (and the source behind it) and the end of Death itself.

As such, I remain hopeful about the end. I believe God wins. I believe that God ultimately triumphs over evil, chaos and death. I believe that the world will flourish under God's reign. I believe in the marriage between Heaven and Earth, when the curse will be lifted and shalom will be restored. I believe, as the end of Revelation poetically indicates to us, in a City of God—an expansion of God's sacred garden—which radiates with

God's glory. I believe that this city's gates will never be shut (Rev 21:25), and that the leaves of the trees, which grow on the banks of the River of Life that flows from the heart of this world order, are for the healing of all the *nations* of the world (Rev 22:2).

Of course, I have to ask a rather obvious question: who are these nations, these other people, that are outside of this city that represents God's Kingdom? Who are these people before whom God's gates will never close, and to whom God sends healing?

I have a great hunch that God is not forcing his way on people, but also, that there will come a time when people will not be able to fill the world with self any longer. And for those people, those who wish to dominate, to be greedy and violent and who wish to bend the world into their image, such a future—a future where God does not allow oppression, greed and violence to hold sway—will be a living nightmare. Could it be then, that those outside the walls, those who need healing, are those whom God is still trying to reach, those who still need to realise that God's vision for the world is better than their own; those that God will never give up on?

I'm speculating, of course. But I'm moved by hope, an eschatological hope in the ultimate redemption of all things. As heretical as this will initially sound to some people, I believe God will get what he wants. I believe *every* knee will bow and *every* tongue will confess God's lordship. I'm not a pluralist, and I'm not certain that describing myself as a universalist (because of the many meanings it carries) is the best way either. But I'm hopeful that the future is good, because God is good and because the gates of God's city will never close. This doesn't mean that I think ultimate redemption will come easy, far from it. For all of us, the Spirit's call of laying down the Kingdom of Self and taking up the Kingdom of God is no comfortable task. It's a dying process that requires the Spirit's power of resurrection working in us as we resist, or are persecuted by, the world's ever-fading systems of power. But I'm certain that whatever transpires in the finality of this present age and in the fruition of the age to come, will not come to be because all roads lead to God, but because of the all-encompassing victory of Jesus over death and Sin; the Jesus all humanity is called to follow and believe in.

Whatever happens between *now* and the ultimate *then*, our call is to follow Jesus, to trust in his Lamb-like way of salvation and to serve God and humanity as he did. With that in mind, there's another, lesser-known, story of an Old Lady which we can learn a lot from. It goes something like this:

> From the moment that the old, wise woman had begun to load her belongings onto the back of the cart, a crowd had gathered to watch.
>
> "Where are you going?" they asked, as she pulled herself onto the seat and ushered her horse forward.
>
> "To a place of peace, and not fighting", she shouted back.
>
> Wishing to hear more, the curious band of onlookers set off in pursuit.
>
> "A place where competition no longer exists," she continued calling to the throng which was swelling in her wake. "Where striving and the gruelling pursuit of *more* is not required because generosity and contentment flows from every citizen and in every home. A community where mercy and justice reign, and inequality no longer exists. A place where people are valued and not dehumanised, nor treated as commodities. A city of rest and work, of flourishing and life. Where poverty is no more, war is extinct, and love is law."
>
> Captivated by her vision, the whole town was soon in tow with what little belongings they had. Every washerwoman, every Banker, every child and every Landlord. As they left, the promise of a new start rekindled friendships; debts were forgiven, loans were cancelled and old treasures shared without interest. All sang of their glorious new future together as they followed the old woman's cart to the outskirts of their town.

But then the wise woman stopped. Turned her horse and cart about, and began to ride back down the well-trodden and familiar cobbled lane.

When she got back to the centre of the town, she climbed down from her seat, unloaded the cart of her meagre belongings, and started back to the door of her home.

Confused, the crowd asked, "What's wrong?"

"Nothing", she replied with a smile, "we've arrived."[252]

We can all come back from this, Rick Grimes assures us, adding that none of us are too far gone for redemption.

No. Rick Grimes is not a theologian, or a church Pastor, or a real person. But I think his words have weight to them.

Rick Grimes is a main character in one of my favourite TV shows; *The Walking Dead* (TWD). For those who have never heard of the show, TWD is an apocalyptic alternative of our present world, where a viral epidemic has transformed the majority of humanity into walking, flesh-eating zombies. Adding to this epidemic's ferocity is the nature of its transmission; this virus isn't spread through the usual means of being bitten by a zombie. Apparently, in this version of the world, you're already infected. Everyone carries a latent, genetic mutation that is triggered upon death. Anyone whose heart stops beating, regardless of the cause, transforms into a creature that feeds on the life of others.

Now I know what you're thinking: but this isn't your typical zombie-genre trash TV show. And that's mainly because the show's title isn't a description of the dead, but of the living, as they, in their determination to survive, begin to lose all sense of their humanity. The world order they had previously lived under has collapsed; taking all their luxuries, laws and sense of national identity along with it. In this vacuum, the human outlook becomes one of 'Cain versus Abel', as other survivors pose more of a threat than the zombies. Hate, envy, violence, suspicion, division and greed run rife over this dystopian, desolate landscape, to such an extent that the Apostle John's description (in a New Testament letter called 1 John) would be a very apt depiction of the show: 'a person who has no love is still dead.'[253] The survivors may not be zombies, but their hearts have stopped being moved with compassion for others and they're just as cannibalistic as the hungry dead.

Even the group that Rick Grimes leads—the group that the show closely follows—began as a rag-tag bunch of good people who were trying to protect themselves from all the bad people. For the first few seasons, their hope was to find a place where they could live in relative peace and practise the ethos of the old world they had lost. Maybe, in the long run, they reason, given enough time and enough hard lessons, the world will stabilise and return to the way it was. Hence Rick's motivational speech about how it is still not too late for the world to turn back (repent) to the way things were.

However, it's been a good number of seasons since we last heard Rick Grimes speak of his redemptive hope. As the show has progressed, as Rick's group has experienced the harsh, abrasive society they live in, their hope has fallen away. And with it, their active expression of the world order they hoped for has also faded. They too have become untrusting, vengeful and militant. They, too, are dead.

As I said in the last section, what we believe about tomorrow always feeds back into today. This is a truth that always pulls my mind to these apocalyptic films and TV shows because, more often than not, these stories seem to paint a bleak picture of the future. If you take a handful of examples, you'll see what I mean. In the depictions of such films as *Children Of Men, The Walking Dead, Elysium, Mad Max, The Terminator, The Book of Eli*—if you cast aside the science-fiction for the moment—the writers seem to suspect that whatever road we venture down, it will still result in a world filled with war, poverty, prejudice and injustice, because the dominant ethic will still be one of man versus man, brother versus brother, Cain versus Abel.

In reality, the writers of these films aren't attempting to predict the future of the world; they're trying to get us to take a look at our humanity. They're aware that the nature of our humanity stems from the nature of our hopes, and they're calling us to take responsibility for the future we are nurturing in our present-day behaviour.

In other words, are we, like the early Rick Grimes, convinced that this world can change, and are we able therefore to exhibit that change? Or are we more like the later Rick Grimes, who, unconvinced that the world's destiny is good, plays by the current world's rules and allows the way it is run to infect his heart?

## ARE WE THERE YET?

For me, the thrust of this question is the underlying stimulus behind the Apostle John writing to the early church in the New Testament letter entitled, 1 John.

No, John wasn't writing his *The Walking Dead* fan-theories to the early church. But like John the Seer in writing Revelation, John the Apostle is trying to pastorally guide the church in its praxis, as it exists in the tension between the birth of God's dream (through the incarnation) and its eventual culmination.

One of John's key themes is to encourage the church to keep looking at Jesus, to trust in and reflect the image of God we see being made manifest in Jesus' life. There's a problem with this though, as some other voices had crept into the church claiming that Jesus wasn't God in the flesh. This teaching suggested that Jesus wasn't fully God *and* fully human, but just an ordinary human being that God (as a Spirit) selected as a vessel. In some sense, this portrayal of Jesus makes him look more like the Old Testament judge Samson, who would, on occasion, have God's power surge through him with extraordinary effects. Like Samson then, Jesus could be viewed as a human *possessed* by the Spirit of God, but he wouldn't be considered as God incarnate.

Such ideas allow people to take Jesus' life and dissect it into two pieces; 'this bit was God in action, and that other stuff was the fallible man, Jesus.' This then wreaks all sorts of havoc with how we are meant to imitate what we have seen as disciples, as we attempt to image God in the world. Did Jesus reflect and embody God's full nature, or was Jesus just another refraction and distortion of the full truth? If Jesus' life is something we can dissect, in order that his humanity can be discounted, then we inevitably lose our benchmark for what a human life of love, a life that honours God, a life that best expresses God's nature and dream, looks like. We're left stumbling in the dark because if Jesus isn't it, has the Kingdom come at all? Are we still waiting for divine life? Are we left to sing Johnny Mathis' *When A Child Is Born* forever?

I really hope not.

So the Apostle is writing to encourage these believers to hold onto the truth that they have been taught, and have already experienced, and not to be deceived by these false, 'Jesus is not the Messiah' (Anti-Christ) ideas. John is reminding the church he loves of the Jesus he has personally walked with, touched and listened to, saying, 'This one who is life from God was shown to us, and we have seen him. [H]e *is* the one who is eternal life'[254]

For John, Jesus is the future reality coming into the present. He is Eternal Life—He is the age to come. Jesus' arrival has shattered the old world order, which is now fading away, and a new world order has arrived. So we don't have to stumble in the dark, but we can walk in the light of Jesus' Kingdom example and life. And because we belong to Jesus, we are, to use John's words, to 'stop loving this evil world and all that it offers you...'[255]

When John talks of *not loving the world*, he's not talking about creation. Nor is it the world of Art, Technology, Science or people. He's speaking of the systems and ideas that influence how the world is run. In other words, John is calling the church out of the old world and into the future.

Unlike us today, John doesn't attempt to predict the nature of the future. He paints no imaginative, futuristic cityscapes, nor does he attempt to guess at what technological innovations there'll be. Like the writers of apocalyptic TV shows, John's more concerned with the nature of the *future humanity*. So when John describes what lies ahead for us, he paradoxically points backwards to the incarnation of God in Christ. 'We can't even imagine what we will be like when Christ returns', John says, 'But we do know that when he comes, we will be like [Jesus], for we will see him as he is.'[256]

John is saying that at the end of it all, humanity, like Jesus, will embody the dream of God on Earth; we will reflect the divine image perfectly. And because of this—because we will look like that kind of humanity *then*—John encourages the church to also pursue the way of Jesus *now*, in this life

In 1 John 3:3, John says something which might seem unusual. He says that those who believe that we will look like Jesus one day will keep themselves pure. The Greek word translated as *pure (hagnos)* shouldn't be twisted by those who think this is about some modern 'purity culture'. This word is better understood as *chaste*. It's not about trying to keep ourselves squeaky clean, but keeping ourselves *reserved* (consecrated) for a purpose.[257] There's old-world marriage symbolism here, that when two people prepared for marriage, then their lives prior to the actual ceremony spoke of the marriage that was to come. Their present reality spoke of their future reality.

As John goes on to say in the third chapter of his letter, if we don't believe that our personal future—that humanity's corporate future—looks like the humanity we see displayed in Jesus, then ultimately we'll carry on in Sin; we'll carry on in our violent, idolatrous fashion and be unfaithful to the ancient vocation to love. Without taking our betrothal seriously, we'll imitate Cain instead of Christ.

Cain, John says, hated his brother and became an instrument of evil and ultimately a zombie to his impulse to dominate. And in this *death-life*—a life void of self-emptying love for others—Cain perpetuated death by killing his brother, Abel.[258] In contrast to this, John encourages us to pursue the way of self-emptying love in this present age, telling us that we do so because we know what love looks like, and what lengths love goes to, because 'Christ gave up his life for us. And so we also ought to give up our lives for our brothers and sisters.'[259]

To rephrase John's message; we are to be a faithful embodiment of the marriage of Heaven and Earth. Our lives and our allegiances belong to love, because the future belongs to love.

Maybe you laughed at that? I wouldn't blame you if you did. I'll be straight with you: on some days, it makes me want to laugh, too. But could it be that we, like Rick Grimes, Cain and the church in John's day, have allowed ourselves to become blinded by cynicism and now find ourselves stumbling in the dark? To hope is, after all, a revolutionary act. The thing is, if I can be convinced that something terrible is going to happen then I'll always prepare for it by altering my habits, choices and lifestyles dramatically for what is to come. And if I can be motivated to prepare for a future that is worse, or that has the same problems as today, then what about a future which is better? Shouldn't I prepare for this? If I don't, then the lack of any shift in my present-day praxis voices what I believe about the future; I'm expressing my doubt in this world being any different.

What if the future of the world doesn't belong to hate, violence, greed, prejudice and injustice? What if the future doesn't belong to those who want to live like Cain? What if the ultimate future of the world belongs to the lamb-like love that is shown to us in the life and death of Jesus? If we believe in a future without death, without tears, without war, without hate, without corruption, then shouldn't we prepare for that now? Shouldn't this stop us living like Cain because we realise there's ultimately no future, no eternity, in that dead lifestyle?

## A COLONY OF LIGHT

John isn't the only Apostle trying to guide the church through this tricky terrain of *now* and *then*. Paul the Apostle repeatedly touches on it in his own writings.

In particular, in his letter to the believers at Philippi, Paul asks whether there's any hope in belonging to Christ. And if there is, then the church is to live in accordance with this future hope. To paraphrase Paul, he instructs them 'to love each other; stand together and not apart. Stop being motivated by your own selfish ambition and vanity. Be humble. Stop viewing others as either inferior or superior (in fact, get rid of the human league table altogether). And all of you be eager to remember what is important to others, whilst being willing to forget what's important to you.'[260]

As you can see, this isn't an imperial, Cain-like mentality. Such advice flies in the face of those voices (including those from within the church) that encourage us to do whatever we feel, whenever we feel like, with no consideration for anybody else. Paul was calling the church to exhibit God's cruciform way, and in order to make his point, Paul, just like John did, points back to Christ's own attitude by quoting an early Church hymn:

> Though he was God,
>
> he did not demand and cling to his rights as God.
>
> He made himself nothing;
>
> He took the humble position of a slave and appeared in human form.
>
> And in human form, he obediently humbled himself even further by dying a criminal's death on a cross.
>
> Because of this,
>
> God raised him up to the heights of heaven
>
> and gave him a name that is above every other name,
>
> so that at the name of Jesus every knee will bow,
>
> in heaven and on earth and under the earth,
>
> and every tongue will confess
>
> that Jesus Christ is Lord,
>
> to the glory of God the Father.[261]

It's hard not to see echoes in this poem of what John the Seer was telling us in Revelation about the Lamb of God.[262] This hymn is not about Jesus taking a break from being God. As we saw in Part Two of this book, God has always laid down the power to dominate—God doesn't cling to and demand his rights as God. God doesn't use his status as God as a means of manipulating or coercing people to do what he wants. And in Jesus, God gave us the perfect exhibition of this cruciform nature.

According to this Hymn (and the Gospels) Jesus, in his equality with God, didn't see this equality as something to take advantage of and exploit people through. Unlike many who have risen to power or believed themselves to be of divine stock and status, Jesus, who was actually divine, didn't try and conquer the world through military might or spectacle.[263] For Jesus—to paraphrase the Dutch priest, Henri Nouwen—there were no countries to be conquered, or ideologies to be enforced, or any people to be subjugated. There were only children, women and men, who needed to be loved. Unlike Caesar, Jesus used power to *serve* humanity, and never demanded tribute.

As we look upon the incarnate God, voluntarily dying upon the cross, we should realise that this is the true meaning of who God is. Through the act of self-emptying love, all power, all glory, all tribute and all authority belongs to Jesus. And one day, *every* knee will bow in allegiance to God—not out of terror or subjugation, but from the realisation that God, by not imposing his right to rule, is the only one who is truly worthy of all praise and honour.

Again, Paul's reason for reminding the church of this cruciform posture of God is because he wants them (and, by extension, us) to reflect it. It's this theology of God that defines our ethics and informs us of how we are to implement (work out) this salvation (saving work) of God in our world today. But Paul, more than anyone, knows that this feat is only possible if we allow God's Spirit to work through us.[264]

It goes without saying, that living a cruciform life—a life which doesn't seek to grasp at status or dominance, or to imitate the dog-eat-dog world around us—doesn't come naturally. We cannot be divine image bearers on our own. Bearing the divine image means being infused with and led by God's life.

Paul also instructs the church to refrain from complaining and arguing (which usually stem from a desire to grasp for power and dominance). Instead, '[we] are to live clean, innocent lives as children of God in a dark world full of crooked and perverse people. [Letting our] lives shine brightly before them.'[265] Like John's use of the word *pure*, Paul's use of the word *perverse* is also prone to being misread, as we fill in the meanings of both words with our own, diametrically opposed definitions of what classifies as pure or perverse behaviour. But we can't read our own moral whims, based on the lens of our own culture, into either of these words. The Greek word Paul uses is *diastrepho*, and it means *twisted*—or more accurately: *internal looking* and *self-seeking*. Hopefully, you can see how this fits with the human story of turning our backs on the vocation to be God's image bearers in the world. Paul is saying that in a world that had become dark and chaotic through self-seeking, we must be light by becoming self-emptying.

This luminous life is not tyrannical. This radiant way of living doesn't use its power, its titles, or its authority and rank to enclose the world within its will. This life imitates God and pours itself out on behalf of the world. This life is Christ-like and anti-Caesar.

Because the church of history couldn't grasp this reality, the failed project known as Christendom was spawned. We hungered for imperial power and militant rule, so we colluded with governments and empires. Sure, there will be some voices saying that it wasn't all bad. But the history of Europe, through the voices of the deprived and the oppressed, speaks clearly enough of the brutality of a church possessed with the desire to grasp for power. More than Abel's blood, the blood of the Dark Ages testifies to the church's perverse tendency to image Cain. In short, we exhibited an infatuation with power that was Anti-Christ and Caesar-like.

Paul, from personal experience, knows that dominance and violence don't save the world or reflect God's rule. Prior to becoming a follower of Jesus, he used violence to prevent the first-century church from speaking about Jesus. Until, that is, he had a dazzling vision of Jesus that turned his world upside down. The encounter he had with Jesus, and the revelation of his sacrifice on a cross, totally transformed Paul's picture of what God is like and how God rules. Paul, writing his letter to Philippi from prison, had transformed into someone who was willing to suffer on behalf of others, instead of using his authority to impose suffering on others.

Like Paul, we are to be inspired to imitate God's use of power; living a life of service and self-giving love, as seen in the life, death and resurrection of Jesus. Living this way humiliates the strong-armed use of power around us in our imperial age.

'Above all,' Paul counsels the church, 'you must live as citizens (a colony) of heaven, conducting yourselves in a manner worthy of the Good News about Christ'.[266] As we fix our thoughts on the future—on what is true, honourable, lovely and beautiful—we are to reflect what we see into the present.[267] But if we don't—if all we see is what the world is like now, instead of what it can and will be—then, like Rick Grimes, we risk falling back into the Cain versus Abel system of rule. Without looking at how God reigns, we will operate under the confusion of the Old Lady, sending the scales of injustice deeper into inequality and self-absorption, and shunning the work of being peacemakers.

Contrary to what those who believe in the Rapture espouse, the Spirit of God doesn't take us away from the world, but deeper into its darkest recesses in order that God's light and hope can be shed there. So I have to ask: Have we turned inward and become perverse, instead of turning outward and becoming compassionate? Have we sought self-righteous purity and moralism more than chastity to the Lamb?

# 7.3 | THE GOLDEN AGE?

I know many of our churches aren't empires in the geographical sense, but do we hunger for power and influence? Do we long for control? Do we desire tribute and wealth? Like the ancient rulers of Christendom, do we believe that the church's political and material promotion in the world is a sign of God's Kingdom on Earth? Do we think that God's Kingdom dream is a 'better' version of empire, instead of an alternative to it? Even though we might have accepted that the mission of God is not about *our* personal transcendence or escape from this world, do we believe that it is still about our ascent and promotion within this world? Instead of seeking the lower places—the posture of service toward humanity—are we still seeking seats of honour?

Is it possible that when some Christians in the West anxiously talk of losing their Religious Liberty, they're revealing that they're worried about losing their religion's seat of privilege at an empire's table? Maybe—I suggest, treading as delicately as I can—losing our seat would help us speak up for the voiceless and oppressed, because only then would we be able to truly see, hear and empathise with those who are oppressed? But I've digressed.

To a certain extent, our theology textbooks already betray the answers to all of the questions above.

When I was training for ministry, there was one particular heading in my Old Testament Survey books that stuck out like a sore thumb. It's not limited to textbooks either. I see this heading cropping up in study Bibles and general writing on Christian ethics.

The heading is this; *The Golden Age of Israel.*

'Golden Age'—that's saying something. Not so much about the actual period in Israel's history, but about *our* reading of that history and *our* aspirations for the future. After all, this isn't a term the Bible uses to describe this specific period. We—the West—have put this name on it. And when we used the label *The Golden Age of Israel,* it revealed a lot about how we believe the Kingdom of God will arrive, look and function. Like an ancient Rorschach test, what we see in this era of history reveals more of our heart's desire than of the desires of God's heart.

For those who are confused right now as to what this is, the title of the 'Golden Age' is often applied to the reigns of Israel's most famous monarchs, King David and his son, King Solomon.

During the reigns of these two rulers, the nation of Israel appeared to hit its peak, politically, economically, territorially. Under David, the tribal system of Israel was centralised under one monarch, and the city of Jerusalem became the centre point of the Israelite Kingdom. Not only did David politically unify his own nation, but due to his military prowess, local, non-Israelite nations also came into the fold, through either political allegiances or conquest.

Under Solomon, the wealth of the kingdom grew substantially. And as the wealth and riches rolled in, the influence and fame of Solomon grew as well, as many of the world's nations came and paid him homage and tribute, or so we're told. With all this wealth and resource at his fingertips, Solomon set about the grandest construction scheme since the nation's birth. Not only did he construct himself a fine palace, but, following the dream of his father, Solomon also had the first Temple constructed. This wasn't just some dainty little affair; this Temple spoke of the opulence of Israel, and the God who had apparently raised them to such heights. We're talking golden instruments, statues and wall coverings! You've seen nothing like this on MTV's *Cribs*, I assure you.

Prior to the Temple, God's presence had dwelt in a tent called *The Tabernacle*. The Tabernacle had been moved throughout the wilderness years, but was permanently pitched at Shiloh once the people of Israel had settled in Canaan. But Solomon's tactic of building a Temple, following his father's initiative of bringing the Ark of the Covenant to Jerusalem, meant that you now had to travel to the capital to meet with God and make your sacrifices. So not only did the Davidic Age centralise the political power, it also moved the religious power into its courts. In David and Solomon, religious and political power became bedfellows.[268] And the rest of the story following their era, and how this entanglement caused problems for Israel, is full of trends that went from bad to worse. But I'm jumping ahead to stories I won't touch on here.

The age of David and Solomon is famous in the biblical narrative. And yet, it was far from perfect. If we're looking at this period as God's dream becoming reality, then we need to look again.

As we saw from Part Six, David, according to the Jewish historians who wrote the book of Chronicles, was prohibited by God from building a Temple due to his bloody hands. He was as brilliant at deriving war strategies as he was at penning Psalms. And that should worry us.

Solomon, despite all his wisdom and wealth, wasn't any better. Under Solomon, slavery boomed. The foreigners, whom the Law of Moses said must be treated with respect, soon found themselves being involuntarily conscripted into Solomon's ever-growing labour force.[269] The first Temple, whether we care to admit it or not, was built using slavery. Not only did slave labour boom, but Solomon's stockpile of war weapons (chariots, horses, soldiers) also grew, and although he didn't draft any of his own countrymen into forced labour (or perhaps he did, as we'll see in a moment), he did draft them into his standing armies. To top it all, Solomon also traded in weapons of warfare with the Egyptians, the Hittites and the kings of Aram.[270] In other words, like most powerful nations today, Solomon sold arms—he empowered wars in other territories.

And, dare I add, the plight of women wasn't great either in this era. Due to either political allegiances via marriage, or just plain patriarchal dominance, both of these men contributed their fair share toward the objectification of women. David, it is said, had quite a number of wives and concubines, but it is written that Solomon had seven hundred wives and three hundred concubines![271]

A long time before all of this, the prophet Samuel had warned the people of Israel of what would happen if they ever had a king: Sons would be drafted into the military, daughters would be taken as trophies, and the country's resources—food, materials, animals, land—would all go as tribute to the king's household.[272] Every one of these predictions was fulfilled under David and Solomon. Strangely, to some extent, Israel's first king, Saul, did a better job than his successors. But this apparent "Golden Age" was only the start of the growing corruption and subsequent oppression that the people of Israel experienced at the hands of those who led them.

Ultimately, David and Solomon followed the ways of the empires that surrounded them. They saw what they did and had, and followed suit, conforming to the customs and behaviour of their world order.

What's most striking is that it was only the *foreign rulers* that admired and coveted Solomon's commonwealth, whilst his own citizens despised it. Immediately after his death, the people of Israel cried out to Solomon's heir, Rehoboam, for relief, claiming that Solomon had been a tyrant who had put them under harsh labour demands and heavy taxation.[273] Rehoboam's refusal to grant their request for compassion resulted in a split of the Israelite Kingdom that would never heal.

Heavy taxes.

Misogynistic objectification.

Slavery.

Military domination and arms deals.

Whose idea of paradise is this?

If it's ours—if this is what we think the Golden Age is a restoration of— then we need serious heart surgery.

When you think about it, this "Golden Age" isn't all that dissimilar to what some say is the ethos behind the "Make America Great Again" campaign, or the goal of most world super-powers. It's an era forged through military conquests and dominance, it's politically centralised, economically wealthy, and it boasts the ongoing spread of its extension through the construction of fine buildings (whose doorways give shelter to the homeless and marginalised that aren't allowed in them). Such an empire is the envy of the world, and yet it's built on the death or subjugation of its enemies, the removal of people's liberties, heavy taxation of the oppressed (both at home and away) and the objectification of its citizens.

Christendom didn't look all that different in its vision than Solomon's empire. For some, this is what "blessing" looked like. For some, the 'Christianization' of the world would happen the same way: conquer, subjugate, tax and rule. And the more control we took, the more our idea of 'the divine right to rule' came with it. Such dominance, we thought, could only have been given to us from God. Many ruling super-powers of the past, having all these hallmarks of wealth, buildings and territorial power, were also quick to claim that they had risen to power by divine appointment. Surely, we thought, this is what God wants for the Church; this is how God wishes to see his dream come to pass?

But whose dream is this; God's or man's?

Is this the Kingdom, or is it more of Babel?

Jesus challenged some of his fellow Jews for having the same perception of what God's Golden Age would look like. At one point, Jesus, referring to himself, told his audience that someone far greater than Solomon was amongst them.[274] In other words, a more glorious vision of God's Kingdom had arrived. But they refused to listen to him; they found it difficult to believe Jesus was greater than Solomon. After all, where was the political power? Where was the military might? Where was the tribute from other nations? Where were the finery, the palaces and the wealth?

The dream of God was among them, and they missed it because their vision of the future was framed by the idea of dominance and wealth.

We may scoff at their ignorance and foolishness, but are we any different in our expectations?

When I look at some of the Mega-church building projects and the wealth they contain, or when I hear what some prosperity teaches spout, or when I listen to the undercurrent of those who yearn for Christendom long gone and who wish to 'take this land back for Jesus'; or when I see the glint of desire that sparks in the eyes of people as they hear about the wealth and power of Solomon…, I often conclude that we're no different at all.

What kind of future does our national vision, or our own individual dreams, or even our local church's vision paint? Does it resemble the heartache of God for captives to be released and the oppressed liberated? Or is our vision drenched in the human saliva of the Davidic Golden Age? If we're honest with ourselves, we would see that Jesus's Kingdom Manifesto doesn't match with our fantasies about what 'running the show' looks like.

# 7.4 | AN UPSIDE DOWN MANIFESTO

You may think that Jesus says nothing against these imperial urges of ours, but you'd be mistaken, especially when we consider the contents of the most famous sermon(s) in history.

The Sermon on the Mount and the Sermon on the Plain are Jesus' contrast between imperialistic values and the values of the Kingdom of God. This famous manifesto can be found in both Matthew's and Luke's gospels, and we've already looked at a good portion of Luke's Sermon on the Plain in Part Four of this book, when we looked at Jesus' call for us to love our enemies.[275] But we're going to dive into this important text one final time.

Both of Jesus' sermons commence with what are known as the *Beatitudes*. But Luke's Sermon on the Plain has a more condensed section of verses that follow the pattern '*Blessed are those who* _____' in comparison to Matthew's Sermon of the Mount, and to this Luke appends a section of verses which follow another pattern: '*Woe to those who* _____'. The New King James translation puts them this way:

> Blessed are you poor,
>> For yours is the Kingdom of God.
> Blessed are you who hunger now,
>> For you shall be filled.
> Blessed are you who weep now,
>> For you shall laugh.
> Blessed are you when men hate you,
>> And when they exclude you,
>> And revile you, and cast out your name as evil,
>> For the Son of Man's sake.
> Rejoice in that day and leap for joy!
>> For indeed your reward is great in heaven.
>> For in like manner their fathers did to the prophets.

> But woe to you who are rich,
>
> > For you have received your consolation.
>
> Woe to you who are full,
>
> > For you shall hunger.
>
> Woe to you who laugh now,
>
> > For you shall mourn and weep.
>
> Woe to you when all men speak well of you,
>
> > For so did their fathers to the false prophets.[276]

These words are of great importance to the tension we find ourselves living in. For those who think being favoured by God means having fine buildings, political clout and great wealth, this section turns that imperialist way of thinking on its head.

To make that clearer to us, the word *Bless* that Jesus uses here is not conveying the sense of *to bless*; to wish for something good to happen in someone's life. Neither is this a first-century version of the modern, patronising 'Aww, bless' when we encounter someone who's down on his or her luck. If the gospel writer transmitting Jesus' message had wanted to convey that idea—the idea of a blessing to come, or wanting to see something blessed—he would have used the Greek word *eulogeō*. Instead, Jesus uses the word *makarios*, which isn't about invoking a blessing, but spelling out the blessèd state people are *already* experiencing.[277]

The first statement ('Blessed are the poor...') affirms the awareness of triumph and position that already exists, whilst the second statement ('For yours is the Kingdom of God') affirms the future, the hope, that allows that sense of victory to exist in the present. Or, to say that in the way that we've already said it earlier in this chapter, their view of the future feeds back into their present. The poor rejoice now because they know that they will receive the Kingdom of God, and they know that those who think that they're building it through their subjugation of the poor won't. They know their status in God's Kingdom, and they are blessed by it.

This may seem backwards to us, I know. We prefer to receive first, and then we'll rejoice afterwards (as long as we're happy with what we've given). And even when we do know that something is on its way, we're normally discontented and agitated until it arrives.

As a child, I'd happily wait all morning for my parents to prepare a Sunday roast by feeding my anticipation on the aromas flowing from the kitchen. Nowadays, I'm impatient with the microwave because it takes seven minutes to warm up the pre-prepared pizza I bought at the local corner shop. In such a hyper-speed age, waiting seems like hard work. Convenience is the way we like it, and hope is something that is in short supply. We want it now. We've been taught that we can have it now. And we're not happy until we've got it. Having it *later* can cause us to have a crisis of faith.

This could be the key reason that the prosperity/power versions of the gospel have spread and reached such epidemic proportions; its message endorses and manipulates our consumer patterns of thinking. Instead of calling us to hope and to exhibit and rejoice in that hope, they've encouraged us to be discontented and to grab.

Sure, some prosperity streams don't strictly state that we receive before we rejoice. Some teach it the other way around: rejoice first and then you'll receive. But this isn't what Jesus is saying, either. He's not teaching, 'Praise first and then you'll be paid'. He's not saying to the poor, 'Cheer up, and then you'll get the Kingdom!' He's stating that those who are assured concerning what God will do in the future are blessed with a sense of confidence in the present. They're not fearful, they're trusting.

We've been taught to fear, instead of how to trust. This teaching comes not only through the teachers of the "prosperity gospel", but equally through our media advertisements. In order to motivate us into buying things, corporations have had to convince us that we are already lacking in some way. We have become indoctrinated with the terror of being left behind, not only through the ideas of Rapture Theology, but also in the everyday sense of the term.

Fear is what drives the economics of most empires: fear that there is not enough for us; fear that we'll be overlooked; fear of insignificance; fear of losing our personal/national power, position, prosperity, etc. Fear leads to irrationality. Fear leads to greed. Fear leads to violence, hate, tribalism and suffering. Fear leads us into a dark way of being human, to riff on the oracle Yoda's ideas. Fear has fuelled the rat-races and power-plays of every human micro-kingdom or empire. Fear causes us to grab, like a mob of consumers on a Black Friday shopping spree, instead of being content or generous.

The Beatitudes call us away from these inclinations towards Self-help and Help-yourself. In place of an economical lifestyle that encourages us to grab-what-we-can, we are to be motivated by the politics of God's Kingdom. Being blessed—trusting in God's triumph—causes us to take a different trajectory in comparison to the power games that the little emperors of this world play. And because we place our hope in this blessing, we don't live out of fear, we trust in love.

Having said all that, Jesus' sentiments about the plight of the poor may seem a little heartless to us. To be clear here, Jesus is not being a sadist. Jesus is not saying that poverty is great. He's not telling the poor to stop complaining about being poor, and start being happy about it instead—absolutely not. Jesus was angry at injustice and he spoke out against it many times. We're not called to ignore it either.

Those poor that are blessed aren't rejoicing at being poor. They're blessed through the knowledge that God's way will eventually win out and that the hierarchies that have produced their plight will be overturned. Instead of chasing a position in the current system, using this current world order's means, they're trusting in their status in God. They're taking heart in their trials and sorrows because they believe that through Jesus, God has overcome the world.[278]

Such hope is not a pipe-dream that has been conjured up to mute dissenting voices; Jesus is not out to silence or negate the voices of those who have been sidelined or subdued by the systematic evils of the world. This isn't a placebo-promise that drugs those with few freedoms to make them accept their lot in life. Neither are Jesus' words to be taken as granting permission or advocating tolerance for abusive circumstances. Nor is this a motto which discourages us from working towards justice, as if we should dismiss tackling poverty because that will dissolve the "blessèd" status with which some have been "gifted".

The Beatitudes are about redemptive hope, a prophetic hope that emerges from a Spirit-led imagination. This divine hope is a rebuttal to passivity in the face of injustice, and the catalyst for redemptive action and song in those who hold to it. This hope inspires the same kind of faith that the Creation Poem kindled in those living in the shadows of the Ancient Near East's oppressive social narratives; similarly, we learn that we belong to a world formed in love by a loving God, not by chaos, so that our life's trajectory and value are shaped by this love, not by chaos. This real, living hope, birthed from a vision of God's Kingdom reality, allows us to rise above our Empire-induced status and expose the lies upon which the hierarchies of the world have established themselves. We know that the oppressive powers of the world do not speak for God; they are not representative of God's order and intent. Theirs *isn't* the Kingdom of Heaven.

This hope helps us persevere through hardship, as we ally ourselves to God's dream and exhibit the world order that history will culminate in. Knowing that we are not fighting a losing battle keeps us pressing forward against the systems of oppression that portray themselves as permanent. Against such claims of permanence, we declare that this isn't the way it ought to be and this isn't the way that it will continue to be. We know the future, and we know that the darkness around us—the darkness that masquerades as immovable and immutable—has no future. And we are to punch holes in the darkness that blinds others in despair by being salt and light in a world enveloped in shifting shadows (as Jesus calls his disciples to be in the words which follow Matthew's account of the Beatitudes).

Without such hope, without a vision of a differing way, without knowing we are more than the categories into which the world has pigeon-holed us, we inevitably revert to imitating the way in which the world functions instead of being transformed by the Spirit of God (Romans 12:2). We will become chaotic, and not creative. We will lose our salty, redemptive flavour. Like Rick Grimes, or the Old Lady and her eating habits, or Solomon in all his opulence, we will remain part of the problematic loop, helping the world spin through yet another cycle of oppression.

If unchecked by the truth of our God-given, blessèd vocation, all we'll desire to do is to take over and be on top. All we'll build is more Golden Ages, and not the Age of God. All we'll strive to become is the oppressor of our oppressors. But church, we cannot love others and subjugate others simultaneously. As my friend Fr. Ryan Cook once said in conversation, 'We don't just overthrow the system, but we seek to reconstitute our very way of being human, offering a vision of a world soaked in shalom, a world where violence ceases.'[279]

Living in the light of such hope isn't without risk though. This faith has a cost. In refusing to play by the world's rules, as we wait and work for this world's way to be overturned, we risk becoming destitute, persecuted and cursed. As we express the future in the present, as we announce the beginning of a new order, we risk not looking like Solomon in all his finery, but like Jesus upon a cross.

What I want you to see is that what Jesus does in the 'Blessed are' statements is radical; he aligns the heart of God's Kingdom with those who have been marginalised and exploited by the current power structure. God identifies with the plight of the poor, the vulnerable, the victimised and the humiliated, and distances himself from those who would otherwise claim to have God on their side. And in case we fail to grasp this, Jesus' list of Woes also makes this abundantly clear.

## WOE IS ME

Like the previous list, this list may also worry us. What's Jesus got against those who laugh, for example? And is it wrong to be satisfied, or to have money? As with the state of being blessed, we could misunderstand this list if we're not careful to understand the context.

To help us grasp this context, it will prove helpful for us to go back in time to another Jewish prophetic voice. Way back in the sixth century BC, roughly contemporary with the prophet Jeremiah, we find the voice of Habakkuk.

The once glorious empire that was birthed and seemed to be flourishing under David and Solomon, has had a rocky road ever since. Its citizens have not only had to face the danger of numerous foreign invasions, but, under the weight of a corrupt monarchy, they've also had to endure cruelty and oppression. By the time of Habakkuk, Israel was facing the imminent threat of the Neo-Babylonian Empire coming down upon them. Reeling from the injustice of all this, Habakkuk has a heart-to-heart with God about the state of the world and Israel's place within it. This short, self-titled book of the Old Testament is the record of Habakkuk's totally relatable complaint to the Creator.

In the second chapter, God responds to Habakkuk's complaints by describing the condition and fate of both Israel's and Babylon's oppressive leadership, and their corrupt, imperial practices. (Incidentally, but on topic, this response from God causes Habakkuk, who was once angry at God, to offer up a song of praise for the salvation that was now on its way. Habakkuk *rejoiced*, and was *blessed* by what God was *going* to do.)

God says to Habakkuk, 'Look at the proud! They trust in themselves, and their lives are crooked [perverse—like what we looked at in a previous section]; but the righteous will live by their faith. Wealth is treacherous, and the arrogant are never at rest. They range far and wide, with their mouths opened as wide as death, but they are never satisfied.'[280]

That's a pretty apt description of the self-indulgent and ravenous consumer culture that exists within imperial thinking. But God doesn't stop there. God then goes on to spell out the charges against the oppressive elite more clearly, with his own list of woes, summarised as follows:

Woe to those who get rich through exploiting others.[281]
[cf. *Jesus: Woe to you who are rich.*]

Woe to those who expand their cities (lust for authority and domination/empires) through violence and corruption.[282]
[*Jesus: Woe to you who believe that their lusts are satisfied/full.*]

Woe to those who forcefully get their fellow humans drunk (intoxicated), in order to gloat (laugh) over another's nakedness and vulnerability.[283]
[*Jesus: Woe to you who laugh.*]

Woe to those who trust in idols (images) and false Gods (or as explained in the last chapter, false ideas of God) through believing lies (told by false prophets).[284]
[*Jesus: Woe to you who are false prophets (who project false images of God or of God's ethics.*]

Every single one of these 'Woes', aligns with the sentiment expressed by Jesus in the Sermon on the Plain (as shown in the square brackets above). Jesus' own words, therefore, are a summary of, or a commentary on, God's words as expressed by the prophet Habakkuk. And Jesus' Jewish listeners would have recognised this pattern of '*Woe to you*', and immediately connected Jesus' sermon with Habakkuk's prophetic utterances.

Therefore, it's not that Jesus has an issue with anybody who laughs; Jesus is not the chuckle police. People loved to be around Jesus, and I can't say that about anyone who doesn't know how to laugh. But Jesus, purposely echoing Habakkuk, is speaking against those who gloat at the impoverished predicaments of others, especially when those predicaments have been proverbially poured down the throats of the marginalised by greedy hands.

In the same way, Jesus is not saying that wealth is a bad thing, per se. He's speaking against the exploitative things that people do to others, either indirectly or directly, in order to get at that wealth and the privileged position it will grant them within their society.

God in Habakkuk and Jesus in the Blessings/Sorrows sentiments of the Sermon on the Plain are denouncing the oppressive practices of human empires and calling us to live an alternative way. Both sets of '*Woe to those*' statements are about the predatory, wolf-like traits of humanity.

In light of all this, if we want to understand Habakkuk's statement that the 'righteous shall live by faith' (a statement that is echoed in numerous places throughout the New Testament), then we need to perceive the arrogant and crooked practices he is exposing—practices that are in opposition to 'living in faith'. Equally, because Jesus is giving his 'Blessed' statements in contrast to his 'Woes', he is also making the same distinction about who the righteous (the faithful to God's Kingdom) are, and who the unrighteous are. According to both Habakkuk and Jesus, the faithful are those who *do not*:

> Exploit others,
>> exhibit greed,
>>> commit violence,
>>>> dehumanise others
>>>>> or idolise power.

The righteous are not inward looking, and they put their hope in the character and ethics of God. Living in *faith, in* this context, then—mirroring what the Apostle John also said—is about not being devoid of compassion towards others; it expresses the commonwealth of the Kingdom of God. Or to phrase it the way Habakkuk does, and in a way that we have already seen in this book, such a practice of faith fills the world with the knowledge of the glory of God (Habakkuk 2:14). Such a display of faith presents to the world a tangible image of God's benevolent character and presence.

How does such an agenda operate in this world of ours? Well, Jesus answers that immediately after finishing his woes: 'Therefore, love your enemies!'[285] This leads us right into the passage of Scripture that we explored in Part Four of this book.

Jesus' advice might not seem practical enough for us. But in a world order possessed by fear—a world order which endorses adopting a 'Cain versus Abel' lifestyle, a world order that uses force to get what it wants, a world order that normalises greed, a world order that believes violence is the answer to the problems we face, a world order that requires someone to be at the bottom in order for others to be on top—then loving those that we perceive ourselves to be in competition with is absolutely the best place to start.

The Beatitudes are not platitudes; they are the hallmarks of how God reigns. The best definition of *Faith*, therefore, is allegiance to the Kingship of Christ. *Faith* is having trust in the political and social ideas of God; it's trusting in Jesus' radical notion that loving enemies, resisting domination, and refusing to be greedy will make this world a more beautiful place to live in. Faith is about putting our hope in God's methods of restoring the world to its flourishing status. We're not called to be like David or Solomon; we're called to look like Jesus. We've always been called to look like Jesus, and we're to trust that God's way of being human, as embodied in Christ, is *the* way.

It's telling that Jesus didn't leave us with instructions on how to build fine buildings, or on how to take over the world. Jesus didn't leave us with construction plans, like David did for Solomon. Jesus left us with the Sermon on the Mount, the commandment to love one another and our enemies, and the example of self-sacrifice. Most importantly, instead of monuments, or flags, or national anthems, Jesus left us with a meal; the centrepiece of God's commonwealth is a table.

# 7.5 | THE TABLE AT THE END OF THE WORLD

For me, our dining table is the most important piece of furniture in our home.

Sure, I think our sofa is pretty comfortable and, regardless of where you sit, you're normally guaranteed an unobstructed view of the TV. I also love my bed. I'll repeat that: I. Love. My. Bed. I cherish my bookcases and their contents. I've classified my favourite, twenty-year-old *Purple Ronnie* mug as priceless. I enjoy our fish tank, and my preferred place to sit in the conservatory, and our children's bedrooms, and our garden. I like the overall sense of space and quirkiness we have in our home, and I'm fortunate to have a tiny nook in the corner of it where I can sit and write.

I *despise* the rowing machine, though. But Steph insists that it's good for my health. So it's got to stay, and I have to use it for more than a clothesline.

However, all of these (but especially the rowing machine) pale in comparison to our table.

It's not a grand thing, by any standards. It looks like solid wood, but it's veneered, imitation chipboard. There are only four of us, but we bought a six-seater so we could have guests. At Christmas, we can squeeze in eight; although one of us—normally me—ends up perched on a corner. It's certainly seen better years; the veneer is patchy and stained, where the kids (and an occasional adult) have spilt drink or food. And in some places, where we've tried to remove the stains, the surface has become tacky and cracked.

It is just a normal, everyday, run-of-the-mill table. And to be honest, if we replaced it tomorrow with something less grand, the table would still be the main thing for me.

I'm not smitten with its construction, but rather with its function. For me, the table speaks of home and hospitality. We gather around this table as family and friends. Yes, we come around it as hosts, or Mum and Dad. But when we sit, it's *we* that sit, as we glimpse each other face to face and eye to eye, because the table raises the little ones up, and it brings down the big folk. I love the table, because to share food with others is the most peace-loving, shalom-making, world-beautifying, welcoming human experience there is. I firmly believe that the very best of humanity is made visible when people come and eat together.

In today's culture, it feels as if sex has been hailed as the pinnacle of human experience. And although there's nothing wrong with sex, and I would affirm that we're sexual beings, I would have to draw the line at sex being the greatest experience of our humanity. In my opinion, there's no greater feeling of intimacy than sitting around a table and eating great food in the company of others. It also lasts longer, too—even when it's fast food.

Eating with others *is* the most liberating and collaborative human experience there is. The only other experience that I know that can have this effect is shared suffering; both eating and suffering together strengthen the bedrock of human relationship like nothing else.

Jesus also understood the importance of eating together. But more than the individualistic West, Middle Eastern cultures have always understood this. Eating together in the Middle East isn't solely about the necessity to feed. Sitting and eating together, sharing stories, being made welcome—these are the means of establishing and strengthening the bonds of a community. And as such, mealtimes impact every tier of a Middle Eastern community; in both a negative and a positive way. To share a table with someone is to be extended the greatest honour that the world has to offer, and to be declined a place at a table was a huge insult.

It should come as no surprise then that as a Middle Eastern book, the Bible is full of feasts. To think of it from a certain perspective, the Bible is the story of God's extended invitation for humanity to come and eat together in God's presence, at God's table. As I've said right from the start, the Jewish and Christian dream is not the transcendence and transmigration of humanity into some heavenly sphere; it's about the descent and dwelling of God on Earth. From beginning to end, God has been trying to eat with us and dwell with us.

## SKINS AND SACRIFICES

The story of the garden, way back in Genesis, already hints at this. In Genesis chapter three, after the Man and Woman have eaten the forbidden fruit, God comes walking through the garden seeking humanity.

For some reason, the writer of this narrative wants us to know the time of day for this divine ramble: God is walking in the evening time.[286] But I'm not inclined to see this as a leisurely stroll in the cool evening air, especially when I consider that the main meal in Middle Eastern societies, the *communal* meal, traditionally takes place in the evening. The original hearers of this story (and those in the Middle East today) would naturally have associated this time of day with eating together, and would have known what God was looking to do as he sought out humanity.

God was seeking to share a meal with humanity in the garden of creation. And despite the disruption caused by the discovery of what Adam and Eve had done, I don't think God's pursuit was prevented. Why do I say this? Well, later on in this scene, God is said to have made clothing for Adam and Eve out of animal skins.[287] So I have to ask: What happened to the animal's meat?

It's often been thought that God's killing of the animal(s) in Genesis three, with the explicit purpose of using their skins as a covering of humanity's nakedness, was the first penal substitutionary atoning act in Scripture. For the proponents of such theories, this tale has become the prime example of an angry God's need of a blood offering in order to dispense forgiveness. That is to say, the animals sacrificed are substitutes for Adam and Eve, receiving the punishment they should have incurred because, we are told, God has to vent some form of punishment onto something.

And yet, this doesn't fit the story at all. It's not even majored on in the account. What makes more sense is that the meal of goat, or calf—or whatever it was—was already in mind. It's not that God had to kill some innocent creature in the place of Adam and Eve in order to forgive; God's forgiveness and mercy are expressed in the fact that the Divine did not cancel the table reservations. Like the Crucifixion, this story is not demonstrating God's need for blood. It's the prime example of the non-retractable reach of divine forgiveness. Humanity's act of rebellion does not prevent God from achieving his goal of fellowshipping with them. The Serpent's attempt to sabotage the Creator's dining arrangements—by getting Adam and Eve to snack on something else beforehand—fails, because the Serpent has overlooked the persistent, faithful love of God.

Therefore, it's the meal—the communion of human and Divine—that's the reason for the animal's death. The animal-skin clothing was merely the natural byproduct of the banquet God prepares and draws the hesitant Adam and Eve into. There's no vengeful anger or blood lust in this scenario. The loving God shows grace and persists in the dream of seating humanity at the Divine Table.

It's worth stating that God has never withdrawn the invitation since. God has continued to pursue us with wild abandon, and for this reason, the Bible is full of echoes and symbols of the invitation to feast with God.

For example, the sacrificial system of Moses has as its focal point this same pursuit of sharing a divine meal together. Yes, some of the sacrificial rituals called for an animal to be killed. But the carcass wasn't thrown away as waste, as if the sole purpose of every sacrifice was to present a substitute for one's sins to an embittered God. The culmination of every sacrifice was a meal; the people ate these sacrifices *together* as a shared celebration of God's merciful presence.

This sacrificial feast with God was never meant to be a private, tiered or elitist affair, however. The sacred meal was to be the centrepiece of God's dream in the world; God's Table was supposed to be the place where generosity, justice and equality overflowed. It was an occasion all of Israel were invited to attend and exhibit through sharing their food with one another—and especially with those who depended most upon the sacrificial meals and tithes: the poor, the outcast, the orphaned and the widow of the community. As such, to eat with God had direct consequences for the health of the wider community.

This is why bringing defective offerings, such as a sick animal, was considered such a serious offence within the sacrificial system. To give the vilest of disease-ridden food to God as a sacrifice also meant feeding the lowest in the community rancid and potentially fatal food. There's no love for your neighbour in such an act. There's no desire for communion if you're content with putting poison in the mouth of your kith and kin. And there's no desire for equality if all you're prepared to give is the worst of what you have. Understanding the seriousness of this helps us to appreciate God's grievances with those (especially the ruling classes) who brought diseased animals to the sanctuary. Such acts, vehemently rebuked by the Old Testament prophet, Malachi, spat upon God's dream of sitting and eating with humanity.

Like the Mosaic law and the story of Adam and Eve, the biblical Prophets and Seers also used the imagery of a divine banquet when they spoke of God's dream for creation and us.

The prophet Isaiah imagined God's Golden Age resembling a great banquet, in which all the nations of the world sat in unison together in the presence of God:

> In Jerusalem, the Lord of Heavens Armies will spread a wonderful feast for all the people of the world.
> It will be a delicious banquet with clear, well-aged wine and choice meat.
> There he will remove the cloud of gloom, the shadow of death that hangs over the earth.
> He will swallow up death forever![288]

John the Seer, in the vision recorded in Revelation, also paints Isaiah's portrait of a banquet. John equates the culmination of God's dream with a lavish wedding ceremony, the marriage of Heaven and Earth. As an angelic messenger tells John, '*Blessed* are those who are invited to the wedding feast of the Lamb'.[289]

There's that word *blessed* (*makarios*) again. As mentioned earlier, the knowledge of what happens *then* should feed back into our *now*. We are to rejoice knowing that God wanted to eat with humanity in Eden and that nothing will prevent God from achieving that dream of a meal of global proportions. Furthermore, this blessedness should overflow in our praxis today; we are to practise and demonstrate the ethical implications of God's Table, now.

This isn't merely about eating together, though. The table is a symbol of welcome; it is putting forth a view of humanity that isn't obsessed with hierarchy, self-promotion or tribalism. In a world besotted with hierarchical human pyramids, those who claim to be God's ambassadors are to present a humanity which gathers around the flat, level surface of a Table—God's Table. In this atmosphere, *we are not* the hosts (and therefore we cannot claim some higher status) but merely other pilgrims who have stumbled upon the bountiful provision of a loving God.

In contrast to the empires that seek to control, stratify and oppress, God's table pulls out a chair which brings us all to the same level of status, exalting the lowly little people and bringing the 'high and mighty' down from their thrones.[290] It's not more empire that God desires, or a divine version of empire, but more table-space.

More unity; less uniformity.

More open commensality; less prejudice.

More justice; less inequality and oppression.

More compassion; less egoism and ignorance.

More generosity; less consumerism.

More benevolent image bearers of God; fewer bastardisations.

Less wall-building.

Less dice-throwing.

Less *mining.*

Less fear; more love.

To re-contextualise the words of Psalm 23, whilst keeping the same thrust, God is placing banqueting tables before the garden-desecrating, Babel-building walls of human empires.

## GOD'S GUEST LIST

Unsurprisingly, dining with people was a big endeavour in Jesus' ministry.

Jesus purposely went out of his way to recline and eat with people. Jesus' table—those with whom he shared food and conversation—spoke with a sharp, prophetic edge into his surrounding culture. He purposely ate with those that others shunned. He shared meals with outcasts, prostitutes and the marginalised of his day.

This habit frequently got Jesus in trouble because, according to his food critics, he was eating with the wrong sorts of people; he was choosing to dine with the unclean and the socially unacceptable. Some of his peers had convinced themselves that these people needed to get their acts together before even a whiff of an invite would arrive from God, and that some of them, according to a few firmly held convictions, were altogether too far gone for redemption.[291]

But this never stopped Jesus. Leaning on Isaiah's imagery, he revealed that God had indeed come to feast with *all* people. His intentional inclusiveness at mealtimes was a bold symbolic act. It formed the centrepiece of his declaration that God's Kingdom had been birthed on Earth and that this is what it looked like and how it operated. As writer Zach Hoag points out:

> Jesus rocked the status quo by embracing the nones and dones of his day. And not just embracing them but saying that the kingdom of God will be more like fraternizing with *them* than feasting with *us.*[292]

Jesus did what his opponents couldn't begin to imagine a Holy God doing. Which is odd, because Jesus perfectly mirrors what God did in the story of Adam and Eve: he eats with humanity anyway, regardless of who they are or what they have done. He exemplifies a God who is not out for vengeance, for forgiveness is embodied in Jesus' determined and faithful approach to humanity, and the atonement comes as a fruit of accepting the invitation to join in the feast God is freely providing.

For those who already had certain convictions about who was welcome at God's Table—for those who believed it was for members of their own ethnicity and for those who kept certain purity laws—this open hospitality was a push too far. They adamantly refused to sit and eat with Jesus, because embracing Jesus' expression meant also having to embrace, eat and sit with those whom Jesus chose to embrace, eat and sit with. In refusing Jesus' table, they refused to take their place at the inaugural feast of God's Kingdom. They couldn't see that the Kingdom had come, because it didn't look like what they'd expected.

On one occasion, as Jesus was teaching on the scope of God's Kingdom, a certain individual, filled with joy over his own nation's inclusion and no-one else's, shouted out, 'What a blessing it will be to eat bread in the Kingdom of God!' But instead of shouting, 'Amen!', Jesus responds to this remark by telling a parable that emphasised the wild and grace-filled invitation of God to those whom others didn't want to sit beside.[293] Jesus' parable highlights that God's Table is not insulted or defiled by those who are invited. On the contrary, it's those who make pathetic excuses not to accept the invitation, those who aren't willing to embrace its challenge and share it with others—these are the ones who bring dishonour and disgrace to the table. From Jesus' perspective, some of his own kin were at a greater risk of not getting a seat than those they perceived as being excluded.

God's guest list makes many of us uncomfortable. It's easier to picture our own names being written on some A-list than to imagine that there's no list at all. We're not happy with a seating arrangement that suggests that the last shall be first and those who are first shall be last. There's always that temptation to see ourselves as more deserving of a seat, or to believe that we'll be sat at a higher table than those we feel superior to. And the idea of God taking away our seats of privilege—the idea that God's Table annuls our self-given titles and status—troubles us deeply.

So to get around this slight to our honour, we're often found building our own seats of power, our own tables—our own empires—and attempting to coax God to come and sit with us. We treat God like the new kid in the school canteen. We believe God is staring around the Earth-shaped dining hall, weighing up which table to hang out with. Sometimes, we don't even observe how God moves in this dining hall of life; we just assume God is sat with *us* and not *them*. But God has already prepared a table and has invited those who have been rejected from our tables—the poor, the disadvantaged, the outcast, the demonised and the underdog. They flock to take their seats, as Jesus once said, whilst we cling to our own table.[294] The onus, therefore, is on us to abandon our adolescent, schoolkid behaviour. It is we who must move with humility towards what God is building.

## THE TABLE IS THE NEW ALTAR

In addition to the Cross, the Table is one of its most central and potent symbols of the Church. Jesus left us with the mandate of remembering him with a meal, which some would call the Eucharist, or Communion, or describe using the simple terms of breaking bread together.

It may seem like a simple meal—a piece of bread and a drink of juice or wine—but its meaning is profound. Every time we eat this meal together— each time we come together to embody God's commonwealth—we're declaring the reign of Christ until he returns. We are declaring that the beginning is nigh, that the Kingdom is both here and yet to come. However, this meal becomes an act of hypocrisy if it's only a meal, and not about the dynamics of God's dream being manifested among us as we dwell together in community.

The church in Corinth certainly had issues in this regard. In his letter to this particular church, the Apostle Paul had some serious criticisms about how the Corinthians celebrated the Lord's Supper. Paul wrote that they ate and drank in a way that was unworthy of the Body of Christ, adding, that because of this, some amongst them had become seriously ill or had even died.[295] People were dropping dead, not flourishing, as a direct consequence of how the church partook in the body and blood of Christ.

For many years, some people have allowed this conclusion from Paul to fuel superstitious ideas of us being struck dead if we drink from a communion cup in a flippant fashion. When I was young in my faith, I even imagined the scene looking like the ending moments of *Indiana Jones and the Last Crusade*, when the power-hungry Walter Donovan chooses poorly and drinks from a false Holy Grail, causing his body to rapidly melt away like wax before his bones crumble to dust. I know, some people's imaginations don't go to silly places like mine. But I have met people who do hold to notions of being cursed with some disease (or worse) if they receive communion in a non-reverential way.

Don't get me wrong—I do believe in being reverent when we take communion. But this idea of a curse is certainly not what Paul was getting at.

When Paul writes that some were sick and had died, they did so not because they took Communion the wrong way, but because the Corinthians' practice at mealtimes neglected the Kingdom's ethic of care towards the least among them. Christ's Body (the Church—formed of individuals living in community) was being sinned against because whilst some of them got full and drunk at mealtimes, the vulnerable among them became malnourished. The more fragile members of Christ's Body, those that required more care and covering (as Paul advised elsewhere) were not being shown the compassionate attention that was due to them.[296]

Instead, the Corinthian Church followed the Roman practice of allowing the hosts and honoured guests to eat their fill before passing the remains of the meal down to the next tier of the community (who would then eat their fill before passing the scraps down to those lower than they were). In wishing to honour the hierarchical practices of their own Roman culture, they stopped practising the ethical obligation of God's Table. They continued to spread the curse (the human pyramid of power and control), instead of manifesting God's solution and alternative. The poor were meant to have a place at God's Table, and *not* as the slaves bringing the food. But the rich and powerful in the Corinthian church had made it once again about places of honour. What the Corinthian church was doing was akin to the offering of diseased meat within the Mosaic sacrificial system. They were perpetuating the plight of the poor whilst they celebrated and maintained their own worldly status.

There's an irony in Paul's words to them; they are attempting to celebrate human *worth*, but they end up eating the meal of Christ in an *unworthy* way. As Rodney Reeves states:

> The ground at the Communion table was supposed to be level; no one had the right to act like the host and raise a toast for the Lord [...]. The incarnation was supposed to be God's ultimate act of hospitality: God became man so that man could dine with God. But the Corinthians had turned the Lord's Table into a country club, where certain members received preferential treatment and others were marginalised.[297]

To tackle this, Paul presents them with Jesus' example. On the night he was betrayed, Paul tells them, Jesus, the one who is worthy of all honours, was the one who took the bread and the wine and *served* it to others. Jesus was the Lord, yet in his earthly walk, he laid down his rights and poured out his life for the least. It was this model of service and hospitality that was to be the source of the church's structure, not the Roman Empire. Or to express that using Lucy Peppiatt's words:

> In contrast to the Graeco-Roman table that is highly stratified, where the rich use the meal as an opportunity to display their largesse, the communion table is a new altar where worldly status is irrelevant, where those who have make way for those who have not, where outsiders are welcomed.[298]

Paul wanted the Table to be the altar of the creation temple; the place where the restored image bearers would display God's intent for society, not the place where the old world order was on show.

## PROPHETIC OR PROSTHETIC?

To a certain degree, the motivation for Paul's complaint about Corinth's improper Table practice is an echo of the Prophet Isaiah's complaint about Israel's idea of fasting (as seen in Isaiah 58).

Both communities failed to see that these sacraments were to be a miniature representation, a sacred diorama, of the life of the community beyond the time constraints of a ceremony. For Isaiah and Paul, the observance of such sacred celebrations whilst neglecting their ethical thrust only served to highlight the hypocrisy of the community. In Paul's Corinth and Isaiah's Israel, "religion" had become an empty husk, void of God's concern for the poor, the vulnerable and the marginalised. If we took Isaiah's words and substituted his references to fasting and the temple with the Lord's Supper and church fellowship, we'd see some striking similarities between the two communities:

> "We have [gathered] before you!" they say. "Why aren't you impressed? We have been very hard on ourselves, and you don't even notice it!"
> "I will tell you why!" I respond. "It's because you are [feasting] to please yourselves.
> Even while you [eat together], you keep oppressing your workers. What good [are these meals] when you keep on fighting and

quarrelling? This kind of [celebration] will never get you anywhere with me.

No, this is the kind of [feast] I want: Free those who are wrongly imprisoned; lighten the burden of those who work for you. Let the oppressed go free, and remove the chains that bind people. Share your food with the hungry, and give shelter to the homeless. Give clothes to those who need them, and do not hide from relatives who need your help […]. Remove the heavy yoke of oppression. Stop pointing your finger and spreading vicious rumors! […]. Then your light will shine out from the darkness, and the darkness around you will be as bright as noon."[299]

The prophet Amos also poignantly highlights the hypocrisy of acting devoted to God whilst not giving a care in the world about God's dream:

I can't stand your religious meetings.

I'm fed up with your conferences and conventions.

I want nothing to do with your religion projects, your pretentious slogans and goals.

I'm sick of your fund-raising schemes,

your public relations and image making.

I've had all I can take of your noisy ego-music.

When was the last time you sang to me?

Do you know what I want?

I want justice—oceans of it.

I want fairness—rivers of it.

That's what I want. That's all I want.[300]

These may be ancient voices, but these issues are not things of the past. Modern Christianity teeters on the precipice of being overtly self-absorbed. More than ever, in our Pentecostal, Evangelical, and Charismatic settings, our gatherings often endorse navel-gazing, instead of awakening us to the distress of others. We're not interested in building tables in the wilderness, but like Solomon, we're more excited about building projects and luxury. Like Isaiah's Israel, we gather together asking God to see and hear us, as we pray for a revival in our land, and God replies by telling us to see and hear the oppressed (if we'll bend our ear to listen). We love our entertaining meetings, *our* holy moments, but it's loving our neighbour and our enemy beyond those moments that God is trying to move us toward.

To be clear, gathering together is crucial to our health and maturity as a church. It's not that we should stop meeting together, but we are called to be more than participants in meetings. Table practice is meant to be the mission and nature of the Church. The meal is supposed to be a microcosm of our wider life together.

Scarily, our meetings are indeed an expression of our life beyond the church walls. They always say something about the heart-beat, priorities and depth of our shared life. If all we want is great coffee, entertaining worship, good childcare provision and life-hack teaching—if all we do is view church as something we attend, like the cinema or a restaurant, and not something we are—it will show.

It'll show in how we talk about those we gather with, and those we don't gather with. It'll show in our inclination towards gossip. It'll show in our desire to be accepted whilst we also seek to maintain our right to be unaccepting of others. It'll show in our desire to segregate the ages as much as possible. It'll show in the consumeristic approach and flavour of our complaints about the services we attend. It'll show in our church hopping.[301] It'll show in our non-discerning fascination with the latest trends and our non-discerning neglect of tradition. It'll show in our desire to see others establish and engage in ministries that we can't be bothered giving our own time to. It'll show in the fact that we make our individualism an even higher and more sacred priority and concern than our corporate life. It'll show in our belief that another church-run program is the answer to reaching our local communities, when all that is often required is a willingness to connect to others and maybe even get involved in a community-run program ourselves.

Sadly, some churches have played to our consumeristic tendencies, and as a result, they look more like restaurant franchises than genuine, meal-sharing communities. We turn up to a venue that's glamorous and flashy, we get full on the atmosphere and the well-dressed consumables that are given to us, and then we leave for another week. And we are no closer to community; we are not even transformed in our heart towards others. We leave full of euphoric, hedonistic satisfaction. We leave drunk on self-inclination, so to speak.

In addition to this, we're not all that welcoming either. Some of our restaurant-like churches and the clientele they attract are so exclusive that others cannot feel genuinely welcome. They're too cosmetic and inauthentic. They reek of Botox solutions to life's abrasiveness and excel in teaching how to paint on a smile. We give out spiritual aspirin, instead of acknowledging the pain, past trauma, doubt and burdens that people carry around with them. We share self-help anecdotes and trite mottoes, when instead we should be coming alongside others and journeying with them through these issues. And like the society around us—a society that is often too caught up in the rat-race to do the real work of healing—we neglect tackling the systemic causes of our distress and turmoil. Instead, we medicate with distraction. Some forms of religion are undeniably (to borrow the words of Karl Marx) the opium of the masses.[302]

In our arrogance, we proclaim that God is with us in our franchises. But the prostitute, the poor, the foreigner, the non-hip, the introvert, the contemplative, the discerning and questioning, the prophet, the teacher, the heretic, the heartbroken, all these see no place for themselves at our exclusive restaurant tables. We do no more for them than to increase their sense of isolation because we put on a spectacle instead of setting out a space for them in our lives.

How, I ask, can God be with us, when the broken, the hurt, the oppressed, the scapegoated and the 'ugly' (by this world's fickle standards of aesthetics and fame) are made to feel unwelcome and uncomfortable in our image-conscious, prosthetic-covered, winning-obsessed, "religious" atmosphere?

## TO-GATHER

God, in Jesus, has not acted to gather crowds of individuals into a building once a week, who will then walk away with their "personal saviour" cradled in their isolated hearts. God's table is no cosy, romantic meal for two. Neither is it monotone, monochromatic, or monocultural. God's table is void of all human monopoly. There's no singular here. It's all corporate and corporeal. God desires to dine with *all* of humanity.

There's a continuing trend in everything we've witnessed throughout this section: there was Adam *and* Eve; the *community* of Israel in the Mosaic Law; the *tribes* of the world in Isaiah's vision; and the *diverse* company of *people* that Jesus dined with.

The gravity of this is that I encounter and exhibit something of the breadth and depth of God's dream only when I gather around the table *with others*. So if I'm going to participate in the imaging of God's dream for the world, I must gather with those unlike me, with others who are not of my tribe, or kin, or language. To an extent, I must take my individuality and lose myself within a host of others in order to celebrate the vocation of being a single living stone within the mosaic of God's presentation to the world.

To conclude this entire chapter with a question: Could it be that we're too focused on building our own kingdoms, instead of extending the table of God, because we're unwilling to lay our lives down for others in service, and we're too busy seeking others to service our own lives?

I heard a loud shout from the throne, saying, "Look, God's home is now among his people! He will live with them, and they will be his people. God himself will be with them. He will remove all sorrows, and there will be no more death or sorrow or crying or pain. For the old world and its evils are gone forever." And the one sitting on the throne said, "Look, I am making all things new!"

-Revelation 21:3-5a (NLT)

# ∞ | MASTERPIECE

I have a childlike conviction that the sufferings
will be healed and smoothed over, that the
whole offensive comedy of human contradiction
will disappear like a pitiful mirage [...] and that
ultimately, at the world's finale, in that moment
of eternal harmony, there will occur and be
revealed something so precious that it will suffice
for all hearts, to allay all indignation, to redeem
all human villainy, all bloodshed; it will suffice not
only to make forgiveness possible, but also to
justify everything that has happened with men.
– Fyodor Dostoyevsky[303]

In recent years, due to advances in technology, famous works of art have found themselves being probed to unveil what's hidden beneath their familiar exteriors.

Often, differing versions of the final image are uncovered. As we peel back each scanned layer of paint we can almost trace the revisions that the artist has made on top of previous attempts. But occasionally, as we delve beneath the outer limits, we find something exciting, like a completely different painting altogether.

One famous example of this is Pablo Picasso's *The Blue Room*. Its curators had always been suspicious that something else was going on under its surface, and after the infrared scans were performed, it became clear that this scene of a woman bathing in Picasso's studio was painted over the top of a portrait of a man.[304] Beneath one Picasso masterpiece, there lay an older and previously unknown painting.

This may seem like a peculiar thing. But it's not the first time one Picasso has been discovered under another. Picasso seemed to make a habit of this.

Real canvas wasn't cheap, so when the commissions didn't flood in, like any artist, Picasso still passionately pursued his desire to paint. Instead of canvas, Picasso would use other material such as cardboard, and occasionally, when consumed by the irresistible urge to birth something, Picasso would take an old, already used, unbought painting and paint over the top of that.

Which sounds straightforward, but this isn't an easy thing to do.

As most artists will tell you, canvas matters. What you paint on is just as important as what you paint with. The texture of a surface—whether it's a proper canvas, cardboard or a brick wall—affects and alters the brush strokes the artist applies to it. Whether it's rough, smooth or uneven, or whether there's already another wet or dried brush stroke present, matters greatly.

For those of you who don't paint portraits, you'll still experience something of this when you paint your house walls. Hiding an existing surface inconsistency is far from easy. But painting over it in such a way that you transform it into something else entirely is a masterstroke of genius.

So it speaks wonders of Picasso's skill as an artist that he was able to take the direction and texture of the old brushstrokes and then overlay them with the new brushstrokes, in such a way that an entirely different painting was brought forth from an old one. Picasso was so skilled in this that, to our naked eye, the old portrait had vanished.

This isn't an art lesson, although, I hope it does increase your appreciation of the skill required to paint a masterpiece. But keeping this imagery in mind is helpful to us.

God is an artist far greater than Picasso, and creation is both God's portrait and God's canvas. God is so creative and so faithful to this work of art, that God is able to revolutionise the brushstrokes that others have applied to this canvas—brushstrokes people have used to paint in their own portrait or to sabotage this good work—and still bring it to its beautiful completion. So much so, that at the end of it all—after all the horror that we have witnessed, after all of the wars, the poverty, the disease—we'll all look back in amazement, wondering how God ever managed to accomplish that.

That's not to say that God is happy or apathetic with the horror of the world. Not once does God ever justify the evil that has happened here, nor does God require that evil to happen. But somehow, in some way, God's brushstrokes will put it all right. In Picasso-like style, God is repainting the world, not throwing it out.

Like all metaphors, my analogy of Picasso will be seen to be full of holes if it's pressed too far. So to be clear, I'm not suggesting that God is painting over the problems. God's not trying to perform some great cover-up of history, by sweeping the injustice out of sight. No. God is a creator who redeems, restores and resurrects. Even the most ancient and driest of brushstrokes, will be undone, no matter what their original intent and their consequence.

At the end of his own painful journey, Joseph, the Jewish patriarch, described God's artistic ability in this way: 'God turned into good what you meant for evil.'[305] For Joseph, God neither caused nor endorsed the injustice that had happened to him, but God did subvert its ultimate goal. Joseph's journey reminds us that regardless of how much chaotic graffiti there is—graffiti that has our tag on it—Creation will one day be the masterpiece that God has always desired it to be. The old will be transformed in the presence of the new. All will flourish as it was intended to; all will be beautiful, whole, and good. God's coming judgement is not destructive, it's a renaissance.

Of course, there's a problem with all this. A masterpiece is an end product that we can all stand back from in relative comfort. But being caught up the middle of the process looks and feels like a mess, regardless of how creative a mess it is. Life is a mess. There's still a lot of human *mining* going on. There's still a lot of dice throwing. There's still dominance and greed and oppression and social immobility. If I am honest, it is still flowing even from my own life.

So I have to ask; Can God really take today's darkness, turmoil and loss and turn it all around? Can there be joy in the morning, when it follows so many nights of weeping and pain? Can God fix all this hurt and brokenness and make it whole?

The trajectory of hope in the Bible says, 'yes.' That even from the most shattered fragments of our lives and dreams God can form a beautiful masterpiece. The writers of Scripture take pains in reminding us that the enemy's brushstrokes, or the brushstrokes of greed, oppression and hate, are not enough to prevent God from doing his work. Nothing can separate us from the love of God. Nothing will stop God pursuing the completion of this great masterpiece. Nothing in all the brushstrokes of death, life, time and space, or the hell-bent powers can restrain God's love for this work of art.

In Romans chapter eight, the Apostle Paul speaks of the frustration we feel as we're caught up between this transition of the old painting becoming the new masterpiece. But he's not full of despair. Paul writes with hope about the glory-filled conclusion:

> I don't think the sufferings we are going through now are even worth comparing with the glory that will be revealed to us in the future. The creation waits eagerly for the sons of God to be revealed; for the creation was made subject to frustration — not willingly, but because of the one who subjected it. But it was given a reliable hope that it too would be set free from its bondage to decay and would enjoy the freedom accompanying the glory that God's children will have. We know that until now, the whole creation has been groaning as with the pains of childbirth; and not only it, but we ourselves, who have the first fruits of the Spirit, groan inwardly as we continue waiting eagerly to be made sons — that is, to have our whole bodies redeemed and set free [...].
>
> Similarly, the Spirit helps us in our weakness; for we don't know how to pray the way we should. But the Spirit himself pleads on

our behalf with groanings too deep for words; and the one who searches hearts knows exactly what the Spirit is thinking, because his pleadings for God's people accord with God's will. Furthermore, we know that God causes everything to work together for the good of those who love God and are called in accordance with his purpose [...].[306]

We can't grasp the glory that will be revealed in that finished article. As a part of the canvas, seeing things at a canvas level and experiencing the mess around us, there are many times we feel like saying, 'Where is God in all of this?' But Paul gives us a beautiful, yet unexpected answer: God still resides *with us* and *within us* through the presence of the Spirit, giving us a foretaste of the finished work, filling us with God's vision and intent for the world.

There's a tremendous amount of groaning in this passage of writing from Paul. The canvas of creation groans. We groan. And the Spirit groans. We groan harmoniously together because we sense that the mess surrounding us isn't the finished article. We groan, we feel this mess, because the Spirit groans within us, stopping us from being apathetic or complacent.

This is a passionate, artistic groaning. It's a creative brooding, like the one at the beginning of Scripture where the Spirit of God hovers over a chaos-filled world. Except this time the Spirit isn't hovering *over* the canvas, but *within* it. Like yeast in dough, to use the imagery Jesus gives us in one of his parables, God's Kingdom is present amongst us, moving what is to what ought to be.

God is restoring the masterpiece which he commissioned at the beginning of time, and Jesus was the master brushstroke in this divine renaissance. His life, death and resurrection have initiated the renovation. And the calling of those in Jesus is to be part of the new brushstrokes, the new palette that God is using. As Paul tells us, we are to imitate the pattern, to bear the image of Jesus.[307]

We're not called to complacency. We're not to seek to escape, to control, or to extort this world in order to paint our own dreams.

Living the dream is about partaking in and following the contours and textures laid down in the brushstrokes of Jesus. We are to be conduits for the Spirit-filled hues of love, mercy, hospitality and justice. These are the brushstrokes that will one day culminate in a world free of death and decay, a world that flourishes because the glorious God dwells and eats with humanity.

Before such hope,
I lay down my self-absorption,
I lay down my desire for control,
I lay down my greed and my dice,
Because I'm looking towards something more substantial than a happy ending to my own story.

Before such hope,
We pick up our humanity,
We pick up our communal responsibility to this sacred Temple,
We pick up our desire for Shalom,
Because we are rejoicing in the coming marriage of Heaven and Earth.

The Spirit *and* the Bride say, 'Come.'[308]

# FURTHER READING

## Part 01


Barrett, Matthew, and Caneday, eds., 2013. *Four Views on the Historical Adam.* Grand Rapids, MI: Zondervan.

Enns, Peter, 2014. *The Bible Tells Me So…: Why Defending Scripture Has Made Us Unable To Read It.* San Francisco, CA: HarperOne.

Lennox, John C., 2011. *Seven Days that Divide the World: The Beginning According to Genesis and Science.* Grand Rapids, MI: Zondervan.

Lewis, C. S., 1940. *The Problem of Pain.* London: HarperCollins.

Niditch, Susan, 1985. *Chaos to Cosmos: Studies in Biblical Patterns of Creation.* Chico, CA: Scholars Press.

Tallis, Raymond, 2011. *Aping Mankind: Neuromania, Darwinitis and the Misrepresentation of Humanity.* Durham, UK: Acumen.

Walton, John H., 2009. *The Lost World of Genesis One: Ancient Cosmology and the Origins Debate.* Downers Grove, IL: IVP Academic.

Walton, John H., with a contribution from N. T. Wright, 2015. *The Lost World of Adam and Eve: Genesis 2-3 and the Human Origins Debate.* Downers Grove, IL: InterVarsity Press.

Wright, N. T., 2014. *Surprised By Scripture: Engaging Contemporary Issues.* New York: HarperOne.

# Part 02

For some insights into medieval Church architecture, see chapter 4 of Martyn Whittock's *A Brief History of Life in the Middle Ages* (London: Robinson Press, 2009), pp. 81-84. With regards to Jewish Tabernacle/Temple design, John H Walton's *Lost World of Genesis One*, listed in Part 01 above, has some interesting insights scattered throughout.

Reeves, Rodney, 2011. *Spirituality According to Paul: Imitating the Apostle of Christ*. Rodney Reeves. Downers Grove, IL: InterVarsity Press.

Wright, N. T., 2011. *Simply Jesus: Who he was, What he did, Why it Matters*. London: SPCK.

Wright, N. T., 2012. *How God Became King: Getting to the heart of the Gospels*. London: SPCK.

Zahnd, Brian, 2016. *Water To Wine: Some of My Story*. Spello Press.

# Part 03

Middleton, J. Richard, 2014. *A New Heaven and a New Earth: Reclaiming Biblical Eschatology*. Grand Rapids, MI: Baker Academic.

Wright, N. T., 2003. *The Resurrection of the Son of God*. Vol. 3 of *Christian Origins and the Question of God*. London: SPCK.

# Part 04

Cone, James H., 2013. *The Cross and the Lynching Tree*. Maryknoll, New York: Orbis Books.

Dorling, Daniel, 2015. *Inequality and the 1%*. London: Verso Books.

Lloyd-Roberts, Sue, and Morris, Sarah, 2016. *The War on Women: and the Brave Ones Who Fight Back*. London: Simon & Schuster.

McGuire, Danielle, L., 2011. *At the Dark End of the Street: Black Women, Rape, and Resistance—A New History of the Civil Rights Movement from Rosa Parks to the Rise of Black Power*. New York: Vintage Books.

Rankine, Claudia, 2014. *Citizen: An American Lyric*. London: Penguin.

Stark, Rodney, 1997. *The Rise of Christianity: How the Obscure, Marginal Jesus Movement Became the Dominant Religious Force in the Western World in a Few Centuries*. San Francisco, CA: HarperCollins.

Sen, Amartya, 2006. *Identity & Violence: The Illusion of Destiny*. London: Penguin.

Storkey, Elaine, 2015. *Scars across Humanity: Understanding and Overcoming Violence against Women*. London: SPCK.

Westfall, Cynthia Long, 2016. *Paul and Gender: Reclaiming the Apostle's Vision for Men and Women*. Grand Rapids, MI: Baker Academic.

# Part 05

Just go and love someone who isn't you.

# Part 06

Boyd, Gregory A., 2017. *The Crucifixion of the Warrior God: Interpreting the Old Testament's Violent Portraits of God in the Light of the Cross*. Minneapolis, MN: Fortress Press. (You could also check out Boyd's condensed version of this work published in 2018, *Cross Vision: How the Crucifixion of Jesus Makes Sense of Old Testament Violence*.)

Flood, Derek, 2014. *Disarming Scripture: Cherry-Picking Liberals, Violence-Loving Conservatives, and Why We All Need to Learn to Read the Bible like Jesus Did*. San Francisco, CA: Metanoia Books.

Jersak, Bradley, 2015. *A More Christlike God: A More Beautiful Gospel*. Plain Truth Ministries.

Niditch, Susan, 1993. *War in the Hebrew Bible: A Study in the Ethics of Violence.* Oxford: Oxford University Press.

Sacks, Rabbi Lord Jonathan, 2015. *Not in God's Name: Confronting Religious Violence.* London: Hodder & Stoughton.

Schwager, Raymund SJ., 2000. *Must There Be Scapegoats? Violence and Redemption in the Bible.* New York: The Crossroad Publishing Company.

Sparks, Kenton L., 2008. *God's Word in Human Words: An Evangelical Appropriation of Critical Biblical Scholarship.* Grand Rapids, MI: Baker Academic.

Webb, William J., 2004. *Slaves, Women & Homosexuals: Exploring the Hermeneutics of Cultural Analysis.* Downers Grove, IL: InterVarsity Press.

Wright, Christopher J. H., 2004. *Old Testament Ethics and the People of God.* Downers Grove, IL: InterVarsity Press.

Zahnd, Brian, 2017. *Sinners in the Hands of a Loving God: The Scandalous Truth of the Very Good News.* Colorado Springs, CO: Waterbrook.

# Part 07

Balthasar, Hans Urs von, 2014. *Dare We Hope "That All Men Be Saved"?: with A Short Discourse on Hell.* 2nd ed. Translated by David Kipp and Rev. Lothar Krauth San Francisco: Ignatius Press.

Gorman, Michael J., 2011. *Reading Revelation Responsibly: Uncivil Worship and Witness: Following the Lamb into the New Creation.* Eugene, OR: Cascade Books.

Hedges, Chris, 2009. *Empire of Illusion: The End of Literacy and the Triumph of Spectacle.* New York: Nation Books.

Hoag, Zach, 2017. *The Light Is Winning: Why Religion Just Might Bring Us Back to Life.* Grand Rapids, MI: Zondervan.

Jersak, Bradley, 2009. *Her Gates Will Never be Shut: Hope, Hell and the New Jerusalem.* Eugene, OR: Wipf and Stock.

Peterson, Eugene H., 1991. *Reversed Thunder: The Revelation of John and the Praying Imagination.* New York: HarperCollins.

Rossing, Barbara R., 2004. *The Rapture Exposed: The Message of Hope in the Book of Revelation.* New York: Basic Books.

Wright, N. T., 2008. *Surprised by Hope: Rethinking Heaven, the Resurrection, and the Mission of the Church.* London: SPCK.

# ABOUT THE AUTHOR

Tristan Sherwin is the author of *Love: Expressed* and a teacher at Metro Christian Centre, a multi-ethnic church working in the Greater Manchester region of England.

Tristan and his wife, Steph, live in Bolton, England, with their two sons, Corban and Eaden.

"*Love: Expressed* is a work of dirt-under-your-fingers spirituality"

—Jonathan Martin, author of *Prototype* and *How to Survive a Shipwreck*

# ACKNOWLEDGEMENTS

As always, this book would not have taken any form if it weren't for the help of those formed around me.

A big thanks to those who have endorsed this work; I know that this is a risky project to put your name next to, and so I cherish your words and the great source of encouragement they've been to me. Particular thanks to my Bishop from across the pond, Brian Zahnd. As with my first book, you were the first to reply with an endorsement, and I continue to be bowled over by your solidarity and generosity.

Elaine Storkey's book, *Scars Across Humanity* remains one of the most significant and sobering books I've read. So to have Elaine provide the foreword for this work is still a 'pinch-me-I-must-be-dreaming' kind of experience. Thank you, not only for your contribution, but also for your periodic emails of encouragement!

A word of deep gratitude must also be given to Paul Schofield, Steph (my beautifully-minded better half), my mentor, Bruce Millar, Ryan Cook, Steve Kershaw, and, more recently, Tom King, for being theological sparring-partners. It's a gift to have people to be vulnerable with, who enjoy the wrestle as much as I do, and who know how to wrestle without it turning into a fight. Thank you for the conversations we've had and the conversations to come.

Many thanks to my family at Metro Christian Centre, Bury and Whitefield, for allowing me to share some, but certainly not all, of this with you during our gatherings together, and for being a home. Also, thank you to the Bridge Community Church, Radcliffe; I came to encourage you, but, as it turned out, you've been a huge source of strength to me.

With regards to getting this book into a book, Richard Van Holst's editorial wisdom and sweat have been invaluable. Thank you Richard, for not only helping me to dot the i's and cross the t's, but also for engaging with my work as a theologian; I know that you didn't agree with everything in here, but I'm thrilled that I got you to look up the lyrics of a Spice Girls song! To Amelia Stura: thank you for asking about and grasping my vision for the book's cover art, and for executing it absolutely perfectly! (Also, thanks for the cakes and the Yotsuba&! novels).

Special thanks must also be given to those who read and reviewed my first book, *Love: Expressed*. After publishing it, I felt vulnerable, to say the least, and it's no overstatement to suggest that this book would never have happened if it weren't for your support. Thank you! Thank you! Thank you!

To my sons, Corban and Eaden: thanks for teaching me to see again with a sense of wonder. I know that I'm grumpy sometimes, but I'm proud of you both and you give me great cause for celebration. To Steph: I know.

Last, but not least, thank you, God. Your faithfulness to these melancholic dry bones continues to leave me breathless.

# ENDNOTES

INTRODUCTION

1      Throughout this book I'll be addressing the problem of self-help, *not* self-care. As someone who experienced a painful nervous breakdown through a lack of good self-care, and who has since been dutiful in attending to my health and well-being, I would not dismiss the power of rest, encouragement, or support, nor the importance of learning to say 'no.' Healthy choices are essential. Additionally, God, I feel, wants us to enjoy, delight and savour the goodness and beauty that is inherent within creation.

However, there exists a deluge of 'sausage factory' clichés that drain the appreciation for self and others out of us. Most of these maxims and programmes, instead of fuelling self-love and love of others, just fuel fear, shame and a huge sense of inadequacy. Sure, some of these ideas can come through guilt-inducing doctrines (to which I don't subscribe), such as total depravity or not trusting our emotions. But there are plenty of non-doctrinal teachings, both within the church and outside of it, that masquerade as self-care but are really self-obsession (we'll touch on this more at the start of Part Five). We are in desperate need of healthy rhythms in our lives—so take good care of yourself (and others), and watch which ideologies you feed yourself on.

For me personally, self-care started when I stopped listening to the self-help mantras of 'achieve, attain, accomplish', and when, I must admit, I stopped holding onto to *mine* so tightly.

PART ONE

2      Genesis 1:1 (NLT)

3      St Augustine of Hippo (c. AD 354 - 430), *Confessions* 1.1

4      Bishop Kallistos Ware, *The Orthodox Way*, rev. ed. (Crestwood, NY: St Vladimir's Seminary Press, 1995), p. 53-54. Used with permission.

5      Attributed to Oscar Wilde (AD 1854–1900)

6      Fyodor Dostoyevsky (AD 1821-1881), *The Brothers Karamazov*.

7      I should add here that I mean *science* books, and not the kind of popular scientism that hides in its guise.

8      I am going to be using the term *author* or *writer* a lot when talking about those who first discussed these stories, only because it's an analogy of what we're used to. But the Creation story, and many other stories within Scripture, would have been oral traditions for many generations prior to being written works. So *storyteller(s)* would be a far better description than *author*.

9      Lucius Annaeus Seneca (Seneca the Younger) (c. 4 BC – AD 65), *Quaestiones Naturales*, Book 7, chapter 31. Seneca also went on to say, in the same chapter: 'Nature does not reveal all her secrets at once. We imagine we are initiated in her mysteries: we are, as yet, but hanging around her outer courts.' I think this is also important to remember today.

10      Heliocentric Solar System is a scientific description of the model of our solar system, *heliocentric* meaning that the sun is at the centre and that our planet, along with the others, revolves about it. None of us would challenge this today, especially since modern technological innovations, such as satellites, have observed this movement. But when it was first suggested in the sixteenth century by the Polish monastic astronomer, Nicolaus Copernicus (who, incidentally, based his model on naked-eye observations of the celestial movements as telescopes hadn't yet been invented), it found itself engaged in an uphill struggle to challenge the deep-seated and generally held Ptolemaic system, which said that Earth was the centre of the known universe. Sadly Copernicus died on the very day his *De*

*Revolutionibus Orbium Coelestium* (On the Revolutions of the Heavenly Spheres) was published. However his work laid the foundations for another revolutionary scientific thinker, and devout Catholic, Galileo Galilei, who pushed Copernicus' thinking into the public sphere with the publication of his *Dialogue Concerning Two Chief World Systems*. As the story goes, this led Galileo into a huge theological and scientific fray with the Roman Catholic Church in 1632, which had made the Ptolemaic model of the solar system a tenet of Christian doctrine. In 1633, Galileo was charged with heresy and apparently spent the remaining nine years of his life under house arrest.

11      Galileo Galilei's famous clash with the religious authorities of his time is now the stuff of legends—a story that raises its head every time a conversation about science versus religion takes place. But as Stephen Hawking once pointed out in an interview (see http://www.radiotimes.com/news/2016-01-26/stephen-hawking-my-sense-of-humour-keeps-me-going/), Galileo wasn't only a religious heretic, *but* the scientific heretic of his time. He rebelled against the Aristotelian principles—the ancient Greek philosophies—that had dominance within the scientific community. Dubbed the Father of Modern Physics, Galileo placed an emphasis on observation being the most important factor in discerning and understanding the laws of the Universe. Of course, religious authorities did hold sway within the socio-political world, including the sciences. But to reduce Galileo's argument to being a clash between scientific and religious views is to oversimplify the matter. This was as much a scientific revolution as it was a religious one, a battle between handed down scientific ideas and new scientific observations. Sadly, there were few like Galileo within the theological spheres who were prepared to exorcise the Aristotelian principles (and the principles of his teacher Plato) from the position of authoritative influence they held in Christian doctrine. Although Galileo's discoveries did impact theology, insipid Greek philosophical ideas, and the dualisms they create, have continued to dominate a huge chunk of Western biblical interpretation and theology, instead of Jewish thought which ought to have played

a larger role than it did. Galileo started his revolution five hundred years ago, but we are slowly catching up. I hope this book will add to this.

12    I have to be careful about the word *new* here. Although this Sun-centric arrangement of our solar system was a challenge to the model popularly held, there is rumour of an astronomer called Aristarchus of Samos (c. 310 – 230 BC) who had already proposed that the Earth moved about the Sun. Sadly, it was the views of Claudius Ptolemy (c. 100 - 170 AD) which won out, and remained the dominant view for fifteen thousand years. But who can blame people for the acceptance of these views? After all, from our Earth-bound perspective, as we gaze into the sky above, it does appear that we are still as the heavens shift. Not only did Ptolemy's model align with Earth-bound perception, but his calculations of the celestial movements did produce fairly accurate results.

13    The Sun does move, however, but not in relation to us. As a part of the Milky Way, our entire solar system travels through space on its own orbit about the centre of the galaxy.

14    Even if God doesn't accommodate, people are still going to interpret and filter everything they hear through their own opinions, ideas and cultural frameworks. Trust me. I've preached and taught many times, and it is still surprising (regardless of how clear you feel you have been) how vast the range of ideas people walk away with—ideas which gel with their own thinking, but which are completely different from what has been shared.

15    A reference to Charlie Chaplin's powerful speech in the film *The Great Dictator* (1940).

16    John H. Walton, *The Lost World of Genesis One: Ancient Cosmology and the Origins Debate* (Downers Grove, IL: IVP Academic, 2009), p. 143.

17    For a sample of biblical texts that affirm God as the creator, see Job 38-41, Psalm 104, Isaiah 40:27-28 and John 1:1-13.

18     The real friction is between scientism and religious fundamentalism. Both parties suffer from the inability to accept descriptions of reality outside of their own peripheral vision. Both refuse to allow the other's perception to nuance their own understandings and highlight their own limitations.

19     *Chaos* is an extremely important idea to note because of its use within the Scriptures and by the people of the Ancient Near East (ANE). Chaos is used in many ANE creation myths to describe the state of the cosmos prior to the creation events. Chaos doesn't describe a time when "nothing" existed, but rather a time when what already existed was in a primal disordered, non-functional and purposeless state. At the beginning of the Genesis account, this state is symbolised with the Hebrew words *tōhû* and *bōhû*, often translated as *formless* and *void*. Often within both ANE tradition and Scripture the sea is used as a metaphor for this disordered and confusing force. The mythical sea-creature, Leviathan, is seen as an allegorical personification of this force, a Chaos creature, so to speak. John H. Walton, in his book *The Lost World of Adam and Eve*, also suggests that we should also understand the Serpent of Genesis Three in this light; it is a chaos creature, an embodiment of a force which seeks to unravel the ordered state of creation. In this sense, Genesis could be read as the account of God ordering the cosmos, giving it function, and not a story of *material* origins. Genesis Three could then be read as an account of how this ordering work was halted and began to unwind. As an aside, Babel (as in the Tower of Babel of Genesis 11, and later Babylon—both the city and the metaphor for oppressive Human Empires) also takes its name from *Chaos*; a confused and disorder state.

20     Just because I'm pushing here the idea that God is immanent (involved, present), doesn't mean that I don't hold to an idea of God also being transcendent (beyond and above all this). *Immanent* and *transcendent* are not opposites when talking of God. The Jewish theologian, Abraham Joshua Heschel suggested that it was an oversimplification to force a dichotomy between God's transcendent and immanent nature. As he puts it, God is related in his transcendence, and

transcendent in his immanence (see *The Prophets*, p. 622). Or, to put that another way, although God is distinct from us and beyond us, God chooses to draw close and involves himself with Humanity and history.

In many ways, God's transcendence is an important aspect of the nature of God's involvement (I nod here towards the ideas of J. Richard Middleton, in his book *A New Heaven and a New Earth*). For example, it was the fact that God was immanent (close, involved), but also transcendent—and therefore not in collusion with, nor an endorser of, the oppressive systems of injustice or slavery—that fuelled the Hebrews' knowledge that they could appeal to God for help when they found themselves enslaved in Egypt. In contrast, their appeals to Pharaoh fell on deaf ears because Pharaoh was directly involved in implementing the oppressive system, not transcendent with regard to it.

21      See; Exodus 40, 1 Kings 7:1-8:10, and 2 Chronicles 3:1-5:14.

22      I almost want to put these last two sentences in bold. Maybe you should grab a highlighter or something and, well, highlight them or something.

23      The Hebrew day starts in the evening, not the morning; so God creates mankind on the sixth day of the story, and on that same evening—which is the start of the seventh day—God rests. Some English translations of the Bible are better than others at indicating this way of measuring the span of a day. For example, at the end of each 'creation day', the New King James Version (and also the Complete Jewish Bible) keeps to the original Hebrew syntax of stating *evening* before *morning* to emphasis when the day started and ended. In keeping with this idea of when a day begins and ends, Jewish custom still follows the practice in which the Sabbath day begins on a Friday evening and comes to an end on the following Saturday evening.

As an added aside, you'll notice that the seventh day of the creation account has a beginning but *not* an end. The standard motif of evening followed by morning isn't present. This seventh day is unbounded, demonstrating the eternal reality of God's resting in creation. The Complete Jewish Bible clarifies the end of this final stanza of the creation poem by stating that God rested so that all that God had made would begin to produce of itself.

24      Genesis 1:26-27 (NLT). See also Genesis 5:1-2.

25      Genesis 2:7 (NLT) [italics mine].

26      This bestowing of the Spirit is also true of the event that took place at the Feast of Pentecost, as recorded in Acts 2:1-13. In Acts chapter two, God pours himself out upon his people, breathing his very likeness into them, fulfilling Joel's prophecy that God would pour out the Divine Spirit on all people regardless of age, gender and ethnicity. (Joel 2:28-29, Acts 2:17-18). All people are called to this, and not just a certain few who happen to possess some particular human attributes. Pentecost is an awakening event, which consists of anointing *dead* stones to form *living* stones. It's not one gender receiving more than the other, or one nationality getting less than any other. At Pentecost, God enters humanity afresh through the work of Christ, and does so with the purpose of reclaiming, restoring, resurrecting and recommissioning humanity to bear the divine image within his temple of creation. Pentecost was a re-enactment of the original endeavour of Genesis (also see endnote 79).

27      From Disney's *The Lion King* (1994), for those who don't get the reference. For those who did, like me, you probably now have the soundtrack playing in your head. Sorry.

28      Romans 8:20.

29      Psalm 14:2-3 (NLT).

30      Genesis 3:9.

31      Romans 3:23 (NLT).

32    I took this number from Jamie A. Davies' book *Life Unfolding: How the Human Body Creates Itself* (Oxford: Oxford University Press, 2014). See especially chapter 17, entitled "Making Friends and Facing Enemies". If you want to explore this internal zoo more closely and why it is vital to our quality of life, you could also check out the following: *The Human Superorganism: How the Microbiome is Revolutionizing the Pursuit of a Healthy Life*, by Rodney R. Dietert (New York, NY: Dutton Books, 2016), and Ed Yong's *I Contain Multitudes: The Microbes Within Us and a Grander View of Life* (Vintage, 2017). Happy reading (and eating afterwards)!

33    2 Samuel 14:14b (NLT, 2015 ed.). I know I used this verse in my first book, but I can't help using it again; it's an amazing verse.

34    Colossians 1:15a, 16b-17, 19-20 (NLT, 2015 ed.) [square brackets and italics mine].

35    See John 1:1-14.

36    See Scot McKnight, *A Community Called Atonement* (Nashville, TN: Abingdon Press, 2007), p. 21.

37    2 Corinthians 3:18 (NLT).

38    2 Corinthians 5:15 & 17 (NLT) [square brackets mine].

39    Ephesians 2:10 (NLT).

## PART TWO

40    The Roman historian Tacitus (c. AD 56 - 117), apparently quoting the words of Gaius Julius Civilis, who led the Batavian rebellion against Rome in AD 69. The full quote is, 'Courage is the peculiar excellence of man, and the gods are on the side of the stronger [*deos fortioribus adesse*]'. Taken from Tacitus's *The Histories*, 4.17.

41    Paraphrase of a quote spoken by the character Shades in the Netflix and Marvel TV show *Luke Cage*, Season 1, 2016.

42    Jürgen Moltmann, *The Crucified God: The Cross of Christ as the Foundation and Criticism of Christian Theology* (London: SCM Press, 2015). (© Jürgen Moltmann, 2015. Used by permission rights@hymnsam.co.uk').

43    James H. Cone, *The Cross and the Lynching Tree* (Maryknoll, Kew York: Orbis Books, 2013), p. xiv-xv. Used by permission of Orbis Books.

44    See Matthew 27:35; Mark 15:24; Luke 23:34; John 19:23-24.

45    For another example of how casting lots was connected to invoking God's will, you need only turn to Acts 1:26. Some may also wish to quote Proverbs 16:33 in support of this idea, 'We may throw the dice, but the LORD determines how they fall' (NLT).

46    Luke 23:34 (NLT).

47    1 Corinthians 1:23-24 (NKJV). A few verses on from this, Paul would also add, 'For I decided to know nothing among you except Jesus Christ, and him crucified.' (1 Corinthians 2:2, NRSV).

48    St Athanasius of Alexandria (c. AD 295 – 373), *On the Incarnation*.

49    Yes, there is a sense of sarcasm in this.

50    Mark 8:27b (NLT). And for the rest of this section I will be focussing on this story contained between Mark 8:27-9:1. You can also read this story in Luke 9:18-27, and Matthew 16:13-28.

51    Mark 8:38-9:1 (NLT, 2015 ed.) [square brackets mine].

52    Walter Wink, *Jesus and Nonviolence: A Third Way* (Minneapolis, MN: Fortress Press, 2003), p. 72. Used with permission.

53    What I mean when I use the term *metaphorised history*, in this context, is that what we read in Genesis Two and Three *is* the story of humanity, but that doesn't mean that it is what we would see transpiring if we travelled back in time and captured the events on film. I'm riffing on the ideas of Jesus scholar Marcus J.

Borg here. It's not that this story is telling us lies, but that history has been converted to symbols and "simplified" into a form that captures and articulates the thrust of the events so that, like good art and poetry, we can get to the truth of the matter in a more distilled form. Some scholars use the word *Myth* to convey this way of thinking (such as C. S. Lewis; *God in the Dock* [London: Collins, 1978]), while others would prefer the term *Parable*.

54     Philippians 2:6 (NLT).

55     James 3:16 (NLT) [italics and square brackets mine].

56     James 3:15, 17.

57     1 Corinthians 1:23-24.

58     For some examples see Romans 6:3-11; Colossians 2 and 3 (which have it as a consistent theme); 2 Corinthians 5:14; Galatians 2:19-20.

59     Rachel Held Evans, *Searching For Sunday: Loving, Leaving and Finding the Church* (Nashville, TN: Nelson Books, 2015), p. 21. Used by permission of Thomas Nelson. www.thomasnelson.com

60     Galatians 2:19-20.

**PART THREE**

61     Genesis 1:28 (RSV). God's commission to humanity within the creation poem.

62     Our eldest son, Corban Sherwin, said this as we explored the ruined remains of the zoological gardens at Rivington Pike, Lancashire, England. 4th May 2017.

63     Friedrich Nietzsche, *Die Fröhliche Wissenschaft* (The Gay Science/The Joyful Wisdom), 1882.

64     I am conveniently forgetting Tim Burton's attempt in 2001. Sorry Tim—but I love everything else you've done (especially *Sleepy Hollow*).

65    See Isaiah 66:1-2 for example. Also note that this particular verse records God boasting that his Temple is better than any Temple that people could build, and that his creation Temple consists of *both* Heaven *and* Earth. God doesn't designate one as being his dwelling place while the other is not; both are his and both form his realm of authority.

66    See John 5:17. I also touch on this passage, and what it means to keep the Sabbath, in my first book *Love: Expressed*, see chapter 6 "Expressed through Sabbath" (Bloomington, IN: WestBow Press, 2015).

67    It's also why we called our second child Eaden. It's pronounced Aiden, but the spelling evokes the meaning of Eden, a place of delight. On most days, he lives up to his namesake.

68    Genesis 2:8-15.

69    For the whole Earth being already filled with the glory of God, as well as the creation story, see Isaiah 6:3.

70    Habakkuk 2:14.

71    Professor Phyllis Trible notes that the Hebrew verb translated *till/tend*, is *'bd* (which means to serve) and the verb *keep/care*, is *šmr* (which describes a protective act, not a possessive role). Trible concludes that the nature of this vocation is not to plunder and rape creation, but to attentively care for it. See Phyllis Trible, *God and the Rhetoric of Sexuality* (Minneapolis ,MN: Fortress Press, 1978), p. 85.

72    In many ways, this is the story that Jesus tells in Mark 12:1-8, about the vineyard and the rebellious tenants. And although, in its immediate context, it refers to the Jewish leadership, this story of Israel's rebellion in the Promised Land is also a microcosm of humanity's story within the world.

73    Exodus 14:15-31.

74    Genesis 8:1-2.

75    It's interesting that the first thing Noah does after the flood in response to this commission is to become a farmer and plant a vineyard. It's gardening all over again. But yet again, instead of being the birthing place of the sacred, this garden/vineyard also becomes an environment which displays human shame and nakedness.

76    Eventually, *Babel* develops into a popular biblical label for all world orders and empires opposed to God's intent for the world. And geopolitically, this Babel plain becomes the home turf to one of world history's oppressively militant imperial heavyweights: the Babylonian Empire.

77    Some other traditional interpretations of this story also highlight this. For example, an intertestamental text called the *Book of Jubilees*, says that the people intended to use the tower to ascend into Heaven (see, Jubilees 10:19). Another first-century text pushes this further and suggests that the people intended to "pierce" Heaven in order to see what it was made of (an idiomatic way of expressing the desire to start a fight) (see 3 Baruch 3:7-8).

78    Tellingly, Genesis 10:8-12 speaks of Nimrod, a descendent of Noah's son, Ham. According to this text, Nimrod had *already* founded the beginning of an empire at Babel, which then extended its reign (or should we say grip) into the surrounding nations. Since Nimrod was an acclaimed warrior, it's likely that this extension took place through waging wars and subjugating other people groups. Therefore, by the time we get to Genesis 11, the people present at Babel could be Nimrod's people, including biological kin and the people he has subjugated to speak the same language.

Also, in light of a previous note (76), it could be that the recorder of this text wishes to use this story as a backdrop to the origins of the Babylonian Empire, and by extension, all oppressive world orders (depending on when we understand this text to have been put down in its final written from, and if we assume this was penned during Israel's exile in Babylon).

79    Understanding the gift of languages as a *restorative* act is important for how we also understand the scene in Acts 2, where God gives the disciples the gift of speaking in unknown languages. Often, because we see the Genesis 11 account of confusing the languages as a punishment (people won't be able to understand each other), Acts 2 is then understood as a reversal of this (people can now understand each other). However, what if Acts 2 is not a reversal of Genesis 11, but a *reaffirmation* of God's redemptive actions in Genesis 11? In other words, as with Babel, God is saying that his glory is not restricted to one nation or one language, and that the world in all its diversity (all tribes, all tongues, all peoples) is to display the glory of God in creation. (See also Revelation 5:9-10, 7:9-10 and Ephesians 3:10 for further reflection).

80    Isaiah 2:2-5.

81    Isaiah 25:6-8 (see also Isaiah 65:17-25).

82    Isaiah 27:1 (see also Psalm 89:10).

83    Isaiah 26:19.

84    Ezekiel 40 – 48, especially Ezekiel 47:9 (NLT). See also Ezekiel 36:35.

*Eschatology* is the theological word for the study of the End Times, or last things. My hope is that through this book, and others mentioned in the Further Reading section, we will come to see this 'end' not as a bad thing, nor understand it as an end where things cease to exist. This end is the beginning, and it is beautiful. This is an end to death and chaos.

85    Micah 4:1-5.

86    As examples see, Jeremiah 31, Ezekiel 36 – 37, Hosea 14, Amos 9:13-15, Micah 2:12 – 13 and Zephaniah 3.

87    The poetic books of Job, Psalms, Proverbs and Ecclesiastes are good places to start for this mix of sentiment.

88    The Wisdom of Solomon 1:12-15 (NRSV).

89    The Wisdom of Solomon 5:17-23.

90    2 Esdras 76, 112.

91    See Sirach 16:26 – 17:2, 17: 30 – 18:14, 38:16-23 and 41:1-4, 11-13.

92    For Mary, see Luke 1:46-55. For Hannah see 1 Samuel 2:1-10.

93    Luke 1:67-79.

94    Luke 1:78-79 (NLT).

95    Luke 2:25-31.

96    Matthew 1:21.

97    John 10:10.

98    John 11:25-26.

99    John 3:16-17 (NLT).

100    Ephesians 1:9-10.

101    Romans 8:18-23.

102    For some example texts on the church's life together, see Acts 2:43-47, 4:32-37. Also, for a great sociological study of the early church's community life I would highly recommend Rodney Stark's *The Rise of Christianity: How the Obscure, Marginal Jesus Movement Became the Dominant Religious Force in the Western World in a Few Centuries* (San Francisco, HarperCollins, 1997).

103    Acts 2:38-40.

104    Acts 3:20-21 (NLT) [italics mine].

105    For examples, Acts 7:2-56, 10:34-47, 13:13-42, 17:16-31. I should also add that the thrust of this preaching, and of the book of Acts, is the declaration of Jesus' ascension and Kingship over the world—this-world.

106    Revelation 21:3 (NLT).

107    Revelation 21:5 (NLT).

108    Compare 1 Kings 6:19-20, Ezekiel 41:4, Revelation 21:16.

109    Habakkuk 2:14, Isaiah 11:9b-10.

110    At this point, the warning of God to Cain springs to mind. After God chooses not to accept Cain's offering of farm produce (and we're not sure why God refused this—but it needn't be read as a refusal stemming from displeasure), Cain goes off in an angry, dejected grump. Unsurprisingly, God pursues a relationship with Cain, and tells Cain to be careful of the way in which he reacts, or responds and *interprets* God's refusal of his offering. God tells Cain to, 'Watch out!', but God is not saying that he is the one that Cain needs to watch out for. Cain's real enemy, as God goes on to indicate, is Sin. As the NLT translates it, 'Sin is waiting to attack and destroy you, and you must subdue it' (Genesis 4:7b)

111    John 20:1-18.

112    See Isaiah 58:6-14, 59:4-8, 61:8, Amos 5:6-15, Micah 6: 8, Proverbs 31: 8 as examples.

113    The blessing of Jesus as given in John 14:27 (NKJV) [text in brackets is mine].

114    Matthew 5:9 (NLT) [text in brackets and italics are mine].

## PART FOUR

115    Howard Thurman, *The Search for Common Ground* (Richmond, IN: Friends United Press, 1986). Used by permission of Friends United Press.

116    God's question to Cain after the murder of Abel in Genesis 4:9.

117    Attributed to the novelist Alexandre Dumas, père (AD 1802-1870).

118    See Rabbi Lord Jonathan Sacks, *Not In God's Name: Confronting Religious Violence* (London: Hodder & Stoughton, An Hachette UK Company, 2015), p. 147.

119    See Hebrews 11:8-10.

120    For the details of the call to Abram/Abraham and Sarai/Sarah see Genesis 12:1-3, 17:1-6, 15-21 and 18:10-15, 17-19.

121    For examples of the prophetic critique—Israel's critique of itself—see: Isaiah 58:3 – 59:16, Ezekiel 22:1-16, 34, Amos 2:4-8, 5:6-15, Micah 2:1-2, 6:6 – 7:6, Habakkuk 2:4-17, Zephaniah 3:1-5, Zechariah 7:4-10.

122    Isaiah 9:6-7 (NLT).

123    Luke 4:17-20 (NLT).

124    Luke 4:21 (NLT).

125    Isaiah 61:1-2 (NLT). Scholar Kenneth E. Bailey, in his book, *Jesus Through Middle Eastern Eyes: Cultural Studies in the Gospels* (London: SPCK, 2008), also notes that the people would have expected Jesus to continue reading all the way up to verse 7 of Isaiah 61. Bailey states that Jesus' omission of part of a verse would have obviously upset people, but the omission of the next two stanzas of Isaiah's poem would have been even more abrasive to their world view (see Bailey, chapter 12, especially p. 152).

126    See Luke 12:54-59. By the way, when Jesus says this, he is not discussing the relationship between humanity and God. Jesus is talking (in parable) to those Jews who desire to participate in the revolt against Roman rule through military action. Jesus knows that if they seek violent revolution, and start the ball rolling down that track, then Rome will push back with greater violence and subjugate them even more. Which, as I said, is what happened in AD 70.

127    Luke 12:52.

128    I know this is a long aside. But I have to spell this out because some people, who have read the aforementioned words of Jesus, have taken those words and used them as "divine consent" to wage war and not to work for peace, even

though peace-making is what we are called to. Some people have used these words as permission to draw lines. Some, sadly, have hijacked these words for use within their abusive forms of personal evangelism, which seek to aggravate and upset people. We are not to see Jesus' words as his consent for us to be argumentative, violent, oppressive or aggressive. Nor is this consent for us to violate people's privacy or to force our opinions on people, and then, when they react against our invasion, say that their reaction is a demonstration of their offense to God's Kingdom, when in actuality it is our rudeness, abrasiveness, crudity and forcefulness that are at fault (in combination with our arrogance, ignorance and inability to hold an amiable conversation), not the Kingdom of God. As the Apostle Peter wrote, we should be ready to share our hope when asked and should do so with tenderness, compassion and humility (see 1 Peter 3:15). We could also mention Paul's advice in 1 Thessalonians 4:11.

129    2 Corinthians 2:15-16.

130    This saying is attributed to St. Francis within the early Franciscan text *The Legend of the Three Companions*, paragraph 58, circa 13c.

131    Luke 6:27-36 (NLT, 2015 ed.) [italics mine].

132    See Psalms 145:20, 58:6-11, 55:23 as examples. Or, for an example that clearly cuts against Jesus' words; '[God] hates everyone who loves violence. He rains down blazing coals on the wicked, punishing them with burning sulfur and scorching winds' (Psalm 11:5-6, NLT).

133    In a similar way, Jesus' words in Matthew 5:43-45, which say that God sends rain on the just and unjust alike, also contravene the ideas presented in Deuteronomy 11:16-17.

134    Luke 6:36-38.

135    Howard Thurman, *The Search for Common Ground*. Used by permission of Friends United Press.

136    Luke 6:39 (NLT).

137    As well as this chapter, there are also three blog posts I have written that exemplify this point. You can find them at my blog site; tristansherwin.wordpress.com. They're entitled: Spit, Mud and Divine Stereotypes; "The Mange", Exclusion and Stigmas; and A Tale of Two Banquets.

138    See Luke 4:23-28.

139    Luke 4:29-30 (NLT, 2015 ed.).

140    Ephesians 2:4-7 (NLT).

141    The story I'm about to explore can be found in Luke 9:43-56.

142    See Luke 9:28-43.

143    Luke 9:48 (NLT) [italics mine].

144    Luke 9:50 (NLT).

145    This notorious story can be found in Genesis 19.

146    Some versions of this passage show James and John making their request by invoking Elijah's ministry into it ("Can we call down fire, like Elijah did?"). I've understood this as them recalling the competition at Mount Carmel (see 1 Kings 18). But there is another account in 2 Kings 1 where Elijah calls down fire upon other humans as proof of his "divine favour". Of course, this could be the story to which the disciples are referring, and not the sacrificial fire of 1 Kings 18. If this is the case, I think the point I'm making would still be valid—more so, as James' and John's request would still be seen as an attempt to demonstrate who are God's people and who are not.

147    Acts 2:3 (NLT).

148    1 John 4:7 (NLT).

149    John 15:13.

150    Claudia Rankine, *Citizen: An American Lyric* (London: Penguin Books, 2014), p. 135. [Reprinted with the permission of The Permissions Company, LLC on behalf of Graywolf Press, www.graywolfpress.org. And with permission from Penguin Books Ltd. Copyright © Claudia Rankine, 2015]

151    Genesis 4:10 (NLT).

152    Jesus' conclusion to his Parable of the Great Banquet, in Matthew 22:14. Often, this line is understood as putting a positive emphasis on the *chosen* few (the opposite of what I have suggested in my sentence). However, it shouldn't be forgotten that, in the telling of this story, Jesus is conversing with some Pharisees who believed their status at the feast of the Kingdom was based on being chosen. Like other religious leaders, they didn't like the open commensality of Jesus' table, and Jesus tells this parable to challenge their idea of how God's invitation looks; the host of this feast invites the *many*, the *whosoever*, in this story. It's the *many* who should be seen as the positive, and the 'few [who] are chosen' should be seen as a criticism of holding to ideas of being included, whilst many are excluded.

153    Luke 2:14 (KJV).

**PART FIVE**

154    As sung by the character Calaf in the opera *Turandot*, by Giacomo Puccini (AD 1858-1924). Translated, it means, 'no one sleeps, no one sleeps'.

155    John 3:30 (NLT). John the Baptist's comparison of his ministry with that of Jesus.

156    Attributed to the novelist Victor Hugo (AD 1802-1885).

157    *Feudal Brandlords* is the term that journalist Naomi Klein uses in her book, *No Logo*, "Chapter 7, Mergers and Synergy: The Creation of Commercial Utopias", 10th anniversary ed. (London: 4th Estate Books, 2010), p. 149.

158    Matthew 4:9 (NLT) [italics mine].

159   This story can be found in the chapter called 'The Mirror of Erised', in J. K. Rowling's *Harry Potter and the Philosopher's Stone.* (or, for my American audience, *Harry Potter and the Sorcerer's Stone*). 1997.

160   George R. R. Martin, *A Game of Thrones*. This particular scene can be found in the chapter called *Eddard*—which doesn't help. So if you have the paperback HarperVoyager 2014 edition, you'll find this conversation at the bottom of page 299. If not, happy hunting!

161   In part, I do get this, but only in part, and only in certain contexts. Universalise this advice though, allow it to be true in whatever context, and it can be dangerous. I can, hand on heart, speak only of myself, but there are parts of me that need to be shut down, not switched on. There are desires, habits, and oppressive and objectifying perspectives of others that would be unhealthy and dangerous to encourage in me—things that should be rejected and called out. I might be out of hand to say this, but it's Christ-likeness that I've been called to learn and follow; not my whims or whatever I feel is true to *me*. We need to exercise wisdom, making certain that we are listening to the right voices with the right motives. Not all encouragement is good for us, nor is all criticism is bad.

162   Jeremiah 29:11.

163   Joseph's story runs from chapter 37 of Genesis all the way to the end of the book at chapter 50.

164   Genesis 50:4-6.

165   *Telos* is the Greek term for end goal, or purpose.

166   Genesis 50:20.

167   Romans 8:35-39.

168   It's OK, feel free to sing. I won't stop you.

169    I'm going to follow the account in Matthew 19:16-30. But you can also read this story in Mark 10:17 and Luke 18:18.

170    The Ten Commandments can be found in Exodus 20:1-17 and Deuteronomy 5:6-21.

171    If you don't celebrate Justin Bieber, please feel free to insert the name of your own preferred celebrity here instead.

172    As Jesus explained in one of his parables, '[T]o all those who have, more will be given; but from those who have nothing, even what they have will be taken away (Luke 19:26, NRSV). Although I do believe Jesus expressed this same sentiment in other places and by it meant to say that our hunger for God will be met with revelation from God (see Matt. 13:12, Mark 4:24-25, and a similar parable to this one in Matt. 25:14-30), could it be that in this specific parable Jesus is not talking about the Kingdom of God? Perhaps Jesus tells this parable to demonstrate the corrupt ways in which worldly empires are built and maintained through oppression and violence? I'll leave this as food for thought. But maybe the hero of this particular tale is not the King (who deprives his servants and slaughters those who reject him, and which is hardly a reflection of the benevolent God we see exhibited in Jesus), but that one servant who refuses to extend and collude with this king's malign agenda and manifesto? I'm probably wrong, but I think it's worth considering.

173    1 John 4:9-12, 19.

PART SIX

174    Exodus 3:14 (NLT, 2015 ed.). God's name, as revealed to Moses from the burning bush.

175    Frankenstein's Creation/Monster in Mary Shelley, *Frankenstein; or, The Modern Prometheus*, Volume 2, Chapter 7 (1818).

176    Arthur Schopenhauer (AD 1788-1860), *Studies In Pessimism: The Essays*.

177   Attributed to St Gregory of Nyssa (c. AD 335–394).

178   Luke 23:23, 34 (NLT).

179   This quote is taken from the beginning of chapter 3 ("The Night Shadows") of *A Tale of Two Cities*.

180   If you want to get to the root of this deep, existential mystery, then your first port of call would be to listen to the song "Wannabe" (1996) by the Spice Girls. The choice is yours.

181   Richard Rohr with Mike Morrell, *The Divine Dance: The Trinity and Your Transformation* (London: SPCK, 2016), p. 27. Reproduced with permission of The Licensor through PLSclear.

182   Marcus du Sautoy, *What We Cannot Know: Explorations at the Edge of Knowledge*, Hardback (London: 4th Estate. An imprint of HarperCollins Publishers, 2016), p. 410. [italics mine]. Reprinted by permission of HarperCollins Publishers Ltd. [For US, Canada and Philippine territories: Excerpt(s) from THE GREAT UNKNOWN: SEVEN JOURNEYS TO THE FRONTIERS OF SCIENCE by Marcus du Sautoy, copyright © 2016 by Marcus du Sautoy. Used by permission of Viking Books, an imprint of Penguin Publishing Group, a division of Penguin Random House LLC. All rights reserved].

As a further aside, the philosopher and polymath, Raymond Tallis (who happens to be one of my favourite writers), also makes this bastardisation (to use Sautoy's term) his central reason for being an atheist. He terms the mishmash of ideas that describe a monotheistic God as being an "ontological monstrosity", akin to a Chimera, as if someone has stuck the back end of a microbe to the front end of a giant [see his essay, "Why I Am an Atheist", *In Defence of Wonder: and Other Philosophical Reflections* (Durham, UK: Acumen Publishing, 2012), pp. 213-224].

183   Genesis 3:10 (NIV).

184   Romans 1:25a (NLT, 2015 ed.).

185    The "curses" (as they have been called through the years) given in Genesis 3:14-17, are not to be seen as God inflicting suffering and subjugation on humanity. This is God spelling out the self-induced consequences of their behaviour. This is what a world without paradise looks like; it is a world where humanity has refused to image God's likeness. Like the Old Testament prophets, God is merely forth-telling, not foretelling.

186    Genesis 3:23 (NLT) [italics mine].

187    You can read the story we are about to explore in Exodus 32.

188    Exodus 32:14 (NLT) [italics mine].

189    Exodus 32:26b-27 (NLT).

190    It's important to highlight how Moses goes about this, too. Moses, as we've seen, declares that *God told him* that the "innocent" people should pick up their swords and slaughter everybody else. But when did God mention this? All God had said previously was that he intended to destroy the people for their disobedience, but God never spelt out the means of doing so.

Of course, we may wonder how God would have gone about destroying the people if Moses had not persuaded God otherwise. However, God would not have needed to employ violence to carry out his original judgement against the people. After all, later on within this story, God punishes a whole generation of Hebrews by prohibiting their entrance into the Promised Land because of their disobedience (Numbers 14:26-30). In this case, God does not *actively* destroy anybody; God allows everybody to live out their full life cycle and die of natural causes within the Sinai wilderness. To add nuance to this thought, the end of the passage in Exodus 32 declares that God sent a plague upon the people to punish them for worshipping the image that Aaron had made (verse 35)—if God's judgement had been the violent sword that Moses declared, then why send this plague (if that is what God did)? Tellingly, the account doesn't record how many (if any) died from this plague.

I'm saying this because even if Moses was right in falling back on God's previous decision (and I don't believe he was), Moses still puts words in God's mouth and assumes that God's punishment should be carried out by actively instigating a violent, bloody massacre.

191    Numbers 20:12 (NLT) [italics mine].

192    By the way, if you want a great little book on God's grace in the Old Testament (an idea which is often wrongly attributed exclusively to God's portrayal in the New Testament) then Preston Sprinkle's book, *Charis: God's Scandalous Grace for Us* (Colorado Springs, CO: David C. Cook, 2014) would be a good place to start. If you want a great book on the Old Testament's representation of a God who speaks out against injustice and oppression etc., then you could read the Old Testament (especially the Prophets), or you could pick up anything by the excellent Old Testament scholar, Walter Brueggemann. There's also some great insights in Abraham Joshua Heschel's *The Prophets* (Harper Perennial Classics, 2001).

193    Rabbi Lord Jonathan Sacks, *Not In God's Name: Confronting Religious Violence* (London: Hodder & Stoughton, 2015), p. 103. © Jonathan Sacks 2015. Reproduced by permission of Hodder and Stoughton Limited, and Used by permission of Schocken Books, an imprint of Knopf Doubleday Publishing Group, a division of Penguin Random House LLC. All rights reserved.

194    Hebrews 4:12 (NLT) [italics mine]. We could, of course, go into a discussion about what the author is referring to as 'the word of God' (and have a similar conversation over the verse in 2 Timothy 3:16). This is an important conversation, rightly deserving a book of its own. If this is something you want to explore, then here are a couple of starters (in addition to the books already listed in the further reading section): Kenton L. Sparks, *Sacred Word, Broken Word: Biblical Authority and the Dark Side of Scripture* (Grand Rapids, MI: Eerdmans, 2011); Christian Smith,

*The Bible Made Impossible: Why Biblicism Is Not a Truly Evangelical Reading of Scripture* (Grand Rapids, MI: Brazos, 2011).

195    *The Handmaid's Tale* (London: Vintage, 2017), p. xiv.

196    John 1:10-18 (NLT).

197    That's why it's important to hold to the fact that Jesus' life, death and resurrection are *according to the Scriptures*, as the New Testament writers tell us. The writers of the New Testament weren't referring to or including their own words when they said this, but to the Hebrew Bible, the Law and the Prophets (i.e. The Old Testament). They knew that what happened in and through Jesus makes no sense if it is detached from the narrative trajectory and hopes of the Old Testament. Sadly, as history has shown, when we have unplugged Jesus from the contexts of the Hebrew Bible, we'll instead read his story according to the Greek philosopher Plato, or Dante's Inferno, or Tim LaHaye's hideous *Left Behind* series, and then totally miss how Jesus solves the real problem, which is our dissonance with God.

198    Strangely, Christianity has had a certain resistance to talking about Scripture in this way, whereas our parent religion—Judaism—has, in the main, always shown an ability to discuss and interpret the Scriptures more fluidly, with the understanding that there is an unfolding taking place across the whole. And yet, contradictory to this, the central claim of historic Christianity, that has separated it from Judaism, is the doctrine of the divinity of Jesus and the fuller revelation of God which he has brought to us.

199    As a thought experiment, if you wrote down the story of your own inspired encounters with God, would it look cohesive? Would your theologies remain consistent throughout the chapters of your life? Has God always looked the same? I'm going to guess that the answer would be no (and you've had the benefit of more than two millennia's worth of theological abstractions). Personally speaking, I've only been on this road for twenty years and my 'convictions' have changed an

awful lot in that time. Not only has my view of God changed, but looking back on my experiences of God, I can also see that in many instances I may have walked away with the wrong impressions.

Let's take this thought experiment a step further, and stop making it about you or me as individuals, and let's enlarge it to include the journey of every member of your local church. When you do this, is our corporate experience of God now less cohesive, or more consistent? Do you all share the same views on God? Has your church's picture of God changed over time? Again, I'm going with it being less cohesive and it having changed over time—especially if we incorporate the history of your local church into the longer history of Christianity and its many streams. Now increase that number of people to a nation, like Israel, who exist in some culture which has numerous other understandings of god(s), and increase the time frame from a lifetime to over a thousand years.

Am I making my point?

200   Raymund Schwager, SJ, *Must There Be Scapegoats? Violence and Redemption in the Bible* (New York: Crossroad Publishing Company, 2000), p.209. Used with permission.

201   Under commandment number two (see Exodus 20:5-6, Deuteronomy 5:9).

202   It's worth noting that castration didn't only happen as a result of ceremonial rituals, but it could also occur through torture or war. In all cases, the thrust of the Mosaic command is not about viewing people who were eunuchs in a negative light, but rather about desacralizing violent acts that others thought would please God and thus be endorsed by God.

203   As an example of a revision to the sacrificial system, the limits that Moses imposed on it are revealing. It's telling that Deuteronomy 12:13 forbids sacrifices being offered anywhere people fancied and, through the development of priesthood, by anyone who wanted to. Pagan sacrificial sites could be established

in any place (with mountain tops being preferred), but the Mosaic Law stated that one place only could be the official site: the Tabernacle (also see Leviticus 17:1-9). As an extra aside on this point, but in keeping with this section's theme, the existence of this law still didn't prevent the prophet Elijah (who wasn't a priest) from building a sacrificial altar on top of Mount Carmel which, at that time, was a pagan sacrificial site to the god Baal (see 1 Kings 18).

204 I should point out that suggesting the sacrificial rituals were something God appropriated is not a new, radical theology. As a few examples: Justin Martyr (AD 100-165), posited that God accommodated the sacrifices to keep Israel—who were used to a culture of sacrifice—away from sacrificing to false deities and practicing idolatry (see, *Dialogue of Trypho* 19, *ANF* 1:204). And Gregory of Nazianzus (AD 330-390) argued that God adopted the primitive religious behaviours that the people were accustomed to and gradually moved them through several changes that moved away from the necessity of sacrifice (*Orations* 5.25, *NPNF2* 7:325-26). The famous French physicist, mathematician and Catholic theologian, Blaise Pascal (AD 1623-1662), commenting on Jeremiah 7:22, insightfully noted, similar to Justin Martyr, that it was not until the Israelites had sacrificed to the Golden Calf that God appropriated the sacrifices, in an attempt to put 'an evil custom to good use' (*Pensées*, 713, Brunschvicq ed.).

205  Psalm 40:6 (NLT) [italics mine].

206  Psalm 51:16-17 (NLT). See also Isaiah 1: 10-17, which also stresses that what God desired wasn't sacrifices, but a change of heart and the justice that flows from this.

207  Hosea 6:6 (NLT) [italics mine]. Jesus quotes this particular verse in Matthew 9:13. This same sentiment is echoed in Psalm 50:8-14, 23.

208  The New Testament writer of Hebrews would echo these thoughts, and would even go as far as to say that the sacrifices were impotent in achieving the forgiveness of sin. See Hebrews 10:1-10.

209    Compare the account of 2 Samuel 7 with 1 Chronicles 28 (esp. verse 3).

210    See Matthew 5:21, 27, 31, 33, 38, and 43.

211 Derek Flood, *Disarming Scripture: Cherry-Picking Liberals, Violence-Loving Conservatives, and Why We All Need to Learn to Read the Bible like Jesus Did* (San Francisco, CA: Metanoia Books, 2014).

212    Or, as Jesus put it, when discussing the matter of divorce in Mark 10:6, these laws reflected the hardness of our own hearts towards the full revelation and intent of God.

213    For example, see Leviticus 19:18 & 33, Deuteronomy 10:18-19, 15:13-14, 23:15-16, 24:17-22, 26:12-15.

214    See Micah 6:8, for example.

215    Genesis 9:6.

216    Matthew 26:52b (NLT).

217    Genesis 9:6.

218    Genesis 4:11-16.

219    Jonah 4:2 (NKJV) [italics mine].

220    Taken from the NLT [italics mine]. Also see Exodus 33:11.

221    The other Gospel writers, Matthew, Mark and Luke (whose writings are known as the Synoptic Gospels), also make this exact same point, although they do so in a different style. In contrast to John, who states it as bluntly as he can, the Synoptic accounts relay the transfiguration of Jesus on top of a mountain (See Matthew 17:1-13, Mark 9:2-13, and Luke 9:28-36. Also see 2 Peter 1:16-19). In this powerful story, Moses (representing the Torah/Law) and Elijah (representing the Prophets) appear and have a conversation with Jesus. Eventually though, despite Peter's desire to build shelters for all three of these great men, Moses and Elijah

fade away, leaving Jesus on his own. Peter wants to show equal honour to all three of them; his offer to build them each a shelter reveals his idea of them all having equal authority. But at that moment, a cloud covers the sky and a voice is heard saying, 'This is my son; listen to him'. Or, another way of saying that is, 'This is my likeness; this is my representative; listen to him'. In other words, it is Jesus, not Moses and Elijah, nor the Law and the Prophets (the Old Testament), that reveals the true likeness of God to us. That's not to say that the Synoptic authors suggested that we toss out the Old Testament—absolutely not. Their accounts of Jesus' life are brimming with ecstatic echoes of the Hebrew Scriptures. Rather, like John, they saw Jesus as the interpretative lens and focal point of what had been said before. Jesus, God incarnate, is the last and final word on what God is like—not Moses, nor the Prophets. Jesus is the testimony (the Testament) of God's character. So what the old testimony says of God must be measured against what Christ shows of God, and if it doesn't fit, then it's not of God.

Ergo, Moses' ideas of God can't be used to overrule what God has shown us in Jesus. It's Jesus who is the revealed Word of God, not the Bible. For example, this means we can look back at the "divine" commissioning of Joshua to slaughter the Canaanites, and say this wasn't God. I can believe that Joshua believed he was acting in accordance to what he thought was God's will, but this doesn't fit with what we are shown through Jesus. Especially a Jesus who teaches us that God is kind to the wicked, a Jesus who teaches us to love our enemies because then we exhibit what God is like, a Jesus who rebukes his disciples for wanting to burn down a village, and a Jesus who speaks forgiveness over his killers.

This may sound revolutionary—and it is, I suppose. But this is the central claim of Christianity: Jesus shows us God's exact likeness; Jesus is the self-disclosure of God (see also Hebrews 1:1-3).

222    Again, I need to stress that I don't believe that the violent portraits of God within the Old Testament should be thrown away or dismissed; they're not in the

Scriptures by accident, but for our instruction, and, if viewed through the Cross of Christ, they speak of the same sin-bearing God that we witness at the crucifixion. In this sense, I'm in total agreement with Greg Boyd when he suggests (referencing Walter Wink) 'that the violence attributed to God in the OT was actually "projected onto God" by "Yahweh's followers"... [and] the presence of these projections in the inspired witness to God's covenantal faithfulness [the Scriptures] is a testament to God's covenantal faithfulness and his self-sacrificial, sin-bearing nature' [*The Crucifixion of the Warrior God: Interpreting the Old Testament's Violent Portraits of God in Light of the Cross*, Volume 2 (Minneapolis, MN: Fortress Press, 2017), p. 689. Used with permission].

What is meant by that is, by allowing the people to project their sin (their idolatry) upon the Divine nature, these texts work like "literary crosses", to use Boyd's term. These texts expose our nature and inclination to violence, but by bearing these projections (Sin), they also testify of the same non-coercive, self-emptying, loving, faithful God that is revealed in the crucified Christ. How the cross achieves this double agenda will be the focus of the next section, and although I won't go back to re-examine the violent Old Testament scenes, they could be seen in the same light.

I only came to Boyd's work after completing the final draft of this manuscript, but I would recommend it for those who wish to delve further into his "Cruciform Hermeneutic" of the violent texts of the Bible.

I also want to add (again, stressing a point that I have already made), that I am not saying that the New Testament story is about a different God as the Old. The God who was happy to sit and eat with the leaders of the Hebrew nation on the top of Mount Sinai (see Exodus 24:9-11), and who physically wrestled Jacob, is the same God who was equally as happy to rub muddy-spittle into humanity's blind eyes in order to restore our sight. As such, I'm not endorsing a supersessionist position of a simplistic and inaccurate dualism between the God of the Old and the God of the

New. It's much more complex than that. The God of the Hebrew Bible is not a villain, as I hope this section has made clear. I've purposely used the Old Testament in dialogue with itself to demonstrate that there is a conversation of discovery taking place among its authors. As I've hinted, these stories tell us something of where God's people were at theologically, and, as Kenton Sparks highlights in his book *God's Word in Human Words* (see the Further Reading section), the Old Testament doesn't just present one theological perspective but numerous perspectives.

223    I'm not going to explain. But if you want to know more, type the words *Skywalker* and *Seagulls* into an Internet search-engine.

224    This scene is from Star Wars; *The Empire Strikes Back*. Lucasfilm. 1980.

225    Acts 4:27 (NLT).

226    Isaiah 53:3-7 (CJB). The full section is found in Isaiah 52:13-53:12

227    I know someone is going to want to quote Jesus' last words given in Matthew 27:46 and Mark 16:34 ('My God, My God, why have you forsaken me?') as being against this idea. However, Jesus' final words are a recital of the opening verse from Psalm 22—an important Messianic Psalm. And so it's not that Jesus is only saying these nine words, but, as Jewish custom expects, the full thrust of the Psalm is invoked and would begin to echo into his listeners' ears. (Or, if you hold to the view that Jesus didn't say these words, the Gospel writers are using this verse to invoke the whole Psalm.) If you read Psalm 22, you will see that it is not God who has physically abandoned the Psalmist to a painful plight, but that the suffering is being inflicted by other humans wishing to victimise and scapegoat the Psalmist. Also, the Psalm concludes, not on a note of feeling abandonment by God, but on a note of confidence that God will vindicate the one suffering; God will rescue the Psalmist and put his enemies to shame.

Some people refute this suggestion that the entire psalm is being invoked through Jesus' quoting of its opening verse, but it's insightful to also take note of the response of those hearing Jesus say these words. None of the bystanders say, 'Yes, you are forsaken!' Some of them think he's calling out for the Old Testament prophet Elijah to come and rescue him. Whereas a few others interpret Jesus's cry as being one of thirst, probably mishearing his words, and begin to lift up a wine-soaked sponge to Jesus' lips. As they do so, though, those who thought that Jesus was calling for Elijah intervene, saying, 'Leave him alone. Let's see whether Elijah will come and save him' (Matt. 27:49). Again, it's telling that those who hear Jesus' cry of "Eli, Eli, lema sabachthani" are anticipating a rescue. In other words, although they miss the connection with Psalm 22, his immediate listeners begin to look for Jesus' vindication from this violent death *via* an act of divine intervention. In short, it's not a question of divine forsakenness that hangs in the atmosphere after these words are spoken in Matthew and Mark, but hope: will God rescue the one suffering and how will God go about it?

Additionally, it's crucial to remember that only Matthew and Mark record this so-called "cry of dereliction", as some have come to name it.

Luke's Gospel only records Jesus quoting the first of half of Psalm 31:15 (Luke 23:46: 'Father, into your hands I entrust my spirit'), which, in line with what I have said above, is also a cry for vindication and rescue, especially as the verse concludes with, 'Rescue me, LORD, for you are a faithful God'.

John's Gospel, on the other hand, has Jesus saying, 'I am thirsty' (John 19:28) and then records the bystanders lifting up a wine-soaked sponge to his lips. In this way, John's narrative helps to shed light on why, in Matthew and Mark's account, some people offer Jesus a drink of wine after he quotes Psalm 22:1; the fifteenth verse of this Psalm also has the psalmist poetically expressing his thirst for rescue and vindication by saying, 'My tongue sticks to the roof of my mouth'. Therefore, based on John's record, it could be argued that the bystanders at the crucifixion in

Matthew and Mark's gospel *do* understand Jesus to be invoking more of Psalm 22 than the first verse alone.

228    Attributed to the Roman playwright, Titus Maccius Plautus (c. 254 - 184 BC), from his comedy *Asinaria*. The full quote is: 'Man is wolf to man, when he doesn't know what sort he is'.

229    T. F. Torrance, *Incarnation: The Person and Life of Christ* (Downers Grove, IL: IVP Academic, 2008), pp. 245-246.

230    See Hebrews 12:24.

231    Bishop Kallistos Ware, *The Orthodox Way*, rev. ed., "Chapter 4, God as Man" (Crestwood, NY: St Vladimir's Seminary Press, 1995), pp. 81-82. Used with permission.

232    I feel the need to add here an important endnote, which needs to be stressed, but without interrupting the flow of the section. *I do not believe in the total depravity of humanity. Nor do I believe in the total depravity of the material creation, either.* Unlike Augustine, I do not think all mankind is derived from condemned stock whose first nature is evil and carnal (*City Of God*, 15:1), and unlike Calvin, I certainly do not think that, 'their whole nature is a seed of sin; hence, it can only be hateful and abhorrent to God' (*Institutes*, II.1.8). I believe we are *inherently* good, and that God loves us. I believe we are conceived with the divine intent of being a blessing to the world. We are all made for God's glory; all of us are called to be a part of this global, beautiful divine-image-bearing mosaic of humanity. I do hope that this has been clear, though implicit, in this book so far.

We need to see that our humanness is not abhorrent to God, or untouchable, or rotten to the core. Skin, sinews, bones, blood—God is OK with all of this. God's work throughout the Bible, culminating in Christ, is not to turn us into angels (or God) but to restore us to our vocation as human beings in a material world. We're called to embody the marriage of Heaven and Earth.

The problem is not our flesh-life, material existence. The issue is with our idolatry, that is, what we believe—what we give allegiance—which then informs our acts. We are not depraved, but we can, and we do, behave under the influence. We are influenced by the false images we have conceived, the idols we have made, the projections (the dreams or nightmares or world views) of our imaginations, and the messages we absorb from society's false prophets. For example, think about the damaging influence that the false standards and conceptions of beauty, power and success have put us under. Think about how something like pornography has distorted sex into masturbation and sexual beings into sex dolls that sexual acts are performed upon (and, in our twisted patriarchal culture, it's usually women who are perceived as the sex dolls as a result). Think about how power and prestige are dressed up and displayed, nationally or individually, through military strength and affluent materialism; think about the 'dog-eat-dog' world this continues to create in its wake.

These views, these images, have shaped our world and continue to drive how our world is run, subsequently creating systems in which people are objectified, impoverished and deprived of human dignity and real choice. The mass of our world's population finds itself being the canvas for the images and ideals of a few.

The truth is that even in our apparently atheistic and secular age, idolatry continues to shape the face of the world. Our wrongful images create a way of viewing life and enslave us to it. In this sense then, it's not that we are punished *for* our Sin (idolatry), we are punished *by* it. It distorts how we view others, ourselves and the world we live in, and as a result, these distortions manifest through our actions towards others, ourselves and the world we live in.

So God has to deal with our idolatry and the dark powers behind our idolatry in order to deal with the sinful acts that flow from it. If all God does is forgive us, without dealing with our enslavement, then we're still in bondage; we will still reflect what we worship. What I want us to grasp is that the incarnation is not about making forgiveness available. God already made forgiveness available within the stories we read in both the Old and New Testaments. *The incarnation is about liberation*; it smashes our idolatry to pieces and frees us from our enslavement to Sin.

Of course, in mentioning 'the dark powers' some might wonder why I haven't touched on these more within the scope of this book. To be specific, why have I focused more on human agency than on the role Satan etc.? Well, in short, it's not because I deem that conversation unnecessary, and it's certainly not because of any disbelief in dark, corrupting powers. That conversation is definitely important. However, within this book, humanity's culpability and agency has been my focus.

## PART SEVEN

233    Spoken by Antonio in Act 2, Scene 1 of William Shakespeare's *The Tempest*.

234    H. G. Wells, *'The Discovery of the Future'*, *Nature 65*, 326 (1902). Used as an epigraph in Carl Sagan, *Cosmos*, Who Speaks For Earth? (New York: Ballantine Books, 2013), p. 336.

235    Julian of Norwich (AD 1342-1416). Taken from the Short Text of *Revelations of Divine Love*.

236    Abraham J. Heschel, *The Prophets* (New York, NY: Harper Perennial Classics, 2001), p. 231 (Copyright © 1962 by Abraham Heschel. Reprinted by permission of HarperCollins Publishers).

237    These are Jesus' words to his disciples, in John 13:34-35.

238    The term 'Second Coming' does not imply that Jesus has temporarily abandoned us; Christ's ascension should not be understood this way. The Ascension is not describing Jesus' departure and withdrawal, but his enthronement

over all creation (for example see 1 Peter 3:22, Colossians 3:1-4, and Philippians 2:9-11).

239    See Hebrews 13:8.

240    John 10:10.

241    Barbara R. Rossing, *The Rapture Exposed: The Message of Hope in the Book of Revelation*, "The Invention of the Rapture" (New York: Basic Books, 2004), p. 35. Reprinted by permission of Basic Books, an imprint of Perseus Books, LLC, a subsidiary of Hachette Book Group, Inc.

242    The letter already makes this purpose clear. Its opening verse states, 'This is a revelation of Jesus Christ'.

243    See N. T. Wright, *The New Testament and The People of God*, "The Hope of Israel" (London: SPCK, 1992), p. 333. Also see, N. T. Wright, *Jesus and The Victory of God*, "Stories and the Kingdom (3): Judgement and Vindication" (London: SPCK, 1996). For some more information on the Apocalyptic genre and movement, also see Larry R. Helyer *Exploring Jewish Literature of the Second Temple Period*, "Apolcalypticism: Hope for Hard Times" (Downers Grove, IL: InterVarsity Press, 2002).

244    See Revelation 17

245    To paraphrase and expand slightly Professor Michael J. Gorman's seven attributes of Babylon/Empire [see Michael J. Gorman, *Reading Revelation Responsibly: Uncivil Worship and Witness; Following the Lamb Into the New Creation*, "Revelation 17-18: A Theological Account of Empire ("Babylon") and its Fate" (Eugene, OR: Cascade Books 2011), pp. 145-146]:

(i)    It's a system of right-handed domination that both seduces the already powerful with the idea of more power, and intoxicates the disempowered, common masses with the idea that more power and prosperity equates to better security. Material greed and consumerism is treated as a healthy compulsion which, in the main, goes unnoticed because of its normalisation.

(ii)    It's both territorially grand and ideologically expansive. It creates a pseudo-ecumenism of politics and religion, but ultimately, its priority is on nationalism; both politics and religion are subservient to the Empire's agenda and projected image. It's self-promoting, and blasphemous in its claims to divine rights. Civil symbols are treated as sacred, and must be sworn allegiance to.

(iii)   It presents in a way which looks attractive, and which will be beneficial to its subjects, but this is a mask to hide its abominations (both within its own borders and globally). Its masquerade is a PR stunt to distract the discerning away from noticing its cruelty to creation and humanity; this includes abuse, objectification and oppression of defenceless humans, trafficking, sweat shops, unsustainable use of the world's resources, etc.

(iv)    Although it claims a divine sanction, or divine status, to do what it wants to, Empire is always ultimately opposed to God and those who prophetically witness to God's use of power, as seen in Christ. Empires will seek to silence or eradicate anything or anyone that challenges their self-promoted rule. Counter-imperial voices are treated as treasonous and blasphemous.

(v)     Empires expand through the compliance of the conquered. As they seek to be more centralised in their power, those on the margins increase in number, as their rights, lands, and liberties are traded for promises of protection. This manifests in a trickle-down economy, which never delivers, but which promises its citizens the right to more as long as they surrender more of their rights into the hands of the few.

(vi)    Empires often perish through self-inflicted wounds. Subjects often revolt against the systems they once empowered as and when the system's masquerade comes to light. Some understand this reversal, this self-collapse, as God's judgement.

(vii)     All world empires—the historical realities—are short-term incarnations of a more powerful and lasting ideology of what we call *Empire*.

If we wanted to define what that ideology of *Empire* is, then I believe Old Testament scholar Walter Brueggemann's definition is useful: "What [...] many scholars call empire, I want to call *totalism*. That means a totally contained socioeconomic, political, educational, cultural system, outside of which there is nothing imaginable, there is nothing thinkable, there is nothing sayable, there is nothing doable. That's where we live. That was the regime of Pharaoh, that was the regime of Nebuchadnezzar, that was the regime of the Persians, that was the regime of the Romans, that is the regime of the market ideology in which we live. We live in a totalism that has monopolized all the money, all the technology, all the imagination. The money interests control the media, the courts, increasingly the universities, and have co-opted much of the church." [Walter Brueggemann, Faith and Culture Conference, "Out of Babylon", Word of Life Church, St Joseph, Mo., 2015, http://www.wolc.com/conferenceaudio/. As quoted in Zach Hoag's book *The Light is Winning* (Grand Rapids, MI: Zondervan, 2017), pp. 189-190.]

246   Revelation 1:8 and 22:13.

247   See Tom Wright, *Simply Jesus: Who he was, What he did, Why it Matters* (London: SPCK, 2011).

248   Revelation 12: 11.

249   Michael J. Gorman, *Reading Revelation Responsibly: Uncivil Worship and Witness; Following the Lamb Into the New Creation* (Eugene, OR: Cascade Books, 2011), p. 76. Used with permission.

250   I'm not going to go into a discussion on Hell, and what that means, in this chapter, or this book. Not because I think it's unimportant—quite the opposite. So I

want to take this opportunity to encourage you to read some of the other books mentioned in the Further Reading section for this chapter, especially Bradley Jersak's *Her Gates Will Never Be Shut: Hope, Hell and the New Jerusalem*, which is an excellent and thorough treatment of this topic.

251    Revelation 18:2.

252    *The Road for Paradise*, by C. B. Wishern. (Can be found at https://medium.com/@CBWishern/the-road-for-paradise-a0530ca177c9).    Used with permission.

253    1 John 3:14 (NLT).

254    1 John 1:2 (NLT) [italics mine].

255    1 John 2:15 (NLT).

256    1 John 3:2 (NLT).

257    Or, to use the Apostle Peter's language (when quoting Leviticus), 'We are to be holy as God is holy'; we are to set ourselves apart for and to God's purposes (see 1 Peter 1:13-16).

258    1 John 3:11-13.

259    1 John 3:16 (NLT).

260    My paraphrase of Paul's advice in Philippians 2:3.

261    Philippians 2:6-11 (NLT).

262    It also echoes the culmination of the *Servant Song* of Isaiah 53:1-12, a part of which, we looked at in the final section of Part Six.

263    As in the Book of Revelation with its portrayal of Rome as a whore and its contrast with the Lamb-like rulership of God, there's another shove against Rome and Caesar here in the New Testament writings.

264    Philippians 2:12-13.

265   Philippians 2:14-15 (NLT)

266   Philippians 1:27 (NLT, 2015 ed.) [brackets mine].

267   Philippians 4:8.

268   Of course, this is an over-simplification. There has always been a marriage between religion and politics throughout the history of world empires. In the ancient world everything was religio-political or theopolitcal—only in the modern world (and maybe just the modern West) has one escaped the control of the other (or maybe not, depending on how you analyse politics and the influence of religion, and vice-versa). The real change in the Davidic Age of Israel wasn't the marriage of religion and politics *per se*, but how the religious arena (the Temple and its Priesthood) came to be under the direct control and influence of a hereditary Monarchy. It used to be that God elected the leaders, but now the bloodline presided over that choice, and it was the heirs of this bloodline who elected which God to worship. So, if the ruling Monarchy chose to worship other deities, such as Baal or Ashtoreth, then the "official" state religion would also change at the mercy of their whims (to summarise the histories of the Kings, as recorded in the books of 1 & 2 Kings). This would be one factor explaining why the function of the Prophets in bearing God's voice (and not the Priesthood) becomes dominant from this moment onwards in the narrative of Israel's history.

269   Compare Deuteronomy 10:17-19 with 1 Kings 9:15-23.

270   See 1 Kings 10:26-29.

271   1 Kings 11:3.

272   See 1 Samuel 8:10-18.

273   See 1 Kings 12.

274   Matthew 12:42.

275   See Matthew 5 – 7 and Luke 6:20 – 49. Matthew's account is what scholars and theologians call the Sermon on the Mount. Luke's account is generally known as the Sermon on the Plain.

276   Luke 6:20 – 26 (NKJV).

277   This insight comes from scholars Kenneth E. Bailey and Raymond Brown in Kenneth E. Bailey, *Jesus Through Middle Eastern Eyes: Cultural Studies in the Gospels*, "Part Two, The Beatitudes" (London: SPCK, 2008). Also note that this word *makarios* is used in both Matthew's and Luke's records of the Beatitudes.

278   John 16:33.

279   Fr. Ryan Cook is a great guy and priest, who was working with a beautiful picture of God's Kingdom in Liverpool, UK, when I first met him. He's since moved back to his native Canada, and he still ranks high in my list of favourite Canadians; right next to the singer Bryan Adams and the author Sarah Bessey. You can follow him on Instagram; @racook. I've used his sentiment with his permission, of course.

280   Habakkuk 2:4-5a (NLT) [comments in brackets are mine].

281   Habakkuk 2:9-11.

282   Habakkuk 2:12-14.

283   Habakkuk 2:15-17.

284   Habakkuk 2:18-20.

285   Luke 6:27.

286   Genesis 3:8.

287   Genesis 3:21.

288   Isaiah 25:6-8a (NLT, 2015 ed.).

289   Revelation 19:7-9a (NLT).

290   I am using Mary's words recorded in Luke 1:52.

291   See Luke 15:1-2, Luke 5:27-31 (cf. Matthew 9:9).

292   Zach Hoag, *The Light is Winning: Why Religion Just Might Bring us Back to Life* (Grand Rapids, MI: Zondervan, 2017), p. 53. Used by permission of Zondervan. www.Zondervan.com

293   Luke 14:15-24.

294   Matthew 21:31.

295   1 Corinthians 11:27 and 29. My writing in the next few segments is based on 1 Corinthians 11:17-34.

296   See 1 Corinthians 12:18-27.

297   Rodney Reeves, *Spirituality According to Paul: Imitating the Apostle of Christ*, "Common Bonds: Worship as Corporate Reality" (Downers Grove, IL: InterVarsity Press, 2011), p. 124.

298   Lucy Peppiatt, *Women and Worship at Corinth: Paul's Rhetorical Arguments in 1 Corinthians* (Eugene, OR: Cascade Books, 2015), p. 75. Used with permission.

299   Isaiah 58:2-4, 6-7, 9-10 (NLT, 2015 ed.) [square brackets mine].

300   Amos 5:21-24 (The Message).

301   Don't get me wrong, there are many, many good reasons for leaving a church. Such as: corruption, abuse, over-controlling leadership, incompatible doctrinal differences, hypocrisy, hate-preaching and prejudiced behaviour or structure etc. I'm only tackling our consumerism here.

302   Karl Marx's famous quote comes from the introduction to his work, *A Contribution to the Critique of Hegel's Philosophy of Right* (Published in 1843, 1844).

## EPILOGUE: MASTERPIECE

303   Fyodor Dostoyevsky (AD 1821-1881), *The Brothers Karamazov*.

304   You can read more on this at: http://www.bbc.co.uk/news/entertainment-arts-27884323

305   Genesis 50:20 (NLT).

306   Romans 8:18-28 (CJB).

307   Romans 8:29.

308   Revelation 22:17.